MW00965433

References for the Rest of Us

COMPUTER BOOK SERIES FROM IDG

Are you intimidated and confused by computers? Do you find that traditional manuals are overloaded with technical details you'll never use? Do your friends and family always call you to fix simple problems on their PCs? Then the *...For Dummies™* computer book series from IDG is for you.

...For Dummies books are written for those frustrated computer users who know they aren't really dumb but find that PC hardware, software, and indeed the unique vocabulary of computing make them feel helpless. *...For Dummies* books use a lighthearted approach, a down-to-earth style, and even cartoons and humorous icons to diffuse computer novices' fears and build their confidence. Lighthearted but not lightweight, these books are a perfect survival guide to anyone forced to use a computer.

"I like my copy so much I told friends; now they bought copies."

Irene C., Orwell, Ohio

"Quick, concise, nontechnical, and humorous."

Jay A., Elburn, IL

"Thanks, I needed this book. Now I can sleep at night."

Robin F., British Columbia, Canada

Already, hundreds of thousands of satisfied readers agree. They have made *...For Dummies* books the #1 introductory level computer book series and have written asking for more. So if you're looking for the most fun and easy way to learn about computers, look to *...For Dummies* books to give you a helping hand.

IDG BOOKS

MORE

WORDPERFECT 6
FOR WINDOWS
FOR
DUMMIES™

by Margaret Levine Young & David C. Kay

IDG Books Worldwide, Inc.
An International Data Group Company

San Mateo, California ♦ Indianapolis, Indiana ♦ Boston, Massachusetts

MORE WordPerfect 6 For Windows For Dummies

Published by
IDG Books Worldwide, Inc.
An International Data Group Company
155 Bovet Road, Suite 310
San Mateo, CA 94402

Library of Congress Catalog Card No.: 94-78908

ISBN 1-56884-206-6

Printed in the United States of America

10 9 8 7 6 5 4 3 2 1

1B/QZ/RS/ZU

Distributed in the United States by IDG Books Worldwide, Inc.

Distributed in Canada by Macmillan of Canada, a Division of Canada Publishing Corporation; by Computer and Technical Books in Miami, Florida, for South America and the Caribbean; by Longman Singapore in Singapore, Malaysia, Thailand, and Korea; by Toppan Co. Ltd. in Japan; by Asia Computerworld in Hong Kong; by Woodslane Pty. Ltd. in Australia and New Zealand; and by Transworld Publishers Ltd. in the U.K. and Ireland.

For general information on IDG Books in the U.S., including information on discounts and premiums, contact IDG Books 800-434-3422 or 415-312-0650.

For information on where to purchase IDG Books outside the U.S., contact Christina Turner at 415-312-0633.

For information on translations, contact Marc Jeffrey Mikulich, Foreign Rights Manager, at IDG Books Worldwide; FAX NUMBER 415-286-2747.

For sales inquiries and special prices for bulk quantities, write to the address above or call IDG Books Worldwide at 415-312-0650.

For information on using IDG Books in the classroom, or ordering examination copies, contact Jim Kelly at 800-434-2086.

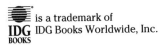 is a trademark of
IDG Books Worldwide, Inc.

About the Authors

Margaret Levine Young

Unlike most of her peers in that mid-30-something bracket, Margaret Levine Young was exposed to computers at an early age. In high school, she got into a computer club known as the R.E.S.I.S.T.O.R.S. "We were a group of kids who spent all day Saturday together in a barn fooling around on three computers that ran on vacuum tubes." Their goal, she admits, was to do language processing "so that the computers could make smart-aleck remarks back to us."

Although Levine got into computers for fun and because "my brother did," she stayed in the field through college, graduating from Yale with a degree in computer science. She was one of the first microcomputer managers in the early '80s and was placed in charge of all PCs at Columbia Pictures.

Since then, Levine has written eight other computer books, including the original *WordPerfect For Windows For Dummies*, her first book with coauthor Dave Kay. "We've known each other for a long time, but Dave is funnier than I am," she says. "Each of us does a chapter, and then we pass them back and forth on the modem. I love writing...*For Dummies* books because I can write the way I think. It's fun being able to say: this is important, but you can forget about That."

Oh, by the way, Levine also met her future husband in the R.E.S.I.S.T.O.R.S., and her other passion is her children, Meg and (the as-yet-unborn) Baby 2.0. She loves gardening, "anything to do with eating," and wandering the Amazon, which she periodically revisits.

David C. Kay

Like his co-author, Dave Kay spent his teenage years fooling around with electronics, watching vacuum tubes glow in his ham radio equipment, in the dark of his basement. Hoping to make a career out of such activities, he became an electrical engineer, only to end up doing more teaching, talking, and writing than engineering. Life changed in 1984 for Kay when he decided he was too comfortable being employed and needed to start his own business. Now a "marketing communications consultant" (promotional writer) for the software and electronics industries, Kay enjoys "being able to tell the unadorned truth about software" through *Dummies* books.

This is Kay's fourth computer book, but he's keeping his coauthoring status "in the family." He coauthored his first book with Margaret Levine Young's brother, John Levine. "It's a lot faster and more fun to coauthor," he says. "Margaret's a better writer than I am, but I'm Meg's godfather so Margaret has to put up with me."

As far as WordPerfect goes, Kay says that he's impressed with how far the company has taken the new version of the program. "It has a lot of great new capabilities — but also an equal number of new peculiarities."

In his spare time, Kay likes to paint, sketch, and sing; he's also an inventor–"wannabe." One of his long-term goals is to write about nature awareness; in particular, how to read human and animal tracks. "I've been studying this stuff for a couple of years, playing with tracks in a sandbox by the back door. I'm almost good enough to track farm equipment now. Another couple of decades and I expect to move on to the heavier mammals, like whales."

Dedication

What brother or sister could pass up the opportunity to dedicate a *Dummies* book to a sibling? Therefore, we would like to dedicate this book to our siblings: to John Levine, a *Dummies* kind of guy in his own right, who got us into this *Dummies* business in the first place; and to Tom and Pam Kay, who engaged Dave in *Dummies*-style punnery at a very tender age, and who have been inspirational in their own, very different ways.

Welcome to the world of IDG Books Worldwide.

IDG Books Worldwide, Inc., is a subsidiary of International Data Group, the world's largest publisher of business and computer-related information and the leading global provider of information services on information technology. IDG was founded more than 25 years ago and now employs more than 5,700 people worldwide. IDG publishes more than 200 computer publications in 63 countries (see listing below). Forty million people read one or more IDG publications each month.

Launched in 1990, IDG Books is today the fastest-growing publisher of computer and business books in the United States. We are proud to have received 3 awards from the Computer Press Association in recognition of editorial excellence, and our best-selling ...*For Dummies* series has more than 10 million copies in print with translations in more than 20 languages. IDG Books, through a recent joint venture with IDG's Hi-Tech Beijing, became the first U.S. publisher to publish a computer book in the People's Republic of China. In record time, IDG Books has become the first choice for millions of readers around the world who want to learn how to better manage their businesses.

Our mission is simple: Every IDG book is designed to bring extra value and skill-building instructions to the reader. Our books are written by experts who understand and care about our readers. The knowledge base of our editorial staff comes from years of experience in publishing, education, and journalism — experience which we use to produce books for the '90s. In short, we care about books, so we attract the best people. We devote special attention to details such as audience, interior design, use of icons, and illustrations. And because we use an efficient process of authoring, editing, and desktop publishing our books electronically, we can spend more time ensuring superior content and spend less time on the technicalities of making books.

You can count on our commitment to deliver high-quality books at competitive prices on topics customers want to read about. At IDG, we value quality, and we have been delivering quality for more than 25 years. You'll find no better book on a subject than an IDG book.

John J. Kilcullen

John Kilcullen
President and CEO
IDG Books Worldwide, Inc.

Acknowledgments

We would like to thank Jordan Young and Katy Weeks, spouses *extraordinaire*. Also: Matt Wagner, Bill Gladstone, our still-tolerant families, and our ever-vigilant editors at IDG books, especially Project Editor Kathy Cox, Technical Editor Michael Partington, and the always-supportive Mary Bednarek. Margy would like to give three cheers for Lexington Playcare Center, without which she would have gotten no work done on this book.

As ever, we are indebted to Dan Gookin, the originator of the *...For Dummies* series. His irreverent style and deep knowledge of software still set the standard for *Dummies* authors.

(The publisher would like to give special thanks to Patrick J. McGovern, without whom this book would not have been possible.)

Credits

Publisher
David Solomon

Managing Editor
Mary Bednarek

Acquisitions Editor
Janna Custer

Production Director
Beth Jenkins

Senior Editors
Tracy L. Barr
Sandra Blackthorn
Diane Graves Steele

Associate Production Coordinator
Valery Bourke

Production Quality Control
Steve Peake

Associate Acquisitions Editor
Megg Bonar

Editorial Assistant
Laura Schaible

Project Editor
Kathleen M. Cox

Technical Reviewer
Michael J. Partington

Production Staff
Tony Augsburger
Paul Belcastro
J. Tyler Connor
Drew R. Moore
Carla Radzikinas
Patricia R. Reynolds
Gina Scott

Proofreader
Henry Lazarek

Indexer
Sherry Massey

Book Design
University Graphics

Cover Design
Kavish + Kavish

Contents at a Glance

Cartoons at a Glance
By Rich Tennant

page xxvi

page 369

page 105

page 392

page 317

page 64

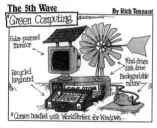

page 263

page 166

page 285

page 7

Table of Contents

Chapter 13: Writing the Great American Novel
(or the Long American Business Report) 233

Part III: More Dealing with the Outside World *263*

Chapter 14: Files from Outer Space 265

Introduction

● ●

Welcome to *MORE WordPerfect 6 For Windows For Dummies*, the book for people who find themselves in a more deeply committed relationship with WordPerfect than they ever imagined. Do you (reader) take this software (WordPerfect) to be your constant companion and friend, 'til hard-disk crash do you part?

Good grief, we hope not! But if you've been hacking away in WordPerfect and are now ready to see some spiffier-looking results and find some more convenient ways to do things, this is the book you want.

About This Book

WordPerfect promises to be able to turn out some pretty nice-looking documents, with tables, charts, and graphics. It also promises to do some tricks you just never used to be able to do by yourself with a word processor but had to get somebody else to do for you, like fine-tuning the way your text looks. It even promises to be able to do some hyper-cool, way-extreme, turn-of-the-millennium stuff like electronic documents, multimedia, and hooking up your documents to spreadsheets and databases.

Promises, promises. Let's see if we can get the software to *deliver*. In this book, we show you how to get WordPerfect to deliver on such tasks as

- Inserting, positioning, and fine-tuning graphics
- Making good-looking tables
- Turning good-looking tables into spiffy charts
- Fine-tuning your text's appearance
- Writing scientific papers with equations
- Creating letters, faxes, memos, and other short stuff
- Creating brochures, fliers, posters, slides, and newsletters
- Creating really big documents, like books
- Simplifying big documents with automatic numbering, indexing, and cross-referencing

✔ Dealing with the non-WordPerfect world

✔ Putting data from spreadsheets and databases into your documents

✔ Making WordPerfect's menus, keyboards, and buttons work better for you

✔ Making WordPerfect do your routine tasks automatically

How to Use This Book

This is not some sort of home-study course where you have to wade through a bunch of lessons before you can actually do something useful. Nope. We pretty much get right down to it. Just look something up in the Index or Table of Contents and start reading. Look for Tooty the Owl for a step-by-step Tootorial.

We even try to keep the number of cross-references to a minimum, so you don't have to flip around so much. We avoid computer jargon wherever possible, but in case some wise guy starts speaking WordPerfect or computer gibberish to you, there's even a glossary in the back.

You don't have to have this book's immediate predecessor, *WordPerfect For Windows For Dummies*, but you may want to check it out. It starts right from the beginning and takes you through a lot of important basics. *This* book amplifies on some important but somewhat more advanced features.

This book contains lots of step-by-step instructions. When we want you to type something, it appears in **bold type**. On-screen messages look like this. When we suggest that you press two keys at the same time, such as the Ctrl key and the O key, we use a plus sign like this: Ctrl+O.

When you have to choose commands from WordPerfect's menu bar, we use a special symbol to separate one part of the command from the next: ⇨. For example, if we tell you to choose the File⇨Open command, that means that you choose the first part of the command (File) from the menu bar, then choose the second part (Open) from the drop-down menu that appears.

Who We Think You Are

We think you are a wonderful, intelligent, and practical human being. After all, you have bought, or are about to buy this book, right? Proof positive.

Moreover, we think you are probably someone who has been kicking around in WordPerfect for Windows for a while. You're doing some perfectly adequate documents, but you've also got a few problems you'd like to solve. Or you're really itching to do something a little snazzier — maybe there's something that you used to know how to do in your old word processor but haven't figured out in WordPerfect.

We also think you're the kind of person who is not completely, utterly in love with software. That is, we think you are a sane, normal person who does not think that playing with software all night is more fun than playing with your kid, your dog, or even your toes.

Finally, we think that you probably have someone you can call upon to help you with the one or two really gnarly things that crop up. We call this person your "guru," but in reality he or she is probably a computer-savvy adolescent in your home or some poor, overworked engineer in your company.

How This Book Is Organized

Dummies books like this one are always divided up into "parts," where the chapters of each part relate to one particular topic (more or less). The order of the parts isn't particularly important here — you don't have to read them in order — but there is a sort of logic to it.

First, we tell you more about a bunch of important features, like graphics and tables and typography, that you might use in darn near anything. Then we show you how to use these and other features in a variety of practical real-life documents and how to deal with the rest of the real-life, non-WordPerfect world. Next, we get into some of the gee-whiz stuff like automation and customization and then finish up with a grab bag of useful tips and tricks.

But, as we say, you can just look something up in the Index and start reading. Don't worry about the order of things. In fact, don't worry at all. Read the cartoons first.

Here are the parts of this book:

Part I: Glorious Graphics

One of the first things folks want to do once they've learned the basics is to put graphics in their documents. So, Part I has the blow-by-blow descriptions of how to brighten up your documents with graphics of all kinds: charts, graphs, clip art, text boxes, do-it-yourself drawings, TextArt, and watermarks. Here's how to draw, insert, and size your graphics; move them around; brighten them up; border them; caption them; and generally fool around with them until they behave themselves.

Part II: More Tantalizing Text

If part of your job is producing a final, ready-to-print, typographically correct document, with tables and figures and equations and everything, Part II is for you. Here's how to create and format tables, fine-tune the typography, do scientific equations, and put together every kind of document from the shortest memo to gigrondous, multichapter books.

Part III: More Dealing with the Outside World

Alas, gone are the happy days when everyone used the same word processor: a #2 Ticonderoga pencil and a pad of lined paper. It's been downhill since then. It seems that there are special programs for everything: spreadsheets, databases, graphics, mathematics. And everybody uses something different. Then there's the great Macintosh/PC divide. What do you do when you need to put it all together?

Turn to Part III! Here's where we show how to exchange files with folks who use different software. This is also where we show you how you can grab something from another program, like a spreadsheet, and pop it into a WordPerfect document. And, taking this idea to the almost ridiculous extreme, we even talk about how to pop moving pictures or sound into your document!

Part IV: More Automation and Customization

If you're spending so much time working in WordPerfect that you feel "lashed to the oars" like a galley slave, declare your independence by perusing Part IV. Even if you would just like WordPerfect to work a little more efficiently for you, this is the place to go. Learn how to reduce a frequently used set of commands to a single keystroke with macros. Change the keyboard and Button Bars around to suit your fancy. Even learn how to create hypertext electronic documents that provide automatic cross-referencing.

Part V: Shortcuts and Tips Galore

While this sounds like it describes how to make more money as a waiter, it's not. Here is a compendium of more good stuff in WordPerfect and our own little ideas on how to make things work better for you. Plus, we tell you where to turn for more information on WordPerfect.

Icons Used in This Book

Look around — icons are everywhere! You can hardly toast a slice of bread any more without having to interpret abstract little pictures that are supposed to mean something. It's like living in an ancient Egyptian tomb! So instead of using cryptic, abstract icons where you can't tell if the symbol means toast, puree, or spin-dry, we use actual pictures in our icons. They're much cuter than the ones on your toaster, too! Here's what they mean:

If there's an easier or faster way to do something, it appears with this icon next to it.

Here's Tooty the Owl (he's so cute, we felt we had to name him) to give you the step-by-step on how to do something.

Mr. Science, here, alerts you to the sort of stuff that people who secretly like software really want to know. It's not required reading unless you are trying to date someone like that (or are already married to one).

When we think your brain is so busy with what we've just said that it's likely to forget something we said earlier, we use this icon to remind you.

This icon subtly suggests that something may go wrong if you're not careful about something. We even tell you what those somethings are.

Where to Go from Here

Our favorite place to go from here is the Contents at a Glance, somewhere in the front of all Dummies books. (Actually, our more favorite place is Cartoons at a Glance, which is similarly located. Well, truthfully, our most favorite place is this nearby ice cream place ...) Contents at a Glance gives you an idea of what the individual chapters are in each part of the book.

If you've got some specific topic that's really gnawing at your brain and you won't be able to eat, sleep, or rest until you figure it out, check the Index. Or see a doctor or something. Good heavens!

Otherwise, drag a comfortable chair up to your PC, fire up WordPerfect, and thumb through the book until you find something fun! Feeling whimsical? Check out TextArt in Chapter 5. Feeling ambitious? See Chapters 12 and 13 on large documents. The important thing is — get going!

Part I
More Glorious Graphics

The 5th Wave   By Rich Tennant

"YES, I THINK IT'S AN ERROR MESSAGE."

In this part ...

You asked for more graphics, you got more graphics! Here's the inside scoop on how to insert pictures, add lines, apply borders and fills, draw pictures, design charts, create TextArt, use 256 stunning colors, and turn your 256 stunning colors into 256 shades of drab on your black-and-white printer! Whatever!

"What do you mean?" you say; "When did I ever ask for more graphics?" Well, perhaps not you, personally. But a lot of folks who read *WordPerfect For Windows For Dummies* asked for more graphics. How do we know? Well, in a stunning coup of logic, IDG Books actually *sends readers' comments to the authors!* That's right, we get copies of every, single, gosh-darned comment that people make on that IDG Books Worldwide Registration Card at the back of the book that you have ignored until now. And we get your addresses, too, so be nice!

So here you go. We've put graphics first so you can master this important skill before we get into serious text stuff and document-building in Part II. Go wild!

Chapter 1

More Graphics Boxes for Illustrations and Sidebars

• •

In This Chapter

▶ Getting a box

▶ Putting text in a box

▶ Picturing your box

▶ Using watermarks

▶ Piling boxes on top of boxes

▶ Moving, sizing, and deleting boxes

▶ Creating captions

▶ Using special graphics tools

• •

As any three-year-old knows, a box is one of the greatest joys in life. Give a kid a box, and she can turn it into a castle, camel, or birthday cake. Give her some crayons, and she will soon have a box full of colorful words and pictures. (In the case of our favorite three-year-old, Meg, the words will be in "Meggish," but impressive nonetheless.)

Not to be outclassed by a three-year-old, WordPerfect uses boxes to help you display castles, camels, and birthday cakes, and to provide sidebars for the colorful words in your document. But unless you know the tricks of these boxes, you may soon find yourself muttering certain other kinds of colorful words!

In this chapter, we tell you how to have fun with illustrations, sidebars, and watermarks, using the various boxes WordPerfect provides. We're not going to talk about how to make pictures, graphs, or "TextArt," though. See Chapters 3, 4, and 5 for that. Also, see Chapter 9 for information on equations and their boxes.

TIP

Improving your view

You can't see any graphics in WordPerfect un- less Graphics is enabled in the View menu. Click on View, and make sure there's a check mark next to Graphics. You'll also generally find it helpful to choose either Page view (press Alt+F5) or Two- page view from the View menu. You can turn off Graphics again if WordPerfect gets too slow to live with, but you won't see the actual images.

How to Get a Box

As with Chinese take-out food, boxes come automatically. Any time you do graphics — or, more accurately, any time you create or insert something using the commands under Graphics in the main menu bar — your work will appear in a WordPerfect box. (Some of these commands, like Draw, Chart, and TextArt, also have buttons on the standard Button Bar, so you get a box if you use those buttons, too.) The text in your document flows around that box in ways that you can control, if you like.

Unlike Chinese take-out, your box will have a border, although it doesn't have to. In addition, when you click on the box, a temporary rectangular frame appears, to tell you that the box is selected. A four-headed arrow indicates you can drag the box around wherever you like (more or less). *Handles* (little squares) appear around the frame that you can click on and drag to change its size. To work on the contents of the box, simply double-click on it.

When you are working with the contents of a box, some of the commands on the main menu bar are unavailable ("grayed out"). To re-enable them, just click anywhere outside the box (in the main body of text). Also, when you have created a box, WordPerfect generally displays one of its specialty menus, called the Graphics Box Feature Bar, on the WordPerfect window. This has useful commands that we discuss later in this chapter; the commands are duplicated in a QuickMenu that appears when you click with the right mouse button on a box.

Different Styles of Box

There are actually different styles of box you can use, depending on what's in the box and how you're going to use the contents. Whenever you make illustra- tions with WordPerfect's Draw, TextArt, Figure, or Text Box features, for instance, WordPerfect automatically uses *styles* of box appropriate for each different type of illustration. Most of these styles work pretty much the same way, so if you learn how to handle one, you've learned to handle them all. (This isn't true for Equations and Watermarks, though, as you'll see later in this chapter.)

Table 1-1 lists the different styles of box and what they're used for, but you'll probably use only a few:

Table 1-1	Styles of Boxes
Style	*What It's Used for*
Figure	Illustrations based on graphics files (like clip art).
Text	Sidebars (blocks of text separate from main text).
Equation	Equations you want to use like an illustration.
Table	No practical use that we can see.
User	Anything, formatted in some particular way you prefer.
Button	Hypertext! See Chapter 20.
Watermark	Graphics that faintly underlay your text.
Inline equation	Equations you want to appear in the text.
OLE object	Something pasted from another Windows program. Try not to think about it.

Let's start with one of the easiest to understand — the Text box. If you're just experimenting with boxes, start with the Text box to give you something to play with.

Text in a box (creating sidebars)

Some text deserves to be in a box (and sometimes that box deserves to be buried six feet underground). In informal documents, like magazine articles, newsletters, and this book, there are always some topics that are peripheral to the main discussion. These traditionally go into "sidebars" (like our "Technical Stuff" blurbs) in boxes. The sidebar usually appears (you guessed it) off to the *side* of the page, often shaped like a *bar*. The rest of the text in the document has to flow gracefully around the sidebar. You get to decide where the sidebar goes and how the main text flows.

Sometimes sidebars have fancy-schmancy borders, or backgrounds, or columns, or they read sideways (like reply cards sometimes do on advertisements). WordPerfect can do a lot of this fancy stuff for you.

It's easiest to start with the box, then put text into it. If you already have the text, just "cut" it out of your document (select it and press Ctrl+X); this puts the text on the Windows Clipboard until you're ready to use it. You can then paste this Clipboard text (by pressing Ctrl+V) into the box instead of typing it directly in (discussed in Step 4, below).

Putting text in a box

To create a Text box, do the following:

1. **Make sure you're in page view (select <u>V</u>iew⇨<u>P</u>age or press Alt+F5).**

   You don't absolutely have to be in page view, but it makes life easier: first, because you can see immediately where your box is located; second, because we describe how things work in page view, not draft view.

   It may also help if you *zoom back* a bit, so you can see more of the page at once. Choose <u>V</u>iew⇨<u>Z</u>oom from the menu bar and click on Page <u>W</u>idth. When you're done with your box, you can reset <u>V</u>iew⇨<u>Z</u>oom to <u>1</u>00% or whatever other zoom you like.

2. **Click in your text at the point where you want your Text box.**

   Note: You can't actually do this. You want the box to appear off to one side, right? And *you can't click over there!* So what the heck kind of stupid feature is this, anyway?! Calm down; just decide which paragraph should be more or less in the vicinity of the Text box, and click anywhere in that paragraph.

3. **Select <u>G</u>raphics⇨Text Box from the main menu bar.**

   Or click on the Text Box button on the Button Bar. (Don't mistake the Text Box button for the TextArt button, which is fun to use, but a little too much fun. We're doing serious work, here.)

   Amazingly, a Text Box appears and the text in your paragraph wraps cozily around it. The box is gift-wrapped with ugly little bars at the top and bottom, like in Figure 1-1. There are also odd little squares around it. These are the handles we talked about earlier. Ignore them for the moment; they aren't really going to appear in your document.

4. **Type the text you want in the box.**

   Your cursor is now blinking meaningfully inside the box, to suggest you type something there. Do so. (If the document window appears to have suddenly gone blank, you didn't succeed at Step 1 and you're in the draft view! So type something anyway, and when you're done, click on the <u>C</u>lose button in the Feature Bar above your text.) If you like, you can do anything you may normally do to text, such as change fonts or paragraph layout, add bullets, or even put your text in columns.

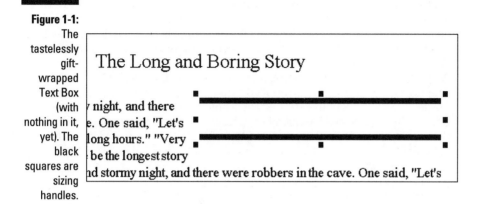

Figure 1-1: The tastelessly gift-wrapped Text Box (with nothing in it, yet). The black squares are sizing handles.

Note that WordPerfect has sneaked in one of its cute little Feature Bars at the top of your WordPerfect window. Did you ask for this? No, it's just WordPerfect being helpful. This particular Feature Bar is the Graphics Box Feature Bar, and it crops up periodically and stays up until you click on its Close button. The Graphics Box Feature Bar lets you do lots of cute tricks such as run text sideways, apply a caption, or change the border. For more information, see "Fancy Boxes with the Feature Bar and QuickMenu" later in this chapter.

5. Go back to work.

That is, click anywhere outside of the Text box. The little squares around the box go away, and you're done. You've got a Text box. Fun's over.

From here on out, Text boxes work pretty much like every other box. So to caption, position, border, fill, or wrap document text around Text boxes, read the other sections of this chapter, beginning with "Fancy Boxes with the Feature Bar and QuickMenu."

Illustrating your sidebar

Sidebars being lighthearted sorts of things, people often like to put pictures in them. Well, just do it. That's right, just do it! Get your cursor into the text of the Text box (double-click on the Text box if your cursor is currently in the main document) and choose Figure from the Graphics menu on the main menu bar. You may have to make your Text box wider if you want text alongside the illustration.

Figure 1-2 shows just how weird you can get with sidebars. We'll give you the fast rundown here using commands we haven't explained yet; come back here after you've read further in this chapter. To make this sidebar, we created a

Text box by clicking Text Box on the Button Bar, typed the text, then inserted a graphic file with the Graphics⇨Figure command. We changed the butterfly's color fills to white with the QuickMenu's Image Tools command, then created a caption for the graphic using the QuickMenu's Create Caption command.

We centered the caption inside the border with the Caption button on the Graphics Box Feature Bar; we applied a new border to the Text box with the Border/Fill button and then turned the whole Text box sideways with the Content button. To read about all commands for doing this stuff, see "Fancy Boxes with the Feature Bar and QuickMenu" and other sections later in this chapter.

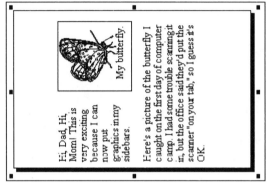

Figure 1-2:
Getting
seriously
weird with
sidebars.

Pictures in a box

Quite probably, the original *raison d'etre* (which we assume is French for "reason for eating," of which there are many in France) for boxes in WordPerfect was to handle pictures. Then the WordPerfect engineers got excited by this concept of boxes. (Hey, give them a break; things get a little slow outside of sugar beet season in Orem, Utah.) They started adding Text boxes and other stuff. So let's take a look at the original exciting idea, a picture in a box.

To put a picture (by which we mean any sort of graphics image) in your document, do the following:

1. **Switch to the page view (select View⇨Page, or press Alt+F5).**

   You don't absolutely have to do this, but it makes life easier because you immediately see where your box is located.

2. **Click in your text at the point where you want your picture.**

   Note: You can't actually do this. The best you can do is decide which paragraph should be more or less in the vicinity of the picture, and click anywhere in that paragraph. It doesn't matter where, the result is the same.

3. **Select G̲raphics⇨F̲igure from the main menu bar (or click on the Figure button in the Button Bar).**

   You see one of WordPerfect's file selection dialog boxes, very much like the ones for opening or saving a file. All it probably shows you, though, are WordPerfect-type graphics files (ending in .WPG) in WordPerfect's graphics directory.

   If you want a different type of image file (like a Windows "bitmap" file: one that ends in .BMP), click on the box labeled List Files of T̲ype and click on a different type from the list shown. WordPerfect (fully installed) will let you choose from about 15 different types of graphics files.

   If the image file you want is not in the current directory (or disk drive), you can change directories just as you do when you open a document file.

4. **Double-click on the file you want under the Filen̲ame box.**

   It's always tricky guessing what's in a file by its filename, so you may find it nice to use WordPerfect's previewer to help you pick the right one. Click on the Vie̲w button, and any file you click on in the file list appears in a separate window.

   Once you see the image you want, click on the OK button in the Insert Image dialog box. The view window disappears and the image appears in a new box in your document. Odd little squares (that are handles for sizing) appear around it. Ignore those squares for the moment; they aren't really going to appear in your document.

5. **Go back to work.**

   That is, click anywhere outside of the box. The little squares around the box go away, and you're done.

When you change the lines, shapes, and colored areas of a drawing, you "edit" it, in WordPerfect lingo. WordPerfect's idea of editing a picture is to put it into the WP Draw program, which you run by double-clicking on the graphics box.

Keeping your document file size down

The easy way is, when you are about to specify the graphics file (Steps 3 and 4 in the preceding tootorial), click on the little box labeled, "I̲mage on disk" in the lower-left corner of the dialog box. This option avoids having WordPerfect copy the image into your document; it just reads the image from the graphics file when you open the document. This means, however, that if you move the image file to another directory, WordPerfect won't be able to find it. It also means that if you give your document to someone else, you have to give them the graphics file, too, and they have to put it in an identically-named directory with an identical path (like `C:\WPWIN60\GRAPHICS`).

Cutting and pasting pictures from other programs

Maybe it's because we're old PC fogeys, but we are always astounded that this actually works. And it does, most of the time. Let's say you have created a picture of Zimbo The Chimp, your local zoo's mascot, in Windows Paintbrush. (Paintbrush comes with Windows, and generally hides in the Accessories group in your Program Manager.) You can select an area of your picture of Zimbo (with the Paintbrush scissors icon), copy it to the Windows Clipboard (Ctrl+C), then paste it (Ctrl+V) wherever your cursor is in WordPerfect. It will automatically be put in a Figure box. Unfortunately, when you go to edit Zimbo's picture by double-clicking on it, you will get WP Draw, not Paintbrush. If you insist on getting the original tool when you double-click, you may have to use something called "linking," described in Chapter 16.

Watermarks

Watermarks are sort of like tatoos for your document: in bad taste when overdone, and definitely a breed apart from other types of graphics. They are images or text that appear faintly in the background of your document; they generally appear on every page or odd/even pages. You can't create them, select them, or control them quite the same way you do for other types of box. Although they do use the Graphics Box Feature Bar, they also have their own, special controls. Here are a few basic facts about Watermarks:

- ✔ Watermarks work sort of like headers and footers, if you're familiar with those. If you're not, read on.

- ✔ There are two official Watermarks, named A and B. You can use either one, or both, on any page. You might have one Watermark (a logo, for instance) on the top-left corner of the page and another Watermark on the bottom right. If you were doing a book or pamphlet, you could assign A to appear only on odd-numbered pages, positioned on the right, and B to appear on even-numbered pages, on the left. That way, the Watermarks would always be on the outside edge.

- ✔ Watermarks can change as you go along: Just create a new A or B Watermark at the point in the document where you want the change. You can also make either A or B stop at any point by turning the Watermark off.

- ✔ Watermarks are generally pictures (image files) but can also be text or text files.

✔ You can have additional, "unofficial" watermark-ish images besides A and B, but the Layout⇨Watermark controls won't recognize them. You make these images by changing a regular graphics box to the Watermark style. See "Changing the Style of Your Box," later in this chapter.

✔ The official controls for official Watermarks are found under Layout⇨ Watermark in the menu bar.

✔ You can't easily select an official Watermark by clicking on it. You can, however, select it by clicking with your right mouse button at the top of the page (in page view, not draft) and choosing Watermark from the QuickMenu.

Making a Watermark (slosh)

Watermarks are a bit trickier to create than your typical bathtub ring. They are easier to scrub out (stop), however. Here's how to make 'em.

It's best to go about creating a Watermark in page view (Alt+F5) or two-page view (choose View⇨Two Page from the menu bar).

1. **Choose Layout⇨Watermark in the menu bar.**

   Or, click with the right mouse button at the very top of your document and choose Watermark.

2. **Select Watermark A or Watermark B from the dialog box that appears.**

3. **Click on the Create button.**

   A Watermark Feature Bar appears, with the buttons Figure, File, Placement, Next, Previous, and Close. Your document text disappears, replaced by a special viewing window for Watermarks.

4. **To create a graphics Watermark, click on the Figure button in the Feature Bar.**

   An Insert Image dialog box appears, very much like the dialog boxes for opening or saving a file. All it usually shows you, though, are WordPerfect-type graphics files (ending in .WPG) in WordPerfect's graphics directory. Choose a file and click on OK.

   If you want a different type of image file (like a Windows bitmap file, ending in .BMP), click on the box labeled List Files of Type and click on a different type from the list shown. WordPerfect (fully installed) will let you choose from about 15 different types of graphic files.

   — and/or —

4. **To put text in a Watermark, just type. To use text from a file, click on the File button in the Feature Bar and choose a document file.**

   To alter the shading of the text, press F9 and change the font shading from the 25% value that WordPerfect normally uses for Watermarks. (You never noticed you could change text shading, did you? WordPerfect is full of cute little surprises.)

5. For graphics watermarks, a Graphics Box Feature Bar now appears so you can fine-tune appearances. Click on Close when you're done.

The Graphics Box Feature Bar lets you control the Watermark's position on the page, its size, and other attributes. See "Fancy Boxes with the Feature Bar and QuickMenu," later in this chapter.

If you can't see the image, try moving the vertical and horizontal sliders on the right and bottom sides of the window.

6. Specify the page placement of your Watermark.

Click on the Placement button on the Watermark Feature Bar. A little dialog box lets you choose between Odd Pages, Even Pages, or Every Page.

7. Click on Close on the Watermark Feature Bar.

WordPerfect returns you to your regular document view.

Editing Watermarks (glug, glug)

To edit a Watermark, choose Layout⇨Watermark in the menu bar and select the Watermark you want to change: A or B. (It doesn't much matter where in the document your cursor is; your edit will affect the Watermark in effect on that page.) Then, click on the Edit button instead of the Create button in the Watermark dialog box. You are now looking at the special viewing window for Watermarks.

Now, to edit a graphics Watermark, press Shift+F11 (or choose Graphics⇨Edit Box from the menu bar) to get a Graphics Box Feature Bar. You can rotate the Watermark, shrink it, change contrast, whatever. See "Fancy Boxes with the Feature Bar and QuickMenu," later in this chapter. Close this Feature Bar when you're done. To edit a text Watermark, do as you would in editing text in a normal document.

Close the Watermark Feature Bar when you're done.

Discontinuing, suppressing, and delaying Watermarks (splash)

To stop (discontinue) a Watermark at any point, place your cursor on the page where you no longer want the Watermark. Then choose Layout⇨Watermark in the menu bar and select the Watermark you want to discontinue: A or B. Finally, click on the Discontinue button. To discontinue both Watermarks, you have to do this twice, once for each one.

There are two polite ways of getting rid of Watermarks temporarily. You can suppress them (turn them off for a while) or delay them (make them start some number of pages after the beginning).

✔ **Suppress.** This approach keeps a Watermark from appearing on a particular page. Put your cursor on that page, choose Layout⇨Page⇨Suppress, and then choose the Watermark you want to suppress from the dialog box that appears.

✔ **Delay.** Use this approach only when you don't want the Watermark to start for several pages. *Before* you create the Watermark, choose Layout⇨Page⇨Delay Codes from the menu bar. Specify the number of pages to delay in the dialog box. Then click on Watermark in the Delay Codes Feature Bar to create a Watermark.

Equations in a box

Equations in WordPerfect are Truly Weird. They are weird largely because of the Equation Editor (which is what you see when you choose Equation under Graphics on the main menu bar). To most writers, this is a horrifying name that combines the terror of the words *equation* and *editor*. As you might surmise, the Equation Editor is neither particularly friendly nor fun to use. Since the weirdness of equations is primarily typographic in nature (that is, you naturally will make many weird typos), we talk about equations in Chapter 9, "More Typographic Mysteries."

The graphics box that equations appear in is, however, not weird at all. It takes two forms, either the *equation* style or the *inline equation* style.

The equation style box is *anchored* to the paragraph your cursor was in when you created the equation. (See "Positioning Your Box," later in this chapter, for more on anchoring.) The box's position is at the top of that paragraph, against the left border. Its height depends on the text of the equation, and its width is the full width of the paragraph. It has no border or fill. You can change any of these or other aspects of an equation box by using the commands described in following sections.

The inline equation style differs from the equation style in that it is anchored to the position in the text where your cursor was when you created the equation, and its width is determined by the width of the equation. You can change the appearance of an inline equation box in the same way you can for a regular equation box.

Button boxes

Hey, our grandmothers had button boxes! How *avant-garde* of them!

Button-style boxes are generally used for doing hypertext, which we talk more about in our discussion of hypertext in Chapter 20. You don't get a button-style box unless you create something called a hypertext link.

Such boxes give the appearance of a push-button by using a special "button" style border and "button fill." The button size is determined by the text that is selected when you create a hypertext link. Button position is anchored to that same text, so the button moves with the text in the paragraph.

You can change the appearance of a button, if you like, using the commands described in following sections.

Fancy Boxes with the Feature Bar and QuickMenu

Someone really should start naming real bars after the bars in WordPerfect. Instead of a TV in the corner above the bartender's head, the Graphics Box Feature Bar would have ... what, a big computer monitor, displaying multimedia graphics instead of football games? Sounds fun, but as it turns out, the Graphics Box Feature Bar (and its sidekick, the Graphics Box QuickMenu) is almost as much fun. With it, you can deliver some pretty fancy effects and spend vast amounts of otherwise useful time dressing up your boxes.

The Graphics Box Feature Bar

The Graphics Box Feature Bar is simply another WordPerfect menu bar sort of thing. It looks like Figure 1-3.

Figure 1-3:
The
Graphics
Box Feature
Bar lets you
do exotic
things to
boxes.

Here are a few important things to know about the Graphics Box Feature Bar:

✔ The Graphics Box Feature Bar is a tool for doing nifty stuff to a box, like putting on a caption, changing the border, turning text sideways, anchoring your box differently, changing the way text wraps around the box, or positioning or sizing the box precisely. There's a QuickMenu that does the same stuff, however, that we think is easier.

✔ WordPerfect puts the Feature Bar up on your screen automatically when you create certain styles of box: Text, Table, and Custom.

✔ You can deliberately ask for the Feature Bar by selecting a box, then using the Graphics⇨Edit Box command. Alternatively, you can press Shift+F11, or choose Feature Bar from the QuickMenu (see Figure 1-4).

✔ To work with another box in your document, use the Next and Prev buttons to jump to them, or click on the box you want to work on. The Graphics Box Feature Bar stays on your screen until you click on its Close button.

✔ If you go to use the Graphics commands in the menu bar and find them all grayed out, it's probably because the Graphics Box Feature Bar is on your screen, and a box is currently selected. Click somewhere outside of any graphics box, and all will be well.

Are you among the rodent-haters (mouse-averse)? The sort of person that uses Alt-key combinations, rather than the mouse, to choose from WordPerfect menus and dialog boxes? Then know this about Feature Bars: To select a Feature Bar button, like Close, without using the mouse, you have to press Alt+*Shift*+the key (C in the case of Close).

Table 1-2 shows what the buttons in the Feature Bar do.

Table 1-2	Graphics Box Feature Bar Buttons
Button	*What It's for*
?	Nothing. It's utterly worthless, unless you want Help.
Caption	Put/edit a caption on your box.
Content	Change/edit what's in the box and specify how it's positioned in the box.
Position	Position (and anchor) the box on the page.
Size	Change the box dimensions.
Border/Fill	Change the border or apply a background.
Wrap	Change how text flows around the box.

(continued)

Table 1-2 (continued)	
Button	**What It's for**
S*t*yle	Change box style, for example, from Figure to Watermark.
Too*l*s	Use special graphics tools (appears with images only).
*N*ext	Move to the next box in the document.
P*r*ev	Move to the previous box in the document.
*C*lose	Exit the graphics box and remove the Feature Bar.

For a closer look at how these buttons work, read the sections after the following one. For a better alternative to the Graphics Box Feature Bar, read the next section.

The QuickMenu — an easier way to do stuff to boxes

There's another, easier way to do the same nifty stuff the Feature Bar does. Position your cursor on the box you want to change and use the QuickMenu (the thing you get when you press the right-hand button on your mouse). The bottom selections in the QuickMenu are the same ones as on the Feature Bar! The top ones change slightly, depending on what kind of box you've selected. (The QuickMenu also unselfishly offers to provide a Feature Bar, by the way, if you would prefer that way of doing things.) See Figure 1-4 for an example of a QuickMenu for a Text box.

Figure 1-4: The QuickMenu approach to working on boxes. (We've shown the mouse, too, just to remind you how to get a QuickMenu.)

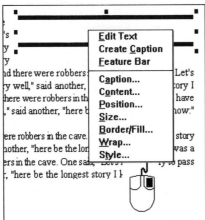

For a closer look at these choices in the QuickMenu (and their corresponding buttons in the Graphics Box Feature Bar), read on.

Captioning Your Box

Never, never try to caption your box by just typing regular old text outside the box. We know it looks like the easiest way; but like most easy answers, it is wrong, inadequate, and an early sign of moral decay. Worse, it will cause you to work harder because you will be constantly fooling with your captions to get them to work right — if you edit the text at all, the caption is likely to move to the wrong place, instead of staying nicely next to or below the box. Dummies avoid hard work at all costs.

Before you start captioning, we suggest you make sure you are looking at your document in page view. Press Alt+F5. (Trust us, it's just easier that way, and that's the view we assume you're using.)

To create a plain and simple caption (left justified under your box, that is), do the following:

1. **Click on your box, using the right mouse button, and choose Create Caption (*not* Caption) from the QuickMenu (see Figure 1-5).**

Figure 1-5:
For a quick caption, click on Create Caption in the QuickMenu. (Now say this out loud, five times, real fast.)

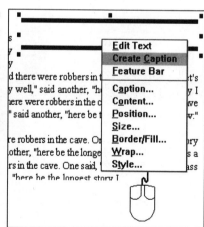

A space opens up under your box, with the cursor (insertion point) so you can type. And, good grief — there's a number or something like "Figure 1" already there! WordPerfect is being helpful again. The number is an illustration *counter* maintained automagically by WordPerfect, a separate count for each type (style) of box. If you have several boxes of the same type (like Figure), they will all be sequentially figure-numbered for you if you use this WordPerfect-supplied number. See Chapter 13, "Writing the Great American Novel (or the Long American Business Report)" for more information on numbering and counters.

2. **Replace or add to the caption as you see fit.**

   Delete the numbered caption if you like; add or substitute your own text. When you finish, click outside the box, in the main text.

3. **If you later decide to change the caption, repeat Step 1, except that Create Caption has become Edit Caption in the QuickMenu (pretty tricky, huh?).**

   If you decide to eliminate the caption altogether, read on.

To create a fancier caption (like center it or put it along the side or top) or eliminate the caption, you need the very clever Box Caption dialog box shown in Figure 1-6. To see this dialog box, click on your box with the right mouse button and choose Caption (not Create Caption or Edit Caption) off the QuickMenu. (Or, if the Graphics Box Feature Bar is present, as shown in Figure 1-3, click on the Caption button.) Either way, you'll get the Box Caption dialog box shown in Figure 1-6.

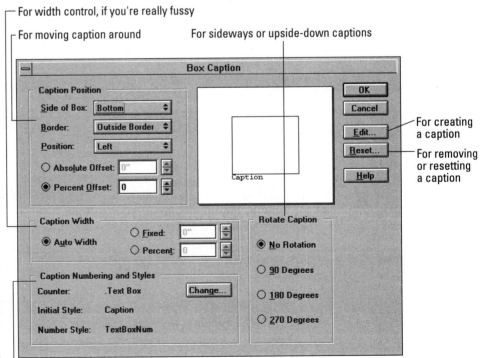

For width control, if you're really fussy

For moving caption around   For sideways or upside-down captions

For creating a caption

For removing or resetting a caption

Figure 1-6: The amazingly clever captioning dialog box.

For automatically numbered captions

When you see the Box Caption dialog box, here are things you can do:

- ✔ **To enter or change caption text:** Click on the Edit button. (If you're not using page view, you will get a special window to make your edits. Click the Close button on that window when you're done.) To get rid of a caption, click the Reset button.

- ✔ **To move the caption to the top or a side:** Click and hold on the Side of Box button (at the top left); drag the highlight to left, right, or top. To make the now-disoriented caption run the right direction, click on the selections in the Rotate Caption area until the caption looks right.

- ✔ **If you are nit-pickingly fussy:** You can adjust where the caption falls with respect to the border by using the Border button; or align the caption along the side by using the Position button and offset settings; or change its width by using the Caption Width stuff. Honestly! This is for people who part their hair with calipers!

- ✔ **If you want a Text box to have a "Figure number" caption** (or do some other "wrong" type of caption)**:** Click on the Change button in the Caption Numbering and Styles area of the dialog box and choose the counter you want.

Positioning Your Box

Well, maybe your box looks spiffy, but it's in the wrong place. Who ya gonna call?

There are two ways to change the size or location of a box (except for boxes in the hands of a three-year-old, in which case there are googles of possibilities). There is the precise, tidy way, described later in this section, and the quick-and-dirty way. We describe the precise, tidy way in "Sizing Your Box," somewhere following.

The quick-and-dirty way to size, move, or delete boxes

The quick-and-dirty way to size, move, or delete boxes works like this:

1. **Click on the box, once.**

   Your mouse cursor changes into a four-way arrow (when it's in the box).

2. **Click and drag the box to the desired location.**

   WordPerfect adjusts the text wrapping, as best it can, around the box. Note that some styles of box may refuse to go into the margins. This has to do with how the box is anchored: "Character"-anchored boxes will not go into the margins. See "The precise, tidy way to move your box" to learn more about anchors and changing anchors. This discussion also reveals how to position a box using exact dimensions, like "one inch from the margin."

3. **To change box size, click and drag a handle.**

   Handles are the little squares around the box. To change box dimensions, position your mouse cursor over a handle; the cursor changes to a two-headed arrow. Click and drag the handle to adjust the size of the box.

   To change the width only, click and drag the center handle on the left or right sides of the box.

   To change the height only, click and drag the center handle on the top or bottom sides of the box.

   To change the width and height at the same time, use the handles in the corners of the box. You drag the two sides that meet in that corner.

   If you change the dimensions of a Text box (especially if you change the height), you may cut off some text. To fix this, see "The precise, tidy way to size your box" in the next section.

To delete a box, click on it once to select it; then press the Delete (Del) key. (If you're currently working in a Text box, first click in the text outside the box. If you're working in that box while in WordPerfect's draft view, click on Close first, before clicking on the box border.)

The precise, tidy way to move your box

The precise, tidy way to move your box is to use the Position command. You can find it in either the QuickMenu or the Graphics Box Feature Bar. We prefer the QuickMenu approach shown in Figure 1-4. (It consists of clicking on your graphics box, using the right mouse button and choosing Position off the QuickMenu that appears.) When you do this, you get a Box Position dialog box like that shown in Figure 1-7.

The buttons in the Box Placement area control *anchoring.* Anchoring controls how your box moves when you add or delete text from your document. The three choices work like this:

Page Anchor: Your box stays in a given position on the page you put it on. (It's not tied to the page number, though. The box moves if additional pages are created or inserted before that page.) Page anchoring is like bolting your boat to the pier — great as long as you don't mind the tides rising and falling around it. The only type of box that WordPerfect normally anchors like this is the Watermark.

Anchoring ties your box to some text.

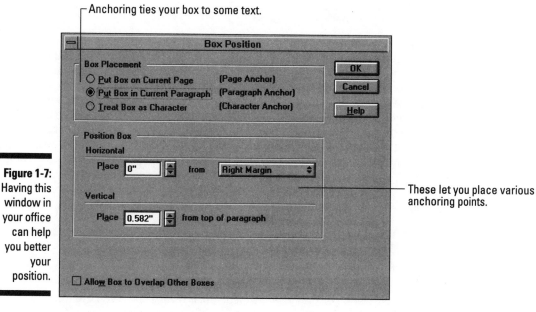

Figure 1-7:
Having this
window in
your office
can help
you better
your
position.

These let you place various
anchoring points.

Paragraph Anchor: Your box floats up or down with a given paragraph, fixed at
some vertical distance like 2 cm above the chosen paragraph. The paragraph is
the one your cursor was in just before you created the box. (The horizontal
position can be relative to the page edges, the margins, or the center of the
associated paragraph.) Most boxes are initially set up by WordPerfect to have
this kind of anchor. Since most illustrations have an explanatory paragraph,
this anchor works out pretty well.

If you change a box to paragraph anchoring, the positioning controls may
occasionally not give accurate results with the new anchoring. If so, cut the box
out (click on it and press Ctrl+X) and paste it before the first character of the
paragraph (click there and press Ctrl+V).

Character Anchor: Your box moves up and down and left and right, drifting like
a jellyfish with the vast, shining sea of text that is your document. It is attached
to the point in your text where your cursor was when you created the box. This
is good for inline equations, hypertext buttons, and *illuminated texts,* like Bibles,
where the first character is an illustration that depicts, say, the life of Saint
Peter. (If you decide to do the life of St. Peter in WP Draw, drop us a line.)

The controls in the Position Box area let you decide exactly where that box
goes with respect to, umm, whatever it has respect to, like a margin or a
paragraph. (The labels on the controls change a bit depending on how you
anchor your box.)

The precise, tidy way to size your box

There are two ways to change the size of a box. (For a box containing fragile chinaware, the traditional way to change its size is to have a sofa fall on top of it in a moving company's van. Do not try this with your PC.) The quick-and-dirty way to size graphics boxes is described in the earlier section, "The quick-and-dirty way to size, move, or delete boxes." The precise, tidy way is to use the Size command in either the QuickMenu or the Graphics Box Feature Bar. We prefer the QuickMenu approach shown back in Figure 1-4. (It consists of clicking on your graphics box, using the right mouse button, and choosing Size off the QuickMenu that appears.) When you do this, you get a Box Size dialog box .

Here's how the Box Size dialog box works:

✔ The Set option lets you type in an exact dimension or adjust the value chosen by WordPerfect.

✔ The Full option means, for the width dimension, that the box should be between the left and right margins (or the column margins, if you're using columns). For the height dimension, it means "between the top and bottom margins."

✔ The Size to Content option makes the box dimensions the same as in the original illustration file, if the content is graphics. For Text boxes, this can get a little weird, so you probably shouldn't do it.

Oddly, the Box Size dialog box doesn't let you distort the image (squish it or expand it), if that's what you want to do. To do that, you have to turn off the check mark in the Preserve Image Width/Height Ratio checkbox, which is in the Box Content dialog box. Use the Content button on the Graphics Box Feature Bar or QuickMenu to get that box.

Stacking boxes

A feature that can be either (1) useful or (2) a pain in the posterior is the ability to overlay boxes on top of each other. Simply click on the box you want on top and drag it over the other box. If you are using WP Draw artwork (files ending in .WPD), where the background is transparent, you can do some cute stuff by overlaying boxes because the underlying image shows through. See Chapter 3 for more on WP Draw.

You could put the butterfly (which comes with WordPerfect stored in a file named BUTERFLY.WPG) on top of one of the bubbles being blown by the cute little girl in BUBBLES.WPG (which also comes with WordPerfect). (You'll have to shrink the butterfly box and remove its border, though.) You can also overlay a Text box on a graphics image, or put a sunset behind your equation, if you are so motivated. But be careful, your text may not be legible if you put it right on top of the non-white portion of the image.

If you really don't want your boxes to overlay each other, choose Position from the Graphics Box Feature Bar or QuickMenu and click on the box labeled Allow Box to Overlap Other Boxes to turn it off. WordPerfect will figure out a new placement as best as it can.

Changing How You Fill Your Box (the Content Command)

OK, you've got a box; what if you want to use a different picture or text (the "content" of the box)? Or what if you want to move it around or rotate the content within the box? The cleverly-named Content command lets you fool around with these aspects of the content.

If all you want to do is *edit* or *modify* the text or graphics in your box, then don't use the Content command; simply double-click on the box. You get whatever you need to do the job for the type of content you have. (For graphics, for instance, double-clicking probably lands you in WP Draw, where you can scribble all over your graphic to your heart's content. See Chapter 3 for more on WP Draw.)

The easiest way to use the Content command is to click on the graphics box with the right mouse button and choose Content off the QuickMenu that appears. (Alternatively, if the Graphics Box Feature Bar is displayed, click on the Content button there.)

You will get a dialog box that looks a lot like Figure 1-8. That figure shows the Box Content dialog box for a Text-style box; it will look a little different for other types of boxes, but not significantly.

Here's how it works:

- ✔ **To fill your box from a file** (a file containing text, an equation, or graphics): Type the filename (and path) in the Filename box. Click on the file icon next to the Filename box if you want to use the familiar WordPerfect Select File dialog box instead of typing a long path and filename.

- ✔ **To edit the text or image:** Click on the Edit button. (This is the same as double-clicking on the box from the document.) Note that, for images, this will probably land you in WP Draw.

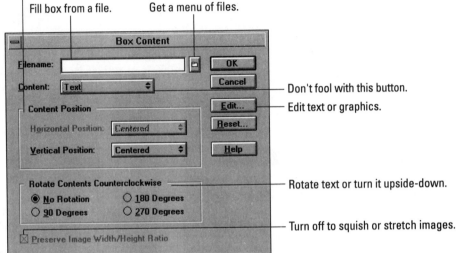

Change position of stuff inside box.

Fill box from a file.　　Get a menu of files.

Don't fool with this button.

Edit text or graphics.

Rotate text or turn it upside-down.

Turn off to squish or stretch images.

Figure 1-8: The Box Content dialog box, for changing how your box is filled.

✔ **To reposition text or an image *within* the box** (you may have a square image in a rectangular box, for instance): Use the Content Position buttons. These let you position the content against the left, right, top, or bottom sides, or centered between sides. Text, however, can't be positioned horizontally this way; use the usual line formatting commands. (Click at the start of the line, then press Alt+F7 for right-justified, Shift+F7 for centered.)

✔ **To run a Text box sideways or upside down** (which happens sometimes when you make fliers): Fool with the Rotate Contents stuff. This doesn't work for graphics; you have to use the special graphics tools to do that. (See "Special Graphics Tools for Boxes with Images," later in this chapter.)

✔ **To squish or stretch the contents of a box to fit the box's dimensions:** Turn off the Preserve Image Width/Height Ratio checkbox by clicking on it. (Normally this option is checked so that you don't mess up an image's appearance.)

Do *not* fool with the Content button in this dialog box, unless you're willing to turn in your Dummies membership card. It lets you change the *type* of contents. If you want a different type of content (like graphics instead of text), delete the entire box and start over again.

For more information on specific things you can do in different types of box, read that particular section (like "Text in a box").

Borders and Fills for Your Box

Borders and fills are the "frosting on the cake" for your box. For that matter, you can actually make your box look like a frosted cake. You can spend so much time doing this that your boss may even become a bit frosted. (In which case, at least you'll know how to fancy up your résumé.) The truth of the matter is, borders and fills are dangerously easy and inviting in WordPerfect, so would you show a little restraint, please?

Having said that, we'll say no more right here. Borders and fills are the same for graphics boxes as they are for paragraphs or anything else in WordPerfect. So, for information on borders and fills, see Chapter 2.

Wrapping Text around Your Box

Not since our parents wrapped our birthday gifts in the Sunday funnies has wrapping text around a box been so much fun! WordPerfect lets you do some pretty fancy text-wrapping, just like the $800 page-layout programs. Normally, WordPerfect wraps text around the side of the box with the most room. This is OK, but sometimes you want to force text to fit on the skinny side or wrap around both sides or not wrap at all. WordPerfect lets you do these things, but it also lets you do even cooler wraps (phatter raps?), like wrap text around the shape of a picture! Figure 1-9 shows an example of this.

The Long and Boring Story

night, and there were robbers in the
e a story to pass the long
nother, "here be the longest
rk and stormy night, and there
One said, "Let's have a story to
y well," said another, "here be
It was a dark and stormy
ers in the cave. One said,
the long hours." "Very
e the longest story I know."

Figure 1-9: Rapping with Mr. Coyote.

To tell WordPerfect how to wrap, click on the graphics box with your right mouse button and choose <u>W</u>rap off the QuickMenu that appears. (Or, choose <u>W</u>rap on the Graphics Box Feature Bar if that's displayed.) You'll get the fairly straightforward Wrap Text dialog box.

The selections on the right side (in the Wrap Text Around area) are pretty self-evident, we think. They let you wrap text around the right, left, both sides, or the largest side. (Largest side means the side with the most room between the box and the margin.)

The type of wrap selections on the left side may need a little explanation, despite the helpful pictures:

Square   Wrap text around the rectangular box.

Contour   Follow the image's shape, not the box's; deletes the border.

Neither Side   No text on either side for the width of the page or column.

No wrap   Superimpose the text right over the image!

Note that the contour wrap works best for WP Draw graphics. (Irregularly shaped "cutouts" that you Edit⇨Copy from Windows Paintbrush will work too!) Other images are often boringly rectangular, even if they don't look it.

Changing the Style of Your Box

In general, don't do it.

Don't do it, that is, if your intention is to change a box that was created in one style (say, Figure) to another style (say Text). Here's why. There is a selection labeled Style on the QuickMenu and on the Graphics Box Feature Bar. Yes, in theory, Style lets you change a box from, say, a Figure style to a Text style. In reality, you can get things rather bollixed up by doing this, particularly if you are using automatically-numbered captions. If you change a style, you get something with the appearance of the new style (like a Watermark), but WordPerfect may not actually recognize it as such (that is, the Watermark commands don't affect it).

 If what you had in mind was not changing a box from one style to another, but changing the appearance of a style, that's just fine. For instance, if you want all Figure boxes to have a new, special border, you can "edit" the graphics style using the Graphic⇨Graphics Styles command. See "Creating or customizing a graphic style," in Chapter 6 for more information on this.

We suggest that if you want to change the style of a box, just delete the existing box (click on it and press the Delete key) and put in a new box of the right style. About the only good reasons for most people to change the style of a box are to change an Equation box to an Inline Equation box or to make a Text or Figure box fade into the background like a watermark (without really being a true WordPerfect Watermark).

You may be tempted to change a box's style in order to use the automatic figure numbering of a different style: if you want your Text boxes to have Figure numbers, for instance. There's a better solution, though, than changing the box style. See "Captioning Your Box," earlier in this chapter.

Still want to change the style of a box? OK, here's how:

1. **Click on the graphics box with the right mouse button and choose Style from the QuickMenu that appears.**

   In the Box Style dialog box that appears, the Style list shows the possible styles for your box. The box's current style is highlighted.

2. **Double-click on the Style you want for your box.**

   Your box is now in the new style.

Special Graphics Tools for Boxes with Images

For graphics fanatics, WordPerfect has an amazing little toolbox. It's only available for graphics images, not Text boxes or Equations or anything else. You can get this toolbox through the Image Tools selection on the QuickMenu (click with your right mouse button on the box with the image in it). This toolbox is also available under Tools on the Graphics Box Feature Bar.

This elf-sized toolbox (also called a tool *palette*), shown in Figure 1-10, appears next to your graphics box.

Figure 1-10:
Cryptic little
buttons in
the Image
Tools
toolbox.

This minuscule set of itsy-bitsy buttons lets you do things like

- ✔ Rotate the image (within the box) about a point that you specify.
- ✔ Move the image within the box.
- ✔ Make the image larger or smaller within the box.
- ✔ Change colors to their complements or to black-and-white.
- ✔ Create a "negative" image (black to white and vice versa).
- ✔ Make filled, colored areas transparent or solid white.
- ✔ Flip the image left/right or top/bottom.
- ✔ Adjust contrast and brightness.
- ✔ Edit the image in WP Draw.
- ✔ Reset the image after you're done mucking it up.

The buttons are indeed tiny and pretty cryptic; but, fortunately, WordPerfect will remind you what they mean. Just move the mouse pointer over a button, and a description appears at the top of your WordPerfect window.

Even so, it's a little hard to tell what you're supposed to do after you click on a button. Here's a breakdown of what to do, by button:

Rotate: Little squares with L-brackets on their corners appear around the image (within the border of the box). Think of these brackets as being attached to the corners of the image. Click and drag any of these to rotate the image around its center. To change the centerpoint of rotation, find a little plus sign in a circle in the middle of the image. (Think of this as a pin stuck through the image and into the paper.) Click and drag this symbol where you want it; then rotate the image. (To rotate Zimbo The Chimp around his nose, for instance, put the plus sign symbol on his nose.)

Move: The move button is pretty simple. Just click and drag the image; parts of the image disappear behind the box, but they're still there. This effect of the image disappearing behind the box lets you crop the image.

Pointer: This gives you a pointer so that you can change the size and location of the image box (the same way you do it without the toolbox — click and drag the box handles).

Scale: Actually, the scale button is three tools in one that appear when you click on the magnifying glass icon.

The first tool (the magnifying glass with the + sign) lets you expand an area of the image (like, if you want Zimbo's left eyeball to fill the box). Click on this tool; you get crosshairs in the image, which you can now move. Position the crosshairs where you want one corner of the image; click there, then drag them to where you want the opposite corner to be.

The second tool (the arrows) lets you expand or shrink the whole image. Click on this tool and you get a slider. Slide up for a smaller image, down for larger. (Go easy on larger; the image can get so large that WordPerfect slows to a crawl!)

The third tool (1:1) resets the image to its original size and proportions.

Complement: The complement button gives you a sort of color negative of your image. It's a fairly useless tool, as far as we can tell, unless you just have a strong dislike for the colors in your image. (Or maybe somebody digitized a color negative for you, and you want the positive? Or maybe you're just into seriously "rad" colors.)

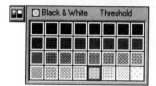 **Black & White:** This button lets you change color to black-and-white. Choose this tool, and you get the box shown here. Click in the tiny checkbox that says Black & White, and WordPerfect will guess at a good translation. If you yourself want to fool with the translation of color to shading, click on one of the shaded boxes. Lighter boxes make lighter areas go to white. (Click again on the checkbox, and your image returns to color.)

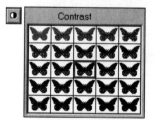 **Contrast:** The contrast button gives all you entomologists out there a thrill, with its display of butterflies. Oh yes, it also lets you pick a contrast level, as represented by the variously contrasty bugs. Pick one.

Brightness: Brightness adjusts, well, ... brightness. It uses the same butterfly gimmick as in Contrast.

Reset: Reset puts everything back the way it was before you first started messing things up with the toolbox. Remember that this will undo *everything*, even the stuff you did right.

Fill: Mostly useful for WP Draw graphics (files ending in .WPG), this tool lets you change a *filled* drawing (colored in-between the lines) to a line drawing. The right-hand butterfly makes filled areas solid white. The middle one makes the filled areas transparent; the box fill shows through. (Even more interesting, if you move this box on top of another box, the underlying box also shows through!)

Mirror vertical or horizontal: This button simply flips the image left-for-right (the left button) or upside-down (the right button).

WP Draw: This button brings up WP Draw with the image already in it.

Image settings: This button lets you control everything about the image from a single dialog box and lets you use numbers (like angles in degrees). This button is essentially all the tools combined. Click here and you get the dialog box shown in Figure 1-11.

This area changes with what you select in the top area.

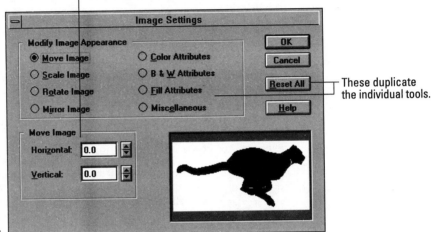

These duplicate the individual tools.

Figure 1-11:
The Image
Settings
dialog box
lets you
specify
things with
numbers.

Thanks to WordPerfect's hardworking Department of Redundancy Department, the Image Settings dialog box duplicates all the functions of the toolbox. The Move Image area in Figure 1-11 changes, depending on what attribute you select in the area above it. This dialog box lets you set attributes like rotation, but it uses numbers — like a scale factor (in percent) or rotation (in degrees) — rather than just doing things visually, as you do with the individual tools.

Chapter 2

More Lines, Borders, and Fills

. . . .

In This Chapter

▶ Using standard lines

▶ Creating custom lines

▶ Applying standard borders and fills

▶ Customizing borders

. . . .

There's nothing like a few good lines to liven things up (like "What's a nice sentence like you doing in a sidebar like this?"). Borders and fills, too ("I'm from across the border" or "Can I get you a refill?"). Especially if your document doesn't have any other graphics, then lines, borders, and fills add whatchacall "visual interest." With WordPerfect, you can put lines under headlines, down the middle of columns, at the end of columns, ... wherever. We suppose that if you use enough lines and stuff, your subject can be mind-numbingly dull, and still be interesting. Hmmm, maybe we should use more lines in this book.

Lines, borders, and fills crop up at various places throughout WordPerfect. Lines have their own menu selection under Graphics on the menu bar; they also appear in the Header/Footer Feature Bar and probably some other places we've forgotten. Borders are a somewhat more hidden option, as are fills (patterned backgrounds), which are done in the same dialog box as borders. The option Border/Fill appears under the Layout selection of the menu bar, in Paragraph, Page, and Columns. It also appears in the Feature Bars and QuickMenus for graphics and text boxes of all kinds. The dialog boxes for borders and fills vary only slightly between, say, paragraphs and text boxes — certainly not enough to worry about.

Standard Lines

Mercifully, we won't continue the obvious pun suggested by this section title. Standard lines in WordPerfect are one of two types:

- ✔ A horizontal line running the width of the page (or column or header) along the bottom of the line of text where your cursor is (press Ctrl+F11)
- ✔ A vertical line running the height of the page, wherever your cursor is (press Ctrl+Shift+F11)

Simple, huh. You can alternatively use <u>H</u>orizontal Line or <u>V</u>ertical Line, under <u>G</u>raphics in the menu bar, instead of Ctrl+F11 or Ctrl+Shift+F11.

Here are a few things you should know about these lines:

- ✔ The standard horizontal line is attached to the line of text your cursor was in when you created the line. If that text moves, the horizontal line moves.
- ✔ The horizontal line goes right at the bottom of the line of text, making the text look like an underlined font, which probably isn't what you want. If you want any space between the standard horizontal line and the text, you have to move the line. Click on it and drag.
- ✔ Unfortunately, if you move the horizontal line for any reason (like to get space between it and the text), it assumes a specific vertical location on the page — for example, 2.52 inches from the top. It no longer moves with the line of text, so if the text moves, you have to move the line yourself. That's just the way it is.
- ✔ The standard vertical line stays in a fixed horizontal position on the page (the position where your cursor was when you created the line — the *original insertion point*). It doesn't move left or right with the text. However, if you move the text containing the original insertion point to another page, the vertical line goes with it. (See the sidebar "Connections between graphic lines and text," if you're curious.)

To move a line of any kind (standard or custom, horizontal or vertical), click on it and drag. To position it more accurately, double-click on it, and you will get the Edit Graphics Line dialog box. See "Custom Lines" for more information.

To adjust line thickness or height, click once on the line to select it. Then drag one of the six handles (little black boxes) on the dashed border shown around the line. (End boxes make the line longer or shorter; middle boxes make it thicker or thinner; corner boxes do both dimensions at once.)

To delete a line, click on it and press Delete.

Connections between graphic lines and text

Even though graphic lines that have a specified position on the page (like 3.14 inches from the top) do not move with your text, there's still an "attachment" between a line and a particular chunk of text. That is because there's a secret graphic line code embedded in the text. As a result, if you move the line of text your cursor was in when you created the line to another page, the graphic line goes to the identical position on that new page. Surprise!

Custom Lines

When you want a line that's shorter, longer, thinner, thicker, another style (like dashed), another color, differently positioned, or generally weirder than the standard lines described previously, you want a *custom* line.

You can create a custom line in two ways:

1. **Adjust the line on the spot.**

   Start out with a standard line, then drag its length, thickness, or position.

2. **Use the Edit Graphics Line dialog box, shown in Figure 2-1 (or its cousin, the Create Graphics Line dialog box). You can get this box in four different ways:**

   • Double-click on an existing standard line.

   • Click with the right mouse button on a standard line and choose Edit Horizontal (or Vertical) Line from the QuickMenu.

   • Click on a standard line and choose Graphics⇨Edit Line from the menu bar.

   • Create a custom line from the start by choosing Graphics⇨Custom Line from the menu bar. This gives you a Create Graphics Line dialog box that works just like the Edit Graphics Line dialog box.

Any of these four approaches gets you the same Edit Graphics Line dialog box. (Actually sometimes it's called Create Graphics Line, but it's identical.)

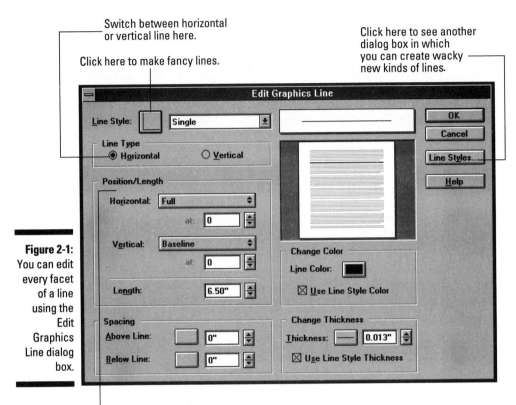

Switch between horizontal or vertical line here.

Click here to make fancy lines.

Click here to see another dialog box in which you can create wacky new kinds of lines.

Figure 2-1: You can edit every facet of a line using the Edit Graphics Line dialog box.

Change these settings to tell WordPerfect exactly where to put the line.

Mucking around with your lines

Here are some of the ways you can muck around with your lines in the Edit Graphics Line dialog box (shown in Figure 2-1):

- ✔ For a different kind of line, click on the Line Style button (in the upper-left corner of the dialog box). A cute little selection chart pops up, shown in Figure 2-2. If you don't like any of these, see "Customizing line styles," later in this chapter.

- ✔ To change a line from horizontal to vertical or vice versa, click on one of the selections in the Line Type area, Horizontal or Vertical. (Not Horizontal or Vertical in the Position/Length area.)

Figure 2-2:
When you click on Line Style in the Edit Graphics Line dialog box, you get to pick out a new style.

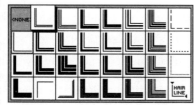

✔ To position the line horizontally, go to the Position/Length area and click and hold on the button next to Horizontal. The button will display different selections, depending upon whether your Line Type is Horizontal or Vertical:

For horizontal lines, you can choose among horizontal positions of Left, Right, Centered, Set, or Full. Left and Right push the line against a margin. Set lets you specify a distance from the left edge of the paper in the *at* box. Full actually specifies the length: fully across the page or column (from margin to margin). Full is the setting for standard lines.

For vertical lines, you can choose among horizontal positions Set, Left, Right, Centered, or Column Aligned. Left, right, and centered are with respect to the margins. Column Aligned puts a line down a column. Set lets you specify a distance from the left edge in the *at* box. Set is the setting for standard lines.

Note that if you Set a line right to the edge of the paper, most printers can't physically print there (unless the paper is small). WordPerfect restricts you to the printable area on the page.

✔ To position the line vertically, go to the Position/Length area, then click and hold on the pop-up button next to Vertical.

For horizontal lines, choose Set or Baseline in this pop-up button to set the vertical position. Set lets you specify a distance from the top of the paper (in the *at* box). Baseline puts the line across the bottom of the line of text (the setting for standard lines).

For vertical lines, the choices for vertical position are <u>S</u>et, <u>T</u>op, <u>B</u>ottom, or <u>F</u>ull. <u>T</u>op and <u>B</u>ottom push the line against a margin. <u>S</u>et lets you specify a distance from the top edge of the paper in the *at* box. <u>F</u>ull makes the line run from top margin to bottom margin. <u>F</u>ull is the setting for standard lines.

✔ For line length, click on Le<u>n</u>gth — what else? Set a value.

✔ To put space between a horizontal line and a line of text, you may think you would set the line's <u>A</u>bove Line or <u>B</u>elow Line spacing values. Nope. It doesn't work; these settings are pretty worthless. The easiest way to do this is to add a blank line below or above the text and create a horizontal line there.

✔ To move a vertical line away from the text (into the margin), first use <u>S</u>et or <u>C</u>entered for horizontal position. Then enter a value in the <u>B</u>order Offset box. (Note that spacing for lines between columns is controlled by Layout⇨<u>C</u>olumns, not here.)

✔ Generally, color and line thickness go with the style chosen. But you can change these by clicking on L<u>i</u>ne Color or <u>T</u>hickness and choosing something new from the pop-up box.

✔ For some real excitement (comparatively speaking), click on the Line St<u>y</u>les button (in the upper-right corner of the dialog box). See the next section, "Customizing line styles."

✔ In some early versions of WordPerfect, the little picture in the dialog box doesn't accurately depict what's going on. Click on OK and check your document if you're confused.

Customizing line styles

If you are extremely finicky (or bored), you can customize line styles. You're not limited to the ones we showed earlier, in Figure 2-2. Heavens, no!

1. **Start by creating or editing a line, as we described earlier.**

   This gets you the Edit (or Create) Graphics Line dialog box we just discussed.

2. **In that box, click on the Line St<u>y</u>les button, over on the right side.**

   You now get a Line Styles dialog box (too boring to show here), with a long list of currently available line styles.

3. **If there's a line style listed that you more-or-less like but would like to change a bit, click on the style, then on the <u>E</u>dit button. If you want to create a style from scratch, click on the C<u>r</u>eate button.**

   Either way, you get a dialog box pretty much like the one in Figure 2-3 (the third dialog box in a series since we started this styles-customizing business!)

4. **Follow the numbered directions in Figure 2-3 to make your changes.**

5. **When you're done, click on OK to close this box, and Select to close the next one.**

Now you can use your new style for your current line or any subsequent line; its name appears in the list of Line Styles in the Edit Graphics Line dialog box.

Figure 2-3:
The Create
Line Style
dialog box;
the Edit Line
Style dialog
box is
similar but
doesn't
have a Style
Name box
because it's
for editing
an existing
style, and
those
already
have names.

Type in a unique name for your style.

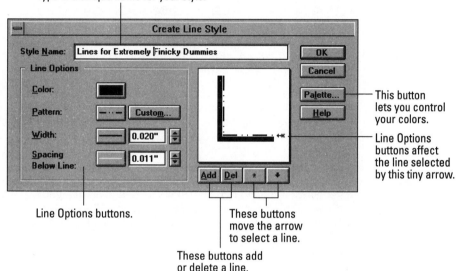

This button
lets you control
your colors.

Line Options
buttons affect
the line selected
by this tiny arrow.

Line Options buttons.

These buttons
move the arrow
to select a line.

These buttons add
or delete a line.

If you are clinically you-know-what compulsive (that is to say, unbelievably persnickety) about lines, you can customize even further. The Pattern control includes a Custom button leading to yet another dialog box. Here you can make up dashed lines from individually numbered line segments, for which you specify length and spacing. (There's gotta be some bored, retired draftsmen hanging out at the WordPerfect labs.) If you want to custom-blend your color, hit the Palette button. We refuse to entertain this subject any more. If you've gone this far, consider that your social life may need a little attention.

Borders and Fills: from Safe to Snazzy

WordPerfect's standard borders put a uniform line style all the way around something: a paragraph, a page, a column, or a graphics box. They're nice, but rather conventional.

Custom borders can go part-way around, or on any combination of sides, and can have different line styles for each side. (The line styles are the same ones we discussed in the last section, as in Figure 2-2, including any custom styles you have made.) Custom borders can also have *drop shadows,* those shadows that make a boxed-in area look like it's three-dimensional or floating off the page. These are, as the kids say, "extreme" (very nice).

Standard borders and fills

✔ **To put a border (or fill) on regular text:** Put your cursor somewhere in that text. (To border or fill a bunch of paragraphs, select all of them.) Choose Layout⇨Paragraph, Page, or Columns from the menu bar, depending on what you're putting a border on. To put a border on a paragraph, for instance, choose Paragraph. Choose Border/Fill from the submenu that appears.

✔ **To put a border (or fill) on a graphics or text box:** Click on the box to select it, then click on the box with your right mouse button and choose Border/Fill from the QuickMenu that appears. (Alternatively, you can choose Border/Fill from the Graphics Box Feature Bar, if that Feature Bar is present.)

You get an exciting and dynamic dialog box, shown in Figure 2-4. It may be called Paragraph Border, or Page Border, or Box Border/Fill Styles, depending on what you are putting a border around, but the effect is the same.

The border dialog box works like this:

✔ For a border, click on the button or box next to Border Style. The button gives you pictures of standard styles; the box gives you a list of standard style names. Choose a style, any style.

✔ For a fill, click on the button or box next to Fill Style. As with borders, choose a fill by picture or by style name. If you use a *gradient* fill (and it will say so in the little fill name box), the colors are controlled by the foreground and background colors, making a gradual transition from one to the other. If you are getting some truly awful color combinations in a gradient fill, try adjusting the foreground and background colors. (Of course, none of this matters much unless you're printing in color, doing hypertext documents, or doing something else gee-whiz that people will only see on color screens.)

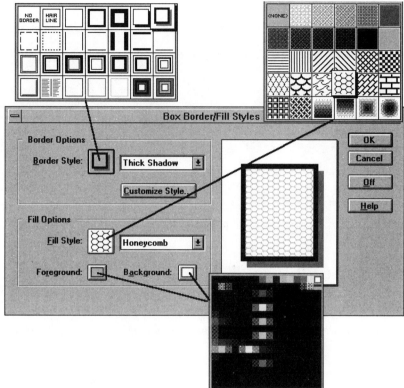

Figure 2-4:
The
fabulously
fun border
and fill
dialog box,
and friends.

✔ To change either of the two colors that make up a fill, click on either the Foreground or Background button. Either button gives you a palette of colors to choose from, but the differences between the colors don't show up too well in black-and-white (as in this book). Foreground controls the color of the lines and dots that make up the fill pattern. Background controls the overall color of the box behind the pattern. If you're using certain types of pictures (like WordPerfect graphics files that end in .WPG), background also refers to the normally-white area underlying the image.

✔ To remove the border and fill, click on the Off button.

The dangers of over-filling

Fill is fun, but it can make the content of your box absolutely illegible. To tone down the fill a bit, choose a weaker foreground color. There's generally a nice gray in the top line of the palette; you might try that. Remember, "Good taste means less filling."

Borders on multiple paragraphs or pages

When you turn on borders or fills and continue to type, you generally continue to get those borders or fills on the new text. If you want to discontinue them at some point, bring up the border dialog box again and click on the <u>O</u>ff button.

If you want to apply borders or fills to a group of already existing paragraphs or pages, select them all first, then turn on borders.

When adjoining paragraphs have a border or fill, the group of paragraphs all get a common border/ fill, with no separations. If you want separators, see the description of customized borders. Add a Separator line to your border style; a double-line line style works nicely for this purpose.

Custom borders

To get fancier borders, click on the <u>C</u>ustomize Style button in the Box Border/ Fill Styles dialog box. (You must have a border style selected for this button to be enabled.) Stand back — you get the mega-overkill dialog box of Figure 2-5.

Figure 2-5 tells most of the story. Here are a few more hints:

✔ When you customize, you are not really changing the named style; you just customize it for this single use. If you customize a paragraph with a red Hairline border style, for instance, and later use Hairline again, it doesn't come up red.

✔ The Li<u>n</u>e Style controls change only those sides that are checked at the top of the box, where it says Select sides to modify. To change just certain sides, click on the checkboxes and turn off the ones you don't want to change. To turn all the sides on or off at once, click on <u>A</u>ll. You can also click on the little triangles in the drawing to turn off or on the lines you specify.

✔ The <u>S</u>eparator line is the line between columns, if you're doing column formatting; it's the line between paragraphs if you select multiple paragraphs for paragraph formatting.

✔ The <u>L</u>ine Styles button (on the right side of the dialog box) does the same thing as the Line Styles button in the Edit Graphic Lines dialog box. See the previous section, "Customizing line styles," for information.

✔ The <u>P</u>alette button is for the incredibly fussy; it lets you blend colors to get just that right shade of red — say, of a Massachusetts Macoun apple in September. If you want to use this feature, see a psychiatrist first; or maybe a cosmetologist.

Click here to control line
style for chosen sides.

Click here to see spacing
on the thumbnail picture.

Turn off the side, you
don't want to modify.

Click here to pick a drop

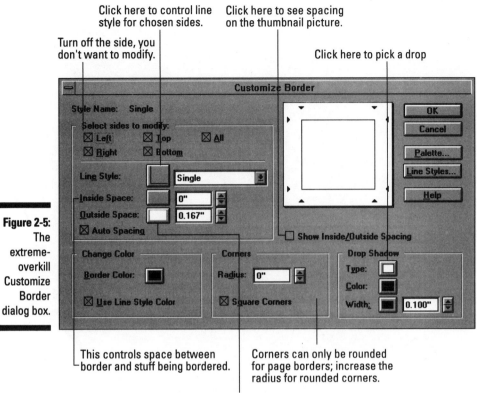

Figure 2-5:
The
extreme-
overkill
Customize
Border
dialog box.

This controls space between
border and stuff being bordered.

Corners can only be rounded
for page borders; increase the
radius for rounded corners.

This controls space between
border and text outside border.

Column "rules" using WordPerfect's borders

If you're doing a newsletter or other multicolumn document, it's sometimes nice to have lines between the columns, called "column rules." In WordPerfect, you can use column rules by choosing Layout⇨Columns⇨Border/Fill, then choosing a Border Style called Column Between (or Column All to box the columns). Adjust this style, if you like, by clicking on the Customize Style button; note that the Column Between style is simply made up of a separator line.

Chapter 3
More WP Draw!

. . . .

In This Chapter

▶ Getting into and out of WP Draw

▶ Staying out of trouble

▶ Using drawing tools

▶ Developing basic business graphics

▶ Using text in WP Draw

▶ Doing graphic fills

▶ Working with clip art

▶ Moving, copying, and modifying WP Draw objects

. . . .

*W*P Draw is WordPerfect's nifty drawing tool for writers. It lets you create drawings and modify clip art, offers some nice special effects, and ... wait a minute. This business of encouraging writers to do graphics has got to stop. We're all in favor of pretty documents and all that, but when software vendors start putting graphics tools as powerful as WP Draw into word processors, we get worried. It's like offering dentistry attachments for power drills. It gives people ideas.

But, you say (and rightly so), our job is to write the operating instructions, not the *Consumer Reports* review. So go ahead, fire up that metaphorical power drill, and have fun. We'll try to help you stay out of trouble.

Getting Into and Out of WP Draw

To get into WP Draw, do any of the following:

✔ If you already have a graphic image in your document that you want to modify, double-click on it.

✔ Or, in the same situation, click with your right mouse button on the image, then choose the top selection on the QuickMenu that appears.

✔ Click on the WP Draw button on the Button Bar to create a new drawing or edit a selected one.

✔ Choose Graphics⇨Draw from the menu bar to create a new drawing or edit a selected one.

To get out of WP Draw, do either of the following:

✔ Choose File⇨Exit and press Enter. This shuts down WP Draw and returns you to your document. WP Draw asks if you want to "Save changes" to your artwork when you do this. If you answer No, everything you've done in this current session with WP Draw will be tossed away. If you were editing an existing drawing, it will remain as it was before you started WP Draw. If you answer Yes, the drawing you're looking at in WP Draw will be copied into your document.

✔ Double-click on the big minus sign in the top-left corner of WP Draw. As with choosing File⇨Exit, WP Draw asks if you want to "Save changes" to your artwork.

✔ Click back in the document window. This leaves WP Draw running so that, unlike when you exit WP Draw, you don't have to wait for WP Draw to update your document file with the new image. This is good if you suddenly have an idea about the text in your document and want to type it in before you forget. You can return to WP Draw at any time by just clicking in the WP Draw window.

Knowledge Is Power (but What Is Truth?)

You can just sort of blunder your way around in WP Draw, but mysterious things will happen. If you want to be a *power* WP Draw user (that is, less confused), here are some important things to know:

About Help: WP Draw is very helpful. When you pass your mouse pointer over a tool, WP Draw gives you a description in the top bar (title bar) of the window. When you use a tool, WP Draw tells you how to do it at the bottom of the window.

About objects: Every shape or chunk of text you work with is an *object* that can be deleted, moved, duplicated, overlaid on other objects, or otherwise mucked-around-with independently from the rest of your drawing.

About selecting: To do anything to an object, you must select it first. Click on the arrow icon at the top-left corner of the tool area; then click on the object. To select a group of objects, either (1) hold down the Ctrl button and click on the objects one at a time, or (2) click and drag a rectangle with the selection tool around the objects you want.

About attributes: When you create shapes or text objects, WP Draw gives them the current *attributes,* like text color, fill color, fill pattern, line thickness and color, and shadow. You may change these with the commands under Attributes on the menu, or with the bottom six tools in the tool strip. If no object is selected when you set these attributes, they're *sticky:* The attributes remain set until you change them, and they affect everything you create after that. To change individual objects, select the objects first, then change their attributes; when you do this, your changes are not sticky (the attributes don't affect subsequent objects).

Draw first, set attributes later: To minimize confusion, it's sometimes best to draw first, not worrying about what colors or shading you see. Then, click on the object with the selection tool (the arrow) and set the colors or other attributes. That way, whatever attributes you set get applied only to that one object; they don't remain set that way for subsequent things you make.

Where the drawing is: When you exit WP Draw and answer Yes to the "Save changes" question, your artwork is saved only in your document (as a linked object, if you care). It's not in a separate file. If you like, you can also create a copy of your work as a separate WordPerfect graphics file using File⇨Save Copy As. This (a new feature of WordPerfect 6.0a) lets you give someone else an image file without having to give the entire document file.

About colors: There are six different *current colors,* separate ones for text and graphics: outline color, fill color, and the secondary color for two-color patterned fills. Since you can set these colors two or three different ways, it's hard to figure out what colors there are and how you set 'em. If you get utterly confused, refer to Table 3-1.

Table 3-1 Color Me Confused: Six Colors and How to Set Them

Color for ...	How You Can Set It:	
	Under Attributes (on the menu)	*Using Tools (on the toolstrip)*
Graphics lines and outlines	Color, then Line Color, or Line, then Line Color	line color tool
Graphics fill	Color, then Fill Foreground	fill color tool
Text (outline and fill)	Color, then Text Color	
Text — outline only	Text, then Color	text tool, then line color tool
Text — fill only	Text, then Foreground Color	text tool, then fill color tool
Second color for fill patterns:		
Graphics	Color, then Fill Background	
Text	Text, then Background Color	

Tools of the Trade

Your drawing tools are the strip of icons down the left side of the WP Draw window, shown in Figure 3-1. Many of these functions are duplicated by commands in the Draw and other menus.

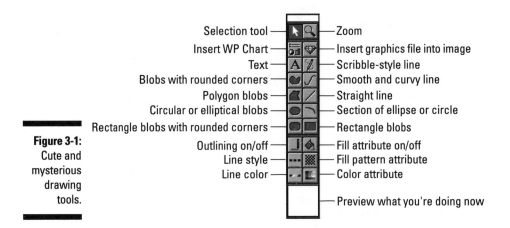

Selection tool — Zoom

Insert WP Chart — Insert graphics file into image

Text — Scribble-style line

Blobs with rounded corners — Smooth and curvy line

Polygon blobs — Straight line

Circular or elliptical blobs — Section of ellipse or circle

Rectangle blobs with rounded corners — Rectangle blobs

Outlining on/off — Fill attribute on/off

Line style — Fill pattern attribute

Line color — Color attribute

— Preview what you're doing now

Figure 3-1:
Cute and mysterious drawing tools.

Business Blob Art

The ugly truth about people doing their own graphics is that most of us will never attempt anything more sophisticated than a bunch of circles and rectangles with lines between them, which here we call *business blob art*. Nevertheless, business blob art can be challenging, so let's take it as an example and learn some of WP Draw's basic tricks.

Fire up WP Draw in any of the squmptzillion ways possible, like clicking on the WP Draw button on the Button Bar. Now you've got a WP Draw screen with a nice, blank "canvas" in the middle. Your drawing tools are neatly arranged down the left side, as shown in Figure 3-1.

The fundamental building blocks are the various blobs and lines created by the tools in Figure 3-1. With these simple tools, plus a little help from the Attributes and Arrange menus, you can create such fine business blob art as shown in Figure 3-2.

Here's how we did it (refer to Figure 3-1 for tool descriptions):

Rounded blob: For the blob representing the new kidney center, click on the blobs-with-rounded-corners tool; move your pointer to where you want the shape to begin. Click and release to start the shape, then repeat that action at various points around the shape you want. A faint line shows how the shape will look when the line closes back to the original point. Double-clicking will close the shape when you're done; don't try to close the shape by clicking back at the original point. Press Esc at any point to abort the shape.

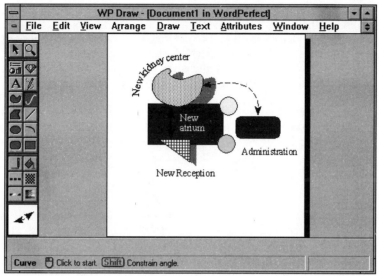

Fill: To create a unique fill pattern and color for that shape, click on the selection tool (arrow), click on the kidney center, and choose Attributes⇨Fill off the menu. From the dialog box that appears, choose a Fill Type of Pattern, then specify a Pattern and a Foreground color.

Always go back to the arrow: To avoid making accidental objects, always click back on the selection tool (arrow) when you're done making something. Otherwise, the tool you selected remains in operation and you're likely to use it accidentally.

Polygon blob (triangle): To create the triangular new reception blob, click on the polygon-blobs tool. Click and release once for each of the three corners. Press Esc if you need to cancel. Double-click to close the shape. Select the shape with the selection arrow and choose Attributes⇨Fill off the menu, as for the other blob, to change the fill; or use the fill pattern and fill color tool.

Shadows: To put shadows on the kidney center and reception blobs, begin by selecting them both. Click on the selection tool; then, holding down the Ctrl button, click on both blobs. Now choose Attributes⇨Shadow off the menu. In the dialog box that appears, choose Shadow On, then use either the slider bars or X and Y Offset to place a shadow. Leave the Transparency On checkbox enabled so that any underlying shapes will not be obscured by the shadow.

Heavy, straight arrow: This is basically a straight line with attributes of greater thickness and two heads. (We have occasionally experienced those attributes ourselves after a hard night bar-hopping in WordPerfect.) If you know you're going to use an attribute repeatedly, like double-headed arrows, you can set up that attribute first, before you make the line or any other shape; we'll do that here. Choose Attributes⇨Line from the menu. In the dialog box that appears, increase the value in the Line Width box. Click and hold on the Arrowhead button, and choose Both Ends from its menu. Close the dialog box (OK) and click on the straight line tool to make the arrow. Click and release once to start the line; hold down the Shift key while you move the mouse for a vertical line (or horizontal, or 45-degree line); double click at the other end.

Rectangular blob (no shadow): Creating the new atrium is a two-step process: creating the shadowless, patternless rectangle, then *arranging* it to the *back,* behind the other blobs. To create it, click on the rectangle-blobs tool. Click where you want one corner and drag to where you want the opposite corner; release the button. The rectangle will overlay the other blobs, for now. Proceed to the next step ...

Move blob into the background: Click on the selection arrow, then click on the *New atrium* rectangle. Choose Arrange⇨Back from the menu.

Rounded-corner rectangle: To make the administration blob, click on the rectangle-blobs-with-rounded-corners tool and do like you did for the regular rectangle.

Circles: (We don't know what these represent; ivory towers of medical learning, maybe?) Click on the circular-or-elliptical-blobs tool. Click at a point where you want the circle's edge to be; holding down the Shift key (to make a circle, not an ellipse), drag away from that point. Release the mouse button. Change the fill color using Attributes⇨Fill off the menu, as before, or use the fill color tool.

Curvy, dashed arrow: As you did for the heavy, straight arrow, adjust the Attributes: In this case, make the line thin and dashed; keep the two arrow-heads. Then choose the curvy line tool. Click and release once to mark one end; then make one or more such clicks along the general path you want (the line doesn't curve until the third point is made). Press Esc to abort at any time. Double-click to mark the other end of the line.

Getting your blobs to march in straight lines

When you've got a lot of blobs to deal with (and don't we all), it's nice if you can keep them in line. The first step is to turn on a grid to guide you. Press Alt+Shift+F8, or choose View⇨Grid. If your blobs are still disorderly, you can force them: Press Alt+F8, or View⇨Snap To Grid. Now, when you create or move blobs, lines, or text, they snap into place. You can change the grid spacing with View⇨Grid Snap Options.

Plain old black text: To make labels like "Administration," you have to enter the text in a special, temporary, editing box. Click on the big A or text tool to begin. See "Stupid Text Tricks" (the next section).

White text over blob: To create colored text (such as white), start just as you do for plain old black text. When you've got the text typed in black, click on the selection tool (arrow) and click on your text to select it. Now, click on the line color tool (bottom left of the tool strip) and choose white from the palette; this changes the text outline to white. Do the same with the fill color tool next to it, so the text will be solid white.

Sexy, curved text: Ha! You've been waiting for this, haven't you. This is tricky, so see "Text that follows a curve" in the next section, "Stupid Text Tricks."

Stupid Text Tricks

Working with text in WP Draw can be a little confusing. Here are the basics, plus some tricks that will get you through the day with minimum distress:

Making text: Click on the big A or text tool. Make a box to type in by clicking where you want one corner of the box (say, the upper-left corner) and dragging to the opposite corner (say, lower right). Type, and text goes in this box. If your text is too large or small or ugly, highlight it and press F9 to change the font (just as you would in a document). You can also change the font and do a bunch of other text stuff with the commands under Text in the menu bar. If you need more or less room in the box for text, drag one of the tiny squares (handles) around the box to resize it. Click anywhere outside the box when you're done.

Editing your text: Click on the selection tool (arrow). Select the text object by clicking on it with this tool, then choose Edit Text from the Edit menu (see Figure 3-3). Edit the text the way you normally would in a document. To change its font or formatting, highlight the text and use commands in the Text menu. Regular keyboard commands like Ctrl+B for boldface and F9 for fonts also work.

Figure 3-3:
The text editing box appears when you create text or use Edit⇨Edit Text.

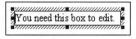
You need this box to edit.

Making text line-wrap properly in the box: If the box is too small, the text will wrap and form a new line. You may not want wrapping, or you may want the text to wrap at a different point. Some solutions are: Use a smaller font; expand the box by dragging its handles (this only works while the box is visible); or press Enter where you would prefer the line to wrap. If you can't see the box, select the text object with the selection tool (arrow) and choose Edit Text from the Edit menu.

Positioning the text in the box: You can center and right-justify your text if you like. If the text box is visible, place your cursor in the line you want positioned and pick from the choices offered by Text⇨Layout or Text⇨Justification. If the text box isn't visible, select the text object with the selection tool (arrow) and choose Edit Text from the Edit menu.

Shrinking/enlarging the entire box of text: If you decide the whole thing ought to be larger or smaller, click on the text object with the selection tool (arrow) and drag one of the handles. Obviously, this makes your choice of font size irrelevant, since the text isn't that size any more. Just remember, if you make every chunk of text a different size using this technique, it gets visually annoying.

Cute colors: It's easiest to change colors after you create your text, rather than before. Select the text object by clicking on it with the selection tool (arrow); to select more than one text object, hold down the Ctrl button while you select. Click on the line color tool (bottom, left on the tool clip) to change the outline color; click on the fill color tool (bottom, right) to change the interior (fill) color.

Text fills: Besides plain colors, you can get patterns, gradient fills, transparency, and other fun stuff. See "More Fills that Thrill," the next section.

Text that follows a curve: There are four parts to getting text to follow a curve or other shape: (1) Type your text normally; (2) create a curved line or other shape where you want the text; (3) select both the text and the curved line together (using the selection tool, hold down the Ctrl key and click on one, then the other); (4) choose Arrange⇨Effects⇨Contour Text to get a Contour Text dialog box; choose a Position for the text on the line, if you like (turn off Display Text Only if you want to see the line), and click on OK. To undo it, choose Arrange⇨Effects⇨Straighten Text.

More Fills that Thrill

The stuff in the middle of a shape or a letter is a *fill*. Analogous to the nutritious creamy filling in your favorite snack cake, fills are a sort of visual treat. You can have a *Pattern* fill (a plain, solid color is also considered a pattern fill), a *Gradient* fill (a gradual transition between two colors), or no fill at all (transparent).

The easiest way to specify a fill is to first create the object (a shape or text), ignoring whatever fill WP Draw gives you. Then go back and change it. There are several ways to do this, so we're going to give you the easiest.

1. **Click on the selection tool (arrow) and click on the object to select it.**

2. **If you only want a solid color, click on the fill on/off tool and choose Fill On, then click on the fill color tool and choose a color.**

3. **For more complex fills, choose Attributes⇨Fill. The Fill Attributes dialog box appears.**

   For a solid color: set Fill Type to Pattern; click on the Pattern button and choose the solid black box; click on the Foreground Color button and choose a color.

   For a patterned fill: set Fill Type to Pattern; click on the Pattern button and choose one; click on the Foreground Color button and choose one color; do the same for Background Color.

   For a gradient fill: set Fill Type to Gradient; click on the Type button and choose a Linear, Circular, or Rectangular pattern (a sample window in the dialog box illustrates these for you). Click on the Center Color and Outer color buttons to choose different colors for your fill.

   For more-exotic gradient fills, adjust the centering of your pattern by clicking the up/down arrows for X Offset and Y Offset. You can also make linear or rectangular shading run in an exciting diagonal fashion (truly!) by adjusting the Angle value in a similar manner. Finally, you can specify how many steps the blending process uses; by clicking on Fixed and specifying a number of steps in that box, you can create shaded bands instead of a continuous transition between colors.

Two kinds of fillings, two ways to change them

WP Draw keeps track of two types of current fill: one for text and another for graphics. It applies these current fills as you create new text and graphics. You can specify them in two ways: Either change the current fill as you go along, or ignore whatever current fill WP Draw gives you, then go back and change the fill on selected objects.

It's probably easier to change fill on selected objects, so that's what we mostly describe in this chapter. If you would rather change the current fill, make sure no object is currently selected. Then use Attributes⇨Fill and, in the ensuing dialog box, set Apply To to Graphics Only, Text Only, or Graphics and Text. Set your fill color and pattern.

To remove a fill altogether, select the object (Step 1 above); then click and hold on the fill on/off tool (the little bucket near the bottom of the tool strip); choose either Fill or No Fill. This gives you a transparent shape or letter (outline only).

You can also turn off the fill attribute before making objects, if you are going to make a bunch of unfilled stuff. Just click with the selection tool anywhere in the blank "canvas" (so there's nothing selected), then click on the bucket. Adorably, the bucket changes between upright (no fill) and pouring (fill) each time you click.

Finally, you can put a background color or gradient fill underlying the entire image, using File⇨Page Layout. If you click on Gradient in the Page Layout dialog box that appears, it works a lot like the Fill Attributes dialog box described previously (in Step 3). For a background color, click on Solid, then the Color button.

Working with Clip Art

One of the best ways for the artistically insecure to create the graphics they need is to edit commercially available artwork, called *clip art* (graphics files). WordPerfect has provided a bunch of clip art, and you can buy additional clip art. Check out the classifieds in the back of your favorite computer magazine or that big heap of literature that came in the WordPerfect box.

A sure way to get yourself into trouble is to start using art that you don't have the right to use. Just because the artwork is in a file and you have that file doesn't mean you can legally use it — even if you modify it. Even scanning printed artwork into your computer doesn't change the legality issue. Make sure you have a license to use the artwork. If you've bought it, it probably came with some sort of license; check the terms. If someone has made it for you, you may have the right to use it, but only once, or not in countries beginning with the letter "Y," or on alternate Tuesdays, depending on the terms of your agreement.

To use clip art other than WordPerfect's (files ending in .WPG), click on the List Files of Type box in the Open File dialog box. (If your clip art is on a diskette, be sure to change the disk drive to A: or B: in that dialog box.) Otherwise, WordPerfect only shows you .WPG files.

There are two ways to work with clip art files in WP Draw:

1. Insert a clip art image as a Figure in your document, then double-click on it to run WP Draw.

TECHNICAL STUFF

Different forms of clip art

Clip art comes in many different forms, or *graphics file formats*. The exact form is usually given by the three-letter extension to the file name. The two main types of format are *vector* and *bitmap*. Vector formats such as WordPerfect's own .WPG format are generally more easy to use than bitmap formats. You can pick them apart and change the parts. Bitmap formats such as Windows Bitmap (.BMP), PC Paintbrush (.PCX), and TIFF are more common, but are harder to modify. You can really only draw on top of those images, not change them. When you use bitmap images in WP Draw, the entire image is an object.

2. In WP Draw, use the *insert graphic file* tool. (It's the diamond icon — why a diamond? Beats us.) Click once if you want to fill the canvas with your image; or, click and drag a rectangle for a smaller image. A file-selection dialog box opens and lets you choose an image. You may find it handy to click on the Vie<u>w</u> button; this lets you preview file contents as you click on file names.

Generally, you should use Method 1. Use Method 2 if you want to include a piece of clip art as an element of another, bigger graphic (like putting a butterfly on Zimbo's nose). Either way, any changes you make won't affect the original clip art file, just the version of it in your document.

You can also cut and paste images from other programs into WP Draw. Imagine you have Windows software that shows you a satellite weather map (isn't imagination wonderful? Actually, you can get up-to-date maps from CompuServe). If the software supports copying and pasting, copy the map image (typically with Ctrl+C) onto the Windows Clipboard. Then, with WP Draw running, paste the weather map with Ctrl+V; in WP Draw it becomes one, single, huge object. Now draw Zimbo on top of the image as the weather-chimp.

Finally, if you're lucky enough to own a scanner, you can read images from paper into WP Draw. Bear in mind that the entire image will be a single, gigundic object. Install your scanner using the scanner manufacturer's instructions. Choose <u>F</u>ile⇨<u>I</u>mage Source Setup to specify the right scanner. (If this menu choice is grayed out or you get an error message, it's because Windows can't find the "driver" software — software that knows about your particular scanner. Time to buy some cookies to bribe your PC guru.) Click on the scanner name in this dialog box; then choose Select. Place your image on the scanner; then choose <u>F</u>ile⇨Ac<u>q</u>uire Image.

Grabbing an image from any Windows program

Here's a crude but effective method for grabbing an image from Windows programs. Windows has a built-in *screen capture* feature that takes a snapshot of the currently active window and puts it on the Clipboard. You can then paste the Clipboard into WP Draw and white-out all but the part you want.

Here's how: With WP Draw running, run the program from which you want to copy an image.

Click in that program's title bar to make sure its window is active. Press Alt+PrintScreen (sometimes shown as PrtScr; generally in the upper right of your keyboard). Now, click in the WP Draw window and press Ctrl+V to insert the image of the window. To white-out parts that you don't want, overlay white-outlined rectangles with white fill.

If you're using WordPerfect's own clip art, you can make changes because the images are made up of various text, line, and shape objects, and you can deal with those separately. If you're using other clip art, like files that end in .BMP, the entire image may be an object, and you can't, say, enlarge Zimbo The Chimp's nose. You can, however, superimpose a new nose made up of a filled ellipse. (A gradient fill makes a nice, round-looking nose, by the way.)

Generally, the fewer the colors, the easier an image is to work with. That's because each patch of color is its own object. If you were going to move one of the butterfly's wings, for instance, you would have to select all the objects in that wing and move them together. Sometimes you can't even do that, because there's a single black background shape behind the entire image. (This provides job security for clip-art artists.)

If you've used the diamond tool (Method 2), your entire image may appear as a single object. If the image is from a .WPG file, you can break it up into individual objects by choosing Arrange⇨Ungroup from the menu.

Some kinds of changes are easy, others just aren't worth the effort. Easy changes are: adding a shape, changing colors and fills, adding titles and other text, and scaling things up or down. But unless you have some artistic talent, great manual dexterity, and lots of time, it's best not to try to change the shapes of complex or realistic images, like butterflies or people.

To change a clip-art image, you can draw new objects on top of it, delete existing objects, or futz around with the colors and fill as we described earlier.

Moving, Copying, and Modifying Objects

Flip 'em, flop 'em, twist and turn 'em; WP Draw lets you do darn near anything to an object. If you muck it up, there's an Undo command under Edit in the menu that undoes your most recent mistake. (You're on your own for earlier mistakes.)

Here's how to mess up perfectly fine artwork in WP Draw. As we said at the beginning, to do anything to an object, you have to select it first. Click on the selection tool (arrow), and then use that to click on the text, line, or shape.

- ✔ **Adding/removing fill:** Select the object, then click and hold on the fill on/off tool (third from the bottom on the right — the paint bucket icon). (Yes, that's what it is.) Choose Fill or No Fill from the tiny little menu.

- ✔ **Adding/removing an outline:** Select the object, then click and hold on the line on/off tool (third from the bottom on the left — the drafting pen icon). (Yes, that's what it is.) Choose Line or No Line from the tiny little menu.

- ✔ **Changing shape:** Select the object, then choose Edit⇨Edit Points off the menu, or click with the right mouse button and choose Edit Points from the QuickMenu. Inflection points appear, marking where you originally clicked the mouse button to make the shape. Click on the inflection points and drag them to change the shape; to drag more than one point, click and drag a rectangle around them, then drag the points.

  Extra credit: A mysterious straight line appears when you click on an inflection point; it goes through the point and has two endpoints. It looks like a skinny see-saw. Drag an endpoint of the see-saw outward for a broader curve; drag it around the pivot point to change the curve's inflection!

  More Extra Credit: Select an inflection point, then click on it or any other point with the right mouse button. With the QuickMenu you can Delete or Add a point, break Open a closed shape, Close a broken shape, change adjoining lines to straight lines (To Line) if they're curved or to curved (Smooth or Symmetrical) if they're straight.

- ✔ **Copying:** Select the object and press Ctrl+C; then press Ctrl+V to paste it. The copy goes inconveniently right on top of the original, where you can't tell it's there. Just move it away to where you want it; the original stays in place.

- ✔ **Deleting:** Select the object; press the Delete key.

- ✔ **Flipping:** To flip an object top-for-bottom or left-for-right, select the object and choose Arrange, then Flip Left/Right or Flip Top/Bottom.

✔ **Grouping/ungrouping:** (Note: "grouping," not "groping"; this is a family book.) When you've drawn a bunch of shapes to represent, say, Zimbo The Chimp (we like Zimbo), you don't want to have to select his nose, his eyes, his mouth, and his uvula every time you have to move him or shrink him. No way; you want to move Zimbo. To do this, *group* his features: Select them all; then choose Arrange⇨Group. Now when you select any part of Zimbo, you get all of him. To move Zimbo, look for a tiny little square somewhere on him and drag that. To fragment him again, use Arrange⇨Ungroup.

✔ **Moving:** To do this, click and drag. If the object has no fill, just an outline, look for a tiny square on the outline and drag that. (You have to use the tiny square for grouped objects, too; see "Grouping/ungrouping.")

✔ **Overlaying:** To put one shape behind another, select it and choose Arrange⇨Back (Front does the opposite); if you're building a stack of several things, realize that objects can only go to the top (front) or bottom (back). The QuickMenu also offers Back and Front.

✔ **Rotating:** Select the object and choose Edit⇨Rotate or click on the object with the right mouse button and choose Rotate off the QuickMenu. Click and drag one of the corner squares that appear around the object. It rotates around the little square-with-tiny-crosshairs currently in the center of the object, which you can also drag and move if you want to rotate around something other than the center.

✔ **Shadowing:** Select the object and choose Attributes⇨Shadow. In the dialog box that appears, choose Shadow On, then use either the slider bars or X and Y Offset to place a shadow. Leave the Transparency On checkbox enabled so that any underlying shapes will not be obscured by the shadow.

✔ **Shrinking/expanding:** Select the object, then drag one of the black squares (handles) that appear around the object. To shrink/expand it without distortion, use the corner handles.

✔ **Skewing:** This is sort of like what happens when you push against a large stack of books on your desk (trust us, we know). Start out as if you were rotating, but instead of dragging a corner square, drag one of the *side* squares that appear around the object.

Overall Image Stuff

As they say in the "dress for success" books, overall image is important. That's why we always wear our best overalls when we write these books.

Here are some things you can do about the big picture.

✔ **Contrast, brightness, warmth:** Sounds like a psychological profile of your family, doesn't it? No? Well, take a picture of them, scan it into WP Draw, and adjust these qualities until you like the way they look. Choose File⇨Adjust Image for a dialog box and fiddle with the values there. *Warmth,* by the way, means redness (versus blueness), sort of. Click on Preview to see how you're doing (you may have to drag the dialog box out of the way). Click on OK when everyone is brighter or whatever.

✔ **Fill:** You can put one of those wild and crazy gradient fills or just a simple color in the background of your drawing (the canvas area) instead of boring white. Choose File⇨Page Layout and click on the Color button to choose a color. For a gradient fill, click on Gradient (not Solid) for Page Color. See Step 3 under "More Fills that Thrill" for more information on how these gradients work.

✔ **Sizing:** Just how big is your picture, anyway? It's hard to tell. To get an idea, turn on the grid with Alt+Shift+F8. Unless you've changed the grid spacing (with Grid/Snap Options), the lines are at one-inch intervals; the dots are at $^1/_4$-inch intervals. But size is an illusion. The size of your picture is usually determined, not by WP Draw, but by the size of the graphics box in your document. Your picture is scaled down to fit the box.

If you don't like this vague sort of stuff, you can specify the exact size when you create the picture, and tell the graphics box not to fool with it. In WP Draw, choose File⇨Page Layout and specify a Width and Height under Page Size. (Your picture will be scaled up or down so everything fits.) In the document, click on the graphics box with the right mouse button and choose Size off the QuickMenu that appears. You get a dialog box. Click on Size to Content in the Width and Height areas, even if it's already checked off. You must repeat this sizing process in the document if you change the size in WP Draw.

✔ **Zooming:** This doesn't actually affect your image, just your view of it. To zoom in on an area, click on the zoom in/out tool (the magnifying glass) and choose the magnifying glass with a + in it. Then drag a rectangle around the area with this tool. The image expands beyond the edges of the WP Draw window; you can get to other areas by sliding the sliders at the bottom and right side of the window. Or, you can zoom back out: Click on the zoom tool again and choose the thing that looks like a blank page.

Got it? Now you know more than any writer ought to know about drawing your own graphics.

Chapter 4

More WP Chart!

Congratulations (sort of)! You are about to enter a new dimension. Here, time and space have no meaning (that is, you can waste lots of both). Swirling galaxies of charts await you in infinite variety, ready to transform your drab, boring numbers into scintillating, tantalizing, glowing graphical representations.

Billions and Billions of Charts

WP Chart offers a mind-numbing selection of charts. (We offer our well-numbed minds as Exhibit A.) If you don't want any of this mental Novocain, skip to "Basic, Simple, Rudimentary, Uncomplicated Charts," later in this chapter.

Chart types and styles

Still with us? Here's the rundown. There are six basic *types* of chart; each is available in several *basic styles*; some have more, others less. There are cute little pictures of types and basic styles on the WP Chart toolstrip at the left side of the WP Chart window.

Then, to add to the mind-numbing choices, you can mix types within a single chart. For instance, you can use a line for one series of data and bars for the rest. WordPerfect offers certain preset combinations, with preset labeling and other stuff, which we'll call *numbered styles*. You, too, can make up your own *custom styles*. Got it? Types, basic styles, and numbered styles. (Not to mention your own custom styles.) We've made up a list, which follows.

Types	Basic Styles	Numbered Styles
Bar	3D/2D	Combinations of types and basic styles, with labeling & formatting
Scatter	Horiz./Vert.	
Line	Bar Cluster/Overlap	
Area	Stacked	
Hi/Lo	Stacked percentages	
Pie	Pie Proportional	

Once you start up WP Chart with the Chart button in WordPerfect's Button Bar (see "Basic, Simple, Rudimentary, Uncomplicated Charts" in the next section), here's where to specify your types, basic styles, and numbered styles:

- ✔ Choose your type in a number of places; in particular, the top seven buttons in the toolstrip or under Chart in the menu bar.
- ✔ Choose both type and numbered style from graphical examples in WP Chart's Gallery. To get the Gallery, use the top button in the toolstrip or the Chart⇨Gallery command.
- ✔ Specify a basic style by means of the Options⇨Layout menu or using the middle set of buttons on the toolstrip.

Chart options

As if all that weren't enough, WordPerfect also lets you fool with the colors and patterns of lines and fills; the width of bars; the fonts, outlining, fill colors, and "boxing" of the text; the labeling, titles, and legends; and the axis grids and tick marks. Had enough? Wait! We haven't talked about drawing on or around your chart in WP Draw! (And guess what — we're not going to! If you want to scribble on your charts, just start WP Chart from WP Draw, and remember that your chart becomes an object in WP Draw. Then read Chapter 3.)

You'll recognize most of the chart types. The best way to understand how WP Chart does the various types is to try them out. Fortunately, WP Chart provides examples of each type. Just launch WP Chart from the Button Bar or menu bar (choose Graphics⇨ Chart) and choose a type by clicking on Chart in the menu bar or one of the cute pictures in the toolstrip on the left side of the WP Chart window.

Rows and columns

When you make a chart, you give WP Chart a table of text and numbers to work with. The trick is to understand how the rows and columns in that table translate into a chart. Here's a quick summary, by chart type.

- ✔ **Bar charts:** Each number in a cell (intersection of a row and column) becomes a bar; column headings become bar labels; columns become clustered or stacked sets of bars; each row (data series) gets a common color or "look"; row headings become color-coded legends.

- ✔ **Line charts:** Each row becomes a line; column headings (in the top row) become labels along the x-axis; each row (data series) gets a common color or "look"; row headings (in the leftmost column) are used to identify the colors in an optional legend.

- ✔ **Area charts:** Rows and columns work just as they do for line charts. The only difference is that the area under the line is filled.

- ✔ **Scatter charts:** These show *y* for a set of *x* values, for instance gas mileage of cars at different speeds. Each row translates into a series of points with its own color, like green points for the "minivans" row, and red points for the "sports cars" row.

- ✔ **Pie charts:** These show proportion; each pair of columns (the left one for labels and the right one for values) is a pie, and each cell in the column is a piece of pie. Multiple columns give multiple pies (up to nine). A proportional pie chart (a basic style of pie chart) shows bigger pies for columns that have larger sums.

- ✔ **Hi/Lo:** For all you stock-market wheeler-dealers, these show stock values (or anything you want to track the same way you would stocks, such as daily temperatures). Each row is a company. A set of four columns gives the high, low, open, and close values, in that order (left to right), for a single day.

Basic, Simple, Rudimentary, Uncomplicated Charts

Now that you've just read about the six billion flavors of chart available in WP Chart, you are undoubtedly saying, "I really don't give a rat's uvula, I just wanna make a bar chart." Hey, we're with you!

Why does it say WP Draw?

Once you get into WP Chart, don't be frustrated by the fact that the title bar on the window says WP Draw. There actually is no such thing as WP Chart; you're really in a Chart Editor within WP Draw; but try not to think about it. It doesn't really matter.

Getting into and out of WP Chart

To get into WP Chart, do any of the following:

✔ Click on the WP Chart button on the Button Bar or choose
Graphics⇨Chart from the menu bar to create a new chart or edit the
selected one.

✔ If you have a table you want to chart, select the entire table, then do one of
the above. The table data, with row and column headings, all goes magi-
cally into a chart.

✔ Click on the WP Draw button or otherwise fire up WP Draw. Then click on
the WP Chart tool (second from the top, left, in the WP Draw toolstrip) and
click once in the canvas area. Or, for a chart that's a small part of a graphic
image, drag a rectangle in the canvas instead of clicking. Your chart will be
fitted into that rectangle. A Create Chart dialog box asks what type of chart
you want; choose anything, you can change your mind later.

✔ If you have a chart already in your document that you want to modify,
double-click on the chart.

✔ Or, in the same situation, click with your right mouse button on the image;
then choose the top selection on the QuickMenu that appears.

To get out of WP Chart, do any of the following:

✔ Click on the Return button on the bottom of the window. (Or, press
Ctrl+F4, or click on File and choose the bottom command in this menu.)
This shuts down WP Chart and returns you to your document (or to WP
Draw, if that's where you started). WP Chart asks if you want to Save
changes to your chart when you do this. Choose Yes unless you want to
discard everything you've done in this WP Chart session.

✔ Double-click on the big minus sign in the top-left corner of the window. As
with pressing Ctrl+F4, WP Chart asks if you want to "Save changes" to your
chart.

✔ Click back in the document window. This leaves WP Chart running, so that,
unlike exiting WP Chart, you don't have to wait for WP Chart to update
your document file with the new image. You can just type. This is good if
you suddenly have an idea about the text in your document and want to
type it in before you forget. You can return to WP Chart at any time by just
clicking in the chart window.

Tools of the trade

OK, besides the menu, what's all this junk in your window? Check out Figure
4-1. There are what looks like a table or spreadsheet on the top, a chart on the
bottom, and a bunch of buttons down the side. Your window actually has two
parts: the data part in the top, where you can type in numbers and headings,
and the chart part in the bottom, where you can see what's going on. If you
need more room for data, just click and drag the heavy black line between the
two parts downward.

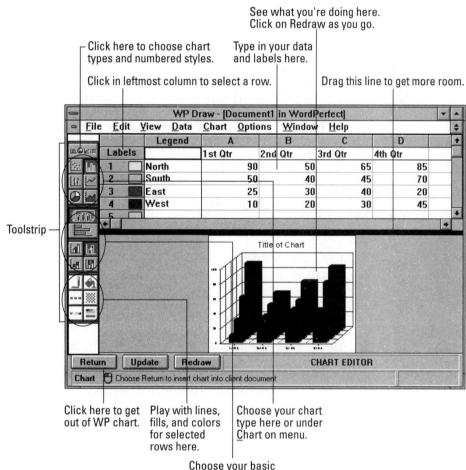

See what you're doing here.
Click on Redraw as you go.

Click here to choose chart
types and numbered styles.

Type in your data
and labels here.

Click in leftmost column to select a row.

Drag this line to get more room.

Figure 4-1:
The chart
command
center, alias
WP Chart,
alias the
Chart Editor
of WP Draw.
You can call
it Charley.

Toolstrip

Click here to get
out of WP chart.

Play with lines,
fills, and colors
for selected
rows here.

Choose your chart
type here or under
Chart on menu.

Choose your basic
chart style here.

You don't actually do anything in the bottom part; it just shows you the chart. It doesn't change automatically when you put in new data, however; you have to click on the Redraw button at the bottom of the window to see the result of data changes.

Basic bar charts

Everybody, but everybody, wants bar charts, so WordPerfect starts you out with an example of one when you fire up WP Chart. If you don't see a bar chart for some reason, click on the bar-chart button in the toolstrip (top, right column), or choose Chart⇨Bar from the menu. Bar charts are good for showing quantities in different categories, like sales in different geographic regions.

Charting your tables: You don't get an example bar chart if you start up WP Chart with a table selected in your document. Instead, your table is duplicated in the top part of the WP Chart window, and the chart automatically illustrates the data. Nice, huh! If you want another type of chart, like a line chart, just change the type. (You have to have your rows, columns, and headings just the way WP Chart wants them for the kind of chart you choose, though. See the following discussion.)

Examine the example data and chart. Notice that

- ✔ Each row of data gets its own color.
- ✔ The top row is reserved for your column labels.
- ✔ The leftmost column is reserved for your "legend," identifying colors with terms such as "North," but right now they don't appear in the chart.

To chart your own data, you can either clear out all the example data and put in your own all at once, or replace the example data one cell at a time. If you're confused about rows and columns, use the cell-at-a-time approach.

To clear out a rectangular area of example data, click in one corner of the area and drag to the opposite corner; press Del, then press Enter when a dialog box appears. To enter new data in a cleared cell or to replace example data in one cell at a time, click in a cell and type your new data (or a legend, or a label).

When you're done entering data, click on Redraw at the bottom of the window.

Put in your own title. Choose Options, then Titles. Type in a new Title in the dialog box that appears. You can also put in a subtitle and label the x-and y-axes in this dialog box. Click on Preview to see results as you go.

When you're done, click on the Return button at the bottom of the window and answer Yes to the Save changes question. If this puts you in WP Draw, click on File⇨Exit to go back to the document.

Here are a few simple variations you may want. Refer to the WP Chart toolstrip in Figure 4-2.

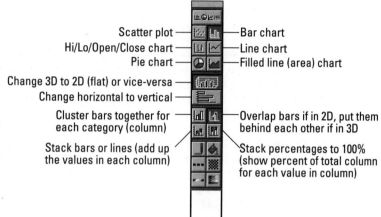

Scatter plot ———— Bar chart
Hi/Lo/Open/Close chart ———— Line chart
Pie chart ———— Filled line (area) chart

Change 3D to 2D (flat) or vice-versa ————
Change horizontal to vertical ————

Cluster bars together for ———— Overlap bars if in 2D, put them
each category (column) behind each other if in 3D

Stack bars or lines (add up ———— Stack percentages to 100%
the values in each column) (show percent of total column
for each value in column)

Figure 4-2:
Variations
on a theme
with the
toolstrip.

✔ For a conventional flat or 2D chart rather than the sexy 3D example, click on the top button of the chart-basic-style buttons; it looks like a vertical bar chart with gridlines. Refer to Figure 4-1. (The words "Toggle 3D/2D chart" appear in the title bar when your mouse pointer crosses this button.) If you change your mind, click on it again.

✔ To change the color or pattern used for a row of data, select the row by clicking in the Labels column (where the color appears). Then click on the color selection button on the bottom right of the toolstrip and pick a color. To change the pattern, click on the checkerboard-looking button just above that and choose a pattern. This is helpful for small charts that will be printed on a black-and-white printer.

✔ To have a legend box that identifies what the colors mean (like "North," "East," and so on in the example), choose Options⇨Legend from the menu. Click in the Display Legend checkbox in the dialog box that appears. Click on the Preview button in that box to see where the legend will go. Click on the Position button to select one of the eight legend positions. Click OK when done.

✔ For a horizontal chart, click on the button that looks like a horizontal bar chart. If you change your mind, click on it again.

✔ For a stacked chart, click on the Stack the bars or lines button. To show what percentage a value (cell) is for each category (column), click on the Stack percentages to 100% button.

✔ For variety's sake, check out some of the standard numbered styles available. Click on the top button of the toolstrip or choose Chart⇨Gallery and click on something you like from the graphical display of examples. Click on Retrieve.

Basic line charts

Line charts are almost as popular as bar charts. They're good for things that vary over time, cost, distance, temperature, or some other continuous variable.

If you start WP Chart from the main menu bar or Button Bar, the first thing you see is a bar chart example. Don't let that stop you; just click on the line-chart button on the toolstrip (second from the top, right column) or choose Chart⇨Line from the menu. If you start WP Chart from your document with a table selected, the data is (are, am, whatever) already in WP Chart's data area. If you start WP Chart from WP Draw, you get to choose Line directly from a dialog box.

Basic line charts work just like basic bar charts. Let's save a tree and not reprint the instructions; just look at the preceding section. Here are a few tips that you may want to think about for line charts, though:

- ✓ Line charts are a little funky-looking in 3D; try 2D. Refer to Figure 4-2.

- ✓ For 2D charts, line style is important. To change line style, first select a row by clicking in the Labels column. Then click on the line style button (second from the bottom on the left) on the toolstrip and pick a style. To change line color, click on the next button down. These are very hard to see unless you expand the chart area of the window (drag the heavy black horizontal line upward).

- ✓ Try an area chart. Click on the area chart button on the toolstrip (just under the line chart button). The bottom row of data gets displayed "in front," so if higher rows have lesser values, they may get covered up.

- ✓ Try a different style. Click on the top button of the toolstrip or choose Chart⇨Gallery and click on something you like from the graphical display of examples. Click on Retrieve.

Basic scatter plots

Scatter plots are useful when presenting statistical data, like the weights of 20 sea turtles at intervals of one month, over a year. Each turtle would get a row; each month's data would be in a column. The scatter plot shows clusters of points at each interval.

If you start WP Chart from the main menu bar or Button Bar, ignore the bar chart example that appears and click on the scatter-plot button on the toolstrip (top, left column), or choose Chart⇨Scatter from the menu. If you start out WP Chart from WP Draw, you get to choose Scatter directly from a dialog box.

Basic scatter plots work similarly to basic bar or line charts, so let's save another tree and not reprint the instructions; take a look at the preceding sections. Here are a few tips for scatter plots, though:

✔ Each row (subject) gets its own color.

✔ The top row is reserved for "X Data"; the beginning and ending values in this row define the range of the *x*-axis (say, from 0 months to 6 months). The intermediate columns give data for whatever *x*-points you obtained your data for (say, 0, 1, 2.5, 3.5, 4, 5.8, and 6 months). Note that WP Chart doesn't require that your data be at even intervals of *x*, but will plot your data at whatever *x*-value heads the column.

✔ You can adjust the intervals along the graph's *x*- and *y*-axes by choosing Options⇨Axis. Select the axis you want to change (X or Y1), set an interval with Major Grid Value, and click on Preview until you get it right.

Basic pie charts

Ahh, nothing like Mom's basic, homemade pie charts to warm the cockles of the heart (warm cockles being essential to good documents). In fact, when you ask WP Chart for a pie chart, it gives you a very fruit-pie-ish example with Bananas, Apples, Pears, and Grapes. (Which raises the question, why does one never see grape pies?)

If you start WP Chart from the main menu bar or Button Bar, ignore the bar chart example. Just click on the pie-chart button on the toolstrip (refer to Figure 4-2) or choose Chart⇨Pie from the menu. If you start out WP Chart from WP Draw, you get to choose Pie directly from a dialog box before entering the Chart Editor.

Here are a few things to observe about these charts:

✔ Each row of data gets a color.

✔ The leftmost white column is for legend information that describes what a given color is all about.

✔ A pair of adjacent columns describes a pie. The left column gives the labels; the right column gives the data.

✔ Only one pie's worth of data is shown in the example. For a second pie, make a second pair of columns. Then click on the button in the toolstrip with the two-pie icon. (This button is grayed-out if there's only one pie's worth of data.)

Here are a few tips for fiddling with basic pie charts. It's really quite similar to fiddling with other types of charts:

- For a conventional flat or 2D chart rather than the sexy 3D example, click on the top button of the chart-basic-style buttons; it (now) looks like a thick pizza. (The words `Toggle 3D/2D pie chart` appear in the title bar when your mouse pointer crosses this button.) If you change your mind, click on the button again.

- To change the color or pattern used for a row of data, select the row by clicking in the leftmost column (where the color appears). Then click on the color selection button on the bottom right of the toolstrip and pick a color. To change the pattern, click on the checkerboard-looking button just above that and choose a pattern. This is helpful for small charts that will be printed on a black-and-white printer.

- To have a legend box that identifies what the colors mean (like "North," "East," and so on in the example), choose Options⇨Legend from the menu. Click in the Display Legend checkbox in the dialog box that appears. Click on the Preview button in that box to see where the legend will go. Click on the Position button to move the legend. Click OK when done.

- To change the labels (like "Banana"), choose Options⇨Labels to get a Pie Chart Labels dialog box. To reposition the labels, click on the Label button in that box. To label pie slices with absolute or percentage values, click and hold on the Value or Percent button and choose Inside or Outside labels. To change the type size or style, click on the Font button. Click on Preview to see what effect you're having; finally, click on OK, and the Pie Chart Labels dialog box goes away.

- For variety's sake, check out some of the standard numbered styles available. Click on the top button of the toolstrip or choose Chart⇨Gallery and click on something you like from the graphical display of examples. Click on Retrieve.

Dealing with Data

While not nearly as much fun as Dialing for Dollars, we must all Deal with Data: the basic numbers and text that we want to chart. We need to somehow get this stuff into WP Chart, shuffle it around, get it graphed, maybe get it printed on the graph as labels, properly format it, blah, blah, blah. As Dummies (not dummies), the question always before us (and probably after us) is: How can we do the most work with the least amount of messing around on the computer?

Getting data into WP Chart

The absolute least-attractive way to get data into WP Chart is by typing it in. If you can at all avoid this, do so. We'll tell you about several nifty ways. But let's get the painful stuff over with first ...

Typing data in

The "plugger's" approach is to type in your data into the data area (top part) of the Chart Editor window (alias WP Chart). No rocket science here. Your mouse pointer becomes a fat + symbol with which you point and click at a cell. A rectangle outlines the current cell. You can also use the navigation (arrow) keys or Tab key to move this rectangle.

Type in values or text; they will replace any existing stuff. Double-click on a cell if you like, and a minuscule dialog box appears in which you can edit the cell's contents.

Don't fret about the format you type values in. Type them any old way you like: with decimal points, without, with dollar signs, in parentheses for debit, scientific notation, whatever. If they have to be printed on the chart in a particular way, you can fix that later.

Just make sure you observe the row and column assignments that WP Chart expects for a given type of chart. Read "Basic, Simple, Rudimentary, Uncompli-cated Charts" preceding, or observe how WP Chart does its examples.

Data from and to tables

If you have your data in a table in your document, congratulations! You may already be a winner! Just select the table or certain cells in the table and fire up WP Chart (click on the WP Chart button, for instance). The selected cells are placed in the data area of the Chart Editor, with a bar-type chart initially displayed.

You can also copy and paste from a table. This is a good way to add data to an existing chart, because you can paste the data where you want it. Select the block of table cells you want, press Ctrl+C to copy, launch WP Chart, click in the cell where you want the top-left corner of the data block to go, and paste with Ctrl+V.

As always, make sure you observe the row and column assignments that WP Chart expects for a given type of chart. For instance, for bar and line charts, you should have a top row of labels and legend data in the leftmost column. Most of us do tables that way, anyway, so it works out nicely. Read the preceding section on basic charts for information on using rows and columns, or observe how WP Chart does its examples.

If you have your data in a chart, but now want it in a table in the document, no problem. Copy the chart, then paste the data into your document, then convert it to table. To do this, select the chart data in WP Chart, press Ctrl+C, click in your document window, and press Ctrl+V to paste. Now you have a table using text and tabs, but not an official table. To convert the unofficial table to an official table, select it and choose Table⇨Create from the document menu.

Importing data

Don't you hate it when somebody gives you data in some other form than the one you need? How can people be so insensitive? Doesn't everybody use WordPerfect? Well, here are some ideas on how you can deal with such rudeness. For more information, see Part III, More Dealing with the Outside World.

- ✔ If they give you a file in some program that you can run (under Windows), do so. Then try copying and pasting the data from that program's window to the WP Chart data area (see the preceding section).

- ✔ If they give you a spreadsheet file with a graph attached, try using the File⇨Import command in WP Chart. In the Import Chart Data dialog box that appears, click on the List Files of Type button and specify Excel, Lotus, PlanPerfect, or Quattro Pro. Then choose your file and click on Import. You can specify a rectangular block (range) of cells to import by giving the row/column address of two opposite corners in the spreadsheet. From cell A2 to cell D22, for instance, is written A2:D22.

- ✔ If they give you a text file (ASCII, pronounced "as-skee," or ANSI, pronounced "ann-see"), and if it supposedly contains only chart data, do the File⇨Import command described above. Choose All Files in List Files of Type, then double-click on your file. Specify ASCII or ANSI in the Text Import box that appears (guess, if you don't know). Also, choose Tab in the Delimiter box, as a first guess. Click on OK. If it doesn't work, try again with other guesses. If they tell you the ASCII or ANSI text file contains more than chart data, try doing an Insert⇨File in the document window (not WP Chart). If you see a table of data, select it, copy it with Ctrl+C, and paste it into WP Chart with Ctrl+V.

Changing data

OK, you've got your data, but maybe it's in the wrong place, or you've got rows where your columns should be. Now you've come to the right place; read on!

Selecting cells

To select a single cell in WP Chart, click in it. To select a bunch of cells, click and drag just as you would select text in a WP document. To select a row, click in the gray, leftmost column of the data area, where the color swatch for the row appears. Likewise, to select a column, click in the gray, top row. To select the entire enchilada, choose Edit➪Select All from the WP Chart menu.

Cutting, pasting, and moving

Cutting and pasting works with WP Chart just as it does anywhere else in Windows. Select something in a window, copy it with Ctrl+C (or cut it out with Ctrl+X) and paste it into the WP Chart window with Ctrl+V. When you paste into WP Chart, make sure you have first clicked in the cell where you want the upper-left corner of your data to go. You can also copy from WP Chart into other windows.

To cut and paste from tables, see the preceding section, "Data from and to tables."

Unfortunately, there's no special command for moving data (except for transposing rows and columns — see the next section). You have to cut and paste data to move it. To exchange one row for another, you need to cut and paste the data in the destination row into a spare row, then cut and paste the new row to the destination, and finally, cut and paste the data in the spare row where you want it.

Switching rows to columns, and vice versa

Nothing is more infuriating than having rows of data where you need columns, and vice versa. Fortunately, WP Chart gives you a way to fix this.

Cut out your data by selecting it and pressing Ctrl+X. Now, click in the cell where you want the first row and first column to begin. Choose Edit➪Paste Transposed from the menu.

If you're importing data, you have the opportunity to bring data in with the rows and columns transposed. Right in the import dialog box, click on Transpose data.

Formatting

Most of the time, you won't care how your numbers are formatted, because they are shown graphically. But, if you display those numbers on the chart as labels, then you do care.

To format, select the data and choose Data⇨Format from the WP Chart menu. A Format dialog box springs up, where you can choose from a list of Formats. First off, you're probably in General format, where lots of options are grayed out because General means "anything goes, who cares." The ####s you see in the list of alternative formats represent digits, so clicking on ($#,###.##) means "dollars and cents, use parentheses for negative numbers."

You can make your own format. You can futz with the precision, pick a number of digits, or choose Floating point; represent negative numbers as you see fit; or display percentages by clicking on Percent. The format automatically becomes "User Defined." Click on OK when you're tired of this.

When you type data into a cell that has been formatted, the formatting doesn't appear until you click in another cell. So don't panic.

Including/excluding

If there's a row or column you don't want to appear in the chart, don't delete it; exclude it. Select the row or column, then choose Data⇨Include Row/Col or Exclude Row/Col. You can also do this for selected multiple rows or columns.

Clearing and deleting

To clear something, select it and press Delete. A cute little Clear dialog box asks if you want to clear the data or its format (or both). If you just clear the data, the format remains for any new data you put in. If you clear the format, that cell reverts to General format.

Elegant and Sophisticated Charts

If you want fancier charts, the first place to look is the Gallery of WP Chart. Click on the top button of the toolstrip to see a bunch of example numbered styles that you, too, can use for your current type of chart. Just double-click on one of these charts in the Chart Gallery dialog box, and pfzap! You've got it. For other types of chart, click on the Chart Types button in this dialog box.

The tricks that WordPerfect uses in its various numbered styles to make a chart more elegant and sophisticated are the WP Chart Options. These let you do things like

✔ Apply data labels and axis labels.

✔ Create a legend (text identifiers for the colors).

✔ Specify grid lines and tick marks.

✔ Use rotated, perspective views of 3D charts. (Zowie!)

✔ Adjust the width and depth of 3D charts.

✔ Mix different types of charting in one chart (like lines and scatter plot).

Size of lines, bars, and 3D depth

To control how "fat" the bars and lines are (and some of them are extremely obese), use the Options⇨Layout command. This command also lets you set the depth of a 3D chart. The other stuff under this command controls the basic styles, which you usually control using the toolstrip.

For line, bar, and scatter plots, the choices work like this:

✔ Width lets you change how wide the bars look. (In 3D, this refers to the view from the front of the chart.)

✔ Depth refers to how deep (or thick) 3D lines, bars, pies, or markers are (viewed from the side of the chart). This also alters the depth of the whole chart.

✔ Height refers to how high 3D lines are (viewed from the front of the chart).

✔ Overlap refers to the amount of overlap when overlapping 2D bar charts are used.

For pie charts, Depth is the same; Size is the overall bigness of a pie; Angle rotates the pie about its center in degrees, and Tilt lays back a 3D chart in degrees.

Exploding pie slices: To move a pie slice out of the pie for special attention, choose a pie Slice by number in the Pie Layout dialog box and set the Distance you want it to be removed from the pie.

Mixed charts

One way to make fancier charts is to change the appearance of an individual row: its type, its color and pattern, the markers used for scatter-plot values, and which of the two possible *y*-axes it plots against. For instance, you may want a scatter plot for your statistical data on plant growth by month, with a line superimposed for average temperature (a separate row of data).

Select a row, and choose Options⇨Series to get a dialog box. Choose a type in the Type box; Marker is what's used for scatter plots (individual points). If you choose a marker or line-and-marker style, choose a marker Type and Size too. Click on Color or Pattern if you want to change those; Line to change the line style; Fill to use a gradient fill or set a pattern background color. Click on Preview to see how your chart looks.

The Axis choices, Y1 and Y2, allow you to use two separate *y*-axes: for instance, one for inches of plant growth and the other for temperature. The second axis is printed on the right side of the chart.

Axis scale, grid lines, and ticks

To control the graphic part of your axes (not the labels), like scale and grid and ticks, use the Options⇨Axis command. (There's also a separate Options⇨Grid/Tick command, but you can do the same thing from Options⇨Axis.)

First, specify what axis you want to play with. In bar, line, and scatter charts, you can have two *y*-axes: Y1 and Y2. You get Y2 only if you use Options⇨Series to specially treat a given row of data. See the preceding section.

The axes of your chart are scaled automatically to your data, unless you change them. To change the overall range, turn off the checkbox in the Auto column for Minimum or Maximum and set new values. To specify the interval at which major gridlines appear (if there are any; see below), set a Major Grid Value. For minor intervals, specify *how many* lines per major interval you want in the Minor Grid Lines box.

To turn on or change gridlines (lines across the whole chart) and tick marks (stubby lines on the axes), click on the Grid/Tick button in the Axis Options dialog box. Specify the axis you're working on, as in the Axis Options dialog box. In the Major box, specify a Grid or Tick line style, and a Color, for major intervals. Under Tick, the settings control whether the tick is inside the axis, outside, or extends to both sides. Do likewise if you want gridlines or ticks on minor intervals. Click on Axis to do more axis work. Click on OK when you're finished.

Axis labels, data labels, and axis titles

At the very least, you should usually display values on your x-and y-axes, so people know what they're looking at. In addition, you may want what WP Chart calls *axis titles*, which let you put descriptive words along the axes. Finally, you may want to label your chart points with the actual value, called a *data label*.

To apply labels, choose Options⇨Labels. On the left of the Labels dialog box that appears, click on the axis you wish to label, or click on Data Labels. Under Options, click on the Display checkbox to disable/enable your chosen label.

For *x*-axes on bar and line charts, where labels tend to be long and interfere with each other, you can have WP Chart stagger your labels. You can also have optional tick marks at major intervals.

Click on the Position button to put your labels above or below the axis or data point.

Click on the Font button to control the font of your labels.

For data labels, you can also control the box around the labels. Click on the Attributes button, and you can specify different box shapes, a fill color or pattern (even gradient!), and the box border color and line style. Mega-overkill, we say!

For axis titles, don't use Options⇨Labels; use Options⇨Titles. Fill in the text boxes for the axes and click on OK.

Legends

Contrary to popular belief, legends are not myths; at least not in WordPerfect. Legends are those little boxes that say what a color (or line style) indicates. Some of the numbered styles in WP Chart include legends, but the basic chart types do not. You have to add them.

Choose Options⇨Legend to get a Legend dialog box, and click on the checkbox in the top-left corner (Display Legend) to wake it up. The Placement choices are pretty self-explanatory. For Orientation: Vertical orientation is the list-like arrangement you normally think of for a legend; Horizontal spreads the legend out horizontally. If you want the box to be called something other than Legend, like "What the Colors Mean," type it into the Name text box; fool with the Font if you like.

If you're fussy about the box, you can put in a pattern, new color, outline color, and line style — even a gradient fill — by clicking on the Attributes button. Go wild. The Series Font button refers to the font of the text that explains each color.

Perspective charts

A rather cool way to show a 3D chart is to show it in perspective by rotating and tilting it a bit. Choose Options⇨Perspective to get a Perspective dialog box. Click on the Right Angle Axes checkbox to turn it off (it aligns the axis with your page's X and Y direction). Adjust the horizontal and vertical tilt by sliding the sliders next to the little viewing window. Click on the Wire Frame View (transparency) checkbox if you want a sort of X-ray view in the viewing window. (This doesn't change your actual chart; if you want the same sort of thing in your actual chart, try selecting your data row and using the Fill On/Off tool — third from the bottom, right — instead.)

Lines, colors, outlines, and fills

The bottom set of tools on the toolstrip is the same set of tools as in WP Draw. These tools are the most convenient way to control the lines, colors, and fills of whatever data series (rows) you have selected.

✔ The L-shaped tool (a pen drawing a line) lets you turn outlines on or off on selected rows.

✔ The paint-bucket tool lets you turn fill on or off for selected rows. A turned-off fill makes things transparent, showing only the outline.

✔ The dotted-line tool lets you change the outline style for selected rows.

✔ The checkerboard tool lets you change the pattern for selected rows.

✔ The rainbow-line tool lets you change line color.

✔ The rainbow-box tool lets you change fill color (foreground color for patterns).

For gradient fills in labels and legends, use the Attributes button in the Labels and Legend dialog boxes; then, again, use the Attributes button in the Attributes dialog box that appears next. Got that? No? We don't blame you.

Captions

Captions are always nice, but you don't create them in WP Chart. You do them in the document itself. When you are done with your chart and are back in WordPerfect itself, click on the graphics box with the right mouse button and choose Caption off the QuickMenu that appears. A Box Caption dialog box springs up; click on Edit to create a caption; a default, automatically numbered figure caption appears at first, which you can change if you like. See Chapter 1 for more information.

Custom styles

For consistency of style, you can save the chart setup you are currently using. It becomes something similar to the numbered styles of WP Chart. Just choose File⇨Save Style and give your style a filename. Later, you can reuse it by choosing File⇨Retrieve Style.

Chapter 5
More TextArt

• •

• •

*O*K, it's playtime. We've had enough of this serious business about illustrations and lines and drawing Zimbo The Chimp. Time to get down to some serious fun, and TextArt (or Text Art) is the most serious fun there is in WordPerfect.

We're obliged to say, however, that while it's a nice, cheap thrill, TextArt doesn't really deserve a chapter of its own. We couldn't figure out what else to do with it, though, so here it is.

What TextArt Is

Well, TextArt is not exactly fine art, nor even FineArt.

TextArt is what you get when you treat text like Silly Putty, molding it into shapes, in various colors, with nice shadows that make it look like it's floating in space. This is stuff that you can't quite do in WP Draw. Although you can wrap text around a shape in WP Draw, you can't make the text itself fill a shape.

TextArt is great for newsletters, presentation "foils" (overhead transparencies), and visually exciting graphics that let you make a point without being a Picasso. It doesn't get much respect, however, in scholarly tomes or government reports.

Figure 5-1 shows a couple of examples of TextArt we cooked up.

Long, long ago in a galaxy far, far away...

A cure for seasickness?

Figure 5-1:
Use TextArt
to liven up
your articles
and reports
or distract
people from
embarrassing
deficiencies
in your
writing.

It's hard to imagine, we know, but one could even improve upon these examples. Copy your TextArt into WP Draw, and you can play with borders, fills, overlaying, underlying, mirroring, and all kindsa stuff. We'll show you a few of these later. First, the fundamentals...

Say "Howdy" to Tex Tart

Let's get this rodeo started, cowpoke. Here's how to do the basic stuff in TextArt.

To create TextArt, do the following:

1. **Click anywhere in the paragraph closest to where you want your TextArt to appear.**

2. **Click on the TextArt button on the Button Bar or choose <u>G</u>raphics⇨ Te<u>x</u>tArt from the menu bar.**

   You get the TextArt dialog box of Figure 5-2.

3. **Type.**

   Your text goes into the Enter <u>T</u>ext box and replaces the word TEXT that's there for an example. Whatever you type appears in the currently selected shape in the big preview box. When you first begin, the current shape is a boring rectangle. You have three lines to type on, up to 58 characters on each line.

4. **Choose a shape.**

   Click on one of the black shapes on the right side of the dialog box. Your text gets redrawn to fill that shape. Sorry, these are the only shapes there are; you can't do your own. If you are possessed of a clear eye, steady hand, and considerable patience, you can, however, edit the shapes of individual letters in WP Draw. See the next section.

   There are four shapes in the lower-right corner that use thin lines; each line in one of these shapes is for a single line in the Enter <u>T</u>ext box. The bottom-right corner's shape, for instance, is for three lines of text.

5. **Choose a color to fill your text.**

   Click on the Te<u>x</u>t button on the upper right and pick a color from the ones shown.

6. **Choose an outline line width and color.**

   Your text is currently outlined in black, but it doesn't have to be. Click on the left button under Outline and choose a line width. The line with an X in it turns off outlining. The line with two arrows is a hairline. Click on the right button and choose a color.

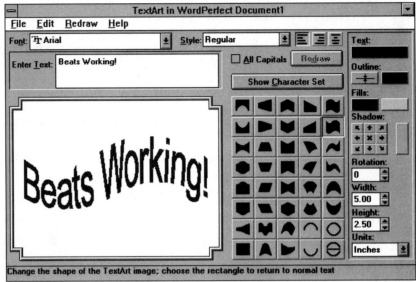

Figure 5-2:
Zwoopy,
loopy text
with the
TextArt
dialog box.

7. **Choose a Width and Height; put new values in these boxes if you don't like the current size.**

8. **Choose File⇨Exit and Return to WordPerfect.**

   You return to your document, where your TextArt appears in a graphics box. At this point, you can treat your TextArt like any other figure: Size it, position it, change or remove the border, or apply a fill (background). See Chapter 1 for excruciating detail about graphics boxes.

   To return to the TextArt editor at any point, just double-click on your text artwork.

Don't be disappointed by the jagged appearance of your TextArt; it doesn't come out that way when it's printed. The text is a lot more readable on paper, too.

If you type a lot of text or use a complex shape, your computer may get really, really, annoyingly slow while you work on the TextArt. If this happens, choose Redraw from the menu and choose Manual instead of the normally selected Auto. Auto means that TextArt is redrawn every time you change something or type a few letters. This redrawing is what makes your computer slow. Manual means that the TextArt is only redrawn when you click on the Redraw button. (The button is a little to the right of the Enter Text box.)

Here are a few things you can do to jazz up your artwork in TextArt.

✔ **Apply a shadow:** Under the word Shadow is a box full of arrow buttons, with an X in the center square. Click on an arrow button, and a shadow appears in the direction pointed by the arrow. Click on it again, and the shadow gets farther away in the same direction. Click on one of the other arrow buttons, and the shadow moves. To change the shadow color, click on the bar to the right of the arrow buttons. To remove the shadow, click on the X button.

✔ **Rotate:** In the Rotation box, type in a rotation in degrees (90 or 270 to run text vertically, for instance) or click on the up- or down-arrow.

✔ **Make it flatter or taller:** By adjusting the width and height, you can reduce or exaggerate the shape. This can help make some things more readable.

✔ **Apply a patterned fill:** Click on the left button under Fills and choose a pattern. Patterns use two colors. One color will be the color you chose earlier for the text, using the Text button. To specify the other color, click on the right button under Fills.

✔ **Use interesting characters and symbols:** Click on the Show Character Set button. A list of all the available characters and symbols appears at the bottom of the TextArt box. Click and hold on a character to enlarge it enough to discern it from the smudges on your screen. Double-click to insert it in your text. Don't worry if all you get in the text box is a black box instead of the symbol you chose; the sample image shows the real thing.

✔ **Use bold or italic type:** Click on the Style button and choose bold or italic, or bold italic.

✔ **Use a different typeface (font):** Click on the Font button. Choose a font, any font. Really ornate fonts will (1) be hard to see, and (2) take a long time to redraw. Keep it simple.

✔ **Right- or center-justify your text:** Click on the justification buttons above the Redraw button. Justification (smooshing text to the left or right or centering it) can make a surprisingly big difference in the readability or impact of your text. Use spaces to help position the text the way you want it.

Don't worry if your TextArt looks a bit out-of-proportion; you can adjust its height-to-width ratio in the document by adjusting the height and width of the graphics box. Click on the TextArt image with the right mouse button and select Image Tools from the QuickMenu that appears. Click on the bottom right tool. Choose Scale Image in the dialog box that appears. Adjust the values in Scale X and Scale Y until the sample image shown there looks the way you want it.

Tricks with TextArt

Heck, if you've wasted this much time doing TextArt, you might as well go whole hog. Here are a few secrets that will help you do some amazing tricks with TextArt.

- ✔ If you cut a TextArt image from its graphics box in your document and paste it into WP Draw, the image becomes a set of objects. You can individually adjust each letter's size, set its colors, whatever you like. When you exit WP Draw and return to the document, the image becomes a WP Draw image, however. You can't get it back into TextArt.

- ✔ If you use the graphics box image tools, you can adjust how your TextArt looks in black-and-white; manipulate the color; scale it; flip it; or position it. In your document (not in the TextArt dialog box), click on the TextArt image with the right mouse button and select Image Tools off the QuickMenu that appears. See Chapter 1, "Special Graphics Tools for Boxes with Images," for more information on using these tools, and Chapter 6 for dealing with color and black-and-white.

- ✔ If you save your work as a TextArt file using File⇨Save Copy As (in the TextArt dialog box), you can easily reuse the resulting file as a figure in subsequent documents. Click on the button next to the Save File As Type text box to see a list of possible graphics file formats. If you save your work as a Windows Metafile, you can use it in other programs. (You can save it as a Windows bitmap, too, but in our version of WordPerfect, there's a bug that makes that image ten times too small! The Metafile format is better, anyway, because it keeps the letters as individual objects, and, like WP Draw, some graphics programs will respect that.)

Let's look at what you can do to TextArt in WP Draw.

1. **To cut a TextArt image from its graphics box in your document, click on it, then press Ctrl+X.**

   (You could copy it instead of cutting it, but then you would end up with two images.)

2. **Launch WP Draw (click on the WP Draw button in the Button Bar, for instance).**

3. **Press Ctrl+V to paste the TextArt into the WP Draw window.**

At this point, your TextArt is a bunch of objects. Note that the outline of each letter is one or more objects; it's not a regular WP Draw object-outline. You can do most of the same things to these objects that you can to things you have drawn. See Chapter 3 for more information on what you can do with objects in WP Draw.

Selecting letters: To select both the letter and its outline together, drag a rectangle around the letter with the selection tool. It's hard to click on the fill part while the outline part is hanging around; you have to separate them or delete the outline part. If you just want to select the outlines, click on them directly. If you're going to do a lot of work in WP Draw, try turning off outlines or fills when you make the TextArt in the first place.

Here are some examples of things you may want to do:

✓ **Individually color or pattern certain letters:** Select a letter (or shadow) and then click on the color selection tool or pattern selection tool (bottom right of the WP Draw toolstrip). Background color for patterned fills is under Attributes⇨Color. Figure 5-3 shows a tasteful example.

Figure 5-3: Quilted letters in WP Draw.

✓ **Apply a gradient fill to letters, using Attributes⇨Fill, then selecting Gradient:** This can enhance a 3D effect; if a letter appears to lean or turn, applying a gradient fill reinforces the illusion. Apply the gradient fill consistently if you do this for multiple letters (as shown in Figure 5-4).

Figure 5-4: Big special effects using gradient fills in WP Draw.

✓ **Change the shape of letter outlines:** You can't change the shape of a TextArt letter's fill unless you select the letter, edit its outline, and replace the original fill with a WP Draw fill. None of this is for the faint of heart.

Select a letter's outline. Choose Edit⇨Edit Points, then drag individual points or selected groups of points around. (You may want to zoom in on the letter first; press F12 and drag a rectangle around the letter to zoom in on it.) To adjust curved shapes, select a group of points. While editing points, drag a rectangle around a group; then drag the group.

The outline of a letter is an open line, not a closed one, so while editing points, click on a point with your right mouse button and choose Close off the QuickMenu. This lets you fill it.

Once you've got some distance between the original fill part of the letter and the new outline, select the fill part of the letter and delete it. Apply a new, WP Draw fill by clicking on the fill on/off tool. If it doesn't fill, you didn't change the shape to a closed line, as above.

Hollow letters, like O, are actually two shapes; put a white fill in the middle one to make it look like a hole. Bring it to the Front to overlay the other shape.

✔ **Change the overall shape of your TextArt:** Create a shape guideline for yourself using one of the line tools and delete it when you're done. Select, click, and drag the letters to move them against your guideline, and stretch them by dragging their sides or corners. If you must, change their shapes as described above. You can see the results of our efforts in Figure 5-5.

Figure 5-5: It wasn't easy, but we did it: a round, gradient-shaded work of text art.

✔ Use clip art for background or to add to your TextArt. Press F4 and choose a file. If you've already pasted the TextArt onto your window, and the clip art covers the TextArt, you may need to use Arrange⇨Back on the clip art.

✔ Wrap WP Draw text around a TextArt letter. (Bizarre, eh?) Why not? Create some text in WP Draw, select both the text and the letter, then choose Arrange⇨Effects⇨Contour Text.

OK, our New England Yankee, Puritan-ethic genes are kicking in. We're having far too much fun and will probably burn for it in heck. Time to move on to some really boring, practical issues. As penance, go to Chapter 7 in Part II and read about tables.

Chapter 6

More General Graphics Stuff

● ●

In This Chapter

▶ Dealing with color in a black-and-white world

▶ Dealing with color in a colorful world

▶ Using graphics styles

▶ Solving miscellaneous graphics problems

● ●

Dealing with Color in a Black-and-White World

While we're really impressed that WordPerfect went to the trouble of creating all this nifty color stuff, we've heard a rumor that everyone out there does not yet have a color printer. Most of the time, it doesn't matter much. WordPerfect and Windows get together and decide on a nice, tasteful shade of gray for each color you use.

Sometimes, however, it gets pretty hard to tell one color from another in shades of gray. This can be confusing when doing charts, in particular; also, colored text. There are a few possible solutions:

✔ Use different patterns (in one or more colors) to fill your charts, drawings, or TextArt (not for regular text).

✔ Choose only from the shades of gray offered in the palette (the second row down on the standard palette).

✔ Change the printing palette to 256 shades of gray. See the first TIP in the following section on how to do this. This palette only affects text, lines, borders, and fills — not graphic images or charts.

✔ Choose colors that come out pretty contrasty in black and white. These are generally the colors between blue and yellow, passing through green. The blue comes out dark, the yellow comes out light. For extremes, you can use black and white.

Here's a couple of things *not* to do:

- ✔ Don't try to use the color-to-black-and-white tool of the toolset for graphics boxes to achieve shades of gray from color. It doesn't do that. It mostly decides what colors are going to end up solid black and what colors solid white, with a very narrow range of gray.

- ✔ Don't spend a lot of time trying different colors in order to get good contrast in black and white. Use one of the solutions we just gave you.

If you've got a bitmap image, such as a scanned-in image or artwork from a graphics file of the PCX or TIFF type, you're pretty much at the mercy of the software and hardware you're using. It decides what color comes out as what shade of gray, subject only to your settings for brightness and contrast (see below).

Here are the few things that you can do that might make the image quality more acceptable:

- ✔ Using the special tools for graphics images (see Chapter 1, "Special Graphics Tools for Boxes with Images"), change the brightness and/or contrast.

- ✔ Using that same set of tools, change the *dithering*. (Dithering is how printers achieve shades of gray or color blending by arranging tiny dots on white paper.) Use the Image Settings tool and click on the Print Parameters button. Generally, you will see that the Dither Method is an Ordered Dither. This is OK for WP Draw and chart images, but often it's not so hot for bitmaps. Click on WordPerfect in the Dither Source box; then choose Error Diffusion as your method. Depending on the type of image and type of printer, you may also be able to try Halftoning as a Dither Method and see if you get any improvement. Your printer's setup may offer other dithering controls; click on the Setup button on the File⇨Select Printer dialog box to see.

- ✔ Change your *printer preferences* to black and white, if it's not already set that way. Choose File⇨Preferences from the WordPerfect menu and double-click on Print. Set the Print Color to Black in the dialog box. This usually results in a bit sharper image if the dithering is set to Error Diffusion, as we just discussed.

- ✔ Try the complementary colors tool. You might get lucky in black and white even if things look bizarre in color on your screen.

Dealing with Color in a Colorful World

If you have a color printer, lucky you. You get to experience the joy of periodically watching your carefully chosen colors turn into muck on your printer. That is, of course, unless you or your company has laid out really serious big bucks for laser color, or dye-sublimation, or one of the other new color technologies.

The truth of the matter is that achieving accurate color on the printed page is a highly tricky art and science. Professional printing companies get paid to do this well, and it's often a problem for them, too. If you're using a color printer in the less-than-a-thousand-dollar range, your results will be colorful, but not particularly accurate or crisp.

If you have problems getting accurate color or crisp images, one basic trick is to stick to the primaries as much as possible. Primary colors are the colors of the inks (or wax, or other consumable material) used in your printer. If these are colors like red, blue, green, and yellow, don't expect to be able to print a wide range of other colors with a lot of quality. If the colors are greenish-blue (cyan), reddish-purple (magenta), and orange (or yellow), you will probably do better. If the ink colors don't include black, don't expect a lot of contrast — black will look brownish.

WordPerfect gives you nonprimary colors by blending. It initially gives you a selection of 256 colors (called a *palette*) to choose from. You can change these by various blending techniques. The colors don't bear a lot of relationship to the colors your printer will print. Certain primary colors on your palette, like pure red or pure cyan, will probably translate into your printer's primaries. Every other color you print will be a mixture of these colors in tiny dots: a dot of cyan; three dots of magenta; 12 dots of yellow, for instance. (In reality, there would also be areas of white and probably dots of black.)

This blending business has its cost. Since to get the exact proportions in our example requires a minimum of 16 dots, a printer using this color can't print features smaller than 4 by 4 dots. So the software that runs the printer has to make a tradeoff: color accuracy versus how small a feature it can print. Professional printers use machines with ten to a hundred times more dots per square inch, so they can do this stuff well. Your printer may have some problems with subtle colors.

Choosing and controlling colors

You choose your colors in dialog boxes for fonts, borders and fills, lines, and WP Draw. They all have buttons that let you choose from the currently available colors.

The place to control the available colors is the *color palette.* There are actually two of these: the printer palette and the presentations palette, although they look and work very much alike. The printer palette lets you control the color of text, borders, and lines, and lets you pick colors by name. When you adjust the printer palette, it stays set until you change it. The presentations palette is what you use in WP Draw and its Chart Editor (WP Chart). When you adjust the presentations palette, it returns to the default palette when you exit. In either palette, though, you can save your adjustments as a named printer or presentations palette file.

When you change the printer palette, it doesn't affect the colors that are already in your document, just the colors subsequently available to you. What you see in your document is (pretty much) what you get.

You can also adjust color to some extent using the special tools for images in graphics boxes. You can control brightness and contrast, for instance. See Chapter 1 for more discussion about these special tools.

The printer palette

There are several places to set the printer palette. In particular: the Font dialog box (press F9), the Border/Fill and Create Line Style dialog boxes, and the Print Preferences dialog box (choose File⇨Preferences⇨Print). They all work with the same palette, so if you change it in one place (like fonts), you change it for all (like borders and graphics lines).

In the Font dialog box, you can choose a color for your text from the printing palette by clicking on Color. If the text is thick enough, you can also control how faded the text looks in that color by adjusting the Shading. To adjust the palette in the Font dialog box, click on the Palette button; you get the Define Color Printing Palette dialog box shown in Figure 6-1.

In a border or fill dialog box, if you're using a graphics style, such as one of the built-in border styles, the color is preset. To choose fill colors, select a fill style, then click on the Foreground or Background buttons. To choose a new border color, click first on the Customize Style button, then on the Border Color button. This is where you can adjust the palette; click on the Palette button to get the dialog box shown in Figure 6-1.

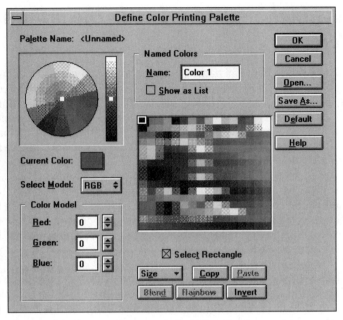

Figure 6-1:
Custom
blending for
fonts, lines,
borders, and
fills;
WordPerfect's
"paint
store" is the
printing
palette
dialog box.

In the Print Preferences dialog box, click on the Define Color Printing Palette button to get the dialog box shown in Figure 6-1.

Changing printing palettes should not change the colors already on your screen. If it does, try saving your document, then exiting from and restarting WordPerfect. Sometimes WordPerfect gets confused. Hey, so do we.

From this Define Color Printing Palette dialog box you can (1) open a printer palette file that gives you a new set of 256 colors, (2) custom-blend one or more colors in this palette, and (3) save your custom-blended colors as a custom palette file.

To try one of the alternative palettes, click on Open and select one of the palettes listed there. To return to your original palette, click on the Default button.

If you use a black-and-white printer, you may want to skip this whole "what shade of gray is this color going to be" business by selecting the 256 Shades of Gray palette that WordPerfect offers.

Individual, named colors in the printing palette

The palette consists of 256 named colors, shown in the center rectangle in the dialog box. They run in order from the top-left to the bottom-right corner. To adjust a single color in the printing palette, first click on it. The color controls on the left now refer to that location in the palette. Note that the color's current name appears in the Name box (where you can edit the name, if you change the color). To see and choose from a list of colors by name and sample swatch, click on the Show as List checkbox.

Use the color wheel on the upper left and the shaded bar next to it to graphically adjust the color you've selected in the palette. The controls in the Color Model box let you do things more scientifically, by controlling the color primaries. (If you're trying to print in your printer's primary colors, the Color Model controls are the place to go.)

First, let's see how to do things graphically (which is always more fun). Click anyplace in the color wheel (or drag the little white square in the middle), and the color currently selected in the palette will change to that color. The bar next to the wheel is the *luminosity* bar (another great bar name). If you move the white square in the middle of this bar, your chosen color and the whole wheel gets lighter or darker. You get pastel colors, for instance, by sliding the square upwards. Normally, luminosity is set right in the middle of the range.

To do things scientifically, use the Color Model controls. These let you set the actual values of the primary colors over a range of 0 to 255 (for the normal setting of Select Model, which is RGB). To get a pure primary color, set one primary to 255 and the others to 0. After adjusting a value, you may have to click on one of the other values to see the effect. Adjusting the proportions of these values is like moving around the color wheel. Adjusting the values for a higher or lower sum while keeping the proportions constant is like sliding around on the luminosity scale. In fact, if you move the graphical controls, you can watch these values change.

If you have a printer with primaries of cyan, magenta, yellow, and black, and you want to specify colors using those primaries, you can change the "color model" (set of primaries) to CMYK to make it easier. Click on Select Model to do this. A more intuitive model — and one that relates well to the graphical controls — is HLS, for hue, lightness, saturation; *hue* is the color (the "o'clock" of the color wheel, 0 to 360 degrees), *lightness* is the same as the luminosity bar (0 to 100), and *saturation* is how murky the color is (distance from the center of the color wheel, 0 to 100). You can use any model with any printer.

If you mess up, just click on the D̲efault button to restore the original palette of colors.

To save your palette with its new color, click on the Save A̲s button. In the Save Color Palette dialog box that appears, type in a N̲ame, like **Ocean pastels**; click in the F̲ilename box, and WordPerfect suggests a filename that you can change if you don't like it.

If you don't save your modified palette, when you click on OK in the Define Color Printing Palette dialog box, WordPerfect notes that the current palette has been modified and asks if you'd like to save the changes. If you choose N̲o, the changes only apply until you exit WordPerfect.

Changing lots of colors at once

If you want to create a new range of colors in your printing palette, there is a ridiculously comprehensive set of features for doing this. The question is, of course, why do it? One conceivable reason is that you want to stay nearer to a couple of colors that can actually be delivered by the primary colors available on your printer. Or else, you may just be in your "blue" period, artistically. Here's a simple example.

To get a palette that gives you shades of a single primary color, click in the upper-left corner (color 1) and give it a pure primary value: say, red=255, green=0, and blue=0. Then click in the lower-right corner (the 256th color) and give it a value of red=0, green=0, blue=0. Click on the Selec̲t Rectangle checkbox and drag a rectangle from the upper-left corner of the palette to the bottom right. Click on the Blen̲d button and wait. Whoa! What's all this green and stuff? It's a lie, that's what. The palette display gets very confused (at least on our screens), but if you click on the S̲how as List checkbox, you see the truth. The truth also appears in the red, green, and blue primary values. Not a hint of green in any color!

For blending purposes, you can also copy and paste two colors from other places on the existing palette. Click on a colored square and then on the C̲opy button; click where you want that color in the palette (the bottom right, usually) and then on the P̲aste button. Do this for the two colors. Now select a rectangle with these guys in the corners and blend as described in the previous paragraph.

If you want fewer (or more) colors when you do this stuff, click on the Si̲ze button and choose something other than 256 colors.

You can save these custom palettes using the Save A̲s button and open them as you need them.

Colors in the WP Draw and Chart palette

WP Draw (and WP Chart, the WP Draw Chart Editor) uses a separate palette from the printing palette and uses a different dialog box. The dialog box that controls this palette is, however, practically identical to the Define Color Printing Palette dialog box. In WP Draw, choose Attributes⇨Color, then click on the Define button. (This action sets the palette for charts, too.)

Use this dialog box just as you did the Define Color Printing Palette dialog box. The Reset button here takes the place of the Default button, and the Block mode of selection here is equivalent to the Select Rectangle checkbox.

Note that the palette has no effect on any bitmap graphics you use, such as scanned images.

To save and retrieve your customized palettes, use the Save As and Retrieve buttons in the Color Attributes dialog box. Note that the printer palette files and the WP Draw palette files are not interchangeable; you can only use .PRC files for WP Draw.

Graphics Styles

Now for a different topic — styles. Nearly every graphics whatsit or thingamajig in WordPerfect uses some sort of style. WordPerfect has styles for lines, borders, fills, all kinds of graphics boxes, and charts (which are a little different, stylewise). Whenever you call up the dialog box for these items, you find buttons for specifying a style. You can use standard official styles, modified official styles, or use styles of your own.

Compared to individually specifying each graphics whatsit in your document, using styles has some advantages: (1) Your documents look more consistent, and (2) you save a lot of work when you want to change things. Rather than changing a whole bunch of illustrations, if they all have the same style you can just change the style.

Let's say you have 20 illustrations in your document. Each one is to be against the left margin, with a thin black border, text wrapping around the right side, and a drop shadow towards the lower-left corner. In blissful ignorance or disdain of graphics box styles, you do this individually to all 20 illustrations. Your boss/editor/spouse/superior-being decides that all illustrations must be against the right margin, with a thin double-line border and no drop shadow. You can (1) scream, cry, and rend your garment because you have to go and change each box, or (2) curse yourself for your ignorance/sloth in not having used a custom box style, which would have saved you. If you had used one, you could change the graphics style the way your boss/editor/spouse/superior-being wants it, and the changes would apply to all your illustrations. Fortunately, you can (3) edit the standard style that's probably already applied to your illustrations.

Whatever graphics you have in your document are already in a standard style. Pictures and stuff are in the Figure style. Text boxes are in the Text Box style. If you want to modify these standard styles, no problem.

Creating or customizing a graphic style

Here's how to create or edit a graphic style for boxes, borders, lines, or fills:

1. Choose Graphics⇨Graphics Styles from the menu bar.

The Graphics Styles dialog box appears, as in Figure 6-2.

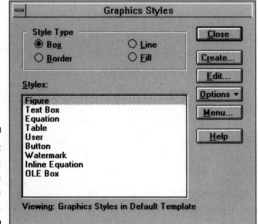

Figure 6-2: Doing graphics in your own style.

2. Choose a Style Type from the dialog box.

The list of Styles changes to show you what's available. If you want to specify an existing border or fill style for graphics boxes, choose Box, not Border or Fill.

3. To edit an existing style, click on a style name, then on Edit.

— or —

3. To create a new style, click on Create.

From here, what you do depends on whether you're creating a line, fill, border, or box style. The Create Line Style dialog box works just like the Graphics Line dialog box described in Chapter 2. Ditto for the border styles. The fill style is a matter of selecting a pattern or gradient and the two colors used in the fill. In any case, once you create the style, just enter a Style Name in the dialog box and click on OK.

For fooling with graphics box styles, the Create or Edit Box Style dialog box, shown in Figure 6-3, has buttons that essentially duplicate the functions of the Graphics Box Feature Bar discussed in Chapter 1 and allow you to include positioning, captioning, borders and fills, text wrap, type and position of content, and image settings like contrast and brightness. Since the exact content of each box differs, there are no controls that allow you to specify exact content.

Figure 6-3:
Creating a custom graphics box style. The Settings button controls different aspects, depending on content: text, image, or equation.

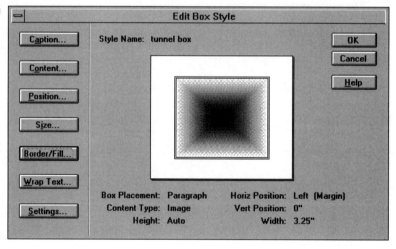

One problem that can arise when using custom box styles is losing the nice, automatic numbering that goes with the built-in .Figure Box, Text Box, and other styles. The official Figure style includes a caption with an automatic counter in it. If you want your custom box style to use this automatic numbering (or share it with other illustrations that use the official Figure style), you must specify the counter.

To specify an automatic counter, click on the Caption button of Figure 6-3. A Box Caption dialog box arises. In the Caption Numbering and Style area of that box, click on the button labeled Change, next to Counter. A tiny Select Counter dialog box opens up; click on .Figure Box (or whichever counter you want) from the Counters window, then click on the Select button. Click on OK to close the Box Caption dialog box. (Don't ask us why there are periods at the beginning of the style names — only the folks at WordPerfect know that. We just report what we see.)

Styles for graphs

If you put a lot of work into getting a graph just right, why waste all that effort on a single graph? Save the setup as a style — not a Graphics Style, but a special kind of style for WP Graphs.

Graph styles save everything but the data: the type of chart, the basic style of it, and all the options: layout, color, special data series, axis specifications, perspective, titles, legends, labels, ... the whole nine yards of cement.

Simply choose File⇨Save Style from the menu and give your style a name. Later, when you work on another chart, use File⇨Retrieve Style to recall it.

Miscellaneous Graphics Problems

Using graphics on your PC is like putting a U-Haul trailer on your car — it's a test of just how much power and performance your system has got and how well it's designed. Undoubtedly, more problems can arise than the ones we've thought of, but ... as in your old school textbooks when, you suspect, the author didn't know the answer either ... these are left as an exercise for the student.

Printer memory

A printer that has always done just fine printing your text documents can suddenly start acting up when you add graphics. If you get partially-printed pages and error messages on your screen, your printer may not have enough memory. This is particularly likely with laser printers. Graphics images require lots and lots of memory, and laser printers have to store an entire page in their memory before printing.

Besides adding memory, other solutions are to scale your graphics down in size (see Chapter 1) or reduce your print quality (printed dots per inch). To reduce your print quality, choose File⇨Print; click and hold on Print Quality in the Print dialog box that appears, and choose Medium (Draft is pretty coarse for most graphics).

Sluggishness

Take two vitamins, a glass of Metamucil, and call The Coffee Connection in the morning. Then there's the problem of *computer* sluggishness. Frankly, anything less powerful than a 33MHz 486 PC with 8MB of RAM is probably going to be a bit sluggish doing graphics in WordPerfect. You may be able to speed things up by switching to Draft view (Ctrl+F5), or removing graphics from the view (View⇨Graphics). Also, close any programs you're running in Windows that you don't need — give WordPerfect as much elbow room as possible.

Printing documents with graphics can be ridiculously slow. If you don't need to see the graphics each time you print, turn them off. When you go to print, check off Do Not Print Graphics in the Print dialog box. If you don't need to print the pages with graphics on them, choose Current Page or Multiple Pages.

Your particular setup of Windows can also make a difference. Armed with a bag of, say, maple-cream-filled doughnuts, ask your PC guru, "Could you please optimize my PC's performance under Windows?" He or she will (after consuming the doughnuts) probably ensure that you are using a "disk cache" like SmartDrive, have a "permanent swap file" of a size that, together with your PC's memory, totals 16MB or more, and that you have "FILES=50" or more in your CONFIG.SYS file. We tell you these things so you can sound knowledgeable to your guru. If you're stuck on an island off the coast of Newfoundland, you have to look them up yourself. (You may also want to consult *Windows for Dummies*, by Andy Rathbone, IDG Books Worldwide).

General printer weirdness

This is like Major printer weirdness, only higher-ranking. Sometimes, graphics stuff just doesn't print right. Your problems may be caused by the *printer driver* you're using.

Printer drivers are chunks of software that know how to run a particular printer. You get a bunch of these with Windows and another bunch with WordPerfect. You may even get a couple with your printer. WordPerfect is happy to run any of these, but sometimes it works better when it uses its own printer drivers. (Sometimes not.)

If you have a different printer driver installed for your type of printer, you can try to use it. Choose File⇨Select Printer. The dialog box that appears shows what drivers are currently available; the one currently selected is highlighted. If you see another driver for the same printer, click on it and then on the Select button. The drivers that come with Windows have little checkered flags; the WordPerfect drivers have little WP icons. If you currently use a Windows driver, click on the Add Printer button and choose WordPerfect. Click on Printer Files in the Add Printer dialog box and see if a new driver for your printer is there. If so, double-click on it.

To install other drivers or to read about solutions to other printing mysteries, see Chapter 22, "Solving Printing Problems," in *WordPerfect For Windows For Dummies*.

Part II
More Tantalizing Text

The 5th Wave   **By Rich Tennant**

"These kidnappers are clever, Lieutenant. Look at this ransom note, the way they got the text to wrap around the victim's photograph. And the fonts! They must be creating their own—must be over 35 typefaces here...."

In this part ...

*P*eople who read the WordPerfect promotional literature are in serious danger of drooling on their keyboards, what with all those tantalizing word-processing features. This is particularly true for people in the business of turning out professional, finished-looking documents. (It's also true for our dog friend, Rusty, but we're not sure if he's reading the literature or just thinking about chewing on it.)

Now that you've mastered graphics in Part I, it's time to move on to all those intriguing text capabilities: tips for making neat tables, tricks for fine-tuning typography, secrets of doing equations, templates for standardizing your documents, features for annotating your document files — even the inside scoop on producing pamphlets or entire books.

Such tantalizing text treats are no longer out of reach. Now you can escape the torment of Tantalus (an early Greek user of WordPerfect) and grasp the finer fruits of word processing. Read on.

Chapter 7
Turning (out) the Tables

● ●

In This Chapter

▶ Reviewing table basics

▶ Formatting rows, columns, and text

▶ Formatting and aligning numbers

▶ Adding lines, borders, and fills

▶ Doing splits and joins

▶ Positioning and sizing the table

▶ Calculating cleverly

● ●

*T*he signs were there when we were all in kindergarten. We should have realized what was going on and rebelled early. Maybe spit out our milk or something. Why did they have us spend so much time putting things in boxes, putting square pegs in square holes, putting our toys in square cubbyholes? It was to train us for our future business careers of endlessly putting things in tables.

Since an awful lot of people seem to spend an awful lot of time doing tables these days, we thought we ought to really get down into it early in this book (while we have the strength). Yes, tables are incredibly boring. Even writing this chapter was a ten-coffee-pot job. But, cheer up — at least tables shouldn't be quite so frustrating any more. Read on.

Tables: A Quick Review

Tables in WordPerfect can be amazingly elaborate. They have buckets of formatting options and the power to do spreadsheet-like tasks. Before we get on to the fancy stuff, though, let's take a quick review.

Using basic table manners

Here's a summary of basic manners for doing tables in WordPerfect.

You can create a table in two ways: the quick way and the long way. The quick way is to use the Power Bar. Click and drag on the icon that looks like a calendar, and you can get a table any size you like. The long way is to use Table⇨Create from the menu bar or press F12 and fill out the dialog box with the number of rows and columns.

To fill out a table, click in any cell and type in your data. Character, line, and paragraph formatting all work pretty much as usual, although the Table⇨Format command (Ctrl+F12) gives a better alternative than doing this the usual way. You can put pictures in the table the same way you would in any other text. To move around in a table, click in a cell or press the Tab key.

Once you have a table, you can adjust its structure. Adjust column widths by dragging the lines between the columns. To format the entire table, use the Table⇨Format command (Ctrl+F12), click on Table in the dialog box that you get, and set the format numerically using that box. To format a row, column, or individual cell, click within it before using the Table⇨Format command; click on Cell, Column, or Row and then specify the formatting you want. To format a bunch of stuff, select it (highlight it) first.

There's a special way to select a cell, row, column, or the whole table, but it requires what occupational therapists call "fine motor control." (Who wants to control a fine motor, that's what we want to know?) Place your mouse pointer in the row or column. Ever so carefully, move the pointer towards the edge of the cell (left edge for a row, top for a column), until the pointer changes into an arrow. Click once for a cell; double-click for a row or column; triple-click for the whole table; quadruple-click repeatedly for carpal tunnel syndrome.

Setting the table: types of formatting

The key to creating good, readable tables (or visually impressive but utterly unreadable tables) is formatting. You can play with three basic types of formatting:

✔ Formatting rows, columns, and text (Table⇨Format, Ctrl+F12, or QuickMenu)

✔ Formatting numbers (Table⇨Number Type, Alt+F12, or QuickMenu)

✔ Formatting the lines and fills (Table⇨Lines/Fill, Shift+F12, or QuickMenu)

We talk about these three in the next few sections. We also discuss some other important things, like breaking up and joining tables, and doing spreadsheet-like mathematics.

Formatting Rows, Columns, and Text

The biggest trouble with tables is usually getting everything to fit nicely. There's always one word in a column that sticks out longer than the rest; or else the table just doesn't fit on the page or in the column. The answer lies within the table version of the Format dialog box. To get one of these boxes, put your cursor in the table and use the Table⇨Format command or Ctrl+F12; or, click in the table, press the right-hand mouse button for a QuickMenu, and choose Format. (You may find life easier if you first zoom out your view of the document to margin width with the View⇨Zoom command.)

The mighty, morphin' Format dialog box actually has three different guises, depending on whether you work on the whole table, a row, a column, or an individual cell. You can't work on a specific row, column, or cell unless your cursor is in it, or you have selected it before you give the Format command.

Here's the sequence of steps to get to the Format dialog box that you need:

1. **Click in the cell, row, or column you want to work on.**

   (Click anywhere to work on the whole table.)

2. **Select (highlight) a group of cells in several rows or columns if you want to work on those rows or columns or on that group of cells only.**

   See "Using basic table manners" for notes on selecting stuff.

3. **Call up the Format dialog box with Ctrl+F12, Table⇨Format, or choose Format off the QuickMenu.**

   Depending on your selection in Step 1 or 2, you get one of the four mutant forms of Format dialog box shown in Figures 7-1 through 7-4.

4. **Check the top row of buttons in the dialog box to make sure you're working on what you want: a cell, column, row, or the entire table.**

   You can switch between the forms by clicking one of the selections in the top row (Cell, Column, Row, or Table).

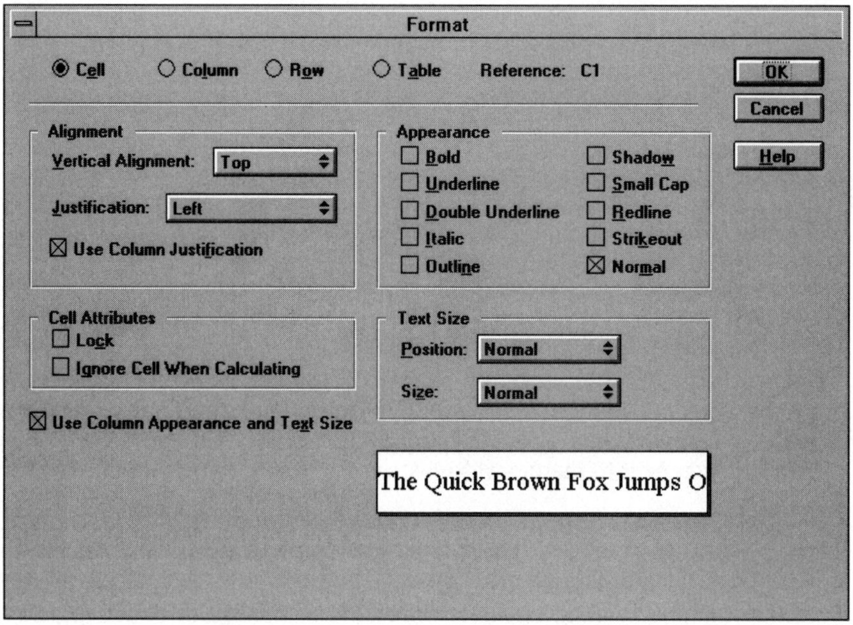

Figure 7-1:
The cell
version of
the Format
box lets you
get picky
about
individual
cells.

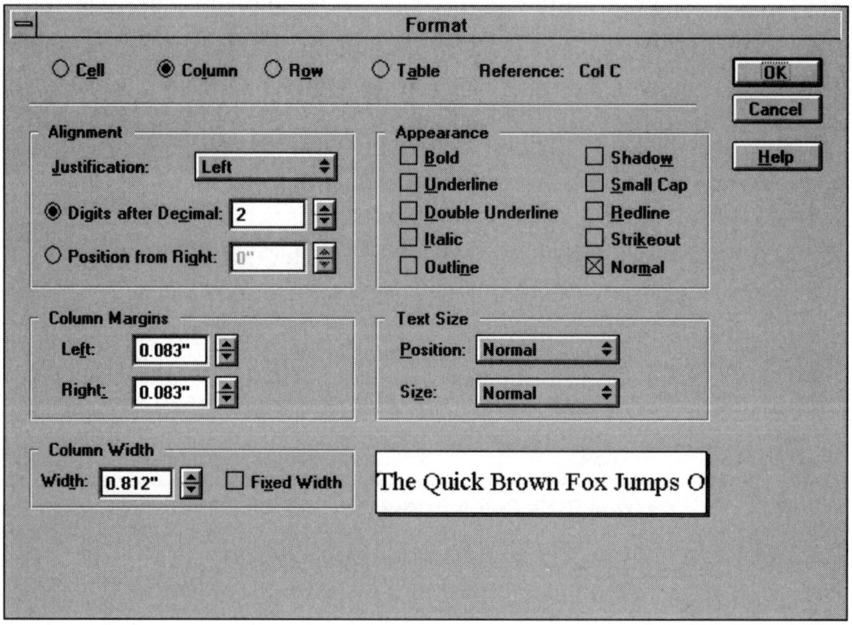

Figure 7-2:
The column
version of
the Format
box looks a
little
different on
the left side.
The right
side lets you
fool with
appearances
on a column
basis.

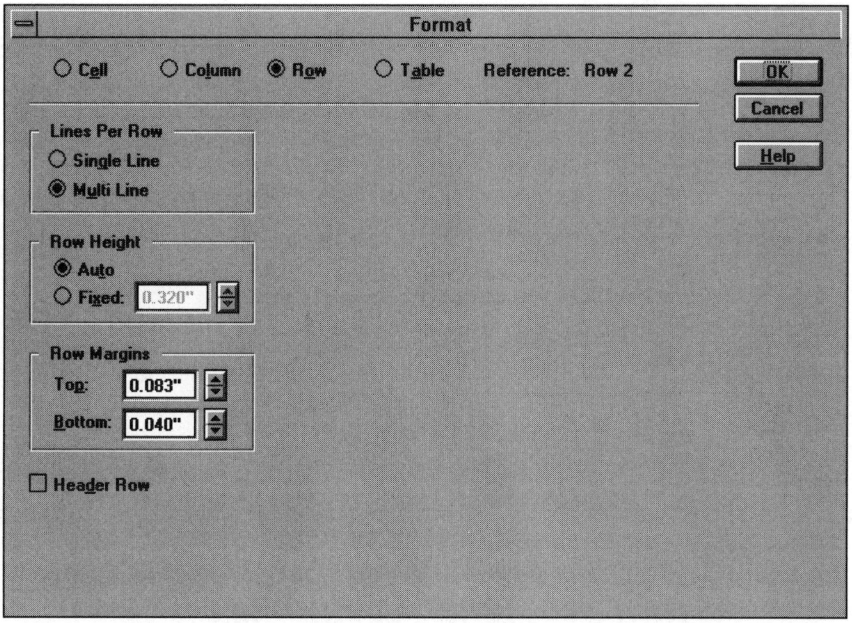

Figure 7-3:
The row
version of
the Format
box. You
can't fool
with text
appearance
on a row-
wise basis.

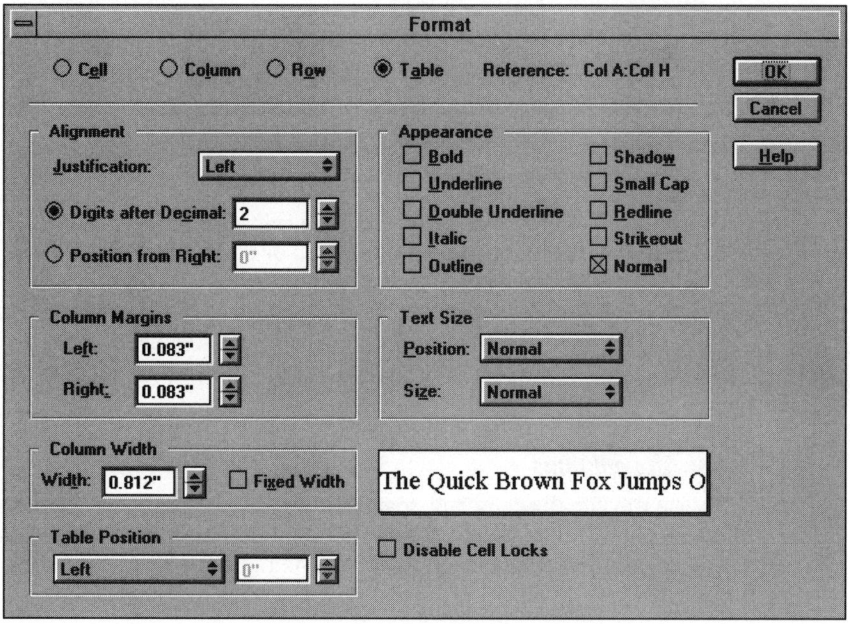

Figure 7-4:
The table
version of
the Format
box lets you
deal with
everything
that's not
specifically
formatted by
row,
column, or
cell.

Now you're ready to format the table or row or column or whatever.

Think first, format second

Before rushing off and formatting your table, decide what part of the table you want to format first: a cell? a bunch of cells? an entire row? an entire column? a group of rows or columns? the whole enchilada?

Most of the time, you can work in any order. But if you're doing a complex table, you'll stay sane longer if you format in this order:

1. **The table in general** (text appearance, table alignment on page, column margins)

2. **Special rows or columns** (text appearance, column widths, row heights, margins)

3. **Special cells** (text appearance, text position in cell, cell locking)

This helps ensure that the formatting you do for an individual cell overrides that for its column or row, and that your column or row formatting overrides that for the table in general.

Width problems (columns)

We don't know about you, but when we sit down at the table we always get width problems. This is also true for the kind of tables one finds in documents. When you create a table (with Table⇨Create, F12, or the table button on the Power Bar), WordPerfect does a great job of giving you nice, even columns running the width of the margins. Unfortunately, this is rarely what you want, but that's not WordPerfect's fault.

As usual, there's a gaggle of methods for dealing with width: dragging lines, using Format dialog boxes, or using the ruler bar. If you prefer using the ruler bar, you'd better turn it on (Alt+Shift+F3 or pick Ruler Bar from the View menu).

Keeping the table a constant width: If you want the overall table to stay exactly the width of the page margins while you adjust specific column widths, you need to set the table position to Full. See the section on "Overall width" a bit later in this chapter.

Specific columns

To use the line-dragging approach, slowly move your mouse pointer across the line between the columns. When the pointer changes to a double-arrow-with-line kind of thingy, click and drag the line right or left. The column edge moves with it.

TIP

Different column widths in different rows

You can't actually have different column widths in different rows (unless you split a cell vertically to get an extra column). But you can make your table look that way: Just make one table right after another; they join together almost seamlessly. You can make the illusion more convincing by turning off the top line of the bottom table. (See "Lines, Borders and Fills," later in this chapter.)

Another approach is to split a cell into two cells or join two to form a single cell. Use Table⇨Split, or Table⇨Join, and see "Splits (and joins) without pain," later in this chapter.

Unfortunately, this approach trades off width with the adjoining column. To avoid affecting the other columns, hold down the Shift key while dragging. Only the width of the column to the left will change.

You can do the same sort of thing with the ruler bar. Drag the down-pointing arrows that mark each column's sides.

To use the dialog box, first see the beginning of this chapter and read about using the different versions of the Format box. (Or select the column and press Ctrl+F12 if you really don't give a snort about the different versions and would just like to get on with it, please.) Down in the lower left-hand corner of the dialog box is the column width setting. To set it, type a width into the box or click like an over-warm cricket on the arrow buttons next to the box.

Another thing sort of related to column width is the column margins. These are the spaces between the left and right sides of the column and the text. You can adjust these in the Format dialog box or on the ruler bar. (To use the ruler bar, click in the column, look in the ruler bar, and adjust the markers there that look like paragraph-width markers.)

Overall width

To change the width of your overalls — or rather, we mean, the width of all columns in the table, you need the table version of the Format dialog box. If you have a moment, see the beginning of this chapter and read about using the different versions of the Format box. In a hurry?

Do the following:

1. **Click anywhere in the table.**
2. **Choose Table⇨Format, press Ctrl+F12, or click with the right mouse button and choose Format from the QuickMenu.**
3. **Click on Table in the top line of the Format dialog box.**

   It should then look like Figure 7-4.

4. **Find the Column Width area in the lower left of the dialog box, and type a number in the box or adjust the width with the up/down-arrow buttons.**
5. **Click OK when you are done changing the formatting.**

There's no way to set the overall width of the table to a specific dimension, like five inches wide, except by adjusting individual column width. You can, however, change the page margin just before a table, then set the margin back to normal after the table. When you create a table, WordPerfect sizes your table to fit in the margins.

You can also set the width to automatically fill the margins. Locate Table Position on the lower left of the table version of the Format dialog box and choose the Full setting. Thereafter, the table stays the width of the margins, automatically adjusting all column widths except those that have been individually set and *Fixed.* (Check off the Fixed Width box in the column version of the Format dialog box; see Figure 7-2.)

It does just what it says. Setting all the column widths at once (by using the table version of the Format dialog box) does just that: changes the width of all the columns in the table, even the ones you set individually. To avoid undoing your individual column settings, set the entire table's column widths first, then set individual columns.

Height problems (rows)

Generally, rows behave themselves pretty well, sitting in neat, um..., rows with their hands folded. This is because WordPerfect automatically makes another line (line-wraps) when the text won't fit within the column width, then adjusts the row height automatically.

Problems arise only if you don't like this. For instance, you may have a table of basically short text (like *melon, apple, pear*) and one nasty, long entry (like *Jerusalem artichoke*). If the long text doesn't fit in your column, the text wraps and makes a single fatter row, thus ruining the artistic consistency of your grocery list and holding you up to public shame and ridicule in the store. There are really only a few good solutions:

🖊 ✔ Make the text smaller (select it and reduce its point size).

✔ Make the column wider (see the previous sections).

✔ Make all the rows higher so they look consistent (to be discussed soon).

✔ Live with it (stop being so darned fussy, or don't buy Jerusalem artichokes).

To make row higher (or less high), you need the table Format dialog box, the rows version (refer to Figure 7-4).

Here's the procedure:

1. Select (highlight) as many rows as you want to change.

If you select the whole table, make sure to select just the table. If the highlighting shows black rectangles with wide white borders in the cells, you've selected more than just the table.

2. Choose T<u>a</u>ble⇨<u>F</u>ormat, press Ctrl+F12, or click with the right mouse button and choose <u>F</u>ormat.

3. Click on R<u>o</u>w in the top line of the Format dialog box that appears to get the row version of the Format dialog box. (Refer to Figure 7-3.)

Now you have two choices for changing your row height. You can either:

• Set the Lines Per Row to Sin<u>g</u>le Line (not so good), or

• Set the Row Height to Fi<u>x</u>ed (better).

The first approach forces your table to cut off long lines of text when they don't fit the cell width in a single line. To fix this, you have to change the font size, so why not do that in the first place?

The second approach lets you set the height of all your rows to a value big enough for two lines, even if you don't need it in some rows. Click on Fi<u>x</u>ed under Row Height and type in or increment the value. (You need more than .517" for normally spaced 12-point text, for example.) You may also want to change rows heights for artistic purposes; to get more white space around your text, for instance.

Also of artistic concern are the Row Margins, controlled through the same dialog box. These provide space between the text and the top and bottom of the row. If the Row Height is set to Au<u>t</u>o, the row height adjusts automatically to the new margins. If Row Height is set to Fi<u>x</u>ed, over-large margins can push your text right out of sight.

For your "header" at the top of the table, there is a special feature. If you bring up the Format dialog box, row version, and click on the box marked Hea<u>d</u>er Row ... nothing happens. Yet. But if you're making a large table that may run over a page break or column break, this is a good feature. It automatically duplicates the header row where your table starts up again on the next page.

Splitting cells: Sometimes it's not exactly a height problem that you have, it's that you need two rows within a cell. Yes, without resorting to mitosis, you can now split cells. Use Table⇨Split. See "Splits (and joins) without pain," later in this chapter.

Formatting and positioning text

Too often, tables are boring and confusing. Partly this is because they look like wallpaper, with every cell in exactly the same typeface, formatted the same way, except for the occasional creative soul who uses (gasp!) boldface type for headings!! Well, with WordPerfect, there's no excuse for this unimaginative conformity. We're revolting! Join us!

You can do a lot of the formatting and positioning of text tables the same way you do with regular text (using the Layout commands). Each cell of the table acts pretty much like a paragraph. But it's generally more convenient to use the Format dialog box.

Fonts 'n' stuff

You can use different typefaces, sizes, and styles in tables just as you normally do in the main body of your text. But if you want to fool around a lot with the looks of your table, it's better first to simply choose a typeface (like Times New Roman) and a size (like 10 point) and enter your data plain: Don't worry about styles, like bold or italics, or positioning, or anything else.

Once you enter your data, use the table Format dialog box to adjust style, size, and position. The Appearance and Text Size areas in the dialog box let you adjust style, size, and position for columns, cells, or the entire table; refer to Figures 7-1, 7-2, and 7-4 and the discussion about them earlier in this chapter.

Here's how to spruce up your table:

1. **Select any portion of the table or the whole thing.**

   Changes at the column and table level don't affect individual cell settings; but to keep your sanity, do the overall table first, then successively smaller parts of the table. Note that you can't change text appearance or size by rows. You have to treat a row as a group of cells: Highlight the entire row, press Ctrl+F12, and click on Cell. (Do this to boldface the table headings in the top row, for instance.)

2. **Choose Table⇨Format, press Ctrl+F12, or click with the right mouse button and choose Format.**

3. **Check and, if necessary, change the top line of the dialog box to Cell, Column, or Table, depending on what you want to format.**

4. Change the font style using the controls in the Appearance or Size area of the box.

These work just like the Appearance, Position, and Relative Size controls in the regular Font dialog box.

Normally, an individual cell takes on the appearance of the overall table. If the column has been formatted, it takes on the appearance of its column. If the cell has been formatted, the cell formatting "wins" over the column and table formatting. So, if you've been playing with an individual cell's appearance using the cell version of the Format dialog box and change your mind, you can reset the cell by clicking on the box labeled "Use Column Appearance and Text Size."

If you are formatting a group of cells that have different Appearance or Size, you will see some checkboxes grayed-out as a reminder. Don't worry about it; whatever you do won't override the individual cell settings.

You! — In the cell! — Assume the position!

One way to help turn an "eye-chart" into a readable table is to do some creative positioning of text and numbers. You can do this using regular line and paragraph formatting, but it's often easier to use the table Format dialog box (Ctrl+F12) — the table, column and cell versions (see the beginning of this chapter). For an example, check out Figure 7-5, which shows a table in progress.

Department	Units produced	Defects	Defect rate	Person to blame
Sprockets				
Left-handed	87516	6	0.00006855889	Chris
Right-handed	95729	13	0.00013580002	Gary
Spindles				
Clockwise	12844	4	0.00031142946	Margy
Counterclockwise	14942	18	0.00120465801	Meg
Mobius	5994	8	0.001334668	Dave

Figure 7-5: Positioning text with quality in mind.

In general, this table is left-justified: By default, stuff is squooshed against the left side of the cell. The Units Produced and Defects columns are right-justified. The heading cells for all columns are left-justified and vertically top-aligned. For clarity, the individual cells describing the types of sprockets and spindles are not only set in small-sized type, but right-justified. The *Appearance* of text in the left column and the cells across the top is set to Bold.

As you've probably figured out, justification (left/right and other forms) is one type of positioning. You can set it either by table, columns, or cells, using the Format dialog box.

Here's the procedure:

1. **Select any portion of the table or the whole thing.**

2. **Choose Table⇨Format, press Ctrl+F12, or click with the right mouse button and choose Format.**

3. **Check, and, if necessary, change the top line of the dialog box to Cell, Column, or Table, depending on what you want to format.**

4. **Look for Justification in the Alignment section of the dialog box (in the cell, column, or table version). Click and hold on the Justification type button; drag to pick a justification from the list.**

   (Decimal align is especially for numbers; see the next section for more information.)

Vertical alignment is another type of positioning, if you have a cell height larger than the text. You can only set vertical alignment using the cell version of the Format dialog box. Click and hold on the Vertical Alignment button; drag to pick top, bottom, or center from the list. The column headings in our example, for instance, are now top-aligned. They could be vertically center-aligned, since the header cells are particularly high.

If you are formatting a group of cells that are not all identically justified or aligned, you will see Mixed in the justification or alignment boxes. Don't worry about it.

Formatting and Aligning Numbers

At first glance, WordPerfect does some mysterious stuff with numbers in tables. For instance, if you type a comma, as in **5,280**, it may disappear. At second glance, this is a nice bit of automatic stuff for making your numbers more readable and saving a lot of typing. You can also align numbers nicely, like along the decimal point.

A little number that's just your type

Part of formatting a number is specifying its type. This is the "punctuation" of a number: how to show a negative number, how many decimal points it uses, and whether it's in regular or scientific notation. Here are the different types you can use. We use negative numbers just so you can see how the sign is handled:

General	-3333.14159
Integer	-3
Fixed	-3.14
Commas	-5,280
Accounting	$ (5,280.00)
Currency	($5,280.00)
Percent	-52.80%
Scientific	-5.28e+03
Text	-3.14
Date/Time	June 16, 1914

The Date/Time number type interprets the number as the number of days since December 31, 1899. Fractions turn into hours if you choose the right format.

Everything starts out as general (which is why commas disappear if you type them into your numbers). Here's the procedure for changing the number type:

1. **Select any portion of the table or the whole thing.**

2. **Choose Table⇨Number Type, press Alt+F12, or click on the table with the right mouse button and choose Number Type.**

   You see the Number Type dialog box.

3. **Check, and, if necessary, change the top line of the dialog box to Cell, Column, or Table, depending on what you want to format.**

4. **Click on the number type you want.**

   A Preview box at the bottom of the dialog box shows you an example.

If you want to design your own format, you're kind of weird, but we like you anyway. Sometimes it's necessary, such as if you want higher precision (more decimal places). Click on a number type something like the one you want. Then click on the Custom button to get a customization dialog box. Here you can increase the decimal places (use Digits After Decimal) or put in foreign currency symbols from Australes to Krone (see Symbol). For dates, you can get 9/15/54, September 15, 1954 (12:00 PM), 15/9/54, whatever. For negative numbers, use parenthesis for money, or CR/DR for credit/debit. If you have a formula, you can round things off. Use commas. Go wild.

The table we were working on in Figure 7-5, previously, could use a bit of number "typing." The Defect rate column would more clearly indicate who gets this month's quality award if the numbers were expressed as a percent. So we (1) select the column; (2) pick Number Type from the QuickMenu; (3) choose Percent off the Number Type box; (4) click on OK, and we get Defect rate numbers like 0.01%, 0.01%, , 0.03%, 0.12%, 0.13%. Not very illuminating; we need more decimal places. So we do the same thing again, but hit the Custom button this time, and change the Digits After Decimal to 4. Now we get Figure 7-6.

Figure 7-6:
Revealing
the quality
champion by
changing
Number
Type to
Percent and
using the
Custom
button to get
4 digits after
the decimal.

Defect rate	Person to blame
0.0069%	Chris
0.0136%	Gary
0.0311%	Margy
0.1205%	Meg
0.1335%	Dave

Keeping your numbers in line

Few things are harder to read than a table full of numbers that don't line up well, especially if they have different numbers of decimal places, like 3.14159 and 31.825.

For numbers like these, there is a special type of justification called Decimal Align — not in the Number Type dialog box, but in the Format dialog box. (It's in the cell, column, and table versions, in the Alignment area. See the pictures of these boxes in Figures 7-1, 7-2, and 7-4 near the beginning of this chapter.) If you use Decimal Align for columns or the whole table, all the numbers will align along the decimal point.

The procedure is:

1. **Select a column to be aligned, or the whole table.**

2. **Choose Table⇨Format, press Ctrl+F12, or click with the right mouse button and choose Format.**

3. **Check, and, if necessary, change the top line of the dialog box to Cell, Column, or Table, depending on what you want to format.**

4. **Look for Justification in the Alignment section of the dialog box (in the cell, column, or table version). Click and hold on the Justification button; drag to pick Decimal align from the list.**

Right next to the Justification button are controls that allow you to position the decimal point where you want it. (Just in the column and table versions, not the cell version.) The most straightforward control to use is Position from Right, which lets you position the decimal point in inches (or other units) from the right edge of the column.

The other control, Digits after Decimal, is a tad strange. It makes the number line-wrap after so many digits. This is really only useful if you also set the Lines Per Row (in the row version of the Format dialog box) to Single Line, which hides the unwanted digits now relegated to the second line. It's probably better to format the Number type (Alt+F12) to Fixed and specify the precision as we described in the preceding section.

Lines, Borders, and Fills

Like just about anything else in WordPerfect, tables can have borders and fills (shading or patterns). Unlike everything else, tables also have rows, columns, and cells, around which there are generally lines (actually called *lines*) and in which there can be separate fills.

The general procedure for adjusting lines, borders, and fills is as follows:

1. **Select any portion of the table, or the whole thing.**

2. **Choose Table⇨Lines/Fill, press Shift+F12, or click on the table with the right mouse button and choose Lines/Fill. You get the Table Lines/Fill dialog box.**

3. **Check, and, if necessary, change the top line of the dialog box to Current Cell or Selection, or Table, depending on what you want to format. It may be best to start with the whole Table.**

4. **Click on the Line Style you want. A preview box at the right shows you an example.**

The dialog box for the Table selection lets you specify

✔ A border around the whole table (Border Lines area)

✔ The interior lines of the table (Default Line Style area)

✔ A fill for the whole table, using two colors (Fill Options area)

The border and line selections work remarkably like the Border/Fill options used for Layout⇨Paragraph and Layout⇨Page and for graphics. See Chapter 2 for more on how to go about choosing borders and fills.

The dialog box for Current Cell or Selection lets you specify lines around the sides of the cell or group of cells. If you select a bunch of cells, you can control the interior lines of that group with Inside or put a separate border around that group with Outside.

Getting rid of lines can be a little tricky. It's easy enough for one cell, row, or column, but doing large areas is not fun, unless you want to get rid of both horizontal and vertical lines. (For that, select the area and set Inside to None.) To get rid of horizontal or vertical lines, you generally have to do one row or column at a time.

Fills are straightforward. Click on the Fill Style button to see a choice of possible fills and select one. Whatever you have selected (a cell, row, column, or whole table) gets filled. As always with fills, it's best to keep them light and unobtrusive. Fills are made with two colors, controlled by the Foreground and Background buttons.

Splits (and Joins) Without Pain

The old song says, "breaking up is hard to do" — which tells you just exactly how much old songs know about it. It's no problem at all to break up *(split)* a table, and you don't even need a lawyer. WordPerfect lets you do two kinds of splits: splitting an entire table into separate, independent tables; and splitting cells horizontally or vertically.

If, "instead of breaking up you wish that you were making up again" (that same old song , which we wish we had never thought of, because it is now stuck in our heads), rejoice! Or rejoince! The Table Join command can piece together tables as long as they have the same number of columns — even if they were never related in the first place.

Splitting a table

To deliberately split a table, you have two choices: the official Table Split method and the unofficial cut-and-paste method.

The official method goes like this:

1. **Put your cursor in the row that's going to be the top row of the new table.**

2. **Choose Table⇨Split from the menu bar, then Table from the drop menu.**

   The table is, technically, split at this point. The trick now is separating the parts.

3. **Turn on Reveal Codes (Alt+F3).**

   If you're not used to seeing WordPerfect's secret codes, you may panic now, but stay with us.

4. **Click in the Codes window just to the right of the box marked** Tbl Off.

5. **Press the Enter key a few times to get some blank lines between the tables. Press Alt+F3 to turn off the scary Codes window.**

Ugh.

The much-easier unofficial method is to cut and paste some rows. Select the bottom rows of the table and cut them to the Windows Clipboard with Ctrl+X. You get a Table Cut/Copy dialog box; choose <u>R</u>ow (then OK). Place your cursor where you want the bottom-half table to go and press Ctrl+V (paste). If the bottom half of the table is to be just after the first table, first press Enter to put in a blank line to separate the tables, then paste.

The utterly rad thing (we're trying to be more cool by not saying "cool" a lot — oops! blew it!) about the cut-and-paste method is that you can also split a table vertically, which you can't do with the official method. Select one or more columns, then Ctrl+X and choose Column. Paste (Ctrl+V) somewhere else in your document, and you've got a new table made of just those columns!

Unfortunately, when you split a table, your headings (like the top row or left column) don't come along. Hey, chill, dude! (Are we getting cooler yet?) Just copy the header row (or column) with Ctrl+C and select Row (or Column) in the ensuing dialog box. Click in the top row (or left column) of your new table and press Ctrl+V to paste.

Splitting cells

Splitting cells (once the exclusive pastime of sociable prisoners, monks, and biologists) is now something any WordPerfect jockey can do. What we're talking about is shown in Figure 7-7, because it's hard to describe in words.

Figure 7-7:
Splitting cells shows the two people responsible for Mobius spindle quality.

Spindles				
Clockwise	12844	4	0.0311%	Margy
Counterclockwise	14942	18	0.1205%	Meg
Mobius	1199	1	0.0834%	Dave
	4196	7	0.1668%	Fred

Cell splitting lets you put two (or more) things in a row or column, where normally there'd only be one. Figure 7-7 shows horizontal cell splitting, but cells can just as easily be split vertically.

To split cells, select them (just put your cursor in it, for a single cell); choose Table⇨Split from the menu bar, then Cell from the drop menu. (You can alternatively click with your right mouse button and choose Split Cell from the QuickMenu.) In the Split Cell dialog box that appears, click on either Rows for a horizontal split, or Columns for a vertical split. You can also specify how many rows or columns the cell will be split into.

Identity crisis: Splitting cells does odd things to the identities of your rows and columns. In Figure 7-7, for instance, there are now more rows in columns B, C, D, and E than in column A. Row 8 consists of the cell with the word "Mobius," and the top row of the split cells (Dave's row). But if you select that row and change, say, its height, both of the rows created by the split will change. Go figure.

Breaking a table

The first problem most people have is keeping their table from splitting — which it will do automatically at a page or column break. Actually, this isn't really splitting, it's more like "breaking" it. Unless you're trying to violate the laws of typographic physics, like squeezing more text on a page than can conceivably fit, there are some nice solutions to this problem. Here are a few ways to keep a table from breaking at the page end:

- ✔ Reduce the point size of your type.
- ✔ Reduce the line height or spacing (Layout⇨Line or Paragraph).
- ✔ Reduce the row margins. See "Height problems (rows)."
- ✔ Select the table and an adjoining paragraph, then apply *block protect* (Layout⇨Page⇨Keep Text Together).

Avoid retyping headers when a table runs over a page. If you must break a table, you can save some work by making the top row an official Header row. In the row version of the table Format dialog box, click on Header Row. This automatically duplicates the header when the table continues on the next page.

Joining tables

May we join your table? Once considered the province of gregarious boulevardiers, joining tables is now something any WordPerfect jockey can do. (It's often discouraged in the finer restaurants, nonetheless.) WordPerfect will let you join two tables horizontally if they have the same number of columns. There is a secret, however.

The first thing is to first get the tables in close proximity. Very, very, close — as in touching each other with absolutely nothing in-between: no blank lines, no characters, and no secret invisible codes. Having accomplished this, the rest is easy.

Put your cursor in the top table and choose T<u>a</u>ble⇨Join, then <u>T</u>able. If you succeed in removing absolutely everything from between the tables, and they have the same number of columns in the joining rows, the tables will join. (As with using certain glues, you have to have absolutely clean and mating surfaces.)

Put your cursor in the *top* table to join two tables.

Quite probably, they will not join. You get an error message complaining that `The table to be joined must immediately follow this table.` Either you put your cursor in the bottom, not the top table, or there is some invisible detritus (like a WordPerfect secret code) between the tables. To surgically extract this splinter of software, place your cursor in the top table at the bottom, rightmost corner and press Alt+F3 to view codes. Click just after the `Tbl Off` code, and if the next code after that is not `Tbl Def`, press the Delete key to get rid of it. Keep this up until there are no codes between `Tbl Off` and `Tbl Def`. Put your cursor back in the top table and try the join again.

Joining (merging) cells

What WordPerfect calls joining cells is actually more like merging cells. It's sort of the inverse of splitting cells: You can combine two or more adjoining cells to form one. Just select the cells and choose T<u>a</u>ble⇨Join from the menu bar, then choose <u>C</u>ell. (You can also choose <u>J</u>oin Cells from the QuickMenu.)

Cutting-and-pasting beats joining

An easier approach that generally works just as well as joining is to select the (entire) table that will go on top, cut it to the Clipboard (Ctrl+X; choose <u>R</u>ows), put your cursor in the top row of the other table, and paste (Ctrl+V).

This approach also lets you join tables side-by-side, for which there is no official method. Just choose <u>C</u>olumns when you cut. When you paste, the columns will be inserted to the left of the column you place your cursor in.

Positioning and Sizing the Table to the Page

To put the table where you want it, the simplest approach is to use the Format dialog box (table version). Refer to Figure 7-4, way back near the beginning of this chapter. (Sorry about that, we've got too much to say to duplicate pictures.)

To position the table, place your cursor anywhere within; press Ctrl+F12 to get a Format box (or use Table⇔Format or the QuickMenu's Format), then click on Table in the top row. In the Table Position area at the bottom left of the Format dialog box, click and hold on the button to choose from Left, Right, Center, Full, or From Left Edge. The From Left Edge selection lets you enter a distance in the adjoining box for the table's distance from the left edge of the paper.

To size the table to fit between the page's side margins, select Full from this Table Position menu. It expands columns that are not otherwise fixed in width, so that the table is exactly as wide as the margins of the page. It stays that way, too, as you adjust column widths, unless you fix all the column widths individually.

Of course, you can always treat a table as an illustration. Just put it in a text box. That way you can move it anywhere at all, have a nice frame around it, caption it, anchor it to the page if you like, and even have an automatic table number in it if you change the graphic style to Table and edit the caption. See Chapter 1 for more on text boxes and captions.

More Calculations

WordPerfect's tables are really very much like spreadsheets in disguise. Like spreadsheets, every cell in the table has a column letter (A, B, C, ...) and row number (1, 2, 3, ...). A group of cells is referred to by its corner cells, separated by a colon, like A1:C5.

Also like spreadsheets, calculations in tables use *formulas,* which are normally invisible. A cell with a formula in it only shows the result of the calculation. A cell with the formula 1+3.14 in it would show 4.14, for instance.

Normally, the formulas are recalculated only at your command; so if you change the data in the table, the results don't change automatically. To recalculate, use the Table⇔Calculate command to get a Calculate dialog box. Click on the Calc Table button — or to recalculate all tables in the document, the Calc Document button. For automatic recalculation, click on either Calculate Table or Calculate Document in the Automatic Calculation Mode area; recalculation then takes place whenever you edit a cell and move your cursor out of that cell. This can make WordPerfect rather slow, however, if you're entering or changing a lot of data.

The Table Formula Feature Bar

You normally can only see or enter the formulas using a special Table Formula Feature Bar, shown in Figure 7-8. But, if you are a real formula hot-shot, you can enter formulas into cells directly if Cell Formula Entry in the Table menu is enabled. Their results are calculated when you then move the cursor out of the cell, and on subsequent recalculations.

Figure 7-8:
The Table Formula Feature Bar reveals the formula behind the scenes in Table A, cell D4.

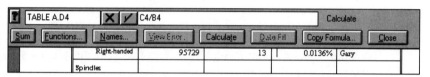

To get one of these beauties, put your cursor in any cell of a table and choose Formula Bar from Table on the main menu bar (or from the QuickMenu — click with the right-hand mouse button).

The white box on the left side tells you what table you're in (WordPerfect enumerates them automatically as A, B, C, and so forth) and what cell. As long as the formula bar says "Calculate" on the right side, you can click in other cells or other tables, hopping around and working with the formulas there.

The white box on the right side is what displays the formula and where you enter the formula. When you start working in this box, WordPerfect enters a special Formula Edit mode and the right side of the bar says Formula Edit instead of Calculate. This means you can't do anything else until you click on either the check mark or the X button.

The button with the check mark tests your formula to make sure it's legitimate and puts the formula in the cell. After you click on this button, WordPerfect re-enters the normal Calculate mode so you can do something besides edit the formula in the current cell. If you make an error that you can't fix, use Edit⇨Undo (Ctrl+Z) to put the cell back as it was.

The button with the X is what you use if you've been editing the formula but change your mind about it and don't want to make those changes to the cell after all. After you click here, WordPerfect re-enters the normal Calculate mode.

The <u>S</u>um button is a convenience feature. It automatically creates a formula summing up the cells above the current cell (tallying a column).

The <u>F</u>unctions button lets you choose from a host of mathematical functions available in WordPerfect, covering basic mathematics and statistics, financial operations, dates and times, logic, and even text operations, like extracting certain text from a cell.

<u>V</u>iew Error will occasionally provide extra help if you make a mistake with math or using a function.

Calcula<u>t</u>e causes all the functions in the document to be recomputed, allowing you to see the result of changes you might have made.

<u>D</u>ata Fill detects a pattern in a row or column of incrementing values and lets you extend that pattern. For instance, if you put the values 1, 2, 3 at the top of a column, select the entire column, and click on <u>D</u>ata Fill, it will continue the sequence right down the column.

Co<u>p</u>y Formula lets you copy a formula from one cell to one or more other cells. Cell addresses used in the formula change accordingly. For example, consider a formula that averages the column above it; if it is copied to the next cell to the right, it averages the column above that cell.

<u>C</u>lose puts away the Feature Bar.

Formulas

Formulas are basically algebra, where the variables are usually cell addresses like C4 and B4 instead of x and y, and the result is what gets displayed in the cell. Cells in other tables can be referred to by their table name and address, such as TABLE B.C4. As with most computer arithmetic, formulas here use * for multiply and / for divide. You can type in numbers, too, like 5,280; not everything in the formula has to be a cell address.

For more-complicated calculations, like net present value, or averages, sums, or arc tangents, there are a host of built-in *functions*. There are far too many for us to describe, but they work like this: There's a name, like NPV for net present value, followed by a list of values for the function to operate on, in parentheses. Values in the list can be numbers or cell addresses (like A5) separated by commas. If the values are in a set of adjacent cells, they can be expressed as a range, like A1:A5 (A1 through A5; a column of numbers). There's a convenient list of all available functions in the Table Formula Feature Bar, in the <u>F</u>unctions button.

TIP

Copy formulas to save work

When you have a series of columns or rows that all need the same basic formula, don't retype a formula for each one — make one and copy it. For instance, when you have a series of columns, each one with a sum or average computed at the bottom, just write the formula for the leftmost column. Click on the Copy Formula button in the formula bar and tell the dialog box how many times to copy it to the right. The new formulas will all work correctly (assuming the data are there above them). See "Copying cells and formulas" at the end of this chapter.

To create a formula (or edit one), click in the formula box. At this point, you can't do anything but work on the formula until you click on the check mark or X button. You can type in formulas as you would type anything else, or you can use special *pointing* features.

One special pointing feature to use while editing is to point at (click in) cells, rather than typing in their addresses. To create the formula in Figure 7-8, we can just point at cell C4, type the / mark, then point at B4 by clicking on it. To enter the formula into the cell, we click on the check mark. You can even point to cells in other tables. Remember, though, you need to click when you point.

Another special pointing feature to use while editing is to point at functions. Click on the Functions button, and you get a Table Functions dialog box. In that box, click on any function listed, then on the Insert button. (To trim down the list, click and hold on the List button and choose the type of functions you're interested in, like Financial.) Replace the variable names, like "Cost," with either numbers or cell addresses.

If you use a function that needs a set of values, like the averaging function AVE(List), you can easily point to a range of cell addresses that serve as the List. Just double-click on List to highlight it, and then highlight (select) the range of cells that contains the values. When you return your cursor to the editing box, the range is entered in terms like A1:C5 (two opposite corners of the range of cells).

Names

To make your formulas easier to read, use names instead of cell addresses. A formula that reads SUM(Sales.January:Sales.March) is a lot more obvious than SUM(B2:B4). You can give names to individual cells, groups of cells, rows, or columns.

Put your cursor in the cell, row, or column you want to name; for a group of cells, select them. Click on the Names button in the formula bar (or choose Table⇨Names from the menu bar). A dialog box appears with table names; your current table is highlighted. Click on the Create button.

A Create Name dialog box appears; type in the name. Indicate exactly what you're naming by choosing Cell/Range, Column, or Row, and click on OK. You return to the table names dialog box and the name is shown; click on Close to exit.

To use the name in typing a formula, click on the Names button. (If the named area is in another table, click on that table listing on the left side.) Click on the correct name on the right side, and then on Insert.

If you've named a row and a column, you can refer to the intersection cell by a combination name. If the row is "Sales," for instance, and the column is "January," you can refer to the intersection cell as "Sales.January." You can either type it in directly or use the Names button described above, twice, typing a period in-between.

Using calculated values in your text

We are absolutely thrilled with this feature, which WordPerfect calls *floating cells*. It lets you use calculated values in your text — not just in a table. These can be calculations based on data in a table or based on data in other floating cells in your text.

Your document may contain a sentence like, "Given our January sales of $24,592 and our yearly goal of $250,000, we are 1.5 percent above target for the month." Now, if some additional sales suddenly turn up (ha!), you would normally have to recompute and retype the numbers. If, on the other hand, you made those three numbers into floating cells (two containing data and one containing a formula), no recomputing is necessary. Just recalculate.

Another use for this feature is simply to refer to a value that appears in a table. For instance, "As shown in Table B, we are 1.5 percent above target for the month." The formula in your floating cell is then just a reference to the correct cell in Table B.

Just be careful with this sort of thing, because if sales go down, your text might read, "... we are -2.3 percent above target ...", and you might not notice until The Monthly Meeting.

To use a floating cell in your text, just position your cursor where you want the cell, and press F12 (or choose Table⇨Create from the menu bar). Pick Floating Cell from the ensuing dialog box.

Type your data into the Table Formula Feature Bar that comes up. When doing the formula, first click in the formula box to get into the edit mode. As you write your formula, you can just point to the data cell by clicking on it in your text. For the example above, the formula would end up looking something like FLOATING CELL A/FLOATING CELL B-1/12.

To get your numbers to look right, use the Table⇨Number Type command (Alt+F12) described earlier. See "Formatting and Aligning Numbers."

To simply repeat a value that appears in a table, create a floating cell. Then click in the formula box to begin editing, and click on the value in the table. Click on the check mark button to enter your data or formula.

Copying cells and formulas

There are two ways to copy things from or within tables: the normal copy-and-paste (Windows Clipboard) approach, or the official Copy Formula approach in the QuickMenu or Table Formula Feature Bar. It turns out that they all work pretty much the same.

For the Clipboard approach, select the area of the table you want to copy and press Ctrl+C. You get a little Table Cut/Copy dialog box, asking whether you are trying to copy the selected bunch of cells or the rows or columns indicated by the selected cells. It guesses what you want from what cells you've selected. If it hasn't guessed your intentions correctly, click on the correct selection. Now put your cursor where you want the upper-left corner of your copied stuff to be and press Ctrl+V.

If you want copies of a single cell, such as when you want to fill a column with copies from the top cell, the same basic process works. Select the cell to be copied (the whole cell, not just the contents) and press Ctrl+C. This time, the little Table Cut/Copy dialog box guesses that you want to copy a Cell (how clever). It also guesses that you want to make a single copy, which is what it means by selecting To Cell. If this is what you want, fine — go paste in the destination cell. If you want multiple copies to fill down the column, click on Down; if you want to fill cells to the right, click five copies, type **5** in the box. Click on OK and the deed is done.

Copying formulas can sometimes yield unexpected results. You may have to read the Technical Stuff in the following sidebar to get things straightened out.

Relative and absolute addresses in copied formulas

If you're not accustomed to spreadsheets, be aware that copying formulas is a magical operation. It generally works the way you want it to, so you don't care. Sometimes, the results are surprising; so it's good to know what's actually going on.

Formulas use cell addresses, right? Like the total of column A, at the bottom of the column, might use the formula SUM(A2:A22). When you copy this formula to column B, does it give you the sum of column A? No way — it sums column B. If you look at the formula with the formula bar, it says SUM(B2:B22). When you copy a formula, its addresses change accordingly. It's as if the formula in our example actually were SUM(the ten cells

immediately above). This is what's called *relative addressing,* having nothing to do with the fact that your relatives move whenever you do.

Usually, this is what you want. Sometimes this doesn't work.

If you don't want relative addressing (you want a formula to refer to, say, cell B1 no matter where you copy it), you must use *absolute addressing.* This means putting the address in brackets, like [B1]. For example, you may have a column of figures based on a single interest rate in cell B1. If you have circumstances where you want the row to change (the number), but not the column (the letter), use the form [B]1. The inverse is B[1].

There is also a Copy command on the QuickMenu that works identically to the Clipboard commands. The Copy Formula button in the formula bar works similarly, except you have to type in the destination cell for a single copy.

Chapter 8

Notable Annotations: Headers, Footnotes, and Comments

• •

In This Chapter

▶ Creating headers and footers

▶ Using footnotes and endnotes

▶ Annotating text with comments

▶ Annotating text with hidden text

• •

*H*ave you noticed increasing numbers of lost souls wandering about your workplace — people flailing the air wildly, muttering to themselves about body parts, like heads and feet? Well, our research has shown that many of these poor unfortunates are business people, students, and professors who have attempted to put headers, footers, footnotes, and other annotations in their documents without proper preparation.

The worst cases are the many poor, trusting folks who attempted to simply (gasp!) *type in* these annotations. Alas, word processing today is WYSIWIG (What You See Is What You Get), not WYGIWYS (What You Get Is What You See). Just because you manage to type text at the bottom of the page that *looks* footnote-ish doesn't mean you *have* a footnote. Gosh, no.

The less-extreme cases are well-meaning folks who just wanted to put footnotes in their theses, or dress up their documents a little. Maybe they tried to make three-part, centered headers. Or add page numbers to the header. Or edit and annotate someone else's text. Very sad.

So, in the interest of social order, as well as of better footnotes, classier headers, and better writer-editor communication (a matter dear to our own hearts), let us explore the joys of these various annotations.

Knowing Your Headers from Your Footers

Headers and footers are those lines of text that appear in the margins at the top or bottom of a page. Every page of this book, for instance, has got a header something like "Chapter 6: Stupid Footnote Tricks."

Headers and footers don't have to be just text; ours have got lines in them, for instance. You can also have page or section numbers if you like. If you're writing a children's book on animals, you could even have pictures of lions, tigers, or bears (oh, my!).

At any point in the document, you can only have two different headers and two different footers: Header A, Header B, Footer A, and Footer B. You can change the text of these at any point in the document by re-creating them. Header B, for instance, could be the same throughout your document; Header A could change with every chapter; Footer A could change whenever you change the topic. Often, people use Header or Footer A for the left pages, Header or Footer B for the right.

You can start headers wherever you like. You can also delay, discontinue, or temporarily suppress headers so that they don't appear where you don't want them. The first page of a chapter, for instance, often has a suppressed header; the headers start on the next page.

You can control the vertical position of your headers and footers on the page by setting the distance between the text and the header. You can control the horizontal position of text with line and paragraph formatting (see the section "Appearance and position of headwear/footwear" later in this chapter).

Making a header or footer

Here's a quick review on how to make a header or footer:

1. **Switch to page view so you can see the headers you create.**

   Choose View⇨Page from the menu bar or press Alt+F5.

2. **Move your cursor to the beginning of your document.**

   Press Ctrl+Home or go to the beginning of whatever page you want the header/footer to begin on.

3. **Choose Layout⇨Header/Footer from the menu bar.**

   Or click with the right mouse button and choose Header/Footer from the QuickMenu.(You get a dialog box for the four types of header/footer.)

TIP

Changing a header/footer in mid-document

Readers appreciate it when a header or footer changes as they go along, telling them what chapter they're in or what topic they're reading about.

To simply have a chapter number that changes, type **Chapter** in your header and click on Number in the Feature Bar. Choose Chapter number off the menu to insert a special code. When you start a new chapter, to make that number change

choose Layout⇨Page⇨Numbering, click on Value in the Numbering Value dialog box, and set a New Chapter Number.

To actually have header text that changes, as this book has, you need to re-create (not edit) one of your headers periodically. Put your cursor on the page where you want the change to take effect and use Layout⇨Header/Footer⇨Create for the header you want to change.

4. Choose one of the four headers/footers.

Use A if you only have one header or footer.

5. Click on the Create button.

You get a Header/Footer Feature Bar, as in Figure 8-1. Your cursor appears in the appropriate top or bottom margin.

6. Type the text.

Use any font, line, or paragraph formatting you like. Heck, put in a picture or a logo if you have one. (See Chapter 1.)

7. Go back to work.

Click anywhere else in the document; click on Close on the Feature Bar if you don't want it any more. If you need to edit a header, choose Layout⇨ Header/Footer from the menu bar again and use the Edit button instead of Create.

Appearance and position of headwear/footwear

Once you have a header or footer, you probably want to fool around with its appearance and position on the page. To do so, make sure you're in page view (Alt+F5), and click in the header/footer. You can use the header on any page. Obtain a Header/Footer Feature Bar from the QuickMenu: With your cursor in the header/footer, click with your right mouse button, and pick Feature bar. The Feature Bar looks like Figure 8-1.

Figure 8-1:
Controlling
your heads
and feets
with the
Header/
Footer
Feature Bar.

You can also use Layout⇨Header/Footer from the menu bar, choose the correct header/footer, and click on the Edit button. Once you have the Feature Bar displayed, here are some things you can do:

✔ **Adjust spacing above or below.**

Click on Distance in the Feature Bar to position your header or footer with respect to the text (the top or bottom margin, actually).

✔ **Specify a different header or footer for left/right pages.**

Technically, you do this for odd- or even-numbered pages, but it generally works out to the same thing (left=even, right=odd). Click on Placement in the Feature Bar. Choose Odd Pages, Even Pages, or Every Page in the ensuing dialog box.

✔ **Put page numbers in your header/footer.**

To display page numbers in a header or footer, put your cursor where you want the number to appear (like after the word Page.) Click on Number in the Feature Bar. Choose the kind of page number you want from the menu that appears. See "Numbering Stuff" in Chapter 12 for more on these numbers. WordPerfect does the numbering automatically.

✔ **Put a graphics line in the header/footer.**

Click on Line in the Feature Bar to create a graphics line. See Chapter 2 for more on graphics lines. (Hint: to adjust spacing between the text and line, choose Set under Vertical. To use a left-, right-, or center-justified line, click on Horizontal, under Position/Length, and then adjust Length.) To change the line once you've created one, double click on the line. Don't click on the Line button again.

For horizontal formatting like centering or indenting, you don't need the Feature Bar.

🗸 **Indent, center, or right-justify text position.**

Place the cursor in your header/footer, just before the text you're positioning. Click the right mouse button and choose Center, Flush Right, or Indent from the QuickMenu that appears. (Shift+F7, Alt+F7, and F7, respectively, also work.)

🗸 **Create a left/right/center three-part header.**

For a header with text on the left, on the right, and in the center, first type all the text, with nothing between the parts. Then place your cursor between the text for left and center, and center-justify, as described above. Similarly, place the cursor between the text for center and left, and choose Flush Right.

🗸 **Make the header/footer margin different from the page margin.**

Header/footer margins change independently from page margins. With your cursor in the header/footer, turn on the ruler bar (Alt+Shift+F3). Drag the left or right margins (the black marks at either end of the white line above the numbered area).

🗸 **Put today's date in the header.**

With your cursor in the header/footer, press Ctrl+Shift+D.

Off with their headers!

There are various humane ways of getting rid of headers and footers — either temporarily or permanently. You can suppress them (turn them off for a while), delay them (make them start some number of pages after the beginning), or discontinue them (stop them altogether).

🗸 **Suppress.** This approach keeps headers/footers from appearing on a particular page. Put your cursor on that page, choose Layout⇨Page⇨Suppress, then choose the header or footer you want to suppress from the dialog box that appears.

🗸 **Delay.** Use this only when you don't want the header or footer to start for several pages. *Before* you create the header or footer, choose Layout⇨Page⇨Delay Codes from the menu bar. Specify the number of pages to delay in the dialog box. Then click on Header/Footer in the Delay Codes Feature Bar to create a header/footer.

🗸 **Discontinue.** Put your cursor on the first page where you do *not* want the header/footer and choose Layout⇨Header/Footer from the menu bar. Choose a header or footer to discontinue and click the Discontinue button in the Headers/Footers dialog box. Repeat for other headers, if you have to.

Restarting headers and footers

When you discontinue headers/footers, WordPerfect inserts an End Header A (or B) code. As a result, you can't easily restart headers afterward. You have to turn on the Reveal Codes view (Alt+F3) and delete the code to do that. If you have to turn off headers/footers for a while, use the Suppress feature.

Likewise, if you find that you need to remove the Suppress code, turn on Reveal Codes and look at the beginning of the page. For the Delay code, look on the page where you created the header/footer.

Footnotes and Endnotes

Moving on from headers to more-sensitive parts of your document's anatomy, let's take a look at footnotes and their more posterior partners, endnotes. (*Endnotes,* by the way, are what we call footnotes when they are printed at the end of a document. They are popular for reference citations and other stuff that would otherwise have to be repeated on each of several pages if they were footnotes.)

If you've never used footnotes in a word-processor before, keep in mind that footnotes aren't attached to a particular page. They're attached to the text that you're annotating. The word processor's job is to put them at the bottom of the page where the annotated text appears (more or less), and do the numbering. Your job is to attach the footnotes to the text and choose the details of how they're going to look.

Two tricks are involved in doing footnotes:

- ✔ Getting the numbering the way you want it
- ✔ Getting the footnote where you want it

There's also the matter of getting that stupid line above the footnote to look right (the separator). That, fortunately, turns out to be pretty easy.

Creating and deleting footnotes/endnotes

Creating a footnote or endnote is so simple, even a Ph.D. candidate can do it:

1. Turn on page view (Alt+F5).

You don't have to do this, but you can see and edit your footnotes more easily this way.

2. **Put your cursor where you want the footnote reference number to appear.**

   Typically, this is just after the word or sentence you are footnoting.

3. **Choose Insert⇨Footnote (or Endnote)⇨Create from the menu bar.**

   Another one of those Feature Bar thingies appears, this time for footnotes. It's nice for zooming around between footnotes, using the Previous and Next buttons; if you delete the footnote reference number by mistake, you can hit the Note Number button to reinsert it. Other than that, you don't need it. Click on Close.

4. **Type your footnote (or endnote) .**

   That number in front of your cursor is the reference number. Don't mess with it, if you know what's good for you.

To delete a footnote, just delete the reference number in the text (not in the footnote). The whole footnote goes away and WordPerfect adjusts the numbering for you.

Notable options

Most people are quite happy with the numbers and formatting that WordPerfect gives them, thank you very much. For the rest of you, however, there are lots of things you can fiddle with. To do so, first click in the text where you want the changes to begin — typically at the start of the document (press Ctrl+Home). Then choose Insert⇨Footnote (or Endnote)⇨Options from the menu bar and get the dialog box shown in Figure 8-2.

There's no place like Ctrl+Home: Before you fool with your footnote options, press Ctrl+Home to put your cursor at the start of the document. Every time you set options, they take effect starting at the current cursor location. So unless you want your footnotes to change appearance or numbering scheme in mid-document, go "home."

Footnote numerology

Footnotes and endnotes normally use regular old arabic numerals. For you European classicists out there, there are also roman numerals and other conventional reference numbering schemes. When you click and hold on Method in the Footnote Options or Endnote Options dialog box, these are some of the numbering schemes you find:

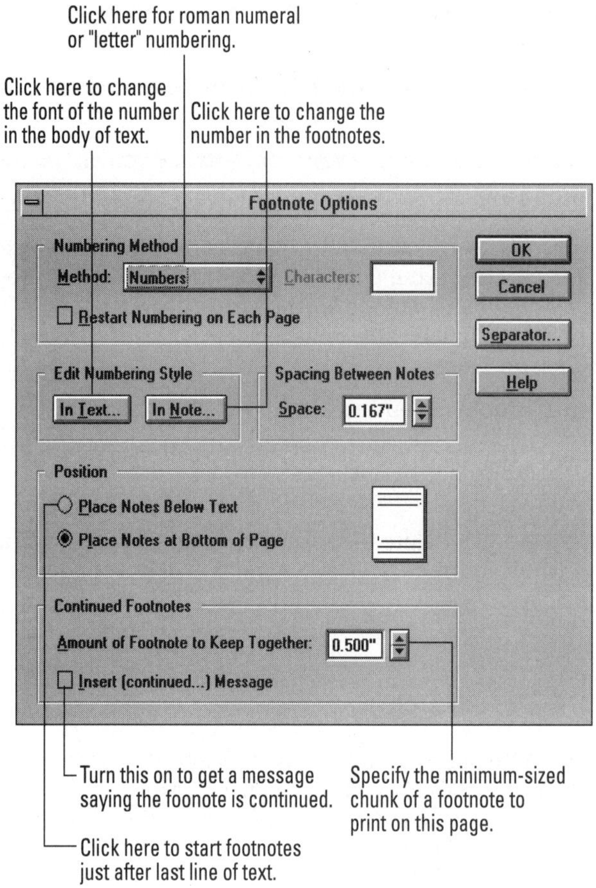

Click here for roman numeral
or "letter" numbering.

Click here to change
the font of the number | Click here to change the
in the body of text. | number in the footnotes.

Figure 8-2:
Doing some
fancy
footnotes
with Insert⇨
Footnote
⇨Options.
Endnote
Options are
similar, but
have fewer
things to
fool with.

Footnote Options

Numbering Method

Method: Numbers   Characters:

☐ Restart Numbering on Each Page

Edit Numbering Style

In Text...   In Note...

Spacing Between Notes

Space: 0.167"

Position

○ Place Notes Below Text

◉ Place Notes at Bottom of Page

Continued Footnotes

Amount of Footnote to Keep Together: 0.500"

☐ Insert (continued...) Message

OK
Cancel
Separator...
Help

Turn this on to get a message
saying the foonote is continued.

Specify the minimum-sized
chunk of a footnote to
print on this page.

Click here to start footnotes
just after last line of text.

1, 2, 3, ...	Numbers
a, b, c, ...	Lowercase Letters (there's Uppercase, too)
i, ii, iii, iv, ...	Lowercase Roman (there's Uppercase, too)
†, ††, †††, ...	Character — use single entry in Characters box, like: † or *
a, e, i, o, u, aa, ee, ...	Character series — use multiple entries in Characters box, like: aeiou

If you want to restart footnote numbering afresh with every page, click in the box labeled Restart Numbering on Each Page. (This is a heck of a good idea if your footnotes are numbered *, **, ***, ****, and so on!) If you want to manually change footnote numbers (not the numbering method) mid-document, place your cursor where you want the change to begin, and use the Insert⇨Footnote⇨New Number command on the menu bar.

If you don't particularly like your numbers in the tiny superscript form, you can change that, too, but it is no fun at all. (WordPerfect shrinks super- and sub-scripts automatically, then fibs about it. If you superscript 12-point text, you get 7.2-point text; WordPerfect still shows it as 12-point, except in the very bottom of the font dialog box.) You can do each number individually, but that's a pain if you have a lot of them. Unfortunately, it's also a pain to change them all at once.

To change how all your footnote numbers will appear in the text, use the buttons in the Edit Numbering Style area of the Footnote Options dialog box, shown in Figure 8-2. Choose Insert⇨Footnote (or Endnote)⇨Options to get the dialog box. Click on In Text. You get the appropriately scary Styles Editor dialog box. "Scary" because (1) it uses WordPerfect's secret codes, and (2) if you're not careful, you can affect all the text following the footnote number!

The menu bar and keyboard commands in this dialog box work just like the main menu bar, but whatever you do applies only to the *style* that WordPerfect uses for footnote numbers. The basic trick is: If you *turn on* some formatting, like a larger type size or boldface, you must turn it off again at the end. For instance, if you press Ctrl+B now in this dialog box, you get a right-pointing code labeled Bold before the other gibberish (codes). This turns on boldface for the footnote number. You must move your cursor to the end of the gibber-ish and press Ctrl+B again to get a left-pointing Bold that turns off boldface.

If you want to change the formatting for the number and/or text of all your footnotes, it works similarly; just use the In Note button (in the Footnote Options dialog box). In the Styles Editor box, click just after the Open Style: Initial Style code and turn on your formatting (press Ctrl+B, for instance). If you only want to format the footnote number (not the text), click after Footnote Num Disp and turn off your formatting (press Ctrl+B, for instance). If you want the rest of the text to have the same formatting, don't turn off the code at all. If you want the rest of the text to have some other formatting, click at the very end of the code gibberish and format away with the menu bar or keyboard commands.

The pain of separation

Separation between footnotes can be set in the Space box of the Footnote Options or Endnote Options dialog box. (Spacing between lines is done with Layout⇨Line Height or Spacing, as for ordinary text. To change spacing for all footnotes at once, use the In Note button as we discussed in the last section.)

WordPerfect positions your footnotes at the bottom of the page, normally. On the last page, as it does on every other page, it leaves space between the footnotes and the text. Because it is the last page, you may not want this space. You can run footnotes right up to the text instead by clicking on Place Notes Below Text in the Footnote Options dialog box. Endnotes are always positioned right up against the text.

When you don't want your Endnotes at the end

If you are doing a single document with several sections or chapters, you may want your endnotes at the end of those sections instead of at the end of the entire document. To do this, put your cursor where you want the endnotes. Choose Insert⁄Endnote⁄Placement from the menu bar to get the Endnote Placement dialog box. To re-start the numbering for the next set, choose Insert Endnotes at Insertion Point and Restart Numbering. This approach works equally well if you place endnotes as you go, or if you wait until later to break up a document into sections, each with its own endnotes.

If you have lots of footnote text, WordPerfect may continue the text on the next page. It generally decides to do this when footnote text approaches half a page in length. You can tell WordPerfect to put a (continued...) message if this happens, and you can control how much of the broken footnote is to be kept together on one page. Refer to Figure 8-2 for details.

Footnotes always come with a separator line between the text and the notes. Endnotes don't. You can control the separator line using the Separator button in the Footnote Options dialog box. This gets you a Line Separator dialog box, which is too boring to reproduce here in such an exciting book. It lets you set space above or below the separator line, position the line horizontally (left, right, centered, or wherever), and specify its length and line style.

Annotating Text with Comments

In the old days, if you were working on a document with editors or other similarly advanced life-forms, you would send your paper document out with a few queries written upon it. It would come back with many helpful comments, scribbled all over your document in colored pencil and connected to your text by a tangle of lines and arrows — and attractively overlaid with coffee-cup stains and cigar ash.

Today, you pass around your document file. If you and your advanced life-form (or forms) are using WordPerfect, you all can make nice, unobtrusive, and legible comments in colored text — right in the document file. Everyone concerned can even have a unique color and initials, so you can easily ignore the comments of people you don't like.

Even better, the comments hide in unobtrusive little balloons in the margin until you make them appear. They don't even print out. Even more better, if your editor comes up with a really socko sentence or two, you can just plunk it right into the document by converting it to text, which we explain later in this chapter.

Creating, editing, or deleting a comment

To create a comment, simply plunk your cursor down right in the offending text and choose Insert⇨Comment⇨Create from the menu bar. Or you can use the QuickMenu instead of the menu bar: Click with the right-hand mouse button in the left margin of the document text and choose Comment.

Distressingly, at this point your document seems to disappear, and you've got yet another one of WordPerfect's amusing little Feature Bars at the top of the document window. Fear not; your document yet lives; it has only removed itself from your presence for the nonce. You are gazing at a special window for writing and editing your comment. Type away. Click on Close when you're done. A little balloon- or box-like icon appears in the margin.

The Feature Bar has nice buttons for inserting the date and time, if you like. If you have set your Environment Preferences, you can also use the Initials and Name buttons instead of typing them (good grief!); see "Personalizing comments" later in this chapter. The Previous and Next buttons let you zip around between comments.

To edit or delete a comment, use the QuickMenu. Click on the comment icon with your right-hand mouse button and choose either Edit or Delete. When you edit, the Feature Bar comes back.

Viewing comments

To view comments, you should probably be in page view (press Alt+F5). You also must be able to see the left margin. Set the zoom to Page Width (use View⇨Zoom).

The comment icons look like the balloons and box in the margin in Figure 8-3. (Not the big balloon in the middle. That comes only when you click on the icon.)

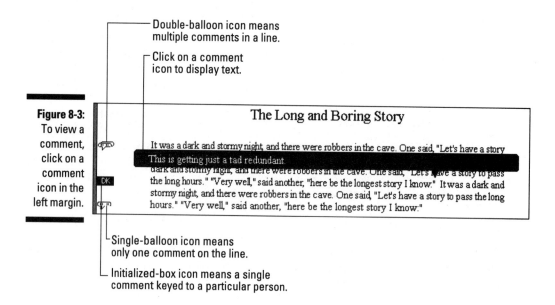

Double-balloon icon means
multiple comments in a line.

Click on a comment
icon to display text.

Figure 8-3:
To view a
comment,
click on a
comment
icon in the
left margin.

The Long and Boring Story

It was a dark and stormy night, and there were robbers in the cave. One said, "Let's have a story

This is getting just a tad redundant.

dark and stormy night, and there were robbers in the cave. One said, "Let's have a story to pass
the long hours." "Very well," said another, "here be the longest story I know." It was a dark and
stormy night, and there were robbers in the cave. One said, "Let's have a story to pass the long
hours." "Very well," said another, "here be the longest story I know."

Single-balloon icon means
only one comment on the line.

Initialized-box icon means a single
comment keyed to a particular person.

Click on a comment icon to view its contents. (Actually, it seems you have to
click somewhere in the left 3/4 of it; otherwise you end up selecting text instead!)
There's only one icon per line; if there's more than one comment per line, a double-
balloon icon appears. If you click on a double-balloon, more balloons will pop up
along the line. (Getting festive, isn't it?) Click on one of them.

By the way, comments are really ugly in draft view. If you're going to use
comments, get used to page view.

Personalizing comments

Comment icons generally appear anonymously, without initials. This is because
people rarely set their WordPerfect Environment Preferences. "The whaaa?"
you say, and rightly so. If you want to have your initials and your very own user
color identifying your comments, do the following: Choose File⇨Preferences
from the menu bar; double-click on the Environment icon; type in your name
and initials where indicated and choose a pretty color with the User Color
button. Click on OK, then Close.

Now put in your comments. Mega-cool, no? Hereafter, any comments made
using your copy of WordPerfect will have these initials and color, unless the
commentator changes the Environment Preferences. (Multiple-comment
icons — the little double-balloon thingies — are excepted, since they could
represent comments from two people.)

Converting comments to text

Good news! When your boss finally tires of debating your phraseology and instead rewrites the sentence for you as a comment, you can easily placate the old buzzard by just converting the comment to text and using it.

While viewing the text of the comment, click on it with your right-hand mouse button. Choose Convert to Text from the QuickMenu that appears. WordPerfect inserts the comment into your text, right where the little pointy part of the text balloon was. Delete the old text and clean things up.

Annotating with Hidden Text

Why you would want to annotate with hidden text when there's such a cute little comment feature, we don't know. Perhaps you have some special reason for secrecy. We won't inquire. Not our business, nope.

Anyway, creating hidden text is as simple as dirt. (Unless you're a soil scientist, in which case it's much, much simpler.) Just type some text, select it, and press F9; click on Hidden in the Appearance area of the Font dialog box.

You may also want to choose another color; this makes it easier to tell hidden text from regular text on your screen. (Color is also apparent when you print — even on a black-and-white printer. To make it subtle, choose a dark blue or green; lighter colors are more obvious.)

Hidden text is not normally visible, to state the obvious. In its invisible state, it does not affect text position or wrapping, page numbers, or anything else we can think of. It's, like, really really gone. To make it appear, choose View⇨Hidden Text from the menu bar. Do it again to make the text disappear.

You can use hidden text to make comments; you can also use it to make conditional text for a document. For instance, you may want to create a report that has two versions: one with certain extra text and one without. (One for the auditors and one for the emergency off-site management meeting, for instance.) Use hidden text for the extra comments. Print the one document with hidden text invisible, the other with it visible. Just don't hand out the wrong versions to the wrong people.

To reconvert hidden text to regular text, you can try to simply reformat it. It's probably best, however, to use the dreaded secret codes approach to avoid leaving stray codes behind, like little land-mines, to corrupt future typing. Yechh. Press Alt+F3 to view secret codes. Look for a code labeled Hidden and drag it out of the codes window to delete it. If you used color, do the same for the Color codes at the beginning and end of the text. Press Alt+F3 again.

Chapter 9
More Typographic Mysteries

● ●

In This Chapter

▶ Understanding "relative sizes" of fonts

▶ What to do when fonts don't come out right

▶ Adjusting spacing between letters (kerning)

▶ Adjusting spacing between words

▶ Fine-tuning line spacing (leading)

▶ Adjusting position of text on the page

▶ Entering the hyphenation zone

▶ Using equations

● ●

Rod Serling, please call your office. The typography of high-powered word processors like WordPerfect is getting just a little Twilight Zone-ish.

The more you use WordPerfect, the more questions arise. Like, just exactly how does WordPerfect decide how much to squoosh lines and letters together? How do you change it? Just how big is a "small" 12-point font? How do you get things to hyphenate properly? How do you get text exactly where you want it? And what the heck is going on in the Equation Editor?

To solve these mysteries, join us as we enter *The Typography Zone*.

Font Phantasms

Fonts can be a little mysterious in WordPerfect, or any word processor for that matter. Two such mysteries in WordPerfect are this business of "relative sizes" of fonts (which appears in the Font dialog box) and the matter of what fonts you see on the screen versus fonts you see on your printed document.

Relative Sizes

Like your relatives, fonts in WordPerfect come in several relative sizes: fine, small, normal, large, very large, and extra large. (Some of our "finest" relatives are "very large.") Some shrinking also goes on when you choose a subscript or superscript. Check out the Font dialog box if you haven't noticed this (press F9 and click and hold on the Relative Size button).

The first question is, What sizes are these, exactly? You've selected a font size, so what is WordPerfect going to give you if you choose, say, "fine"? The second question is, Why use these settings when you can control actual point size?

The answer to the first question is that relative sizes are scaled-down or scaled-up versions of the point size you specify. Unless you change it (and we'll tell you how), the proportions are

Fine:	60%
Small:	80%
Normal:	100%
Large:	120%
Very Large:	150%
Extra Large	200%
Super- or Subscript	60%

When you choose one of these sizes, the Font dialog box tells you what point size your text will appear to be. Look way down at the bottom of the dialog box, where it says `Resulting Font`.

Why would you use these relative sizes when specifying a font, rather than giving the point size? The best reason is to give yourself more freedom in choosing the overall point size of the type in your document. If your document text is 12-point, for instance, and you decide headings should be larger, try using one of the larger relative sizes instead of specifying, say, 14-point type. That way, if you later decide to use smaller type for the document and its headings, you only need to change the point size once, for the whole document, and avoid having to change each heading separately. No matter what point size you choose, your headings will still be proportionately larger, such as 120% larger for Large. (If you use WordPerfect's built-in header styles, this feature is exactly what's used. Heading 1 is Very Large; Heading 2 is Large.)

To change the proportions used for each size, choose File⇨Preferences, double-click on the Print icon, and in the Print Preferences dialog box that appears, change the percentages listed for each size. Click on OK when you're done.

When fonts go bad

WordPerfect is pretty good about printing out the fonts you ask for. There are times, however, when the font you print out doesn't look like the font you asked for, or when your printout doesn't look like someone else's, even though you're using the same file.

These problems are usually because your copy of WordPerfect doesn't have or can't find a particular font called for by the document. If this happens, WordPerfect makes the best guess it can, substituting available fonts for unknown fonts. Even if it can find the font, the font may be usable on the printer only, not on the screen. In this case, the document prints out in the correct font but has to choose a substitute font for the screen.

You can't really fix the problem unless you change the font used in the document to something that WordPerfect has available, or install the font the document needs. Apart from that, if you don't like WordPerfect's substitutions for fonts it can't find, you can change them.

Sneaky font substitutions

WordPerfect does not always use exactly the font you tell it to; it fudges a little to make your life easier. It has internal lists of what fonts to print (*printer fonts*) or display (*display fonts*) when you specify a certain font in your document (*document font*). These lists are called *font mapping tables*. There are three of these that matter to us here, and they appear in the Edit Printer/Document Font Mapping dialog box. (Choose Layout⇨Font⇨Font Map.) Here's what they control:

Document — what printer fonts to use for each font you specify in the current document

Display — what fonts to display on the screen for each printer font used

Automatic Font Change — what fonts to print for different Appearance or Relative Size settings of a printer font

The Automatic Font Change table is pretty sneaky. If you are using a printer font that doesn't come in a certain size or style (say, it only has non-italic Courier) and your document calls for Courier italics, the Automatic Font Change table substitutes a Windows TrueType font (if you have it) called New Courier, which does offer italics.

For basic technical stuff about fonts, see Chapter 8 in *WordPerfect for Windows for Dummies*.

To change these substitutions, you use the Edit Printer/Document Font Mapping dialog box. It's got some scary jargon, but don't panic.

If the document calls for, say, Flea Circus font (which you don't have available), and WordPerfect is substituting New Courier on the printer and on the screen, you can pick a better substitute. Here's how:

1. **Press F9 to bring up the Font dialog box and click on Font Map.**

2. **Click on Document in the Edit Printer/Document Font Mapping dialog box that appears.**

3. **On the left side, in the Document Font area, click in the Font box to choose your weird font (like Flea Circus) from a list.**

4. **On the right side, in the Printer Font area, click in the Face box to choose whatever font you want to substitute for Flea Circus.**

   (You can even use a different style and size here, too, if you want, but that can get pretty mind-boggling in practice.)

5. **Repeat this for each of the different type sizes of Flea Circus used in the document. (Go back to the left side and choose another Size.)**

If you get things horribly mixed up, click on the Automatic Selection checkbox to go back to WordPerfect's original substitution. Nothing you do here takes effect until you click the OK button, anyway, so click on Cancel to give it up altogether.

If the document is printing out in the right font, but the fonts on your screen don't quite match, click on Display. Now for each printer font listed on the left side, you can choose a better display font on the right side.

Typesetting Terrors

It's getting harder to tell the word processors from the page layout programs these days. It's especially true in WordPerfect, where there are a variety of *typesetting* and other typographic features. What these features let you do is to very, very precisely control where your text is printed and how much space is between letters and words. We use the term *twiddling* hereafter as our official term for getting persnickety about your text in a typesetting sort of way. (Because it's a silly word and we like it, that's why.)

Now it's really cool that these features are there, but you really gotta ask yourself, "Who the heck cares?" Well, as far as we can tell, there are three types of text twiddlers:

1. People who are trying to get text to fit better in the space allotted. They either have too much text for the page, column, or text box, and it doesn't fit at all, or they have too little text and it doesn't fill up the space nicely.

2. People who have to print on preprinted forms. These people twiddle text in order to print it in the spaces on the form, or at least not overwrite the preprinted stuff.

3. People who are using WordPerfect to create typographically finicky documents like sales brochures and books, even though they should be using a page layout program and a professional designer; they're too cheap to do that, and why should they anyway when there are these typesetting features in WordPerfect? These people twiddle text simply to make it look and read better.

Twiddling text to make it fit

Making text fit is probably the most common application for text twiddling. Say, for example, you have to keep your company's position paper down to two pages so it can be printed on a single sheet of paper. The position paper, unfortunately, runs a few lines too long. (And, of course, you can't possibly cut any text from this important tome.)

There are lots of non-typographic ways to deal with this, including shrinking your margins (using Layout⇨Margins) and reducing space between paragraphs (using Layout⇨Paragraph⇨Format), but you want this document to look as much like the company standard as possible, so you want to keep your adjustments subtle. Try those solutions first, though. If they don't look so good, try the typographic solutions below:

There are two typographic solutions to the problem of making text fit:

✔ Fine-tune the spacing between lines (adjust the line height or *leading*, pronounced "ledding").

✔ Fine-tune the spacing between words and letters (adjust the automatic *kerning*).

If you're trying to make text fit on a page, adjusting the space between lines probably gives you the biggest bang for your buck. Only if there are paragraphs with very short last lines will adjusting the word and letter spacing help you fit text on a page.

You adjust the line, word, and character spacing from the Word Spacing and Letterspacing dialog box, shown in Figure 9-1. Read on to see how to do these adjustments.

Adjust the Between Lines
value to decrease or increase
space between lines.

Squeeze words together
by decreasing Percent of
Optimal or increasing Pitch
(characters per inch).

Squeeze letters together here
just as for Word Spacing.

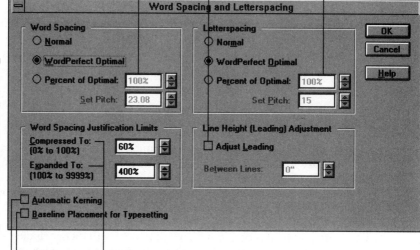

Figure 9-1:
The spacey
world of
Word
Spacing and
Letterspacing
also
includes line
spacing
("leading").

For lines with full justification, these
keep WordPerfect from squeezing
or expanding too much.

Align text across all pages so
facing pages don't look weird.

Clicking here does practically nothing.

Twiddling the spacing between lines

Of course, there is no command in WordPerfect called anything like "adjust distance between lines." That would be too easy. No, there are two ways to do this.

The first way is to change the line height. This is the distance from the baseline (bottom) of one line to the baseline of the next line. Normally, this is automatically set by your choice of font. To change it, first click at the beginning of the document or wherever you want the line height to change. Choose Layout⇨Line⇨Height, click on Fixed in the Line Height dialog box that appears, and adjust the value given there.

The other way is to change the line spacing, which is an *additional* distance between the lines. To adjust that spacing, use the wordspacing and letterspacing command.

To fine-tune line spacing, do the following:

1. **Click at the point in your document where you want the adjustment to begin.**

   Generally, it's best to use the same line spacing for the whole document, so put your cursor at the very beginning of the document.

2. **Choose Layout⇨Typesetting⇨Word/Letterspacing to get the dialog box shown back in Figure 9-1.**

3. **Click in the Adjust Leading checkbox and decrease (or increase) the value back in the Between Lines box.**

   If the value becomes negative, that just means that the value is being subtracted from whatever line height you currently have. Leave some perceptible space or your document will become unreadable.

Twiddling word- or letterspacing

When someone designs a typeface like "Times Roman" or "Galaxy," the type designer has to figure out how much space looks good between the letters. (We imagine Galaxy uses lots of space.) This spacing is pretty subjective, but in the long haul it does make a difference in how comfortable the typeface is to read. The spacing is called *kerning*, probably because it reminds people how kernels of corn can get stuck in the spaces between their teeth. No, really, we have no idea why it's called that — it just is, like "mizzens" and "thwarts" on ships.

WordPerfect apparently has its own opinion about kerning for some typefaces, because there's a place in the Word Spacing and Letterspacing dialog box where you can choose between the designer's kerning (Normal) and WordPerfect Optimal kerning. (Refer to Figure 9-1.) Frankly, we've never seen it make a hoot's worth of difference either way.

You can adjust the kerning for a whole bunch of text at once (like the entire document or a selected paragraph). This is called word and letterspacing. Or, if you're really persnickety, you can individually twiddle one space at a time. This is called "manual kerning," and has nothing to do with getting corn out of your teeth with your hands.

To solve the problem of getting a bunch of text to fit the page, or of making the overall spacing simply look a little better, use WordPerfect's word spacing and letterspacing features. Here's how:

1. **Click where you want the compression (or expansion) to begin.**

   It's generally best to use the same spacing for the whole document, though, so put your cursor at the beginning of the document.

2. **Choose Layout⇨Typesetting⇨Word/Letterspacing to get the dialog box of Figure 9-1.**

3. **Adjust spacing between words by clicking on Percent of Optimal in the Word Spacing box and adjusting the percentage value.**

   A smaller percent-of-optimal gives you less space.

   You can also adjust the spacing between words by increasing or decreasing the *pitch* (characters per inch). This works the opposite of the percent value: Increasing pitch gives you less space.

4. **Adjust spacing between letters by doing the same thing in the Letterspacing box.**

5. **Click on OK to see the results of your efforts.**

A very minor twiddle you can do is to adjust the limits of compression when you have *fully* justified text. (You can't do this unless Layout⇨Justification is set to Full.) This twiddle will only affect appearance; it won't help shrink or enlarge the text overall. To make text fit nicely between the margins, WordPerfect makes tiny spacing adjustments. To keep it from compressing spaces as much, set the Compressed To value higher (in the Word Spacing Justification Limits box). To keep WordPerfect from expanding spaces too much, set the Expanded To value lower.

If you can't tell whether or not you're making a difference when you change word or letterspacing, try pressing Ctrl+Z repeatedly while watching your screen. Ctrl+Z is the undo command and, if pressed repeatedly, will undo and redo your change.

The Truly Finicky can adjust individual spaces between specific letters by using *manual kerning*. Click between the letters in question and choose Layout⇨Typesetting⇨Manual Kerning. A dialog box appears in which you can increase or decrease the spacing. When you do this, WordPerfect inserts one of its notorious codes between just those chosen letters; in this instance, a horizontal advance or HAdv code. You can delete this code without looking in the code window just as you would a space character (click after it and press the Backspace key, for instance).

Twiddling text position on the page

There are times in life when position is very important. One of the more boring instances of this is getting text in the right position. The basic facts of text positioning are that you can move text horizontally or vertically. You can move text relative to other text or relative to the edges of the page. That's it. It may appear more complicated than that, but that's how it works. It's called the Advance feature in WordPerfect.

Advancing text to the correct position is particularly useful when you have to print on preprinted forms. Measure the distance from the left and top edges to the area to be filled in, then set text position relative to these edges. You can even make a template with pre-positioned text as placeholders and use the template whenever you want to print on the form.

To advance text, do the following.

1. **Click just before the text you want to move or position and choose Layout⇨Typesetting⇨Advance.**

    You get the Advance dialog box shown in Figure 9-2.

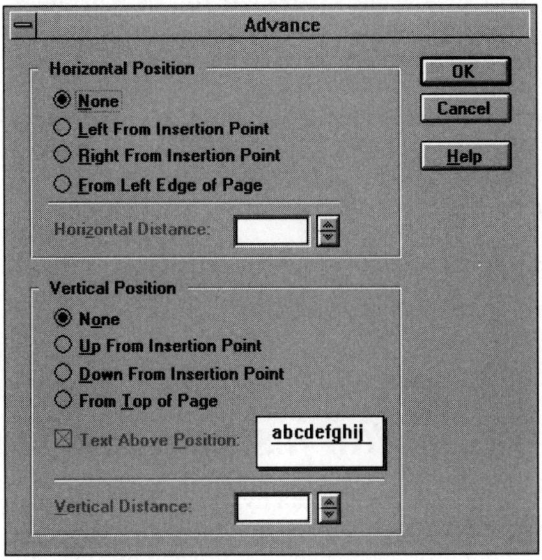

Figure 9-2:
To precisely position text on the page, or just move it around a bit, use the Advance feature.

Advance

Horizontal Position
- ● **None**
- ○ **Left From Insertion Point**
- ○ **Right From Insertion Point**
- ○ **From Left Edge of Page**

Horizontal Distance: [   ]

Vertical Position
- ● **None**
- ○ **Up From Insertion Point**
- ○ **Down From Insertion Point**
- ○ **From Top of Page**

☒ Text Above Position: abcdefghij

Vertical Distance: [   ]

[OK]
[Cancel]
[Help]

Horizontal position affects only a single line's worth of text to the right of the cursor. Vertical position affects all the subsequent text and paragraph- or character-anchored graphics following the cursor.

2. **To position text exactly on the page, choose <u>F</u>rom Left Edge of Page and From <u>T</u>op of Page, then set the distances.**

3. **To just move text up or down, choose one of the other types of position, such as <u>R</u>ight From Insertion Point, and adjust the distances.**

The Advance feature is perfectly capable of positioning text right on top of other text or over graphics boxes that are page-anchored. WordPerfect makes no attempt to move anything else out of the way when you advance text.

Advancing text puts WordPerfect codes HAdv (horizontal advance) or VAdv (vertical advance) where your insertion point is. To see symbols in your document representing these codes, press Ctrl+Shift+F3. You can delete them or copy and paste them if you like.

Hyphenation Hysteria

Hyphens! Soft-hyphens! Em-dashes! En-dashes! You want hyphens, we got hyphens! Hyper-perfect, hyperbolic hyphenation is happening now during hyphen hysteria days at hyphen city, so hop on down!

In other words, hyphenation in WordPerfect is yet another case of overkill. Or is it? Stay tuned ...

First, why hyphenate? Two reasons:

1. To combine words, as in "beech-and-basswood-aged ale"

2. To break words at the end of a line, as in "juxta-position"

So what's wrong with just typing a hyphen?

Good question. When most people need a hyphen, they do what comes naturally: stick in little "minus signs." This is fine for making compound words, like "pie-in-the-sky," but not for breaking words at the end of a line, indicating a range like Monday–Friday, or setting off a phrase — just like this one.

If you do stick a hyphen in the middle of a word, you have given WordPerfect permission to automatically break the word at that point if it needs to. The trouble is, if after you've added or deleted a word or two in the sentence WordPerfect decides *not* to break the word there, you end up with a ridiculous-looking hyphen in the middle of your word. If you want a really infuriating time, try to manually hyphenate a long document with dashes. The automatic word wrapping will ensure an endless stream of incorrectly hyphenated words. Use automatic hyphenation instead, described later in this chapter.

Hyphens versus dashes

There are three hyphen-like symbols, each having its own well-defined role in life:

- ✔ The hyphen: usually found above the equal sign on your keyboard, and which has three identical-looking but differently working forms: "hyphen code" (-), "hard hyphen" (Ctrl+-), and "soft hyphen code" (Ctrl+Shift+-).
- ✔ The em-dash: a rather long dash — used to set off a phrase. This is WordPerfect character 4,34 (press Ctrl+W and type in **4,34** in the Number box).
- ✔ The en-dash: a shorter-than-em dash used for a range of numbers, like 9 – 5.

Here's the scoop on the three forms of hyphen:

When you are combining (compounding) words, like "hard-boiled" or "Jack-in-the-box," use the regular, old hyphen. WordPerfect calls it a *hyphen code*. This allows WordPerfect to legally (under International law) end the line just after the hyphen if the word would otherwise overextend a line. (Just kidding about the law part. It's completely illegal.)

Use the *hard hyphen* (Ctrl+-) when you want to keep the words together on the same line, come hell or high water.

Use the *soft hyphen code* (Ctrl+Shift+-) to indicate where a word should break during automatic hyphenation if WordPerfect attempts to break it. The hyphen is invisible unless the word is actually broken.

The minus sign is not a good minus sign

Since it allows the line to break immediately after it appears, the hyphen that's above the equal sign (and also appears on your numeric keypad) makes a bad minus sign for numbers appearing in a line of text. If your line breaks in the wrong place, it can leave your minus sign on one line and your number on the next. Use a hard hyphen for negative numbers or subtraction instead: Press Ctrl+- (which looks ridiculous in print and means press Ctrl and the "-" key).

Another way to combine words that are OK to break is to use a *hyphenation soft return,* which has nothing to do with tennis. Some compound words take the form of "and/or," "cookie/biscuit," or "Ben&Jerry's." These won't be hurt by breaking them after the slash or other joining character, so you can insert an invisible "OK to break here" mark at that point. To get one of these, though, you have to use Layout⇨Line⇨Other Codes, select Hyphenation Soft Return, and then (in the Other Codes dialog box that appears) click on Insert. While you're here, notice the other cool codes.

Automatic hyphenation

Unless you tell it to, WordPerfect does not break and hyphenate words at the end of a line. Generally, you won't care unless you use columns. Then it gets tough to make nice, even lines out of whole words. Things get particularly weird when you use *full* justification.

```
I t    m a k e s
y o u r  t e x t
look  something
l i k e  t h i s,
```
because WordPerfect is juggling spaces to try to make words fit on a line without breaking them. Even without columns, your text can sometimes look a little squeezed, stretched, or excessively ragged on the right. *Fixed pitch* fonts like Courier take on an especially ragged appearance.

If you want to manually break a word at the end of a line, click where you want the break, then press Ctrl+Shift+- (hold down the Ctrl and Shift button and press the dash, or "minus" key). This inserts a *soft hyphen* that appears if the word needs to break and disappears if it doesn't.

If you want WordPerfect to break words for you, it will be most happy to do so. *You* may become a little disgruntled, but *it* will have a fine time.

Automatic hyphenation in WordPerfect goes as follows. It's a feature that you turn on. But be aware that when this feature is on, WordPerfect will regularly be asking you for help in hyphenation as you write, when you scroll, or during a spell-check. It's best to pretty much complete your document first, then turn on hyphenation.

1. **Put your cursor where you want this word-breaking, automatic hyphenation stuff to commence.**

2. **Choose Layout⇨Line⇨Hyphenation to get the Line Hyphenation dialog box.**

You are now entering the hyphenation zone

To decide what words to try to break at the end of a line during hyphenation, WordPerfect defines a hyphenation zone. It will break words to make lines end within that zone. The zone begins 10% of the column width to the left of the right edge and ends 4% to the right. When you turn on hyphenation, you can change this zone if you like. Setting the percentages higher causes fewer words to be hyphenated but gives you more uneven typography. Lower percentages improve the typography but cause more hyphenation.

3. Click in the Hyphenation On checkbox, then on OK.

WordPerfect scurries off to get its dictionary to see where it can break various words. (The spell-checker files must be installed for automatic hyphenation to work.) If WordPerfect can't find the word, or there is no legal breakpoint given for the word, it asks you for help.

If you really don't want to be asked, when you get done with this Tootorial, choose File⇨Preferences and double-click on the Environment icon from the main menu. Change the Hyphenation Prompt button from When Required to Never. Click on OK to close the dialog box and then Close to exit the Preferences window.

4. When the Position Hyphen dialog box of Figure 9-3 appears while typing, you must decide what to do about the given word. Choose how to break the displayed word or to not break it at all.

Unfortunately, WordPerfect doesn't show you where this word is in the document. You probably want to (1) hyphenate, (2) not hyphenate, or (3) get the heck out of hyphenation, done as follows:

- **WordPerfect suggests a place for a hyphen, which you can change by clicking with your mouse or using the left-right arrow keys on the keyboard. Click on Insert Hyphen to hyphenate there.**

- **If you don't want to break the word at all, click on Ignore Word, and the word will go unbroken to the next line.**

  WordPerfect will never bother you again about this particular word. (It leaves a secret Cancel Hyphenation code in front of the word.)

- **If you really don't want to be bothered with hyphenation right now, click on Suspend Hyphenation.**

  Hyphenation comes back to haunt you when you change your document in any way.

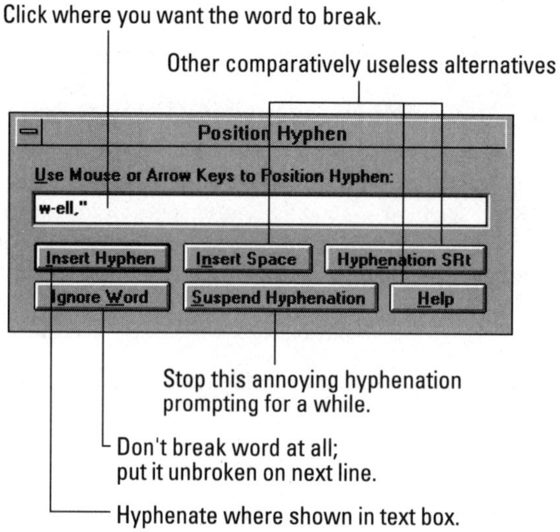

Click where you want the word to break.

Other comparatively useless alternatives

Figure 9-3:
More
hyphenation
choices
than you
really want.

Position Hyphen

<u>U</u>se Mou<u>s</u>e or Arrow Keys to <u>P</u>osition Hyphen:

w-ell."

<u>I</u>nsert Hyphen   In<u>s</u>ert Space   Hyph<u>e</u>nation SRt

<u>I</u>gnore <u>W</u>ord   <u>S</u>uspend Hyphenation   <u>H</u>elp

Stop this annoying hyphenation
prompting for a while.

Don't break word at all;
put it unbroken on next line.

Hyphenate where shown in text box.

- **If the word displayed is a compound word like "hold-up," break it after the existing hyphen using Hyphenation SRt (soft return).**

  WordPerfect should have done this automatically, but sometimes it has a bad hyphenation day.

- **If, for some reason we can't imagine, you want to break the word into two separate words without adding a hyphen, click on I<u>n</u>sert Space.**

5. **If you're all done hyphenating for a while, you can safely turn off hyphenation to avoid being annoyed. (Repeat Step 1.)**

"Hard" characters help avoid breakups

There are "hard" characters you can use if you don't want words to break up at the end of a line. If you don't want your compound words to break at the hyphen, use a *hard hyphen* between them.

Press Ctrl+- for one of these. If you just want to keep words together, like "January 6," use a *hard space* between them: Press Ctrl+Spacebar.

Equation Ectoplasm

Equations are one of the scariest typographic features in WordPerfect. Nonetheless, equations are a tough problem, and WordPerfect deserves a lot of credit for tackling these problematical poltergeists with its Equation Editor. (It rates a "really neat" from one of our spouses who is an engineering student.) As with a good ghost story, people either laugh or scream when they encounter this ectoplasmic editing device.

Introducing the Equation Editor

The reason equations are scary is that you can't just type them in the way they look. (Check your keyboard; no integral signs, right?) Instead, you have to write a description of how they should look, and let WordPerfect materialize them in their final form.

To perform this trick, WordPerfect uses a special Equation Editor, shown in Figure 9-4. To request a seance with the Equation Editor, click where you want the equation to appear, then choose either Graphics⇨Equation or Graphics⇨Inline Equation from the menu bar. Regular equations appear in graphics boxes (see Chapter 1). If you want the equation to appear as part of the text, use inline equations.

If you don't see Equation or Inline Equation in the Graphics menu, you have to add them to the menu. Choose Graphics⇨Graphics Styles, and click on Menu in the dialog box that appears. Choose Equation or Inline Equation in the list that appears. Click on OK, then Close.

The basic operation of the Equation Editor is simple: Enter a description of the equation in the top window, and when you click on the Redisplay button, the equation appears in the bottom window. When you're done, choose File⇨Close, and the equation appears in your document.

Terminology for writing your description

The trick is learning the terminology and language that you use to describe the equation. For instance, to create a cube root symbol, you use the term (or *keyword*) NROOT, followed by a 3. Fortunately, you don't have to memorize the terms — or even type them in, unless you want to. There are several lists of terms, each one rather fancifully called a *palette.* You can display one of these palettes at a time in the left panel of the Equation Editor. You can switch between these palettes by clicking and holding on the Commands button immediately above the panel. You can ignore these palettes and just type in the terms if you know them, or you can double-click on an item in the palette to insert it where the cursor is in the description panel.

Click here for the editor
to redraw the equation.

Describe your equation here.

Choose your equation font here.

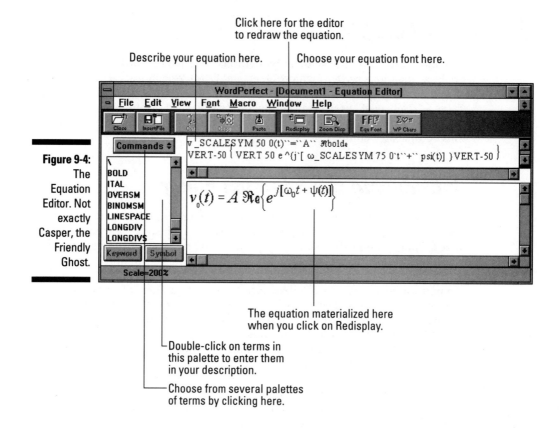

Figure 9-4:
The
Equation
Editor. Not
exactly
Casper, the
Friendly
Ghost.

The equation materialized here
when you click on Redisplay.

Double-click on terms in
this palette to enter them
in your description.

Choose from several palettes
of terms by clicking here.

Here's a thumbnail sketch of what's in the palettes:

Commands   mostly formatting terms (like superscript) and line symbols like
             square root

Large   math and calculus symbols, including scientific and bracketing
             symbols, in two sizes

Symbols   regular-sized math symbols

Greek   the Greek alphabet in upper- and lowercase

Arrows   pretty obvious — a bunch of arrow-like thingies

Sets   all that intersection and union stuff, plus inequalities, transforms,
             and the like

Other   accent marks

Functions   trigonometric, logarithmic, and a few other functions

If you don't care for the way some of the symbols look, or if you don't find what you want, you can also use any of the WordPerfect symbols normally used in ordinary text. Click on the WP Chars button on the Button Bar and select a character set to choose from.

Typing in a description

To type in a description of an equation, just start typing, like $y = mx + b$. (When you type in regular text, the text comes out in italics; to turn the italics off, precede the characters with the FUNC command.) If there's something you need that's not on the keyboard, like a symbol or special formatting, choose the keyword for it from a palette. If your description gets long, you can press Enter to continue on another line; it won't affect your equation at all.

When specifying symbols in your equation description, you can either use the terms for those symbols or copy the symbols themselves from the palette. Click on the symbol in the palette, then on Keyword to insert the term, or Symbol to insert the symbol. Double-clicking always gives you the term.

Don't try to format your equation with the keyboard commands you use in regular document text, like Ctrl+B for bold; use the BOLD command. You also can't change individual font sizes, although you can change the entire equation's font type and size with the Equ Font button. To scale individual characters up or down, use the SCALESYM command followed by a percentage value (no percent sign) such as 50 for $1/2$ size. To offset symbols up or down, left or right, use the VERT and HORZ commands, respectively, which like SCALESYM should be followed by a percentage value. There are also superscript and subscript commands, ^ or SUP, and _ or SUB, respectively.

When you type in regular text, which you need for constants and variables (like x), you can capitalize or not as you see fit, and the equation will match. If you spell out Greek characters like "omega," the case of the character matches the initial case you typed. **OMEGA** or **Omega** creates a capital omega. The word **oMEGA** creates a lowercase omega.

When you want terms in your equation that exactly match the keywords used as commands or symbols by the Equation Editor, you've got a problem. Say, for example, you want the word "sigma." To tell the Editor to read this as a symbol, not a keyword, precede it with a backslash character (no space in-between) as in **\sigma.**

Spaces in the description area are generally ignored, except that you should put them before and after commands and other keywords. To put spaces in your equation, use the tilde (~) symbol, typically on the top left of your keyboard. For tiny ($1/4$) spaces, use the back-accent symbol, usually Shift+~.

The secret of the braces

A key trick is grouping things in your equation. For instance, to show the square root of a^2+b^2, you should get both terms within the radical symbol. To do this, group the terms in curly braces, like this: `{a^2+b^2}`. The whole description would then read `SQRT{a^2+b^2}`.

This grouping stuff is especially important anytime you are going to use some sort of formatting command. If you have to make the entire expression e^j+k a superscript, it needs to be grouped with curly braces.

If you need to use curly brace characters in your equation, use the commands `LEFT\{` and `RIGHT \}`, both of which must appear. Or, click on the WP Chars button and choose from the characters starting at 7,21 in the Math/Scientific Ext. set (which is what we did in Figure 9-4).

Table 9-1 shows some other useful commands besides the ones described previously. Commands affect the characters that follow; sometimes all of them, sometimes just until the command encounters a space. To avoid doubt, group the terms you want affected in {} characters.

Table 9-1   Commonly Used Commands for Equations

To Do This ...	Use This...	Notes
Superscript or subscript	^ or SUP, _ or SUB	
Reduce/enlarge symbol	SCALESYM *pct.*	Where *pct.* is a percent value.
Big fractions, the horiz. bar	OVER	
Square root (radical sign)	SQRT	
Any root of the *n*th power	NROOT *n*	
Position offset by *pct.* %	HORZ *pct.,* or VERT *pct.*	Don't include % symbol.
Character formatting	BOLD or ITAL	
Table of rows	STACK	To end row, use # symbol.
Align rows of numbers	STACKALIGN	Aligns on & symbol mid-number.
Align within group	ALIGNR, ALIGNL	Align with right or left of group.
Matrix	MATRIX	# ends rows; & separates columns.
Limits of integration, etc.	FROM *n*, TO *m*	Put multiple *n*, *m* symbols in {}.

When you're done

Your equation is saved as part of your document when you close the editor with File⇨Close; just double-click on it in the document to edit it again. The equation appears in a graphics box of either the Equation or Inline equation style. See Chapter 1 for information on captioning, bordering, sizing, and other graphics box activities.

If you want to save your equation as a separate file, use File⇨Save As in the Equation Editor and save it with the extension .EQN. To use this file again somewhere else, choose File⇨Insert File in the Equation Editor. Since this command inserts the description from the file wherever your cursor is, you can use an earlier equation as part of new, larger equations.

You can also save the equation as a graphics file, although you won't be able to edit this file with the Equation Editor. Choose File⇨Save As in the Equation Editor and select WordPerfect Graphics 2.0 in the Format area of the Save As dialog box.

Examples

The overall easiest way to understand this stuff is to look at a few examples. In Figure 9-5 are four equations and their descriptions.

$v_0(t) = A \, \Re e\left\{ e^{j[\omega_0 t + \psi(t)]} \right\}$	v _ 0(t)`` =``A`` ℜe VERT-50 ⎰ VERT 50 ⎱ e ^(j`[ ω_SCALESYM 75 0`t``+`` psi(t)] }VERT-50 ⎰
$\dfrac{1}{\overline{w}} = \dfrac{\sum\limits_{m=0}^{\infty} m \, u \, n_0 e^{-\mu kT}}{\sum\limits_{m=0}^{\infty} n_0 e^{-\mu kT}}$	OVERLINE w ~ = ~ { Σ FROM {m=0} TO INF m`u`n_0e ^ {-mu/kT}} OVER {Sigma from {m=0} to ∞ n sub 0e sup {-mu/kT}}
$\operatorname{cof}_{23} \begin{bmatrix} 2 & 4 & 3 \\ 6 & 1 & 8 \\ -2 & 1 & 3 \end{bmatrix} = - \begin{vmatrix} 2 & 4 \\ -2 & 1 \end{vmatrix}$	FUNC cof _23 ~ LEFT[MATRIX {2&4&3#6&1&8# 2&1&3} RIGHT]~ = ~ -``SCALESYM 300 LINE ~MATRIX {2&4#-2&1}~ SCALESYM 300 LINE
$\displaystyle\int_0^{\infty} \dfrac{e^{-nx}}{\sqrt{x}} \, dx = \dfrac{1}{2n}\sqrt{\dfrac{\pi}{n}}$	SCALESYM 300 INT FROM 0 TO SCALESYM 200 INF {{e^{-nx}} OVER SQRT x}~dx``=``1 OVER {2n} SQRT {pi OVER n}

Figure 9-5: Examples of equations and their descriptions in the Equation Editor.

Chapter 10
More Styles and Templates

*I*n Chapters 12 and 17 of *WordPerfect For Windows For Dummies*, we described how to create and use styles and templates. But we failed to let you know how *totally cool* they are. For people who write a lot (like us), styles are a necessity of life. We try never to use regular formatting commands to format a paragraph — instead, we make up a new style. After all, if we use one paragraph that looks like that, chances are there will be another one!

Furthermore, true style aficionados always save their styles for reuse. Once you've formatted one letter just the way you like it, why do it again? You can just save your collection of letter-related styles in a template and use the template whenever you want to write a letter.

For those of you who haven't yet been initiated into the wonders of styles and templates, read on — we review the basics before delving into their ultimate coolness. By the end of this chapter, you too will have a lot of style(s).

The Basics of Style

What's a style? A style is a special type of WordPerfect code that contains as much formatting information as you like. For example, one style code can tell WordPerfect to format a paragraph as bold 14-point Helvetica, centered. Styles have names, like *Heading 1*, or *Fig Caption*, and are usually stored in documents. (Or in templates, but we'll get to that later in this chapter.)

When you use a style, WordPerfect usually sticks in two codes, one to turn the style on and one to turn it off. There are three types of styles:

Character   Affects the text you select (the codes go at the beginning and end of the text to be formatted)

Paragraph   Affects an entire paragraph (the codes go at the beginning and end of the paragraph)

Document   Affects the entire document (if the code is at the top of the document), or the rest of the document (otherwise)

Applying a style

When you install WordPerfect, you get a list of styles for free, with names like *Heading 1* and *Heading 2*. Here's how to apply a style to some text (that is, format the text in accordance with the codes in the style):

1. **If you want to format a hunk of text that is less than a whole paragraph, select the text.**

   To format a whole paragraph, just click anywhere in the paragraph.

2. **Choose Layout⇨Styles from the menu or press Alt+F8.**

   You see the Style List dialog box, shown in Figure 10-1.

3. **Click on a style from the Name list.**

   As you highlight each style, its description, type, and location appear at the bottom of the dialog box.

4. **Click on the Apply button.**

   WordPerfect sticks style codes into your document, and the text is formatted.

If you choose a paragraph type of style, the style applies to the whole paragraph your cursor is in, even if you selected some text. To format a small hunk of text within a paragraph, you have to use a character style.

Speedy styles

Every time you want to apply a style, you have to choose Layout⇔Styles (or press Alt+F8) and double-click on the style you want. There must be a faster way!

There is, though it takes a bit of work to set it up. For styles that you use very frequently, you can write a macro and assign it to a keyboard combination so that you can press, say, Ctrl+1 to apply the *Heading 1* style to the current paragraph.

For instructions on creating macros and assigning them to keys, see Chapters 17 and 18. (This is an area where Microsoft Word aficionados can sneer at WordPerfect, because quick keyboard combinations are an easy-to-use part of Microsoft Word styles.)

In the Style List dialog box, you can also double-click on the style you want — WordPerfect automatically chooses Apply for you.

Click here to select style to use.

Information about the selected style.

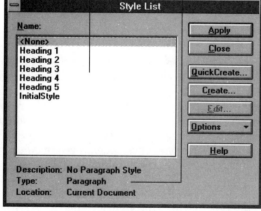

Figure 10-1: This is Mission Control for styles, listing the styles that are available.

It's not my style

If you change your mind and don't want a style to apply after all, you can delete the style codes. You must use the dreaded Reveal Codes window to see and get rid of them. (We described it in Chapter 11 of *WordPerfect for Windows for Dummies*.)

1. **Move your cursor to the beginning of the text you want to un-stylize.**

2. **Choose <u>V</u>iew⇨Reveal <u>C</u>odes from the menu or press Alt+F3.**

   The Reveal Codes window appears at the bottom of the screen, showing the part of your document that contains the unwanted style codes. At the beginning of the text that is formatted with a style, you see a code that says `Char Style` or `Para Style`.

3. **In the Reveal Codes window, move your cursor just to the left of the offending style code and press Delete.**

   Alternatively, you can move the cursor to the *right* of the code and press Backspace. Either way, blow it away.

   When you delete the code that begins a style, WordPerfect automatically deletes the matching ending code.

Another way to delete a style code (or any other code, for that matter) is to drag it right out of the Reveal Codes window. As soon as it hits the outside world, the code shrivels up and dies.

Creating a style

The easiest way to create a style is by using WordPerfect's QuickCreate feature. (I'd like to see a program that came with a SlowCreate feature.) Format some text the way you like it and choose <u>L</u>ayout⇨<u>S</u>tyles from the menu. Click on the QuickCreate button. WordPerfect shows you the Styles Quick Create dialog box. Enter a name for the style, and a description (for your information only), and choose whether it's a character or paragraph style (more on the differences between them in a moment). When you click OK, you've got a new style. Click on <u>A</u>pply in the Style List dialog box and you're done.

You can also create a style by entering the codes that should be included at the beginning and end of the text to which the style is applied. To create a style this way, you use the Styles Editor.

The Styles Editor (doesn't she work for a newspaper?)

One of the very coolest things about styles is what happens when you (or someone else) decide that different fonts, justification, or spacing would look nicer. If you didn't use styles, you'd have to make formatting changes in lots of places in your document. With styles, you make the change in one place: the Styles Editor.

To edit a style or create one from scratch:

1. **Choose Layout⇨Styles from the menu bar or press Alt+F8 to see the Style List.**

2. **To edit an existing style, click on the style you want to edit in the Name list and click on the Edit button. To create a new style, click on the Create button.**

   WordPerfect pops up the Styles Editor, shown in Figure 10-2. If you are editing an existing style, some of the settings may appear in gray, showing that you can't change them. For example, for built-in styles, like *Heading 1*, you can't change the name or type of the style (you can change them for styles you make yourself).

3. **To change the name of the style you are editing or to give a new style a name, edit the current name in the Style Name box.**

   If this box appears in gray, you can't change it.

4. **To change or enter the style's description, edit the contents of the Description box.**

   This appears in the Style List dialog box, to remind you what the style is for.

5. **To switch the style to a different type, click on the Type button and choose a different one.**

   When you create a new style, WordPerfect guesses that you want a paragraph type of style, the most commonly used type.

6. **To choose what happens when you press the Enter key while using the style, click on the arrow in the Enter Key will Chain to: box.**

   If you have applied this style and you are typing text, this action tells WordPerfect what you want it to do when you press Enter. WordPerfect can apply the same style, another style, or it can apply no style to the next paragraph.

Separates codes that work
at beginning of styles from
those that happen at end.

Choose what happens
when you press Enter.

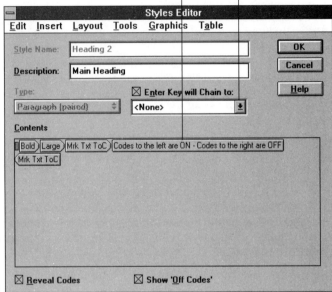

Figure 10-2:
Here's
where you
can fool
around with
the
formatting
of
paragraphs
with style.

7. **To enter or change the codes that take effect when you apply the style, edit the codes in the Contents box.**

   This box contains the actual codes that go into effect when the style turns on or off. Usually, you only need to worry about the codes that turn on at the beginning of the style — WordPerfect turns them off again at the end of the style automagically.

   To enter formatting codes, choose commands from the menu bar right in the Styles Editor dialog box. For example, to set the font, choose Layout⇨Font from the menu. (You may notice that the regular WordPerfect menu bar *disappears* while the Styles Editor is displayed!) You can also type text, if you want text to appear automatically when the style is applied. (You'll see examples later in this chapter.)

8. **When you are done creating or editing the style, click on OK.**

   You return to the Style List dialog box.

9. **Click on Close.**

If you edited an existing style, all the text in that style changes to the new formatting you specified. If you created a new style, you can now apply it just like any other style.

You may see an interesting new comment code that says `Codes to the left are ON - Codes to the right are OFF`. All the codes from the beginning of the box apply at the beginning of the style, that is, where the style is turned on. All the codes after the comment code apply at the end of the style, that is, when the style is turned off.

Style tips

As your document fashion consultants, we'd like to provide some style tips:

- ✔ Use the <u>R</u>eveal Codes option at the bottom left of the Styles Editor dialog box, assuming that you want to see the exact formatting codes your style contains.

- ✔ Any time you think that you might have several paragraphs formatted the same way, create a paragraph style. Any time you foresee having words or phrases formatted the same way, create a character style. Don't waste time doing the same formatting over and over and over...

- ✔ If you aren't sure how your document ought to be formatted, consider making styles with your best guesses. You can always change the codes in the styles later. It's much easier and more reliable to change the formatting codes once in the Styles Editor dialog box, than each time the formatting occurs in your document.

- ✔ If you want control over the exact codes that happen both at the beginning and the end of the style, choose the Show '<u>O</u>ff Codes' box at the bottom of the Styles Editor dialog box. This reveals a comment code that says `Codes to the left are ON - Codes to the right are OFF`. Any text or formatting codes before this comment code happen just before the text to which the style applies. Any text or codes after the comment code happen after the styled text.

If the Reveal Codes option is *not* selected, the comment code disappears and you see a double horizontal line between the "before" codes and the "after" codes.

Types of Styles

When you create or edit a style, WordPerfect lets you choose the type of style: character, paragraph, or document. We hear you asking: What's the diff? Who cares?

A fair question, we must admit. Here are some tips for how and when to use each type of style.

Character styles: specially formatted hunks of text

Character styles are great to use for formatting less than a whole paragraph. Character styles can appear anywhere in your document — like right in the middle of a sentence — so you can use them to format a word or phrase. For example, if you are writing a press release and you want the name of the product to be specially formatted, you can make a style called *Product Name* and define the formatting for it. Then whenever the product name ("Buffalo Chip Ice Cream," or whatever) appears, you apply the style to it.

Some do's and a don't

Here are some do's and a don't for character styles:

- ✔ *Do* decide what should happen when you press the Enter key while you are typing text in this style. When you start a new paragraph, do you want the new paragraph to continue in the same style, switch to another style, or not have a style applied? Usually, with character styles, you want the style to turn off when you press Enter. Tell WordPerfect your decision on this matter by choosing an option from the Enter Key will Chain to: list.

- ✔ *Do* include text if there is text that should appear every time the character style is used. You can enter text to appear either before or after the text to which the style applies. Just put the text before or after the `Codes to the left are ON - Codes to the right are OFF` comment code.

- ✔ *Don't* include paragraph-y type formatting in a character style. For example, don't include commands from the Layout⇨Paragraph or Layout⇨Page commands. If you do, your text gets formatted strangely when you apply the style.

Example: a style for citations

Here's an example of how you can use a character style. Suppose that you plan to create a document that will have lots of citations that look like this: (see "Reefing"). You want each citation to start with an open parenthesis, the word *see*, a space, and a quotation mark. You want each citation to end with another quotation mark and a close parenthesis. You can create a style for your citations and include these standard characters right in the style. Figure 10-3 shows how this Citation style will look in the Styles Editor.

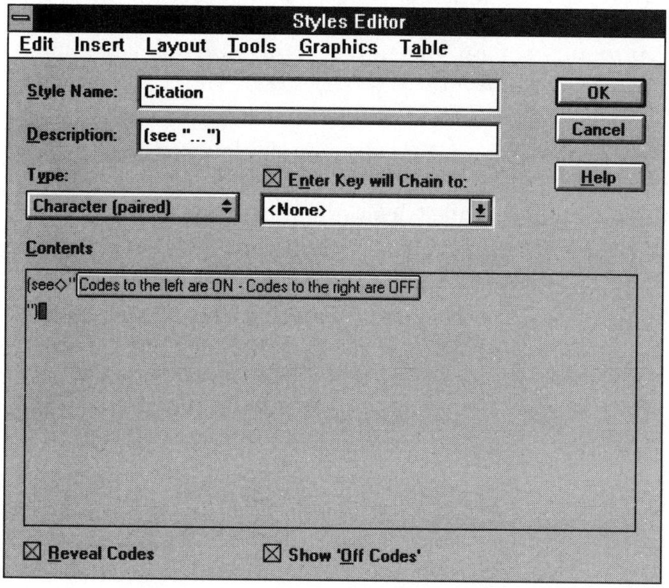

Figure 10-3:
A style for
citations.

In your document, you just type the name of the citation where you want it to go, like this:

```
Reefing
```

When you apply the Citation style to it (by choosing Layout ⇨Styles from the menu, or pressing Alt+F8), you see this:

```
(see "Reefing")
```

Paragraph styles: our favorite style

Paragraph styles are used (as you have already guessed) for formatting that always applies to an entire paragraph. The most popular paragraph styles are those used for headings. Paragraph styles are also good for figure captions and other things that appear in a paragraph by themselves.

When you apply a paragraph style, WordPerfect always puts the beginning and ending codes at the beginning and end of a paragraph, never in the middle. Here are the places your cursor can be when you apply a paragraph style:

- ✔ With your cursor anywhere in the paragraph that you want to apply the style to, WordPerfect turns the style on at the beginning of the paragraph and turns the style off at the end.

- ✔ When you select some text in a paragraph, WordPerfect does the same thing — the style codes go at the beginning and end of the paragraph. That's how paragraph styles work!

- ✔ When you select some text that spans two or more paragraphs, WordPerfect inserts a code to begin the style at the beginning of each paragraph and a code to end the style at the end of each paragraph.

Some tips

Here are some tips for using paragraph styles:

- ✔ Use any character-y or paragraph-y codes that you want, including codes from the Layout⇨Font, Layout⇨Line, and Layout⇨Paragraph menus. But *don't* include page-oriented codes, like those from the Layout⇨Page menu — they won't work the way you expect (or at all).

- ✔ Decide what should happen when you press the Enter key while you are typing text in this style. When you start a new paragraph, do you want the new paragraph to continue in the same style, switch to another style, or not have a style applied? For example, after a *Heading 1* paragraph, you probably want a normal paragraph, not another heading.

- ✔ Include cute little characters for effect (we love 'em!). To insert a special character in the Contents box, choose Insert⇨Character, and choose a character from the WordPerfect Characters box. (See "Inserting Cool Characters" in Chapter 25 of *WordPerfect for Windows for Dummies* if you need information about the WordPerfect Characters box.)

- ✔ Decide how much space to leave above and below the paragraph, especially for headings. We like to leave a little extra space around our headings, usually more space above than below. See the example in the next section for how to control spacing around a heading to a tee.

✔ Include text, lines, or graphics that should appear at the beginning or end of every paragraph in this style. You can enter stuff to appear either before or after the text to which the style applies. Just put the text, line, or graphic before or after the `Codes to the left are ON - Codes to the right are OFF` comment code.

Example: a style for headings

Here's how we set the style for the way we like our first-level heads to appear in many documents. We set the spacing above the heading, below the heading, and between the lines of the heading if the heading spills onto multiple lines. We choose the font, and we mark the heading so that it will be included in the table of contents (just in case we decide later to make a table of contents — see Chapter 12). Figure 10-4 shows how the style codes appear in the Styles Editor.

We've got a bunch of codes here, so let's take it step by step.

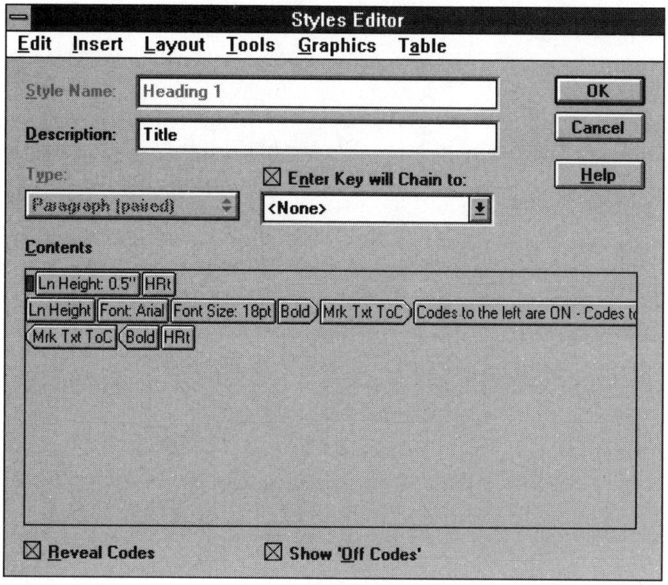

Figure 10-4:
A style for major headings.

Spacing above the heading: We want to leave a lot of blank space above the heading and less blank space below it. We can't just change the line spacing for the heading because if the heading spills over onto two lines, we don't want the lines to be widely spaced. Instead, we set the line height to half an inch and then enter a hard carriage return (to put a half-inch-high blank line above the heading). To set the spacing, at the beginning of the Contents box, we choose

Layout⇨Line⇨Height from the Styles Editor menu bar, click on Fixed, enter .5" for the height, and click on OK. Then we press Enter to insert a hard carriage return (to insert a half-inch-high blank line).

You may think that you insert a code by using the Layout⇨Paragraph⇨Format command and setting the Spacing Between Paragraphs to more than 1, but this leaves space *after* the heading, not before it.

Spacing the lines of the heading itself: If we leave the line height set to half an inch, and the heading extends to more than one line, the heading lines will have a huge gap between them. Not good enough! So after the hard carriage return, we need to set the line height back to automatic (so WordPerfect calculates it based on the size of the font used. To reset the line height, we choose Layout⇨Line⇨Height from the menu bar, choose Auto, and click on OK.

Font: Now we can set the font for the heading itself. We like to use a large sans-serif font for the major heading (kind of like this book, actually), so we choose Layout⇨Font and select 18-point bold Arial.

Table of contents code: (This code is optional, if you never, ever create a table of contents. See Chapter 12 for more on making tables of contents.) The last code at the beginning of the style marks the heading for the table of contents. To set this code, we choose Tools⇨Table of Contents from the menu bar of the Styles Editor dialog box. A Table of Contents dialog box slithers across the bottom of the screen (it's easy to miss if you're not looking for it). Choose Mark 1 to make a *Heading 1* style. (Choose Mark 2 for the *Heading 2* style, and so forth). Then click on Close to make the dialog box slither away.

Spacing below the heading: To add some extra space below the heading, we add a hard carriage return at the very end of the codes, after the `Codes to the left are ON - Codes to the right are OFF` comment code. (Make sure the Show 'Off Codes' box is checked.)

Styles and status

Unless you have been fooling with the information on the status bar (the bottom row of information in the WordPerfect window), it displays the paragraph style, if any, of the current paragraph. (You can decide what is on the status bar — if you forgot, see Chapter 20, section "The status bar," in *WordPerfect for Windows for Dummies*.)

To apply a different paragraph style, you can double-click on the part of the status bar that shows the paragraph style. WordPerfect immediately displays the Style List dialog box, so you can pick a new style.

Oh, and one last thing — because we never want two *Heading 1* paragraphs in a row, we choose *<None>* for the E̲nter Key will Chain to: setting. (If the paragraph after the *Heading 1* paragraph will always use a particular style, you can select that style for the E̲nter Key will Chain to: setting.)

Example: a style for tips

This book has a cute little TIP icon that appears in the left margin whenever we actually say something useful, like this:

See?

You can do almost the same thing and make it easy by using a style. For example, there is a special character that looks like a little pointing hand that you can use as your own TIP icon. Figure 10-5 shows a sample tip style in the Styles Editor.

```
┌─────────────────────────────────────────────────────────────┐
│ ▬                         Styles Editor                      │
│  E̲dit   I̲nsert   L̲ayout   T̲ools   G̲raphics   T̲able          │
│                                                               │
│  S̲tyle Name:  │Tip                              │   ┌──────┐ │
│                                                     │  OK  │ │
│  D̲escription: │pointing hand, then indented     │   └──────┘ │
│                                                     ┌────────┐│
│  T̲ype:              ☒ E̲nter Key will Chain to:      │ Cancel ││
│                                                     └────────┘│
│  │Paragraph (paired) ⬍│  │<None>              ⬍│   ┌──────┐  │
│                                                    │ H̲elp │  │
│  C̲ontents                                          └──────┘  │
│  ┌──────────────────────────────────────────────────────────┐│
│  │▐Hd Left Ind│Hd Back Tab│◄ Left Tab│Italc)Bold)Tip:(Bold(Italc)◇│
│  │                                                          ││
│  │                                                          ││
│  │                                                          ││
│  │                                                          ││
│  │                                                          ││
│  │                                                          ││
│  └──────────────────────────────────────────────────────────┘│
│  ☒ R̲eveal Codes        ☐ Show 'O̲ff Codes'                    │
└─────────────────────────────────────────────────────────────┘
```

Figure 10-5:
A style for
clever tips.

Indentation: We want to indent the text of the tip a bit, to leave some room for the pointing hand icon. To make a hanging indent with the icon in it, choose L̲ayout⇨P̲aragraph⇨H̲anging Indent in the Styles Editor menu bar to insert an indent code and a back-tab code.

The pointing hand: To insert the cute little picture of a hand, choose Insert⇨Character from the Styles Editor menu bar. You see the WordPerfect Characters dialog box, shown in Figure 10-6. Scroll down until you see a character you like, click on the character, then choose Insert and Close. The character appears in the Contents box. Then press Tab to insert a Tab character so that the text that follows is indented with the rest of the paragraph.

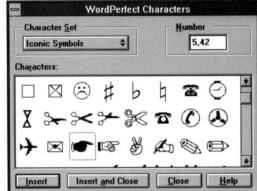

Figure 10-6: WordPerfect's selection of jazzy special characters.

"Tip:" For serious overkill, you can also include the word "Tip" at the beginning of the tip paragraph (for readers who haven't already guessed from the pointing hand that they are about to read something interesting). We decided to make it appear in bold italics (press Ctrl+B and then Ctrl+I, type **Tip:**, press Ctrl+B and Ctrl+I again, and press the spacebar once).

Again, unless you plan to have several tips together, choose *<None>* for the Enter Key will Chain to: setting.

Document styles: formatting the big picture

At last, the final type of style: document styles. As you may have already guessed, document styles are for formatting that applies to the entire document, or at least to more than just one paragraph. Things like page margins, page borders, columns, and other general formatting are good material for a document style.

Unlike character and paragraph styles, when you use a document style, WordPerfect sticks only one secret code into your document, at the position your cursor is in when you apply the style. This is the point at which the style takes effect. There is no endpoint for a document style — it stays in effect until the end of the document or until you apply another document style, whichever comes first. (In WordPerfect-ese, it is an *open* rather than a *paired* style.)

Here are some guides for using document styles:

✔ Use a document style anytime you want an open style, that is, a style with no definite ending. The style doesn't have to apply to the entire document; the style remains in effect just until you apply another document style. For example, if you write reports in three standard sections, each with its own format, you can create three document styles, one for each section. Apply each at the beginning of the section for which it is designed.

✔ Include all the types of formatting that are used in the document. Set the font to the most commonly used font in the document; ditto for Layout Line, Paragraph, and Page commands. Might as well set the margins, justification, and even the watermark, too, if you plan to use one!

We don't use document styles as much as character or paragraph styles because we define templates instead — check out the rest of this chapter! From here on out, we'll talk about using styles in templates, and why you'd want to.

Where Do Styles Come from? Where Do Styles Go?

For centuries, people have wondered where styles come from. Why are long skirts OK now, but unacceptable in the 1960s? And why do men have to go to work with little pieces of silk (or silk-oid products) around their necks? In the real world, no one knows where styles come from.

However, WordPerfect's styles are easier to locate. When you create a style, it is stored in a definite place — in a document or in a template.

Normally, WordPerfect saves any styles you create in the document in which you created them. Simple enough. These styles are usable in this document, and nowhere else. However, what if you want to use the same styles in another document? There are a few ways to do this:

✔ Tell WordPerfect to load some styles from one document to another. In the document that doesn't contain the styles you want to use, choose Layout⇨Styles to see the Style List dialog box, then click on Options and select Retrieve. You can tell WordPerfect the name of the file that contains the styles you want, and whether to retrieve the system styles (*Heading 1*, *Heading 2*, and so on), the user styles (ones you made up), or both.

✔ If you plan on making lots of documents that use the same set of styles, create a template to contain them. (We talk about templates later in this chapter — you're going to love 'em.)

There is also a Save As command in the list you see when you click on Options in the Style List dialog box. The Save As command saves your styles to another file, but it insists on creating a new file. You can do this, but you'll find that it makes more sense to make a template file.

Collecting Styles into a Template

The best place to store the styles you like to use is in a template. (We discussed templates in Chapter 17 of *WordPerfect For Windows For Dummies* — here's more information about them.) A template is a prototype of a document, a blank that you can use whenever you want to make a document. If you create several differently formatted kinds of documents, like letters, memos, faxes, and reports, you can create several differently formatted templates, one for each kind.

You can think of a template as a cookie cutter, a dress pattern, or an architectural blueprint. It contains the general outlines of a document. Every time you use it to make a document, however, you can fill in the details differently.

What style are your initials?

WordPerfect has a special style, called *InitialStyle*, that lives in every document or template you create. It defines what your document looks like if you don't do any other formatting — that is, it defines the default formatting for the document.

There are two ways to define the codes that should be in effect at the beginning of the document:

1. Choose Layout⇨Styles (or press Alt+F8) as usual to see the Style List. Choose the *InitialStyle* style and edit it.

2. Choose Layout⇨Document⇨Initial Codes Style from WordPerfect's menu bar. Amaz-ingly, you are back in the Styles Editor, looking at the *InitialStyle* style.

We don't know why the folks at WordPerfect provided two ways to do the same thing, but they do that a lot.

If you want to use this *InitialStyle* for all new documents you create, check the Use as Default box in the bottom-right corner of the Styles Editor dialog box. (This sticks the *InitialStyle* style into your standard template — we'll tell you what that is at the end of this chapter.)

Templates can contain styles, which is why we bring up the subject. For example, a template for a book chapter may contain all the styles that are used to format the book — chapter headings, major and minor subheadings, figure captions, and the formats used for tables. Templates also can contain text — a memo template can contain the *To, From, Date,* and *Subject* headings that you use in every memo. Templates also can contain graphics, so your memo template can display your company logo at the top.

If you really want to get into some fancy stuff, a template can include macros (prerecorded sequences of keystrokes that you can play back), a specially designed Button Bar that is displayed whenever you edit documents created with the template, and abbreviations that you want WordPerfect to spell out automatically. These advanced topics (almost like actual programming!) are described in Part IV of this book.

You can use templates that already exist, modify existing templates, or make your own.

Where do templates live?

Templates are stored in a special directory, not with the rest of your documents. This directory is usually a subdirectory named `template` in your WordPerfect program directory. For example, if WordPerfect is installed in `C:\WPWIN60`, your templates are in `C:\WPWIN60\TEMPLATE`. You can change this location (although we never do) by using the File⇨Preferences⇨File command, double-clicking on the File icon, and clicking on the Templates option in the File Preferences dialog box.

Templates use a different filename extension from regular WordPerfect documents — *.WPT*. Other than their location and the special filename extension, they are pretty much like regular documents, as you'll see. You can even turn a document into a template by moving it into the template directory and changing its name to use the *.WPT* extension.

When you install WordPerfect, you can install *ExpressDocs*, which are a bunch of templates that WordPerfect programmers set up for you. Some of them are really cool — flip through the ExpressDocs manual to see what they look like and how each works.

The standard template — you're already using it!

Whether you know it or not, you have been using templates ever since you started using WordPerfect. Or rather, you've been using at least one template, the standard template. It's called `standard.wpt`, and it lives in your template directory along with all the other templates. WordPerfect uses this template whenever you create a new document using the File⇨New command.

Every time you use the File⇨New command (or press Ctrl+N) to make a new document, WordPerfect actually creates the new document using the standard template, `standard.wpt`. You can modify the standard template if you like, for example, to change the default font, the margins, the paper size, or whatever. These changes will take effect whenever you create a new document using File⇨New.

There are also some back-door, under-the-table ways to change the standard template. When you use the Styles Editor to edit the *InitialStyle* style, no matter what document or template you are editing, you can check the Use as Default box in the bottom-right corner of the Styles Editor dialog box. This sticks the *InitialStyle* style into your standard template.

You can tell WordPerfect to use a different template as the standard template, although we think this kind of thing causes more confusion than it helps. If you choose File⇨Preferences from the menu bar, double-click on the File icon, and click on the Templates option, you see the dialog box shown in Figure 10-7. You can change the directory where WordPerfect looks for templates, the name of the standard template, and even the filename extension it uses for templates. We don't recommend it, though.

Cutting Out Your Own Template

There's no point making a template from scratch — you probably have a nice-looking document or existing template that you could use to get started. Here are two ways to make a template: first, by starting with a document, and then by starting with a template. (If you don't have a nice looking document to start with, make one, fooling with the formatting until you like the looks of it.)

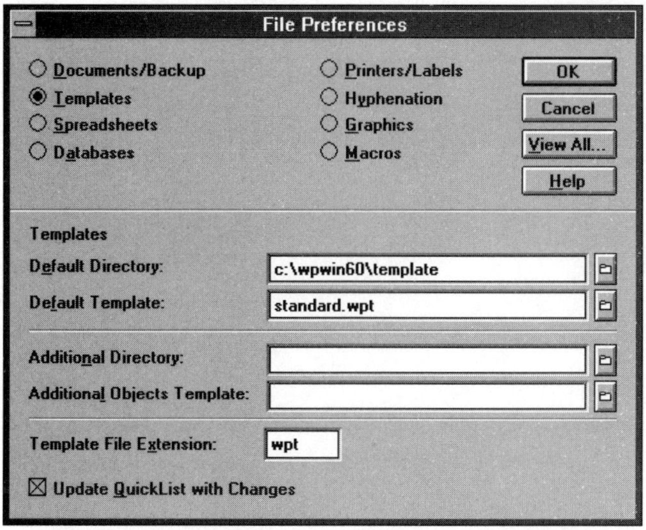

File Preferences	
○ D̲ocuments/Backup ○ P̲rinters/Labels	OK
● T̲emplates ○ H̲yphenation	Cancel
○ S̲preadsheets ○ G̲raphics	View All...
○ D̲atabases ○ M̲acros	Help

Templates

De̲fault Directory: `c:\wpwin60\template`

Def̲ault Template: `standard.wpt`

Additiona̲l Directory:

Additional Objects Template:

Template File E̲xtension: `wpt`

☒ Update Q̲uickList with Changes

Figure 10-7:
Where do templates come from? Where do templates go?

Starting with a document

Here's how to make your own, personal template. As an example, let's make a letter template. We assume that you've already written a few letters and have figured out how you like them formatted.

1. **Open a document that uses the same formatting to be used in the template.**

   That is, choose File⇨Open, or press Ctrl+O, or click on the Open button. Then open a nicely formatted letter that you've already created.

2. **Delete the text of the document, leaving just the stuff that you include in all documents of this type.**

   For a letter template, delete the text of the letter and leave only the stuff that appears in all letters. For example, your document might look like Figure 10-8 (probably not, actually, unless you have the same name and address as one of the authors).

3. **Adjust the formatting if necessary.**

   If the formatting isn't absolutely perfect, spend a minute getting it right. Be sure to set the margins.

Figure 10-8:
A template
for personal
letters.

4. **If you haven't done so already, define styles for the commonly used types of paragraphs.**

   We like to leave a little space between paragraphs in our letters, so we define a *Normal* style that contains a paragraph spacing code, which you can create using the Layout⇨Paragraph⇨Format command in the Styles Editor menu bar. We use this style for the text of the letter, so that extra space automatically appears after each paragraph.

   If you want to indent the first line of each paragraph, you can stick a tab code at the beginning of the style (if pressing the Tab key doesn't insert one in the Contents box, choose Insert⇨Tab from the menu bar in the Styles Editor).

5. **Insert any graphics you want to appear.**

   For example, if you have a graphics file containing a company logo, insert it in your template where you want it to appear in your letter. (See Chapter 1 if you forgot how to do this.)

6. **Insert any special codes that you want to appear.**

   For example, in a letter, you can insert a code that automatically displays today's date. (Choose Insert⇨Date⇨Date Code from WordPerfect's menu bar or press Ctrl+Shift+D.)

7. **Save your document as a template by choosing File⇨Save As or pressing F3. In the Save As dialog box, save the file in your template directory using the .*WPT* extension.**

If you see the QuickList in the dialog box, double-click on Template directory to move directly there. Otherwise, use the Directories box to move to the `template` subdirectory of your WordPerfect Program directory (usually `C:\wpwin60\template`). For the filename, type something like **myletter.wpt.**

WordPerfect comes with a bunch of predefined templates (called ExpressDocs), stored in your template directory. These templates have already taken most of the good filenames. Check to see if there is already a template with the name you are thinking of using. If you use the same name as an existing template, you'll blow the existing one away, which would be a shame — you might want to look at it some day.

Starting with a template

Another good way to make a new template is to start with an existing template. Take a look at the fancy templates that WordPerfect provides with the program — they call them ExpressDocs. (Sounds to us like an emergency medical service, but never mind.)

1. **Choose File⇨Template from the menu bar (or press Ctrl+T or click on the Template button).**

   You see the Templates dialog box, shown in Figure 10-9.

2. **Click on the Options button and choose Create Template.**

   You see the Create Document Template dialog box, shown in Figure 10-10.

3. **In the New Template Name box, enter a name for your new template.**

   You don't have to type the .*WPT* extension — WordPerfect adds it for you.

4. **In the New Template Description box, enter a description of your new template.**

   This description shows up later in the Templates dialog box when you highlight the template name on the list. It can be a nice little reminder of what the template is for.

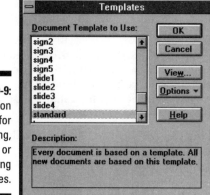

Figure 10-9:
Mission
Control for
making,
editing, or
using
templates.

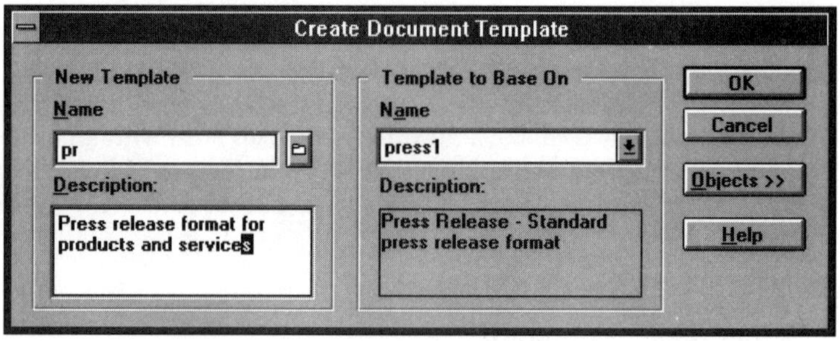

Figure 10-10:
Making a
new
template.

5. **In the Template to Base On Name box, enter the name of the existing template that you want to use as the starting point for the new template.**

   You can click on the down-arrow at the end of the box to see a list of the templates in your template directory.

6. **Click on OK.**

   You return to the regular WordPerfect editing window, and you see your new template, which currently looks exactly like the existing template you chose to base it on. But wait — something is new! Another row of buttons has appeared above the document — it's the Template Feature Bar! (See the sidebar.)

7. **Make changes to the template as necessary.**

   Enter or delete text, so that the text in the template is text that you want to include in every document you create using this template. Similarly, enter or delete graphics and codes. Define or delete styles, so that the list of styles for this template includes only styles that are useful for this type of document.

8. **When you are done, click on the Exit Template button in the Template Feature Bar.**

9. **When WordPerfect asks if you want to save your changes, choose Yes.**

   WordPerfect saves the template, and it disappears from the screen.

Whichever of these two methods you use, you end up with a template that you can use to create as many documents as you like (and even some that you don't like).

The tempting Template Feature Bar

When you use the Create Template or Edit Template commands from the Options button in the Templates dialog box, WordPerfect thoughtfully offers you the Template Feature Bar with the following tasteful buttons:

Create Object: Click on this button to see a menu that lets you choose to create a Style, Macro, Abbreviations, Button Bar, Keyboard, or Menu bar as part of this template. (Alternatively, you can use the regular commands to create these — this button provides a short cut.)

Copy/Remove Object: If you want to copy stuff (styles, macros, abbreviations, and so on) from one template into another, click on this button to display the Copy/Remove Template Objects dialog box. You can tell WordPerfect what template to copy from, which type of object (styles, macros, you know the rest), exactly which objects to copy, and which template to copy them into (it doesn't have to be the template you are currently editing). You can also delete objects from a template.

Associate: Don't think about this button until you've read about creating keyboards, Buttons Bars, menus, and macros (in Part IV).

Description: Click on this button to see or change the description of the template you are working on.

Initial Style: Click on this button if you want to define the *InitialStyle* for the template, using the Styles Editor dialog box.

Exit Template: Click on this button to save the template and close it.

Cookie-Cutter Documents: Using Templates

Time to make the cookies! Once you have made or edited a template (or chosen one from the ExpressDocs templates that come with WordPerfect), it's easy to bake up a tastily formatted document.

1. **Choose File⇨Template from WordPerfect's menu bar, or press Ctrl+T, or click on the Template button on the Button Bar.**

   WordPerfect displays the Templates dialog box, shown back in Figure 10-9.

2. **Double-click on the name of the template you want to use.**

   WordPerfect loads the template. However (and this is a subtle thing), WordPerfect knows that you are planning to make a new document, not just modify the template. Notice that the document name in the title bar of the WordPerfect window is *not* the name of the template — it's something like *Document1*, indicating that you are editing a new document that hasn't been named yet.

3. **Fill in the missing information.**

   For example, if you are using a letter template, go ahead and write the letter, typing in the address, the salutation, and the body of the letter.

   You can also edit the text that you included in the template — it's not carved in stone. For example, if your letter template contains the closing *Very truly yours* and you'd rather use *Hugs and kisses* for this particular letter, you can just change it. Edits to the document don't affect the template — that is, you'll see *Very truly yours* the next time you use the template to write a letter.

   The ExpressDocs templates that come with WordPerfect contain some fancy programming. In many cases, you *can't* edit the text in these templates, because it is actually a "locked cell" in an invisible table — this is a tricky way of making text that can't be edited. (See the sidebar "I can't edit the danged text!" in Chapter 17 of *WordPerfect For Windows For Dummies*.)

4. **Save and print the document as usual.**

In addition to using templates for formatting, styles, text, and graphics, you can really go to town and include macros, special Button Bars, and other fancy things. We explain these features in Part IV of this book, along with how to include these features in your templates.

Chapter 11

More Recipes for Popular Small Documents

*I*n Chapter 19 in *WordPerfect for Windows for Dummies* we told you how to create a variety of small documents — especially some really small ones, like letters, memos, envelopes, and faxes. This chapter contains some more ideas for those of you who like to be terse.

Letters, Faxes, and Memos, Again

We write lots of letters and faxes. Yes, we know it's old-fashioned, but we still do it, at least until everyone in the world has an e-mail account. (We do — if you want to comment on this book, send your comments to us at the Internet address *dummies@iecc.com*).

How to store 'em

It's very wasteful to store each letter, memo, or fax in its own file. Science tells us that if a letter contains 500 characters of text (about 100 words — not a major letter), it takes up 2,850 bytes on your disk. If we double the length of the letter, the file size goes up only to 3,450. If you include a fancy letterhead with a graphic, the file sizes can be much larger. What can we learn from this little exercise in arithmetic? Well, one possibility is to write longer letters, but we're not sure that that's the answer.

Our answer is to store many letters, memos, and faxes in one file. We make one file for each person to whom we write. The first time we write to that person, we just write the letter (or fax or memo), print it, and close the file. Then, every time we want to write again, we do the following:

1. **Select the date of the last letter (or memo or fax) and move it *below* the address and salutation.**

   For memos and faxes, move the date just above where the text begins. We know this seems strange, but wait and see what we're going to do.

2. **With your cursor at the beginning of the date of the last letter (the one you just moved), press Ctrl+Enter to create a page break.**

   Now page two of your document has the date and text of the last letter, memo, or fax. That's all you need to keep — there's no point duplicating your letterhead and the person's address, which is still at the top of page one.

3. **Move up to page one, which is about to become your new letter, memo, or fax.**

   In fact, your letterhead and the person's address are already there!

4. **Type in today's date, or press Ctrl+D to insert it.**

   We don't recommend using Ctrl+Shift+D to insert a date code; if you look at this letter tomorrow, it should be clear that the letter was dated today. Your document should look something like Figure 11-1.

5. **Type the text of the letter, memo, or fax.**

6. **Print the letter, memo, or fax, making sure to print only the pages of the new letter, not past letters.**

   For one-page letters (the best kind), you can use the Print Page button on the Power Bar.

This system puts all of your letters, memos, and faxes to one correspondent in one document, with the most recent letter first — hey, most people file paper letters the same way, with one file folder per correspondent, most recent at the front. It makes it easy to refer to stuff you said to this person before. ("... As per my letter of the 16th, ...") And by storing the letterhead information just once, it saves on disk space.

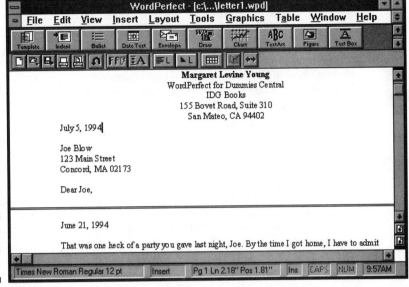

Figure 11-1:
Add your
new letter to
the
beginning of
your file for
this
correspondent.

The page numbering dilemma

For letters, memos, faxes, and the like, page numbering is a tricky problem. One-page letters don't need page numbers — in fact, they look stupid. For multiple-page letters, page numbers are required by most civilized writers. Here's how we handle page numbers for letters and memos, using a footer. (If you prefer your page numbers in headers, follow the same steps, but think "header" whenever we say "footer.")

1. Create a footer that contains the page number.

Using the Layout⇨Header/Footer command, make a Footer A like this:

```
        Page 1
```

or like this:

```
        Joe Blow, Acme Widgets, Page 1
```

Either way, type the text that you want to appear (like **Page** or **Joe Blow**), and use a code to provide the page number (by clicking on the Number button on the Header/Footer Feature Bar and choosing Page Number).

2. **Suppress the footer on page one of the letter.**

   Choose Layout⇨Page⇨Suppress from the menu bar and choose Footer A or Footer B (the footer you just made).

If you use the one-file-per-correspondent method of storing letters, described in the first section of this chapter, you only need to follow these steps once. The new pages you add to the front of the document continue to have the footer suppressed.

Three-Fold Pamphlets

You know the kind of pamphlets we mean — a regular piece of paper (8½ by 11 inches) folded into three panels to make a nice little brochure. It's easy to make these in WordPerfect — just tell it to print sideways on the paper (landscape, in official word-processing parlance), in three sections.

It's not a bad idea to take a piece of blank paper, fold it into three sections, and use it as a mock-up of the brochure. Professional graphics people create these mock-ups all the time — don't be embarrassed. Determine which panel will be the cover, which will have the boring stuff like name, address, and telephone number of the organization producing the brochure, and where you want to put pictures.

Your brochure document will contain two pages, one for the outside of the brochure and one for the inside, as shown in Figure 11-2. One panel of the outside is usually the cover, and the text of the brochure usually starts on the leftmost panel on the inside. Here's how to begin:

1. **With your cursor at the beginning of the document, choose Layout ⇨Page⇨Paper Size.**

   You see the Paper Size dialog box, shown in Figure 11-3.

2. **Choose Letter Landscape from the list of Paper Definitions. Then choose Select.**

   Your list of paper definitions may look different depending on which printer you use.

   WordPerfect creates a paper size code for you and may also stick in a temporary page break (THPg) code — we're not quite sure why. WordPerfect won't let you delete it, so you are forced to have a blank page at the beginning of the document. Oh, well — just ignore this blank page!

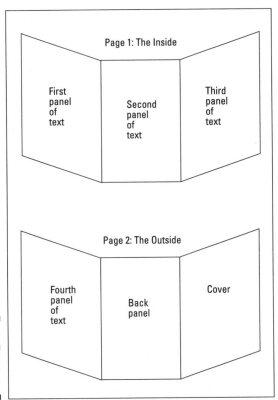

Figure 11-2:
Anatomy of
a three-fold
brochure.

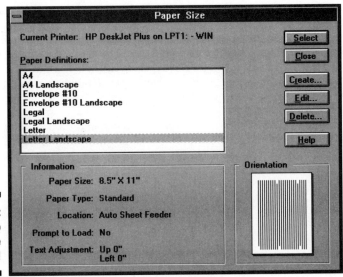

Figure 11-3:
Time to
landscape
your paper!

3. Choose the <u>L</u>ayout⇨<u>C</u>olumns⇨<u>D</u>efine command from the menu bar.

You see the Columns dialog box shown in Figure 11-4.

4. Enter 3 for the <u>C</u>olumns setting and <u>N</u>ewspaper for the type.

For a brochure, you can reduce the spacing between the columns — try 0.25 inch for the <u>S</u>pacing Between Columns setting. Depending on your type size, your columns may be too close together if you set the <u>S</u>pacing Between Columns at much less than that. Try a setting and see how it looks!

5. Click on OK when you are done setting up the columns.

6. Type in or copy in the text of the brochure

If you follow the diagram in Figure 11-2, start with the text that you want to appear on the three inner panels of the brochure. Since you defined the columns as newspaper-type columns, the text can flow from panel to panel. To insert a column break, press Ctrl+Enter.

If your brochure has many headings and subheadings, it's a good idea to use styles, so that headings are formatted consistently. (See Chapter 10 for information on styles.)

7. Type the cover text.

Make sure that the last column on the second page contains the text that you want on the cover. You can also create graphics boxes to contain any graphics that you want to insert (refer to Chapter 1 for more about graphics boxes). Figure 11-5 shows part of a brochure about a church, with the cover text in the lower right of the WordPerfect window.

If your printer can handle legal-size, 8¹/₂ by 14-inch paper, you can create a four-fold brochure. There are several ways to fold a four-fold brochure — accordion-style, folded in half and then in half again, or using a gate-fold where the paper is folded in fourths so that the two ends meet in the middle. Decide which way you plan to fold your brochure before making the brochure in WordPerfect. You should definitely use a piece of scrap paper to make a mock-up, since the order of the panels can be confusing!

Remember, if you need even more space, you can make a pamphlet that consists of several sheets of paper folded in half and stapled together, like a little book. Refer to Chapter 19 in *WordPerfect For Windows For Dummies* for details.

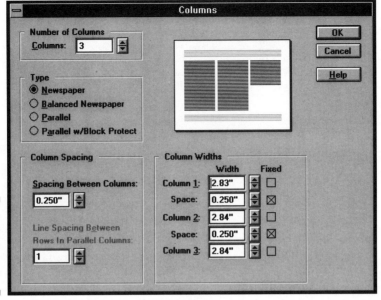

Figure 11-4:
How many
columns
would you
like?

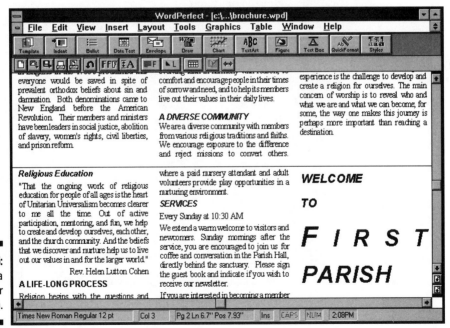

Figure 11-5:
Part of a
brochure for
a church.

Signs and Posters

Everyone needs to make a sign now and again, whether it's for a company staff meeting, a church picnic, or to ask neighbors to look for a lost cat. Naturally, the most attractive and eye-catching signs are created by four-year-olds with large magic markers, but WordPerfect can do a pretty good job, too.

Here's how:

1. **Decide if you want the paper to hang up in its regular orientation or sideways.**

   If you want go with sideways, use the Layout⇨Page⇨Paper Size command to choose the Letter Landscape paper definition (refer to Figure 11-3).

2. **Choose an attractive border, using the Layout⇨Page⇨Border/Fill command.**

   You see the Page Border dialog box, shown in Figure 11-6. Click on the NO BORDER button and choose a good-looking border. Then click on OK. See Chapter 2 for the gory details about borders.

3. **Create a graphics box for each picture you want to include, using the Graphics⇨Figure command.**

   Use clip art, if you have any. Otherwise, you can leave a blank space to glue paper artwork, or let your four-year-old loose with the markers!

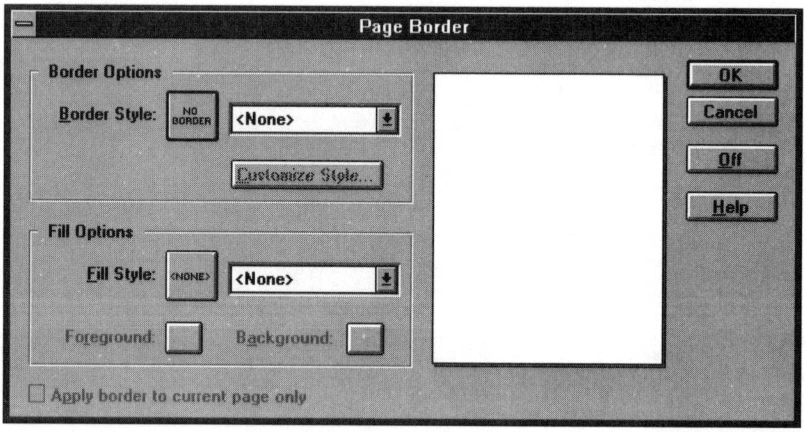

Figure 11-6:
Put a border around your poster.

Page Border
Border Options
Border Style: [NO BORDER] \<None\> ▼
Customize Style...
Fill Options
Fill Style: [\<NONE\>] \<None\> ▼
Foreground: [ ] Background: [ ]
☐ Apply border to current page only

OK
Cancel
Off
Help

4. **Type the text of the poster.**

   Format it using BIG fonts, like maybe 36 or 48 points, so that it will be readable from a distance.

5. **Print the poster.**

   If you want the poster on stiff paper, your printer may not be able to handle it. Print the poster on regular paper and photocopy it onto your poster paper. See Figure 11-7 for an example of what you can do.

If you have a color printer, this is certainly the time to use color. Otherwise, you can consider highlighting parts of the poster using transparent markers or water colors, or at least printing the poster on colored paper. Or you may want to use an interesting graphic as a watermark (see Chapter 1).

Figure 11-7:
Here's a sample poster, using a logo in a graphics box.

Overhead Transparencies and Slides

Most overhead transparencies look horrible, and no one in the audience can read them. There is a simple reason for this:

- ✓ They contain too many words!

To be readable, a transparency should contain no more than eight — yes, that's right, eight — lines of text. Like maybe a title and seven bullet points. The text has to be big. Never just use the pages from your handouts as transparencies. Sorry to sound so doctrinaire — but we've given a lot of lectures in our time. (Of course, our time was about ten years ago, but the nature of eyesight hasn't changed.) See if you can read your transparency at arm's length. If you can, then your transparency will be readable to your audience as well.

If you plan to deliver a talk, you can use WordPerfect to make some snazzy-looking overheads or slides.

1. **Choose the Layout⇨Page⇨Paper Size command and select the Letter Landscape paper definition.**

   Refer to Figure 11-3 to see the Paper Size dialog box.

2. **Use the Layout⇨Page⇨Border/Fill command to put a border around the edge of the page — this always makes your transparencies look more official.**

3. **Create styles for the text — maybe one for titles and another for bullet points.**

   Read Chapter 10 if you haven't used styles before. Choose large, easily readable fonts for your styles — perhaps 24-point Arial. (See Chapter 9 for more about typefaces.)

4. **Save the document.**

   You've got the formatting set. Now you are ready to enter the text.

5. **Type the text of each transparency, pressing Ctrl+Enter to create a page break between them.**

   Remember — eight lines is all you get! If you have the text you plan to read from, or notes for the speech you plan to give, in another document, you can copy the text into this document, but plan to do lots of editing. In the words of the immortal Strunk (author of *Elements of Style*), "Omit needless words!"

6. Print the transparencies.

If your printer can't handle transparencies (and many can't — check the manual), don't despair. Print the document out on plain paper and photocopy the pages onto transparencies. Or go whole-hog and shell out for one of those new-fangled color inkjet printers that can print onto transparencies — they're getting cheaper every day.

Newsletters

There seems to be a newsletter on every conceivable topic these days — one for tightwads; one for stay-at-home-dads; one for folks with every known job, disorder, or software package. Well, maybe it's time for you to put your two cents in and create your own newsletter.

Books have been written about newsletter design (you might want to look at *Looking Good in Print*, Third Edition, by Roger Parker; *Graphic Design for the Electronic Age,* by Jan V. White, published by Watson-Guptill; and *Words into Type*, Third Edition, published by Prentice Hall). But assuming that you've decided on the overall design and the number of pages for your newsletter, here is a way to set up a newsletter format in WordPerfect. Make a blank newsletter, with all the formatting — nameplate, masthead, styles, columns, margins, you name it. Save it as a document or as a template (see Chapter 10).

A newsletter design involves lots of steps, so we break it into stages — headers and footers, column layout, and final details. Be sure to save your document (or template) after almost every step — you may make a mistake, and WordPerfect has been known to flip out when doing complex formatting.

Mastheads and mastfeet

First let's create the masthead (the stuff at the top of the first page, also called a nameplate) and the headers and footers.

1. Choose View⇨Reveal Codes from the menu bar or press Alt+F3.

You are going to need to see the codes you are making because, if they occur in the wrong order, the formatting may not be the way you want it.

2. Set the margins of the pages, using the Layout⇨Margins command (or press Ctrl+F8).

Most newsletters use half-inch margins on all four sides.

3. **Create graphics boxes for the masthead (nameplate) of the newsletter, using the Graphics command.**

   For example, you may create a Figure box to contain a logo and a Text box to contain the title and the date, as shown in Figure 11-8. (For details on making graphics boxes, refer to Chapter 1.)

4. **To position the graphics boxes exactly, click on the Position button on the Graphics Box Feature Bar.**

   You see the Box Position dialog box. For the position of the boxes, choose Put Box on Current Page and set the horizontal and vertical position from the edge of the page. Then click on OK.

5. **To make the boxes exactly the right size, use the Size button on the Graphics Box Feature Bar.**

   You see the Box Size dialog box. You can set the height and width of each box. This is especially useful if you want two boxes next to each other, exactly the same height (as in Figure 11-8).

6. **Close the Graphics Box Feature Bar by clicking on the Close button. Then click in your document so that your graphics box isn't selected any more.**

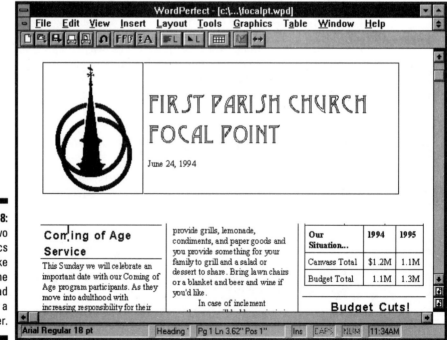

Figure 11-8:
Two graphics boxes make the masthead for a newsletter.

7. **Choose Layout⇨Header/Footer to see the Headers/Footers dialog box.**

   This dialog box lets you choose among Header A (which you can use for headers on odd-numbered pages), Header B (for headers on even-numbered pages), Footer A (footers on odd-numbered pages), and Footer B (footers on even-numbered pages). (Refer to Chapter 10 in *WordPerfect For Windows For Dummies* if you need a refresher.)

8. **For each of the four headers and footers, choose the header or footer from the list, click Create, enter the text of the header or footer, and click on the Close button.**

   You can include the name of the newsletter, the date, the volume and number of the issue (if you number the issues), and the page number. Page numbers should appear on the outer corners of the pages, so put them at the beginning of the line on even-numbered pages and at the end of the line on odd-numbered pages.

9. **Suppress Header A on the first page, using the Layout⇨Page⇨Suppress command.**

   The header would look silly up at the top of the page above the nice masthead you just made.

When you save the newsletter document (or template), make sure that a graphics box isn't selected (if it is, you see little boxes at the corners of the box). Otherwise WordPerfect may decide that you only want to save the graphic, not the whole document!

Columns and lines

Next, let's set up the columnar format you want.

1. **With your cursor just below the masthead, choose the Layout⇨ Columns⇨Define command from the menu bar.**

   Make sure that the cursor is after the margin codes, too. You see the Columns dialog box that was shown in Figure 11-4.

2. **Set the number of columns in the Columns box, choose Newsletter, set the Spacing Between Columns, and click on OK.**

   Many newsletters use three columns with 0.25 inch between columns.

3. **If you want lines between the columns, choose Layout⇨ Columns⇨Border/Fill.**

   You see the Column Border dialog box, which looks more or less the same as Figure 11-6.

4. **Click on the down-arrow to the right of the Border Style box, which probably says** <None>**. Choose Column Between from the list and click on OK.**

   If you have an opinion about the width of the line, change it before clicking on OK. Click on the Customize Style button to display the Customize Border dialog box, fool with the settings you see, especially Line Style, and click on OK.

   After you click on OK again to make the Column Border dialog box go away, you see little stubs of lines between the columns. As you fill text into the columns, these stubs of lines will grow.

Final touches

You've done the main formatting for a newsletter! Here are a few other touches that can make your newsletter look more professional:

1. **Make a table of contents.**

   Make sure that your Heading 1 style contains markers for a table of contents. Put the table of contents in a text box at the bottom of the first page of your newsletter. If you need details on creating an automated table of contents, see Chapter 12.

Newsletter styles

Create paragraph styles for the types of paragraphs you use often in the newsletter, including these:

Heading 1: Used for titles of articles. You may want to leave some extra space around the heading or draw a line above and below it. To draw horizontal lines automatically above and below every article title, choose Layout⇨Paragraph⇨Border/Fill and select Thin Top/Bottom from the drop-down list of border styles.

Heading 2: Used for subtitles to break up long articles.

Caption: Used for figure captions (if you plan to use them).

Bullet: Used for bulleted lists. Use a hanging indent with a bullet character in the left margin.

Sidebar Head: Used for the title of a sidebar (that is, text in a box). You can use a different style from article titles. Take a look at the sidebars in this book — they use a completely different font from the main text.

Sidebar Text: Used for the text of a sidebar.

Table Head: Used for the titles of tables (if you anticipate any tables).

Table Column Head: Used for the column headings in tables.

Table Text: Used for the text of tables.

You'll probably think of other styles that you will use in your particular newsletter.

2. **Make a masthead (that is, a box containing info that identifies who puts out the newsletter).**

   Time for another text box! This one should list the name and address of your organization, the names of folks involved in the newsletter, and subscription information.

3. **If you plan to mail the newsletter without an envelope (that is, the newsletter is a *self-mailer*), make an area for the mailing label, return address, and stamp.**

   Let's say you are making a four-page newsletter that will be printed on one 11-by-17-inch piece of paper, which is folded in half to make an 8½-by-11-inch booklet, then folded in three parts for mailing. Make the bottom third of the back page look like the front of an envelope, showing the address label, your return address, and space for the stamp or bulk mail permit number.

   To do this, create a Text box on the back page that occupies the full width of the page and is three inches high. Position the Text box at the bottom of the page. In the box, type the return address of the organization and any other message that you want to appear. If you use a postal permit, make another Text box to contain the indicia information (post office and number of the permit). The bottom of your newsletter may look like Figure 11-9.

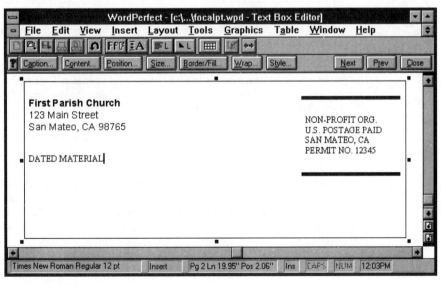

Figure 11-9: The bottom third of the last page of the newsletter, with address and mailing information.

It's news time!

Save your final newsletter format as a document or as a template, preferably the latter. You'll use it each time you create a new issue of the newsletter.

Now you can start entering the text. With luck, you've already got the text in other document files and can copy it into your newsletter. Here are a few hints for making a good-looking newsletter:

✔ Use a few sidebars, maybe one per page, to break up the text. To make a sidebar, create a Text box and type the text into it. You may want to give the Text box a background (a fill) — use a *very* pale gray. (See Chapters 1 and 2 for details on making sidebars and choosing fills.)

✔ Tables are good for breaking up boring-looking text, too. WordPerfect lets you create a table right in a column of text. If you want a table to span two or more columns, put it in a Text box.

✔ Pictures are a great way to liven up your newsletter. If you have a picture in a graphics file, create a Figure box (again, see Chapter 1). If you have the picture on paper, create a blank Text box the same size as the picture and later glue the picture to the final draft.

If you have a picture on paper and the newsletter will be printed by a real professional offset printer, give the blank Text box a totally black fill and don't glue the picture on. Instead, give the picture to the professional printer with instructions on where it should go — he or she can do a much neater job of putting the picture into place.

✔ If you have nothing else to enliven a page of text, use *pull quotes*. Select one or two interesting quotes from the text and create a Text box for each quote. The text boxes can fit within one column or can span two columns. Use a large font for the quotes, so they stand out from the rest of the text.

Newsletters reproduced from your laser printer's output are fine for informal communication, but often lack the crisp look of professionally printed documents. They also generally lack color, unless you have a color printer. Even then, if you are going to have your newsletter printed in quantity, you may be better off not using color in your document. Color reproduction is pretty expensive for a newsletter, especially if you want two-sided documents — get a quote or two from professional printers. For more information on these issues and other issues of working with professional printers, see Chapter 15.

Other General Tips

Here are some other ideas for creating small documents.

The continuing saga

On some letters or other short documents such as press releases, you may like to see the footer *Continued on next page.* However, this footer shouldn't appear on the last page. This is a snap in WordPerfect — create a footer that contains your continuation message. Then suppress the footer on the last page of the document.

Page 17 of 42

Doesn't it look official when each page of a document tells you how many pages you should have in total? It makes a nice cross-check when printing, too, so you know if you've printed the whole thing. Here's how to create a footer (or header) that not only automatically numbers the pages but also displays the total number of pages in the document. (We cadged this hint from *WordPerfect for Windows Magazine* — see Chapter 23 for information about how to get a subscription.)

The trick is to use a *cross-reference* to something on the last page of the document. Cross-references are designed for providing page references, like *For more information on animals that eat their young, see page 134*. We explain cross-references in detail in Chapter 13. For right know, all you need to know is that the thing that the cross-reference refers to (the last page, in this example) is called the *target*.

Here's what to do.

1. **At the very end of the document, create a cross-reference target.**

   Choose Tools⇨Cross-Reference to display the Cross-Reference Feature Bar (another one!). In the Target box on the Feature Bar, type **lastpage**, the name for the target. (You can use another name for the target if you want, but choose one that makes sense!) Then click on the Mark Target button on the Feature Bar. This creates a hidden target code.

2. **Create a header or footer on the page where you want headers or footers to start printing.**

   Choose Layout⇨Header/Footer, choose a header or a footer, and click on Create. Now you see the Header/Footer Feature Bar.

3. **Type** Page **and a space, press Ctrl+Shift+P to insert a page number code, type another space, type** of, **and type another space.**

While you are at it, you may want to click on the Justification button on the Power Bar to tell WordPerfect to center the header or footer line you are creating. Now you are ready for the magic part — the cross-reference code that displays the page number of the last page of the document.

4. **Click the right mouse button anywhere on the Header/Footer Feature Bar and choose Cross-Reference from the QuickMenu that appears.**

Poof! The Header/Footer Feature Bar is replaced by its Cross-Reference counterpart.

5. **Click on the Mark Reference button on the Cross-Reference Feature Bar.**

You see a question mark where you'd like to see the number of pages in the document. What gives? The Target box on the Feature Bar still says *lastpage,* so WordPerfect knows which cross-reference target you want the page number of. The problem is that WordPerfect still has to calculate the number — this process is called *generating* the number. Hang on a sec and we'll be ready to do that.

6. **Click the right mouse button anywhere on the Feature Bar again and choose Header/Footer to return to the Header/Footer Feature Bar.**

7. **Click the Close button on the Header/Footer Feature Bar to tell WordPerfect that you are done typing the text of the header or footer.**

The Feature Bar goes away, to be replaced once again by the Cross-Reference Feature Bar.

8. **Click on the Generate button on the Feature Bar and click OK on the dialog box that follows.**

WordPerfect then spends a few seconds (or a few minutes, if the document is long) checking out the page numbers of your cross-references. Then, poof! It's done.

9. **Click on the Close button on the Cross-Reference Feature Bar.**

Finally, all of your Feature Bars are done.

10. **If you are not already in page view, choose View⇨Page from the menu bar so that you can see your brand-new header or footer.**

If you edit your document further and possibly change the number of pages in the document, be sure to regenerate the cross-references so that the page count will be correct. Before you print the document, choose Tools⇨Generate (Ctrl+F9) from the menu bar and click on OK from the dialog box (this command does the same thing as Step 8 in the steps you just followed).

Chapter 12

Creating Books: The Front Matters

• •

In This Chapter

▶ Title pages and other front matter

▶ Terrific tables of contents

▶ Perfect page numbering

▶ Lists of figures and tables

• •

So, you're writing the Great American Novel. Or for you international readers, it's the Great Bolivian Novel (we're just guessing here). And you've decided to typeset it yourself, using WordPerfect.

A few years ago, this would have been an idiotic idea. "Get a desktop publishing program!" we would have cried. "Word processors can't handle books!"

However, times have changed, features have been added, and WordPerfect has got all the fancy features you could want to handle publishing most types of books. (No, this book wasn't typeset using WordPerfect. IDG Books wouldn't let us, no matter how we begged and pleaded.)

In Chapter 19 of *WordPerfect for Windows for Dummies*, we described some of WordPerfect's big-document features. In this chapter, we review some of the ones we've already talked about (like making a table of contents and an index and using master documents) and we describe some others (like automatically numbering things, and creating lists of figures or tables).

We'll start at the beginning of a book, with the title page, and work our way back. (This stuff is quite reasonably called the *front matter* in book-writing circles.) Seems like a reasonable way to proceed! Chapter 13 discusses the actual text of the book — the stuff after the front matter.

Bound for Binding

Have you ever read a book where you have to crack the binding like crazy to be able to read the beginnings and ends of the lines because they disappear into the center crease of the book? That drives us nuts. Similarly, we've occasionally gotten materials in ring binders in which the holes are punched right through the edges of the text.

Heaven forbid that your fine manuscript should be formatted in such a déclassé manner. If you plan to bind your book, or even punch holes in it to put it in a ring binder, you can leave extra blank space on the bound (or punched) edge of the page. In other words, you need an extra-wide left margin on odd-numbered (right-hand) pages and an extra-wide right margin on even-numbered (left-hand) pages. The bound or punched side of the page is called the *inside edge*, by the way, so what you want is to increase the inside margin.

Amazingly, the WordPerfect folks have thought of this and have a feature just for you. When you create your book document, follow these steps to add some space to the inside margin to allow for binding.

1. **With your cursor at the beginning of the document, choose Layout⇨Page⇨Binding/Duplex from the menu.**

   You see the Binding/Duplexing Options dialog box, shown in Figure 12-1.

2. **If you plan to bind (or punch) your book the regular way, with the long edges of the pages bound, leave Left selected. If you want to make a flipchart-type book, with the short edges of the pages bound, choose Top.**

   The Left setting means exactly what you probably want — WordPerfect sticks extra space on the left side of odd-numbered (right-hand) pages and on the right side of even-numbered (left-hand) pages. The Top setting means that you get extra space at the top of odd-numbered pages and at the bottom of even-numbered pages.

3. **In the Amount box, enter the amount that you want added to the inside margin.**

   A reasonable amount to add is $^1/_4$ or $^1/_2$ inch (.25 inch or .5 inch).

4. **Click on OK.**

5. **Choose Layout⇨Margins from the menu bar.**

   Now enter the margins, *not* including the extra binding amount, as follows.

6. Set the left and right margins.

If you are binding the book along the long edge of the paper, enter the same width for both the left and right margins — the width of the outside margin. Let's say that you entered $^1/_2$ inch for the binding amount, and you want to leave $^3/_4$ inch on the outsides of the pages and $1^1/_4$ inch on the insides. Enter $^3/_4$ inch for the left and right margins. (Wow! Fourth grade math at work!)

If you are binding the book along the short edge of the paper, the left and right margins aren't affected by the binding width so enter whatever margins you want.

7. Set the top and bottom margins.

If you are binding the book along the long edge of the paper, enter whatever top and bottom margins you want. The top and bottom margins aren't affected by the binding width.

If you are binding the book along the short edge of the paper, enter the same width for both the top and bottom margins. Use the width that you want for the edge of the paper away from the binding.

8. Click on OK.

Figure 12-1:
Leave a little
extra space
on the
inside edge
of your
pages, to
allow for the
space that
the binding
takes.

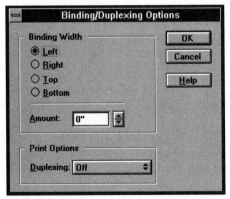

When you look at your document in page or two-page view, the binding width is filled with a gray cross-hatch pattern to remind you that it is there.

The Duplexing setting in the Binding/Duplexing Options dialog box is great if you have a duplex printer, that is, one that prints on both sides of the page. If you have a duplex printer, tell it how you want to bind the book (From Long Edge or From Short Edge). Otherwise, ignore it.

Title Pages and Front Matter

Front matter — it sounds like something discovered by a particle physicist. Yes, there's matter, antimatter, and now — front matter!

However, booksmiths have long used the phrase to refer to all the stuff that you always flip right past at the front of the book. Here are the pages you'll need to make.

The title page

Make a page with the title of book, author, and publisher's name centered tastefully in the middle of the page. (Actually, the publisher info is usually at the bottom of the page). This is page number *i* of the book (that's a roman numeral one), but it doesn't get a page number. However, start page numbering here anyway, so that the page numbers, when they do appear, are correct. (See the section "Funky Page Numbering" at the end of this chapter for details on numbering the pages of the rest of the book.)

Make Header A for the odd-numbered pages and Header B for the even-numbered pages. Be sure that the page numbers appear on the outside corners of the pages. Header A may look like this:

```
Life for Dummies                    Page i
```

while Header B may look like this:

```
Page ii              Life for Dummies
```

Here's how to create these headers:

1. **Choose View⇨Reveal Codes from the menu bar or press Alt+F3.**

   You need to see the secret codes that you are creating to make sure that you get them in the right order.

2. **With your cursor at the tippy-top of the document, choose Layout⇨ Header/Footer from the menu bar.**

3. **Click on Header A and click on the Create button.**

   You return to your document with the Header/Footer Feature Bar displayed.

4. **Type the text of the header, using the Number button on the Feature Bar to provide the page number. Put the page number at the end of the line of text.**

To get WordPerfect to put some text at the beginning of the line and other text at the right end of the same line, type all the text together. Then move your cursor just before the text you want right-aligned and press Alt+F7. Voilà!

5. **Click on the Placement button on the Feature Bar, choose Odd Pages, and click on OK.**

This header will appear only on odd, that is, right-hand, pages.

6. **Click on the Close button on the Feature Bar.**

7. **Repeat these steps for Header B, putting the page number at the beginning of the line and choosing Even Pages for the Placement. Close the Feature Bar.**

8. **Choose Layout⇨Page⇨Numbering, and click on the Options button.**

9. **For the Page setting, choose Lowercase Roman, then click on OK in both dialog boxes.**

Now the page numbers in the headers are small roman numerals instead of arabic ones.

10. **Choose Layout⇨Page⇨Suppress from the menu bar and choose to suppress Header A. Then click on OK.**

Header B won't appear on this page anyway, because this is not an even-numbered page.

11. **Type the title of the book, author(s), and publisher's name; format them nice and big and bold.**

12. **Press Ctrl+Enter to insert a page break after the publisher info.**

Suppress headers on all pages up until the *second* page of the table of contents. (Don't ask why — that's just the way it's done. Look at the front of this book, for example.) And press Ctrl+Enter to insert a page break between each page and the next.

The fine print

Page ii of your book contains copyright information, disclaimers, trademarks, and other small print. Be sure to include the complete name and address of the publisher and the ISBN if you are publishing this for real (if you work for a large company, someone else can probably tell you exactly what information to include on this page). And do include a copyright, like this:

```
Copyright © 1995 by John Quincy Adams. All rights reserved.
```

That's all you have to do to protect your work under copyright laws (if you want to go whole hog, you can fill out an Application for Copyright form and send it with a copy of your book to the Library of Congress.)

Other front stuff

Page iii and following should contain the *About the author* page, if you want one, the dedication, and the acknowledgments. Remember, there are still no page numbers. And don't use *Heading 1* or *Heading 2* styles for the titles or any style that contains codes to include a paragraph in the table of contents. (See the section on styles later in this chapter.)

Styles for Books

We interrupt this exposition about the pages at the front of your book to talk about styles. Why? Because we've gotten up to the table of contents, and before you can make a table of contents, you must decide on the paragraph styles you'll use for the chapter titles and other headings in the book.

What an odd page!

According to ancient book-binding tradition, the table of contents, each chapter, the index, and some other book parts start on odd pages, that is to say, right-hand pages. You can tell WordPerfect to make sure that certain pages appear on odd-numbered pages and to insert a blank page if necessary. Choose Layout⇨Page⇨Force page from the menu bar. Choose Current Page Odd and OK. WordPerfect creates a secret Force Odd formatting code. If the page was originally even numbered, WordPerfect inserts a page break before it to make it into an odd-numbered page.

Some useful styles

Here is a list of some of the paragraph styles you probably need to create:

- ✔ **Part Title:** If your book isn't divided into parts or sections, forget this style. If you make this style, be sure to include table-of-contents codes (described later in this chapter).

- ✔ **Chapter Title:** Actually, this style is for the number and title of the chapter. Include table-of-contents codes.

- ✔ **Major Heading:** This style is for the top-level heading within a chapter. You can use the existing *Heading 1* style for this. Include table-of-contents codes if you want these headings in your table of contents.

- ✔ **Minor Heading:** This style is for the second-level heading within a chapter. You can use the existing *Heading 2* style for this. Include table-of-contents codes if you want these headings in your table of contents. Also if you want further levels of headings, make styles for each level that you want.

- ✔ **Figure Caption:** This is the style for a caption that appears with a figure. Include list-of-figures codes.

- ✔ **Table Caption:** This is the style for a caption that appears with a table. Include list-of-tables codes.

- ✔ **Production Note:** This style is for notes among the authors, editors, and production folks, posing questions, making comments, and giving directions on how text or figures should appear. This text shouldn't appear in the final book — one of the last stages of editing can be to delete all paragraphs that use this style or at least to hide them. You may want to format this style using large characters in a bright color.

- ✔ **Bullet:** This style is for indented paragraphs with bullets.

- ✔ **Sidebar Title:** This style is for the title of a sidebar.

- ✔ **Sidebar Text:** This style is for the text of a sidebar.

- ✔ **Table Column Heads:** This style is for column heads in columnar tables.

- ✔ **Table Text:** This style is for the text in columnar tables.

Define all of these styles in your book document — you'll need them. You can use the names if you like (in fact, some of these names are longer than WordPerfect accepts). You'll probably define a bunch more styles based on the particular subject of your book.

For details on how to create and use styles, see Chapter 10. We covered the basics in Chapter 12 in *WordPerfect For Windows For Dummies*.

Styles for the table of contents

You must include table-of-contents codes in the styles that will be used for headings that should appear in the table of contents. You may want the *Part Title*, *Chapter Title*, *Major Heading*, and *Minor Heading* to be listed in the table of contents. Decide which styles you want to appear there and in which order — WordPerfect can produce tables of contents with up to five levels of headings, from level-1 headings (for the part or chapter titles) to level-5 headings (for the minor sub-sub-headings).

Don't worry if you don't know exactly how many levels of headings you want in the table of contents. Err on the side of too many, because it is easy to tell WordPerfect to include fewer levels.

Once you have made the styles, here are steps for making the headings appear automagically in the table of contents:

1. **Choose Layout⇨Styles (or Alt+F8) from the menu bar.**

   You see the Style List.

2. **Choose a style that you want to appear in the table of contents, like *Chapter Title*, and click on the Edit button.**

   You see the Styles Editor, with the information about the style you chose.

3. **Choose Tools⇨Table of Contents from the Styles Editor menu bar.**

   The Table of Contents Feature Bar appears in its own little window at the bottom of the screen.

4. **Click on the Mark 1, Mark 2, Mark 3, Mark 4, or Mark 5 buttons, according to the level of headings using this style that you want to appear in the table of contents.**

   For example, if your book isn't divided into parts, the chapter title-style headings should be the level-1 headings in your table of contents, so use the Mark 1 button when editing the *Chapter Title* style.

   When you click on a Mark button, a secret code should appear in the Contents box in the Styles Editor. We've had a little trouble getting it to appear sometimes — we click the Mark button like crazy but no codes appear. Our solution is to click on the title bar of the Table of Contents Feature Bar's little window so that the window is selected. *Then* we click on the Mark button.

5. **Click on OK to finish editing the style.**

   You return to the Style List dialog box.

6. **Repeat Steps 2 through 5 for each style that will be used for headings that you want to appear in the table of contents.**

   Use the Mark <u>1</u> button for the first style, the Mark <u>2</u> button for the second style, and so on. Generally, don't mark two different styles for the same table of contents level.

7. **Click on the <u>C</u>lose button on the Style List dialog box.**

   Now your headings are ready to appear in the table of contents.

Tables of Contents

Aha! It's finally time for the table of contents (or *TOC* for short). Due to the Wonders of Modern Technology and because of all the work you just did to include table-of-contents codes in your styles, WordPerfect can generate the table of contents for you.

Making the TOC

Here's how to set up the table-of-contents code:

1. **Make sure that you use styles for the chapter headings in your book and that the chapter heading style contains markings for the table of contents.**

   That is, follow the directions in the preceding section. And use the style that you created when you write the chapters of the book, which we'll get to in a later section of this chapter,

2. **On the table of contents page, type a title for the page (like, maybe, *Table of Contents*, f'rinstance). Then press Enter a time or two, to leave some space below the title.**

   Format the title as you wish, but *don't* use a chapter title style for it! Otherwise, the *Table of Contents* heading will show up in your table of contents.

3. **Below the page title, choose <u>T</u>ools➪Table of <u>C</u>ontents from the menu bar.**

   This command produces the useful Table of Contents Feature Bar (Figure 12-2), this time right under the Power Bar and Button Bar.

Figure 12-2:
This Feature
Bar helps
you set up a
table of
contents.

4. **At the location where you want the table of contents to start, click on
the Define button on the Table of Contents Feature Bar.**

You see the Define Table of Contents dialog box, shown in Figure 12-3.

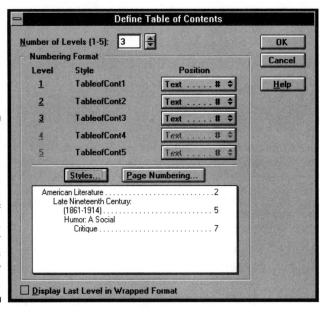

Figure 12-3:
You can
choose up
to five levels
of entries in
your table of
contents,
but two or
three is
usually
enough.

5. **Set the Number of Levels to the number of levels of headings you want to include in the table of contents.**

   If you want only first-level headings (which are usually chapter titles, or perhaps part or section titles if your book is divided into parts like this book), choose 1. If you want to include chapter numbers, major headings, and minor headings, choose 3. (See the section "Styles for the table of contents" earlier in this chapter for how to tell WordPerfect which headings are level 1, level 2, etc.)

6. **For each level you want to include, determine if you want page numbers to appear, and if so, if they should have dot leaders.**

   Unless you change it, each level will appear with the text of the heading, a bunch of dots, and a right-aligned page number. To change this setting for a heading level, click on its *Text.....#* button and choose a different setting.

7. **Click the OK button.**

   WordPerfect sticks the message `<< Table of Contents will generate here >>` into your book. This means that the codes are now in place for a table of contents, but you need to "generate" it.

8. **Click on the Generate button on the Table of Contents Feature Bar, and choose OK on its dialog box.**

   Then WordPerfect sifts through your document, looking for text that is marked with the table-of-contents mark codes that you inserted in your headings styles earlier in this chapter. When it finds such a heading, it notes the page it is on, and copies it to the table of contents, as shown in Figure 12-4. This table of contents replaces the `<< Table of Contents will generate here >>` message.

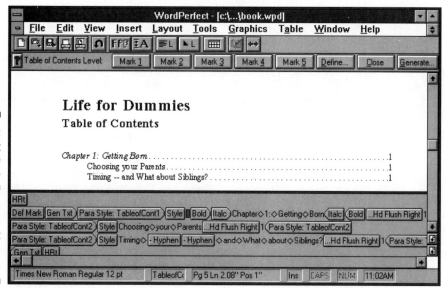

Figure 12-4:
WordPerfect automagically makes your table of contents and sticks in the right page numbers.

9. Click on the Close button to make the TOC Feature Bar go away.

Make sure that the table of contents starts on an odd-numbered (right-hand) page. That's how it's done — add a blank page if necessary by pressing Ctrl+Enter. And suppress the page number for the first page of the TOC. After that, allow those lovely small roman numeral page numbers to show. You should be up to at least page vi.

When you click on the Generate button and click on OK, WordPerfect generates not only the table of contents but also any indexes, tables of authorities, cross-references, and lists that you have defined. These fancy-sounding features are described later in this chapter.

As you edit the text in the book, the pagination will change (dozens, if not hundreds, of times, in our experience). You may also add or delete headings, rearrange chapters, or slice out text that you decide is boring. Whenever you want to update the table of contents, just choose Tools⇨Generate from the menu bar or press Ctrl+F9. Then choose OK in the Generate dialog box.

Changing the TOC definition

What if you decide later that you want a different number of levels in your table of contents, or that you don't want dot leaders? It would be nice if you could edit the settings in the Define Table of Contents dialog box.

Yes, it *would* be nice to edit the settings in the Define Table of Contents dialog box, but you can't do it. There's no way to edit the table of contents definition (if you do, and click on OK, you get a *second* table of contents!). We expected that double-clicking on the Def Mark code in the Reveal Codes window would allow us to edit the definition, but no. (WordPerfect has noted this deficiency as an enhancement request, so who knows? They'll make this possible soon, we're sure.)

So, if you want to change the settings on your table of contents, here's what to do — in a nutshell, blow it away and start over.

1. If you don't already see the Reveal Codes window, choose View⇨Reveal Codes (or press Alt+F3) to display it.

2. Find the Def Mark code in the Reveal Codes window.

This is the code that defines the table of contents. To make sure that this is the right code (and not one that defines something else, like an index), move the cursor directly before it. The code should expand to say something like Def Mark: TOC, 3: Dot Ldr #.

3. Press Del to delete the code.

4. **If you don't already see the Table of Contents Feature Bar, choose Tools⇨Table of Contents from the menu bar to display this Feature Bar.**

5. **Click on the Define button, enter the number of levels you want, choose any other options you want, and click OK.**

   This makes a brand new `Def Mark` code for your table of contents.

6. **Click on the Generate button and choose OK in its dialog box.**

   WordPerfect deletes the old generated table of contents and makes a new one.

Formatting the TOC

You can control the style of the lines in the table of contents. For example, you may want the chapter titles to appear large and bold, with space above them, while headings within chapters appear in normal-sized print. To control this stuff, you can set the styles that WordPerfect uses for them.

WordPerfect uses styles named *TableofCont1, TableofCont2, TableofCont3, TableofCont4,* and *TableofCont5.* You can edit these styles, changing the codes so that the styles look the way you want. Interestingly, if you just choose Layout⇨Styles from the menu bar, these styles don't usually appear on the list of styles. Here's how to edit these styles.

1. **Choose Layout⇨Styles or press Alt+F8 to see the Style List.**

2. **Click on Options, then on Setup.**

   You see the Style Setup dialog box shown in Figure 12-5.

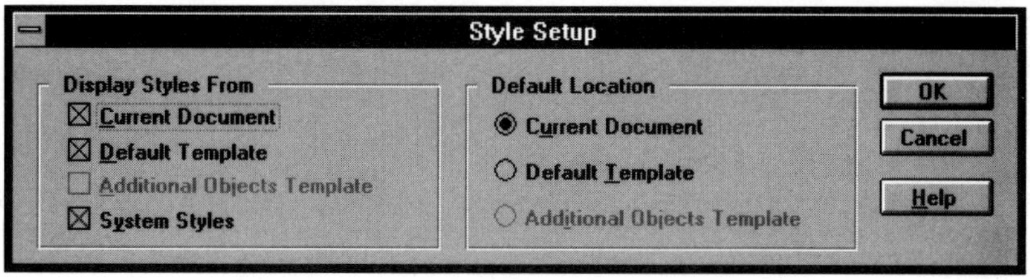

Figure 12-5: What styles should WordPerfect include on the style list?

Style Setup

Display Styles From
☒ Current Document
☒ Default Template
☐ Additional Objects Template
☒ System Styles

Default Location
◉ Current Document
○ Default Template
○ Additional Objects Template

OK   Cancel   Help

3. **Click on the System Styles setting so that an X appears in its box.**

   This setting tells WordPerfect to show you all of its automatically created styles, including those for tables of contents and indexes.

4. **Click on OK.**

   Dozens of mysterious and exciting styles appear in your style list.

5. **Edit the *TableofCont1*, *TableofCont2*, *TableofCon3*, *TableofCont4*, and *TableofCont5* styles just as if they were normal styles.**

   For details about editing styles, see Chapter 10.

When you tell WordPerfect to include system styles on the style list, it shows you *all* the system styles, not just the ones for the table of contents. You can see the styles WordPerfect uses for indexes, figure numbers, the works.

Lists of Figures and Tables

If you are writing a Scholarly Tome or a Business Report, it probably has lots of figures, tables, and other authoritative-looking stuff in it. If you are writing the Great American Novel, you are probably planning to keep the figures and tables to a minimum — at least, you should if your novel's truly Great — so you can just skip this section.

Making a list

WordPerfect can number your figures, text boxes, and tables for you (see Chapter 1). Be sure to use the Caption button on the Graphics Box Feature Bar to enter the captions for your figures — that way, it's easy to make a list of your figure captions with their page numbers.

Here's how to make a list of the figures in your book:

1. **After the table of contents, insert a page on which to make the list of figures.**

   That is, press Ctrl+Enter for a page break at the bottom of the table of contents (after the end of the generated text).

2. **Type a title for the page, like *List of Figures*.**

   Format the title the same way that you formatted the title of the table of contents. Press Enter a time or two after the title to leave some space below it.

3. Choose Tools⇨List from the menu bar.

Surprise! Another Feature Bar — the List Feature Bar! (See Figure 12-6.)

Figure 12-6:
Buttons to
help you
create lists.

Figure 12-6:
Buttons to
help you
create lists.

4. With your cursor where you want the list of figures to begin, click on the Define button on the Feature Bar.

You see the Define List dialog box, shown in Figure 12-7.

5. Click on the Create button.

You see the Create List dialog box, shown in Figure 12-8.

6. In the List box, type a name for this list, like Figures.

WordPerfect lets you define lots of different lists, in case you have lists of figures, tables, equations, references, jokes, recipes, or what-have-you. You give each a name.

7. Change how the page numbers will appear by clicking on the Text....# button.

Or just do nothing, which gives you page numbers with dot leaders — a perennial favorite.

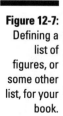

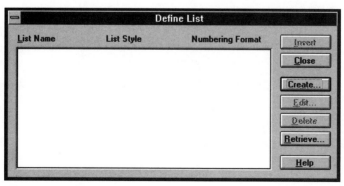

Figure 12-7:
Defining a
list of
figures, or
some other
list, for your
book.

```
┌─────────────────────────────────────────────────────┐
│ ─ │                 Create List                    │▪│
├─────────────────────────────────────────────────────┤
│ List: │                                    │  ┌─────┐│
│                                               │ OK  ││
│ ┌─ Numbering Format ──────────────────────┐  └─────┘│
│ │ Position: │Text . . . . #│ ▲▼│ │Page Numbering...│ ┌──────┐│
│ │                                           │Cancel││
│ │ ┌───────────────────────────────────┐   └──────┘│
│ │ │     Illustrations                  │   ┌──────┐│
│ │ │ Mark Twain Playing Pool........27  │   │ Help ││
│ │ │ Literary Friends...............63  │   └──────┘│
│ │ │ The Young Sam Clemens..........88  │           │
│ │ └───────────────────────────────────┘           │
│ └──────────────────────────────────────────┘       │
│                                                     │
│ ┌─ Current Style ─────────────────────────┐        │
│ │ List                        │Change...│  │        │
│ └──────────────────────────────────────────┘       │
│                                                     │
│ Auto Reference Box Captions: │[None]        │▼│     │
└─────────────────────────────────────────────────────┘
```

Figure 12-8:
You're
making a list
and
checking it
twice!

8. Click on the downward-pointing arrow to the right of the Auto Reference Box Captions box, and choose .Figure Box from the list that WordPerfect displays.

".Figure Box" (complete with the period) is the name of the style that WordPerfect uses for text that you type as the caption of a graphics box that contains a figure.

9. Click on OK.

You return to the Define List dialog box, and the Figures list now appears (highlighted, even) in the list of lists. (Wow — this sounds confusing!)

10. Click on the Insert button.

WordPerfect dismisses the dialog box and sticks a `Def Mark` code for the list into your document where the cursor is. It also inserts the generated text `<< List will generate here >>`.

11. Click on the Generate button and choose OK on its dialog box.

WordPerfect deletes the `<< List will generate here >>` message and creates the list of figures, as shown in Figure 12-9.

12. Click on Close to make the Feature Bar go away.

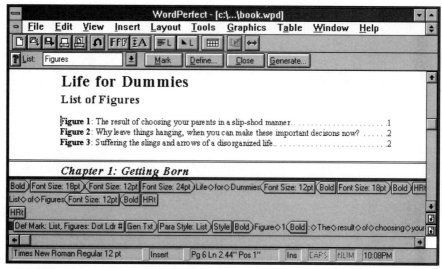

Figure 12-9:
You've got a
little list!

If you move your cursor just before the Def Mark code in the Reveal Codes window, you see something like this: Def Mark: List, Figures: Dot Ldr #. This tells you that this is the definition of a list named *Figures*, and that page numbers appear with dot leaders.

To tell WordPerfect to update the list of figures you just made, choose Tools⇨Generate from the menu bar or press Ctrl+F9. Then choose OK on the Generate dialog box.

Compulsive list-making

Do you know people who make lists wherever they go? Well, you and WordPerfect can do the same thing — you can tell WordPerfect to make a list of *anything* in your document, along with the page numbers the anything is on.

List of tables and tables of lists

You can make a list of the tables in your book the same way that you list your figures. In the Create List dialog box, name your List type something like **Tables**. Choose .Table Box for the Auto Refer- ence Box Captions setting. Then insert a code and generate the list the same way as for a list of figures.

For example, if you are writing a travelogue about your trip around Brazil, with recipes for local dishes interspersed in the text, you may want a list of recipes to appear right after the table of contents. Here's how.

1. **After the table of contents, insert a page on which to make the list of recipes.**

   That is, press Ctrl+Enter for a page break at the bottom of the table of contents (after the end of the generated text).

2. **Type a title for the page, like *List of Figures*.**

   Format the title the same way that you formatted the title of the table of contents. Press Enter a time or two after the title, to leave some space below it.

3. **Choose Tools⇨List from the menu bar.**

   This displays the List Feature Bar.

4. **Click on the Define button.**

   You see the Define List dialog box, shown in Figure 12-7.

5. **Click on the Create button.**

   You see the Create List dialog box, shown in Figure 12-8.

6. **In the List box, type a name for this list, like** Recipes.

   You can choose any name — choose one that makes sense to you.

7. **Change how the page numbers will appear by clicking on the Text....# button.**

   Or just do nothing, which gives you page numbers with dot leaders — a perennial favorite.

8. **Click on OK to dismiss the dialog box.**

   Note that you haven't touched the Auto Reference Box Captions box. This is because you aren't making a list of something that WordPerfect has a special style for, like the various types of graphics boxes.

   You return to the Define List dialog box, and *Recipes* now appears in the list of lists.

9. **Click on the Insert button.**

   WordPerfect dismisses the dialog box and sticks a `Def Mark` code for the list into your document where the cursor is. It also inserts the generated text `<< List will generate here >>`.

10. **In the List box on the List Feature Bar, select the name of the list you just made.**

    That is, click on the downward-pointing arrow to the right of the List box on the Feature Bar and choose the list name from the menu that appears. That's how you tell WordPerfect which list you want to work with.

11. **For each recipe in your book, select the title and click the Mark button.**

    This marks the title to appear on the list. (In the Reveal Codes window, if it is open, you see a `Mrk Text List` code.)

    Better yet, use a style for all the recipe titles and insert the list-marking codes into the style. (In the Styles Editor, choose Tools⇨List to display the List Feature Bar, choose the name of the list from the List box, and click on Mark.)

12. **Click on the Generate button and choose OK in its dialog box.**

    WordPerfect deletes the `<< List will generate here >>` message and makes the list of recipes.

13. **Click on Close to make the Feature Bar go away.**

To change the style of a list, you need to edit the *List* style. To make sure that the style appears in your Style List, follow the instructions in the section "Formatting the TOC" earlier in this chapter. Then edit the *List* style just like any other style.

The End of the Beginning

Well, you've created the title page, dedication, acknowledgments, table of contents, and table of just about everything else. That just about wraps up the front matter of your book. To celebrate, insert a page break (by pressing Ctrl+Enter) after the last page of the front matter.

From here on out, you've got chapters, possibly appendixes, and an index.

If your book has an introduction, it doesn't count as part of the front matter. Instead, it gets a heading and normal arabic page numbers like a regular chapter.

To start numbering the pages using arabic page numbers (like 1,2,3,...) instead of the small roman numerals you used for the front matter, follow these steps.

1. **Move your cursor to the top of the first page on which you want arabic numbers.**

   That's probably the first page of the Introduction or Chapter 1.

2. **Choose** **L**ayout⇨**P**age⇨**N**umbering **from the menu bar.**

   You see the Page Numbering dialog box.

3. **Click on the** **O**ptions **button to see the Page Numbering Options dialog box.**

4. **For the** **P**age **setting, click on the current setting (which is probably** **L**owercase Roman**) and change it to** **N**umbers**.**

5. **Click on OK.**

   You are back in the Page Numbering dialog box.

6. **Click on the** **V**alue **button.**

   You see the Numbering Value dialog box.

7. **In the Page Settings part of the dialog box, change the New** **P**age **Number to 1.**

8. **Click on OK.**

   Once again, you are back in the Page Numbering dialog box.

9. **Click on the** **C**lose **button.**

   All dialog boxes disappear, and the page number of the current page now appears as *1*.

Funky Page Numbering

In lots of books and reports, especially those about technical stuff, the pages are numbered by chapter. That is, the pages in Chapter 1 are numbered *1-1, 1-2, 1-3,* and so on. Chapter 2 starts over again with *2-1, 2-2, 2-3,* and on. Naturally, WordPerfect stands ready to handle this kind of page numbering.

Your pages are numbered...

WordPerfect can number all your pages using the Layout⇨Page⇨Numbering command and the Number button on the Headers/Footers Feature Bar. Nifty! Here's how to put chapter-based page numbers in your headers or footers:

1. **At the top of the first page of Chapter 1, choose Layout⇨Header/Footer and create or edit the header or footer in which you want the page number to appear.**

2. **Type** Page **and a space.**

3. **Choose Number from the Feature Bar and choose Chapter Number from the pop-up menu.**

    You get a secret chapter number code that appears as a 1 in the text.

4. **Type a dash or a period or whatever you want to appear between the chapter number and page number.**

5. **Choose Number from the Feature Bar again and choose Page Number from the pop-up menu.**

    This creates a secret page number code that also appears as a 1. Now your page number looks like *Page 1-1.*

6. **Click on Close in the Feature Bar when you are done editing your header or footer.**

7. **If you are using two headers or footers (A and B) for even and odd pages, repeat Steps 1 through 6 for the other header or footer.**

8. **Page forward through your document until you get to the top of Chapter 2.**

    Assuming that you are in page view, so you can see your headers and footers, you see the page numbers increasing like *1-2, 1-3,* and so on.

9. **At the top of the first page of Chapter 2, choose Layout⇨Page⇨Numbering from the menu bar and choose the Value button.**

    You see the Numbering Value dialog box shown in Figure 12-10.

10. **In the Page Settings section of the dialog box, set the New Page Number back to 1.**

11. **In the Chapter Settings section, set the New Chapter Number.**

    If you are at the beginning of Chapter 2, set this number to 2.

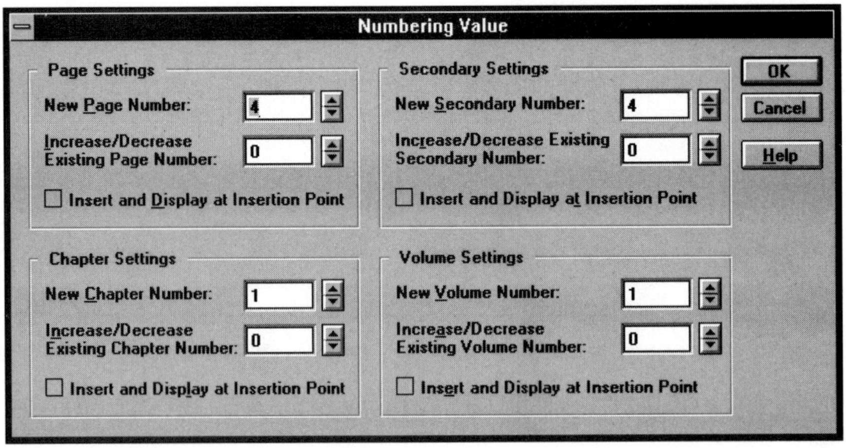

Figure 12-10:
Resetting the chapter and page numbers at the beginning of a new chapter.

Numbering Value		
Page Settings	**Secondary Settings**	OK
New Page Number: 4 ⬍	New Secondary Number: 4 ⬍	Cancel
Increase/Decrease Existing Page Number: 0 ⬍	Increase/Decrease Existing Secondary Number: 0 ⬍	Help
☐ Insert and Display at Insertion Point	☐ Insert and Display at Insertion Point	
Chapter Settings	**Volume Settings**	
New Chapter Number: 1 ⬍	New Volume Number: 1 ⬍	
Increase/Decrease Existing Chapter Number: 0 ⬍	Increase/Decrease Existing Volume Number: 0 ⬍	
☐ Insert and Display at Insertion Point	☐ Insert and Display at Insertion Point	

12. **Choose OK and OK again to exit from all those dialog boxes.**

    The page number for this chapter changes to *Page 2-1* (for Chapter 2, anyway).

13. **Repeat Steps 9 through 12 at the top of the first page of each chapter in your book.**

Now WordPerfect knows the page numbers for all the pages in your book.

If you have front matter (a table of contents, and so on) before the beginning of Chapter 1, follow Steps 9 through 12 for Chapter 1, too. Set the chapter and page numbers both to 1.

Your table of contents, too

When you define the table of contents, you must tell it to use chapter-based page numbers. Otherwise, you see only the page number within the chapter (for example, *1*) instead of the whole page number, that is, *3-1*). Here's how to use chapter-based page numbers in your table of contents.

1. **Follow the directions in the section "Making the TOC" up through Step 6.**

    You are in the Define Table of Contents dialog box.

2. **Choose Page Numbering.**

    You see the Page Number Format dialog box shown in Figure 12-11.

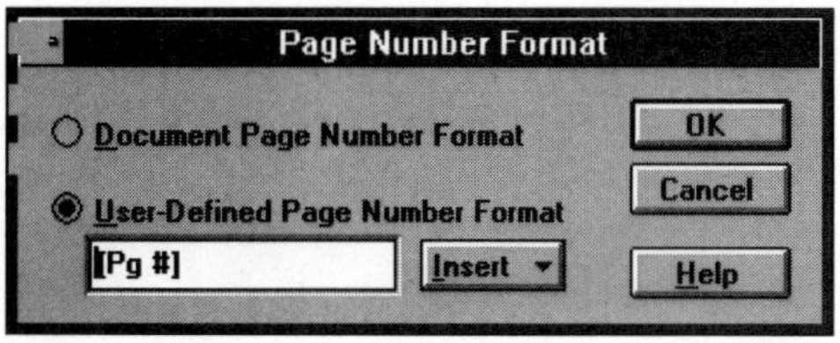

Figure 12-11:
Telling
WordPerfect
what kind of
page
numbers to
use in the
table of
contents.

Page Number Format	
○ Document Page Number Format	OK
● User-Defined Page Number Format	Cancel
[Pg #] Insert ▾	Help

3. **Choose User-Defined Page Number Format.**

   The text box below this setting contains the code [Pg #].

4. **Place your cursor just before the [Pg #] code in the text box.**

5. **Choose Insert, then choose Chapter Number from the little menu.**

   A [Chp #] code appears.

6. **Type a dash to appear between the chapter and page numbers.**

   Now the text box should say:

```
[Chp #]-[Pg #]
```

7. **Click on OK.**

   You return to the Define Table of Contents dialog box.

8. **Follow the rest of the steps in the "Making the TOC" section.**

   When you generate the table of contents, the page numbers include the chapter number. For example, the first page of Chapter 3 appears as *3-1*.

Your page numbers are two-level (that is, chapter number and page number), but your table of contents can have as any many as five levels. The number of levels in the table of contents tells WordPerfect how many levels of headings you want shown in the table of contents. Both the page numbers and the table of contents have *levels*, but their levels don't have much to do with each other.

Chapter 13

Writing the Great American Novel (or the Long American Business Report)

*T*he thing about a book or a major report is that it's, well, *big*. We're talking about thousands and thousands of words, here (Believe us, we know!) If you try to put the entire text of a book into one WordPerfect document, you'll probably run into trouble. Here are some advantages to splitting up something as large as a book into a bunch of smaller documents:

  ✔ Smaller documents are faster to open and save.

  ✔ If different people are working on different chapters, you can pass around the chapters separately.

  ✔ If WordPerfect, Windows, DOS, or the gods eat a document, you have less to lose. It's the old eggs-in-one-basket theory.

The way to split a large document into smaller ones is to use one *master document* and a bunch of *subdocuments*. We talked a little bit about master and subdocuments in Chapter 19 of *WordPerfect for Windows for Dummies*, but we'll go into more detail here.

The Game Plan for Creating Master Documents

Here's the general theory: A *master document* is a document that contains codes that link it to other documents, which are called *subdocuments*. Once you create these subdocument codes in the maser document, you can tell WordPerfect to *expand* the master document, which means that it reads in the contents of all the subdocuments. Now the master document is huge, containing the whole book. Before you save the master document, you can tell WordPerfect to *condense* it, and WordPerfect puts the contents of each subdocument back into the proper file.

For example, check out Figure 13-1. Imagine that you have a document named BOOK.WPD (we do). You store each chapter of the book in a separate file, with names like CHAP1.WPD. Instead of copying the contents of each chapter file into the main book file, you create a link to the chapter file in the main book file. That is, BOOK.WPD contains subdocument codes that refer to INTRO.WPD, CHAP1.WPD, and CHAP2.WPD. This allows you to continue storing each chapter separately, so that different people can work on them, but you can also combine the chapters.

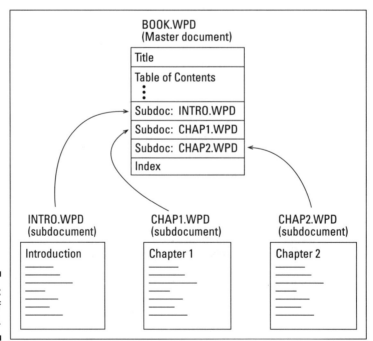

Figure 13-1: Anatomy of a book.

Combining the chapters into one big master document allows WordPerfect to number the pages right through and to create a table of contents, cross-references between chapters, and an index.

It's a good idea to make a template to use for all the chapters in your book so that they use the same formatting and styles. Then create the subdocuments, that is, the chapters. Finally, create the subdocument codes in the master document. You've already made the master document — it's the document you've been working on since the beginning of the chapter, with the title page, table of contents, and so on.

Creating a subdocument template

Here is how to make a template to use for all the subdocuments (chapters) in your book.

1. **Open the document in which you've already set up the styles you want to use in the book.**

   If you've been following the steps since the beginning of Chapter 12, you've already made a document with the styles, title page, table of contents, and so forth. If not, start with a new document and make the styles as described in the section "Styles for Books" in Chapter 12.

2. **Save it as a template in your templates directory.**

   That is, choose File⇨Save As from the menu bar, type in a filename like **CHAPTER.WPT** (be sure to use .WPT as the file extension, so WordPerfect knows that you want to use it as a template), and choose your templates directory (the Template subdirectory of your WordPerfect program directory).

3. **Delete all the text, figures, codes, you name it.**

   Since this is a template, you don't need all the text you've entered for the beginning of the book.

4. **Enter any text or formatting that you will want in every chapter.**

   For example, you can create a code that suppresses the header on the first page of the chapter, and you can enter a line saying **Chapter** that uses your chapter title style.

5. **Save it again (still as a template) and close it.**

Now the template is ready for use. It's chapter time!

Creating your subdocuments

As you write each chapter of the book, use the chapter template that you just made. (That is, choose File⇨Template from the menu bar or press Ctrl+T to create each chapter.) Be sure to use the styles you set up and apply them consistently. Save each chapter as a separate file.

Linking it all together

Now your chapters are ready to link to your master book document. Here's how to link them all together.

1. **Open your master book document.**

   That's the document with the title page, table of contents, and the rest of the front matter, described in Chapter 12. If you haven't made a master document yet, make a new blank document. (You may want to back up and make a template to use for the master document and all the individual chapters.)

2. **Move to the end of the front matter.**

   You should already have inserted a page break and changed the page numbering from small roman numerals to regular arabic numbers (see the section "The End of the Beginning" in Chapter 12).

Divide and conquer

What if you have already got a book in one huge file? It's easy to split it up and use the master document/subdocument system we're describing.

1. Make a chapter template as described in "Creating a subdocument template."

2. Open the master file that contains the entire contents of the book.

3. For each chapter, choose File⇨Template to make a new, blank document using the chap-

ter template. Then copy a chapter from the master file to the new chapter file (using the cut-and-paste commands Edit⇨Copy, or Ctrl+C, and Edit⇨Paste, or Ctrl+V). Save each chapter as a separate document.

4. When you are sure that the contents of all the chapters are safely in the various new chapter files, delete the contents from the master file. (It's not a bad idea to save a copy of the original master file somewhere, just in case.)

---

3. **To make a code for a subdocument you want to include, choose File⇨Master Document⇨Subdocument from the menu bar.**

   You see the Include subdocument dialog box. (We think that "subdocument" should be capitalized in the title of this dialog box, don't you?)

4. **Choose the filename of the chapter and choose Include.**

   WordPerfect creates a secret Subdoc code where your cursor is. Also, if you are in page view, a cute little icon appears in the left margin of your document — an arrow pointing to a piece of paper (see Figure 13-2). This means, "A subdocument will appear here when this document is expanded."

   If you are in draft view, you see a gray comment, saying Subdoc and the full pathname of the file that is included (see Figure 13-3).

5. **With your cursor right after the Subdoc code, press Ctrl+Enter to begin a new page for the next chapter.**

6. **Repeat Steps 3 and 4 for each chapter.**

   If your book or report has sections, appendixes, introductions, prefaces, or whatever, you can make a subdocument for each of these, too.

The sign of a subdocument

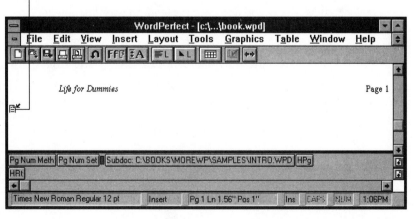

Figure 13-2: A tiny icon tells you that a subdocument has been included here.

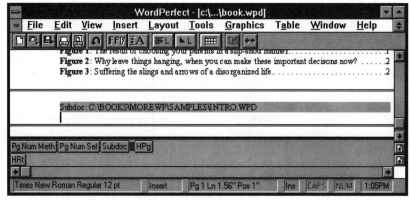

Figure 13-3:
The draft
view of a
subdocument
code.

Expanding and condensing

These Subdoc codes are all very interesting, but where's the text? When will your chapters appear in the master document? Ah — to bring the contents of the subdocuments into your master document, you must *expand* the master document. This expansion brings in all or some of the subdocuments — you can decide. When you want to put the contents back into the subdocuments, you *condense* the master document.

Here's how we expand and condense our master documents.

1. **Open the master document.**

2. **Choose File⇨Master Document⇨Expand Master from the menu bar.**

   You see the Expand Master Document dialog box (shown in Figure 13-4), which lists all the subdocuments that are linked to the master document. Initially, all the subdocuments are selected. If you want to skip any of them, click on the little box with the X in it to make the X go away.

Figure 13-4:
Which sub-
documents
do you wish,
oh master?

Expand Master Document

Subdocuments:
⊠c:\books\morewp\samples\intro.wpd
⊠c:\books\morewp\samples\chapter1.wpd
⊠c:\books\morewp\samples\chapter2.wpd

OK
Cancel
Mark ▼
Help

3. Click on OK.

WordPerfect displays a message that tells you what page it's on as it expands the subdocument codes. Then WordPerfect returns you to your master document, complete with the contents of all the subdocuments you selected.

In page view, WordPerfect inserts those cute little icons in the left margin of the master document at the beginning and end of each subdocument (as in Figure 13-5). In draft mode, you see gray comments at the beginning and end of the subdocument (shown in Figure 13-6). Don't worry — none of these icons or comments will appear when you print the book.

4. Edit the book as necessary.

You can edit the text from the subdocuments — when you condense the master document later, WordPerfect will store your changes back into the chapter files. You can also generate the table of contents, lists, and index.

5. To condense the master document, choose File⇨Master Document⇨Condense Master.

You see the Condense/Save Subdocuments dialog box shown in Figure 13-7. Each subdocument is listed twice — once with the notation `condense` and once with `save`. You can choose which subdocuments to condense out of the master document and which to save back into the subdocument files.

We almost always both condense and save all the subdocuments. It's less confusing that way.

┌─ Subdocument starts here

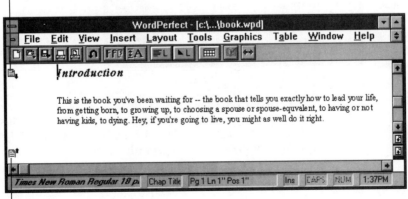

Figure 13-5:
The beginning and ending of a subdocument in page view.

└─ Subdocument ends here

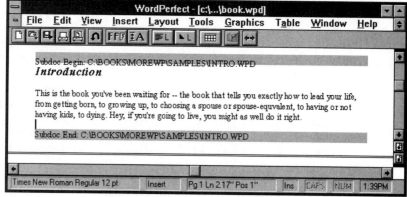

Figure 13-6:
The
beginning
and ending
of a
subdocument
in draft
view.

6. **Click on OK.**

   WordPerfect puts the contents of the various subdocuments back into
   their respective files, leaving the subdocument codes in the master
   document so you can call them back.

7. **Save the master document.**

   It can't hurt.

Figure 13-7:
Decisions,
decisions —
which sub-
documents
do you want
to condense
or save?

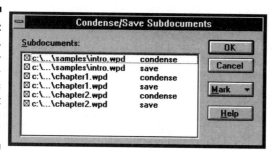

While you are working on a master document, don't open any of its
subdocuments. Either you or WordPerfect (or both) can get confused about
where you have made changes and what's the latest version. Early versions of
WordPerfect for Windows can even get rather upset.

Tips for Editing the Master Document

Here are a few notes on editing and saving master documents and their subdocuments.

- ✔ When you want to save a master document that is expanded, WordPerfect asks if you want to condense it first. If you choose not to condense it, WordPerfect saves all of your changes into the master document, including the contents of the subdocuments. However, WordPerfect does *not* save any changes you made to the subdocuments back into the subdocument files.

- ✔ When you want to edit a chapter, you have to decide whether to edit the subdocument (chapter) file or the master file. If the master file is condensed, or was condensed when you last closed it, then the latest version of the chapter is currently in the chapter file. If the master file is expanded, or was expanded when you last closed it, then the latest version of the chapter is currently in the master file.

  To avoid undue confusion (unless it's already too late), we suggest that you *always* do your editing and saving the same way. We *always* condense our master document before saving it.

- ✔ If you no longer want to include a subdocument in a master document, just delete its Subdoc code. In the Reveal Codes window, move your cursor just before the Subdoc code and make sure that the filename is the one you no longer want to include. Then press the Delete key or drag the code out of the Reveal Codes window (it dies when it leaves).

- ✔ You don't have to expand the master document in order to generate its table of contents, index, and other generated stuff. If you choose Generate from a Feature Bar, WordPerfect automatically expands the master document, generates the table of contents and other generated stuff, and then condenses it again.

- ✔ If you have differently formatted styles in your master document and in your subdocuments, those in the master document win. If a style is defined in two subdocuments, the one in the first subdocument wins. When you condense and save the subdocuments, WordPerfect saves the styles from the master document in the subdocument files. This actually works out rather nicely, since it ensures that the formatting of your whole book is consistent.

Numbering Stuff

Books contain lots of numbers — page numbers, chapter numbers, figure numbers, table numbers, footnote numbers, you name it. WordPerfect can do lots of this numbering for you, so you don't have to worry about having two Figure 13's and no Table 3. To number things, you use a *counter*. (To number kitchens, do you use a kitchen counter?)

WordPerfect has two kinds of counters:

- ✔ **System counters:** WordPerfect automatically numbers the various types of graphics boxes — figures, Text boxes, equations in boxes, user-defined boxes, and tables in boxes. System counters have names that begin with a period (for some odd reason): *.Figure Box, .Table Box, .Text Box, .Equation Box,* and *.User Box.*

- ✔ **Manual counters:** These are counters that you create, using the Insert⇨Other⇨Counter command. You tell WordPerfect where to display these counters, as well as exactly when to increase them.

Just to confuse matters, there are lots of ways that counters (either system or manual) can count:

- ✔ **Regular numbers:** They can count *1, 2, 3,* and so on.

- ✔ **Roman numerals:** They can count *I, II, III,* and so on; or *i, ii, iii,* and so on.

- ✔ **Letters:** They can count *A, B, C,* and so on; or *a, b, c,* and so on.

- ✔ **Multilevels:** They can count with more than one counter, as in an outline. For example, a two-level counter could count *1.1, 1.2, 1.3, 2.1, 2.2,* and so on. When you create a multilevel counter, you can tell WordPerfect how each level of the counter should count, to make counters like this: *I.A.1.a, I.a.1.b, I.a.2.a,* and so on.

Wow! Talk about options! But these options are actually useful — look at the figure numbers in this book, for example, which are two-level (for example, *Figure 13-8*).

Don't use counters for page numbering! We tried it and it didn't work, especially if you want a table of contents and an index. The method described in Chapter 12, the "Funky Page Numbering" section, works great.

Using system counters

It's easy to use system counters — just create graphics boxes and give them captions. (See Chapter 1 for information on how to do so.) When you create a caption for a graphics box, you choose Caption on the Graphics Box Feature Bar. To edit the actual text of the caption, you click on Edit to enter the Caption Editor. At the beginning of the caption, WordPerfect has already inserted a code that provides the number for the box. For example, if you create a Figure box and enter a caption for it, WordPerfect enters a code that says:

```
Open Style: Figure Num; [Bold] Figure  [Box Num Disp] [Bold]
```

In English, this means that using the style Figure Num, it displays (in boldface) the word *Figure*, a space, and the box number.

Don't worry; you don't need to understand why this code looks the way it does. The point is that WordPerfect makes it automagically, and that it works.

Notice that WordPerfect keeps five *separate* counters for the five types of graphics boxes. Figures are numbered separately from Text boxes, which are separated from tables. This is usually the way you want it.

Changing how system counters count

What if you don't want your figures numbered *1,2,3*, but rather *A, B, C,* and so on? You can simply tell WordPerfect to use a different numbering system, like this:

1. **With your cursor at the very beginning of the document (the master document for the book, that is), choose Insert⇨Other⇨Counter from the menu bar.**

   You see the Counter Numbering dialog box, shown in Figure 13-8. The dialog box lists all the counters, both system counters and manual counters, and lets you edit them.

   Actually, we're not sure if it matters where your cursor is when you give this command, since this little operation doesn't seem to create a secret code, but better safe than sorry.

2. **Choose the counter you want to change from the Counter list and then click on the Value button.**

   For example, to change the way figures are numbered, choose *.Figure Box* and then click on the Value button. You see the Set Value/Number Method dialog box, shown in Figure 13-9.

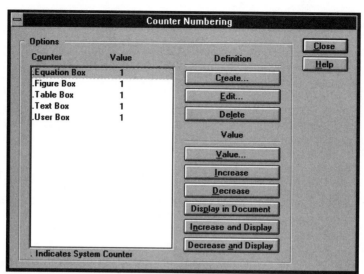

Figure 13-8:
Which
counter do
you want to
fool with?

Figure 13-9:
How would
you like your
system
counter
numbered?

3. **Click on the Single Level Method button, which probably says *Numbers*. Change this setting to the numbering method you want.**

4. **Choose OK, then Close, to get rid of the dialog boxes.**

   Hmm ... what's going on around here. The numbers in your captions haven't changed. They won't change until you generate your document again (the same operation that updates tables of contents, lists, and the like).

5. **Choose Tools⇨Generate from the menu bar or press Ctrl+F9 and click on OK in the Generate dialog box.**

   WordPerfect regenerates all your generatable codes, including the system counters. When it's done, the counters use the new numbering scheme you selected.

   If you want two-level figure numbers, where the first number is the chapter and the second number is the figure within that chapter, then *don't* choose multilevel numbering in the Set Value/Number Method dialog box. Leave the <u>L</u>evels setting at *1*. Multilevel numbering doesn't work the way you may like for system counters — it's really designed for manual counters. Instead, see the section "Funky Page Numbering" in Chapter 12.

If you want a counter to start at a number other than one, you can tell WordPerfect about it. This is useful if you are writing part of a longer report, and someone else's material will come before yours. In the Set Value/Number Method dialog box (refer to Figure 13-8), enter the starting number in the <u>V</u>alue box.

Changing the format of system counters

What if you don't want the captions of your figures to say *Figure* before the figure number? What if you want them to say *Example* instead? No problem — the word *Figure* is stored in a style, which you can easily change. Here are the styles that WordPerfect uses for the five system counters:

- ✔ FigureNum, for figure numbers
- ✔ EquationNum, for equation numbers (that is, numbers for equations in boxes)
- ✔ TblBoxNum, for tables in boxes
- ✔ TextBoxNum, for Text boxes
- ✔ UserBoxNum, for user-defined graphics boxes

If you haven't already done so, tell WordPerfect that you want to be able to see and edit system styles, not just the styles that you make. Follow the steps in the "Formatting the TOC" section in Chapter 12.

Making your own counters

Chapters, sections, examples, cases, recipes — your book may contain lots of things that need to be numbered. And you can number them yourself, just by typing in the numbers by hand, but *you'll be sorry*. As soon as you've typed in all 27 examples, some smart-aleck will suggest that you move Example 26 to just before Example 3. You'll be stuck changing all those numbers by hand.

Instead, get smart and make a counter for each series of numbered stuff in your document — one counter for chapters, one for examples, and one for cases. Then you can tell WordPerfect when to display the counter and when to increment it (that is, bump it up one).

You don't have to create counters to number the figures, Text boxes, and other graphics boxes in your book — WordPerfect does this for you by creating its own system counters, described in the previous section.

Counting on your fingers

Here's how to make a counter, for example, a counter that numbers chapters automatically.

1. **At the beginning of the document (the master document, that is), choose Insert⇨Other⇨Counter from the menu bar.**

   You see the Counter Numbering dialog box, shown in Figure 13-8.

2. **Choose Create.**

   You see the Create Counter Definition dialog box, shown back in Figure 13-10.

3. **For the Counter Name, enter a new name.**

   Like, for example, *Chapter.*

4. **If you want a plain old counter (not a multilevel one), just choose the numbering method by clicking on the Single Level Method setting.**

   If you want regular arabic numbers, leave it alone.

5. **Click on OK.**

   You return to the Counter Numbering dialog box, and your new counter appears on the list of counters, with a starting value of 1.

6. **Click on Close.**

Now your counter exists and is ready for use.

If you want your counter to start at a number other than one, choose the Value button on the Counter Numbering dialog box and enter a different value.

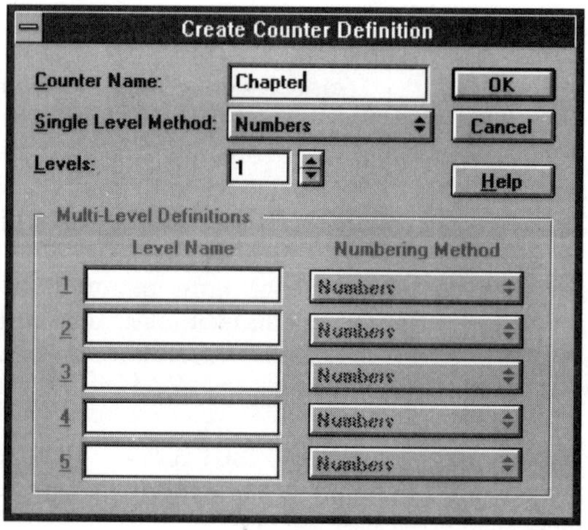

Figure 13-10:
Making your
very own
counter.

Create Counter Definition		
Counter Name:	Chapter	OK
Single Level Method:	Numbers	Cancel
Levels:	1	Help

Multi-Level Definitions

	Level Name	Numbering Method
1		Numbers
2		Numbers
3		Numbers
4		Numbers
5		Numbers

Zeros and ones

If you want a counter to start at one and count upward, there are two ways to do it:

0. When you create the counter, start it with the value 0 (zero). Each time you want to display the counter, use the Increase and Display button in the Counter Numbering dialog box. The counter starts with the value 0, but it gets bumped up to 1 before it is displayed the first time.

1. Start the counter with the value 1. The first time you want to display the counter, use the Display in Document button, so that the first displayed value is still 1. After that, use the Increase and Display button to display values.

The first method may seem a little bizarre (why set the counter and then change it before the first time it's displayed?), but it actually has some advantages. Let's say that you are using the counter to number examples in your text, and you start the counter with the value 1. If you switch the order of the examples later, you can get into trouble. If you move an example that contains the "increase and display" code to become the first example, and the example that contains the "display in document" code becomes a later example, the number will be wrong — it will start with 2 instead of 1, and two examples will have the same number.

Here's the count

When you want this counter to appear, you tell WordPerfect to display it. For example, in the title of each chapter, instead of typing the chapter number, you can display the *Chapter* counter. Here's how:

1. **Move your cursor to wherever you want the chapter number to appear.**

   For example, delete the *1* in the *Chapter 1* title of your first chapter and position your cursor where the *1* was.

2. **Choose Insert⇨Other⇨Counter from the menu bar.**

3. **Select the counter you want to use from the list of counters.**

   You see the current value of the counter next to the counter name.

4. **If you want to insert the current value of the counter, click on Display in Document.**

   — or —

4. **If you want to insert the next value of this counter, click on Increase and Display.**

The first time you use a counter (like in the title of Chapter 1 of your book), you usually use the Display in Document button so that you see the value 1. The value of the counter remains 1 for the rest of the chapter. In the titles for the rest of the chapters in the book, you choose Increase and Display so that WordPerfect bumps the number up by one before displaying it — the next chapter is 2, then 3, and so on.

Changing the count

You can change the value of a counter at any point in the document by choosing the Value button in the Counter Numbering dialog box, then entering a new value. To bump a counter up or down by one, you can choose the Increase or Decrease buttons.

Multilevel counters

OK, you asked for it. Let's say that you want to number your figures like the ones in this book — with the chapter number, a dash, and the number of the figure within the chapter. To number things this way, you need to use a multilevel counter.

Worse still, if you want to use a multilevel counter in the caption for a graphics box, you've got to fool around with a graphics box style, a caption style, and the counter itself. Yikes! (You may think that you could make a regular old counter and stick it into the captions for your graphics boxes, but you'd be wrong. The counter refuses to count if you do that.)

The WordPerfect technical support folks came up with the method (described in the next section) of getting the number to work — it may be complicated, but it works! Thanks, guys!

If you want to number the pages in your book with page numbers *1-1, 1-2, 1-3* in Chapter 1, *2-1, 2-2, 2-3* in Chapter 2, and so forth, there is a *completely* different way to do it. *Don't* use counters! Instead, see the section on "Funky Page Numbering" in Chapter 12.

Setting up a multilevel counter for graphics boxes

Here's how to number figures, Text boxes, tables, or other graphics boxes by chapter.

1. **Choose Graphics⇨Graphics Styles from the menu bar.**

   You see the Graphics Styles dialog box, which is discussed way back in Chapter 6.

2. Select the type of box you are planning to use — for example, Text box — and choose Edit.

You see the Edit Box Style dialog box. Here is where you can tell WordPerfect how you want all the Text boxes (or whichever type of graphics box you chose) to work in this document and other documents created with the same template.

3. Choose Caption.

You see the Box Caption dialog box, shown in Figure 13-11. In the lower-left corner of the dialog box are the Caption Numbering and Styles settings. Here's where you do your dirty work.

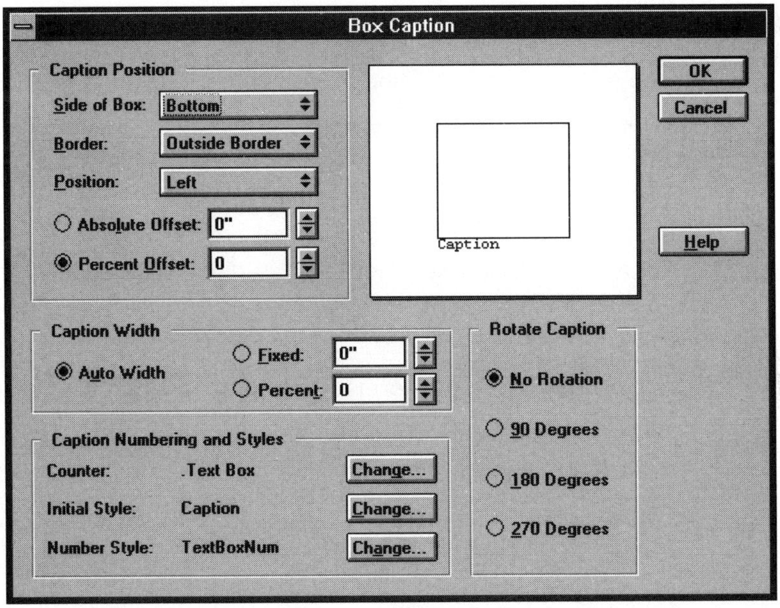

Figure 13-11:
Telling
WordPerfect
how to
caption your
graphics
boxes.

4. Choose the Change button to the right of the Number Style label.

You see the Style List dialog box, described in Chapter 10. You're going to create a new style that displays the type of box numbers you want.

5. Choose Create.

You see the Styles Editor, also described in Chapter 10.

6. For the Style Name, type a name, like Box Caption.

Optionally, you can type a description (it might not be a bad idea — things are getting confusing) like **Box caption that contains chapter number and box number**.

7. **Click on the Type button (which is currently set to Paragraph) and change it to Document.**

   Who knows why this should be a document-type style? Hey, the WordPerfect folks say that this will work.

8. **Click on the Contents box.**

   If the Reveal Codes box isn't already checked, click on it so that you can see all the cool codes you'll be creating.

9. **Type any formatting codes and text that you want to appear before the chapter and box number.**

   For example, press Ctrl+B to make the caption bold, then type **Figure** and a space.

10. **Choose Insert⇨Other⇨Counter from the Styles Editor menu bar.**

    You see the Counter Numbering dialog box, shown back in Figure 13-8.

11. **Choose Create to make a new kind of counter — a two-level graphics box counter.**

    You see the Create Counter Definition dialog box, shown back in Figure 13-10.

12. **For the Counter Name, type something like** Box Number.

13. **Change the Levels to 2.**

    This counter will be a two-level counter, the first level for the chapter number and the second level for the box within the chapter.

14. **Click on OK.**

    You return to the Counter Numbering dialog box.

15. **Choose Level 2 under the counter name you just created (probably *Box Number*) and click on the Value button.**

    You see the Set Value/Number Method dialog box, shown back in Figure 13-9.

16. **Set the starting value for Level 2 to 0 (zero) and click on OK.**

    By starting the value with zero, it will appear as 1 in the first caption, since we'll use the Increase and Display method of displaying the number.

17. **Choose Level 1 under the counter name you just created and choose Display in Document.**

    This tells WordPerfect to display the first part of the counter (the chapter number) in the caption. You are back in the Styles Editor and the Count Disp code (which displays the counter) appears in the Contents box.

18. **Type a dash or period — whichever you want to appear between the chapter number and the box number in the caption.**

    Hmmm... a tough esthetic choice.

19. **Choose Insert➪Other➪Counter from the menu bar.**

    You see the Counter Numbering dialog box yet again.

20. **Choose Level 2 under the counter name you just created and choose Increase and Display.**

    You return to the Styles Editor, and there is a new `Count Disp` code that displays the second part of the counter (the box number).

21. **Turn off any formatting codes that you turned on earlier, in Step 9.**

    For example, press Ctrl+B. This way, the figure number will be bold, and the rest of the caption (the part that you type in separately for each individual box) will not. If you want to see how the caption will look, click on the Reveal Codes box to turn it off.

22. **Choose OK.**

    Your caption style is complete! You return to the Style List dialog box.

23. **Select the style you just created (it's probably already selected) and choose Apply.**

    This tells WordPerfect to use this style for the captions of the type of graphics box that you chose way back in Step 2. You return to the Box Caption dialog box. Your new box caption style appears to the right of the Number Style label in the lower-left corner of the dialog box.

    But wait — you're not done! You need to tell WordPerfect to use the counter you created in Step 11 for this type of graphics box.

24. **Choose the Change button to the right of the Counter label.**

    You see a little Select Counter dialog box.

25. **Choose the counter that you created in Step 11 and choose Select.**

    You return to the Box Caption dialog box, and your counter name appears to the right of the Counter label.

26. **Choose OK to return to the Edit Box Style dialog box.**

27. **Choose OK to go back to the Graphics Styles dialog box.**

28. **Choose Close to get rid of all remaining dialog boxes — free at last!**

Now that you have told WordPerfect in exhaustive detail (we're exhausted, anyway) about how to number your selected type of box, whenever you make one of this type of box, edit the caption (using the Caption button on the Graphics Box Feature Bar). WordPerfect uses your new, fancy numbering for the caption.

Fixing your numbering at the beginning of each chapter

To use chapter-based numbers, you have to tell WordPerfect when a new chapter begins, bumping up the chapter number part of the counter by 1 and resetting the box number part of the counter to 1. Here's what to do at the top of the first page of each chapter, starting with Chapter 2.

1. **Choose Insert⇨Other⇨Counter from the menu bar.**

   You see the now-infamous Counter Numbering dialog box, shown back in Figure 13-8.

2. **Choose the box counter you created and choose Value.**

   You see the ever-popular Set Value/Number Method dialog box, shown back in Figure 13-9.

3. **For Level 1, increase the number by one.**

   This reflects that fact that, since you are at the beginning of a new chapter, the chapter number should increase by one.

4. **For Level 2, set the number to 0.**

   This tells WordPerfect that there have been no boxes so far in this chapter. The next box will be numbered 1.

5. **Choose OK and then Close.**

The boxes in each new chapter will use the new chapter number and box number.

Cross-Referencing Stuff

"For more information on feeding wolverines, see page 632. For a table of related statistics on third-world butterscotch consumption, see Table 14. For details on how to make tiramisu, see footnote 198."

Ah, cross-references. Cross-references are the bane of every author's (and editor's) existence. We don't know about you, but as we write a book, chapters flash in and out of existence as we change our minds and get new ideas. Figures move around. Paragraphs leap from chapter to chapter. This fluidity (not to say disorganization) means that if we write *for more on styles, see Chapter 9*, the reference may well be wrong by the time the book is done. (In fact, it's Chapter 10 now.)

What's a writer to do? Turn to technology! Rather than typing the page number, chapter number, figure number, or table number, you can create a secret code that will *look up* the number for you.

To tell WordPerfect to display the proper cross-reference, you actually enter *two* secret codes:

✔ A *target* code that shows WordPerfect what you want to refer to. For example, if you want to refer to a figure, you create the target code right next to the figure.

✔ A *reference* code that displays the cross-reference. For example, you create the reference code where you want "(see Figure 149.7.3b)" to appear.

Your document can contain lots of different targets and references, so each target has a name, and each reference refers to the name of its target. Confusing enough? Let's try it in real life.

Ready, aim, fire!

Here's how to create a target code and a reference code that refers to it.

1. **Move your cursor right after the thing that you want to refer to.**

   For example, if you want to refer to a graphics box, put the cursor right after it. You may need to use the Reveal Codes window (press Alt+F3) to get the cursor in the right place. If the target is a footnote or endnote, put the cursor in the note.

2. **Display the Cross-Reference Feature Bar (shown in Figure 13-12) by choosing Tools➪Cross-Reference from the menu bar.**

Figure 13-12:
A Feature
Bar for
creating
cross-
reference
targets and
references.

3. **Type a target name in the Target box on the Feature Bar.**

Choose a name that you'll remember — if the target is a table about dolphin mating habits, name it *dolphin mating* or some such thing. You have about 30 characters.

4. **Click on the Mark Target button from the Feature Bar.**

Sounds like you're about to nuke something back to the Stone Ages, doesn't it? Actually, WordPerfect just sticks a secret target code where your cursor is.

In reference to your target

Once you've created a target code, you can make as many references to it as you want. You can create various types of references from the little menu that the Reference button displays:

- ✔ **Page:** Displays the page number that the target is on. If the target is on page 3, you'd see *3*.

- ✔ **Secondary Page:** Forget about secondary page numbers, which we never use.

- ✔ **Chapter:** Displays the chapter number that the target is in, assuming that you use chapter-based page numbering. See the section "Funky Page Numbering" in Chapter 12. If the target is somewhere in Chapter 2, you'd see *2*.

- ✔ **Volume:** Displays the volume number, assuming that you use volume-number-based page numbering, which we've never done. Forget about it.

- ✔ **Paragraph/Outline:** If you use WordPerfect's outline feature to number your paragraphs automatically, this displays the paragraph number that the target is on.

- ✔ **Footnote or Endnote:** Displays the footnote number or endnote number that the target is in. If the target is in footnote 17, you see *17*.

- ✔ **Caption Number:** Displays the graphics box number from the caption of the graphics box the target is in. If the target is in a caption that starts *Figure 5*, you see *Figure 5* (including the word *Figure*).

- ✔ **Counter:** Displays the value of the counter at the point where the target appears. Actually, we've had some trouble getting this one to work.

Here's how to create the various types of references.

1. **Move your cursor to the spot where you want the reference to appear — the page number, chapter number, or what-have-you.**

2. **Type whatever lead-in you want, like** see page **or** for more information, refer to Chapter.

3. **Choose the target you want from the Target list on the Cross-Reference Feature Bar.**

4. **Choose the type of reference you want by clicking on the Reference button on the Feature Bar and choosing from the menu that appears.**

   We described the various types of references at the beginning of this section.

5. **Choose Mark Reference.**

   A question mark appears — not exactly what you wanted. WordPerfect will actually look up the reference the next time you generate the table of contents or whatever.

6. **When you want WordPerfect to look up the reference, choose Tools⇨Generate or press Ctrl+F9 and click on OK.**

You can create as many references to one target as you want, including references of all different types. For example, you may want to see something like this:

```
See Figure 5, which appears in Chapter 2 on page 16.
```

This example contains three references (a caption number reference, a chapter reference, and a page reference) to the same target. You mark the target only once, and then create the three references.

Indexing

Well, we're in the home stretch now — almost at the back of the book. You've got tons of chapters, with page numbers, cross-references, figures, and who-all knows what else. It's time for the index. (We talked a bit about making an index in *WordPerfect For Windows For Dummies*, in the "Recipes for Popular Documents" chapter. But here's a more complete description.)

Making an index involves marking the index terms where they appear in the text (and marking terms that don't actually appear), defining the index where it will appear, and generating the darned thing.

Mark it up

You'll need tons of index entry codes — at least three per page, the old wives' tales say. Here's how to make index entry codes.

1. Open your master document and expand it.

If you are indexing a document that has no subdocuments, you can certainly skip this step!

2. Choose the Tools⇨Index command from the menu bar.

You see the Index Feature Bar, shown in Figure 13-13.

Figure 13-13:
Buttons you use when creating an index.

3. For each word or phrase in the text for which you want an index entry, select the word or phrase and click in the Heading box on the Feature Bar.

WordPerfect copies the text you selected into the Heading box.

4. Edit the text in the Heading box as needed.

For example, if the word is capitalized and you don't want it to appear capitalized in the index, uncapitalize it in the Heading box.

5. Click on the Mark button on the Feature Bar.

WordPerfect creates an Index code in your text.

Sometimes the word or phrase that you want to appear in the index doesn't actually appear at all in the text. For example, for a paragraph about making tiramisu, you may want an index entry that reads *Italian desserts*. Just put your cursor in the text you want to refer to, type the index entry into the Heading box, and choose Mark.

Index heads and subheads

Most indexes have headings and subheadings. For example, if you have a lot of material about dolphins, you may want subheadings like *Dolphins, river* and *Dolphins, Miami*. When WordPerfect creates the index, it will look like this:

```
Dolphins
   Miami, 14
   river, 27
```

To create an index entry with a heading and subheading, enter the text for the heading in the H*e*ading box and the text for the subheading in the *S*ubheading box. Then choose the *M*ark button.

Don't enter *Dolphins, intelligent* in the H*e*ading box. WordPerfect won't know that you want the part after the comma to be a subheading.

Intelligent indexes (or is it indices?)

Making a good index is actually a fine art. People spend their lives learning to make a truly fine index — not too many entries or it will be as long as the book being indexed, but enough entries that the reader can find things quickly. Here are a few tips from the pros:

- Be consistent about capitalization. In some books, all index entries are capitalized. In the *...For Dummies* books, most terms start with small letters, except for names of stuff that are capitalized in the program (like *Styles Editor* or *File Exit command*).

- Be consistent about plurals and verb endings. Most indexes use plurals for all nouns and gerunds (the form that ends with *ing*) for

all verbs. Your index will look stupid if you have some entries under *Dolphin* and others under *Dolphins*.

- Be consistent when you create headings and subheadings. If you create one entry with the heading *White chocolate* and another with the heading *Chocolate* and the subheading *white*, the two entries will appear in different parts of the index. Decide early on what headings will have subheadings.

- Include synonyms, up to a point. If you have a bunch of entries for *Oceans*, you may want to include them under *Seas* as well. Think about what terms the reader may have in mind when looking for information.

Define it

Here's how to define and generate the index.

1. **Go to the end of the document.**

   That's where indexes always live.

2. **Press Ctrl+Enter to insert a page break.**

   You can also force the index to start on an odd-numbered page by choosing Layout⇨Page⇨Force Page and then Current Page Odd.

3. **Type the page heading for the index and press Enter a few times to create a little space.**

4. **Choose Define from the Index Feature Bar.**

   You see the Define Index dialog box, shown in Figure 13-14.

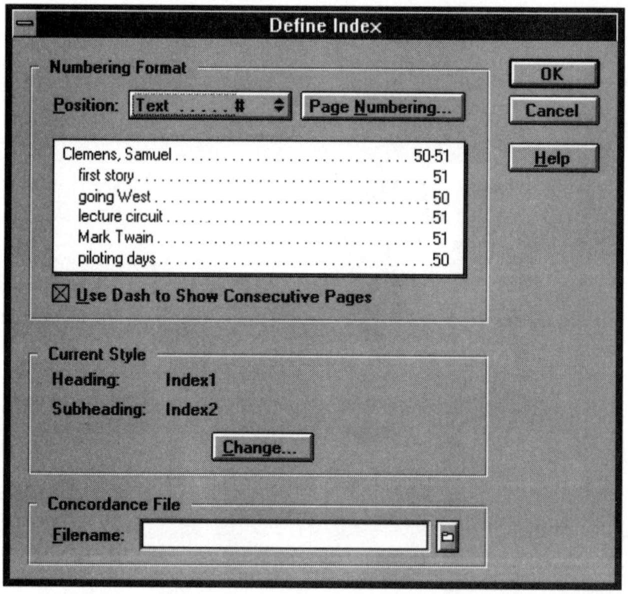

Define Index

Numbering Format

Position: [Text . . . . . # ▲▼]   [Page Numbering...]

[OK] [Cancel] [Help]

Clemens, Samuel	50-51
first story	51
going West	50
lecture circuit	51
Mark Twain	51
piloting days	50

☒ **Use Dash to Show Consecutive Pages**

Current Style
Heading: Index1
Subheading: Index2

[Change...]

Concordance File
Filename: [   ] [□]

Figure 13-14:
Telling
WordPerfect
how to
format your
index.

---

5. **If you want entries to be followed by dots leading to a page number at the right margin, leave the Position setting alone. Otherwise, click on the button that says *Text....# * and choose a different setting.**

   WordPerfect offers several different positions for the page number, including no page number at all.

6. **If you are using chapter-based page numbers (that is, *2-3* for the third page in Chapter 2), choose the Page Numbering button. You see the Page Number Format dialog box.**

   Review the section "Your tables of contents, too" in Chapter 12, if you want to be reminded about how chapter-based page numbering works. The next five steps tell WordPerfect to display chapter-based page numbers in the index, too.

7. **Choose User-Defined Page Number Format.**

   The text box below this setting contains the code [Pg #].

8. **Place your cursor just before the [Pg #] code in the text box.**

9. **Choose Insert, then choose Chapter Number from the little menu.**

   A [Chp #] code appears.

10. **Type a dash to appear between the chapter and page numbers.**

    Now the text box should say:

    ```
    [Chp #]-[Pg #]
    ```

11. **Click on OK.**

    You return to the Define Table of Contents dialog box.

12. **Click on OK again.**

    WordPerfect creates a Def Mark code containing the definition of the index, and you also see the text << Index will generate here >>. This text will be replaced by the actual index when you generate the index in the next step.

13. **Choose Generate from the Feature Bar (or press Ctrl+F9) and choose OK.**

    WordPerfect generates the index, along with any table of contents, cross-reference, or other generatable codes in the document.

    To regenerate the index at any time, choose Tools⇨Generate from the menu bar or press Ctrl+F9.

Fixing the index

The first time you generate your index, it will look as if a truck ran over it. We just thought that we'd warn you. You'll find typos never made before in the history of western civilization. You'll think that a four-year-old broke into your document and added a few index entries.

Not to worry — it's hard to enter index terms consistently and to guess ahead of time what all the major headings will be.

To correct an index, *don't* just edit the generated text. If you do, the next time you generate the index, all of your corrections will be blown away. Instead, you've got to find the index codes in your document and fix them there, which is kind of a pain in the neck. Display the Reveal Codes window so you can see the index entry code, and use the Edit⇨Find⇨Match⇨Codes command to find them. Unfortunately, once you find a bogus index entry code (which looks like `Index: Ultimate Frisbee`), you can't edit it. Instead, you must delete it and make a new one.

Formatting the index

WordPerfect uses two styles for the index: *Index1* for the headings and *Index2* for the subheadings. If you don't like the spacing, font, or indentation of the index, you can change them by editing these styles. (Editing styles is described in more detail in Chapter 10.)

1. **Choose Layout⇨Styles from the menu bar or press Alt+F8.**

   You see the Style List.

2. **Make sure that the *Index1* and *Index2* styles appear. If they don't, choose Options⇨Setup and click in the System Styles box so that it has an X in it. Then choose OK.**

3. **Select the *Index1* style from the Name list in the Style List dialog box and click on the Edit button.**

   Before changing the codes in the Contents box, make a note of what the codes are now so that you can put them back if you don't like your changes.

4. **Make changes to the style and choose OK when you are done.**

5. **Repeat Steps 3 and 4 for the *Index2* style.**

6. **Click on the Close button to leave the Style List dialog box.**

The cheater's way to make an index

Far be it from us to pass judgment on any way that you want to get your work done, but WordPerfect provides a pretty sleazy way to make an index, called a *concordance*. In real life, a concordance is a list of all the words used in your document, with the exception of totally boring words like *the*, *a*, *is*, and the like.

In the world of WordPerfect, a concordance is a list of the words or phrases that you want to include in your index. You enter this list in a separate document. Then when you create the index for your book (or whatever document you are indexing), WordPerfect automatically indexes *all* occurrences of the entries in the concordance, wherever they appear in your document.

The great thing about using a concordance is that it is a quick way to index words or phrases that appear in many places in your document. The sleazy thing about it is that WordPerfect insists on indexing every single instance of the word or phrases, whether or not it makes sense to do so. For example, if you mention flying fish in a passing way in Chapter 2, but the real information about them is in Chapter 6, WordPerfect will index the entry in Chapter 2 anyway. The other sleazy thing about using a concordance is that it only creates index entries for text that actually appears in your document, not for alternative phrasings or synonyms not in your document. If you include *chocolate* in your concordance, WordPerfect won't index *chocolates* or *cocoa*.

Perhaps the best way to use a concordance is together with regular index entries. Use the concordance to list the words and phrases that appear many times in your document and use regular index entries for other words and phrases, rephrasings, and the like.

Here's how to make a concordance.

1. **Start with a new document.**

2. **Type in the entries, one per line, just as you want them to appear in your index.**

3. **Save the file just as you always do.**

   Just in case.

4. **Sort the entries into alphabetical order by choosing Tools⇨Sort (or Alt+F9) and choosing OK.**

   You don't have to do this, but it really speeds up index generation later. WordPerfect sorts the lines in the file into alphabetical order.

5. **Save it again, now that it's sorted.** ·

6. **Define an index, following Steps 1 through 6 in the section "Defining the index" earlier in this chapter.**

   Unfortunately, there is no way to edit an existing index definition. If you have already defined an index, delete the `Def Mark` code for it and make a new one.

7. **For the Concordance File Filename setting in the Define Index dialog box, enter the name of the concordance file.**

   Either type the full filename (including the path, if it is in a different directory from the document you are indexing) or click on the little folder button to the right of the text box. You see the Select File dialog box — choose the concordance file and click OK.

8. **Choose OK to create an index definition.**

9. **Choose Generate from the Feature Bar (or press Ctrl+F9) and choose OK.**

   WordPerfect generates the index, along with any table of contents, cross-reference, or other generatable codes in the document. The index includes all instances of the entries in the concordance file.

Jazzing up your index

Most (if not all) indexes include some things that WordPerfect just can't do for you:

- ✔ Letter headings, that is, a big *A* at the beginning of the entries that begin with *A*, a big *B* at the beginning of the *B* entries, and so forth.

- ✔ *See* and *See also* entries. For example, if you've got lots of entries under *Samba*, and you don't want to repeat them all under *Brazilian music*, you might want an entry that says *Brazilian music, see Samba.*

Who knows why WordPerfect can't do these things automatically. Some other popular Windows word processors we could name can handle these niceties. We suggest that you deluge the WordPerfect support line with demands that letter headings, *See,* and *See also* be included in a future version of WordPerfect for Windows.

In the meantime, once you have generated the index for absolutely the very *last* time, you can edit the generated text of the index, adding letter headings as well as *See* and *See also* entries. But remember — if you choose Tools➪Generate or press Ctrl+F9 in this document, your improvements will be blown away by the newly generated index.

Part III
More Dealing with the Outside World

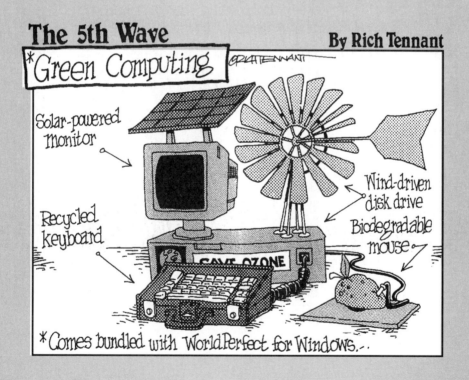

The 5th Wave   By Rich Tennant

*Green Computing

Solar-powered monitor

Recycled keyboard

SAVE OZONE

Wind-driven disk drive

Biodegradable mouse

* Comes bundled with WorldPerfect for Windows...

In this part ...

*I*t's big, it's ugly, and it's out there waiting for you. It's the World Outside of WordPerfect, where people use strange, non-WordPerfect file formats; where Macintosh users sneer at the document files you give them; and where professional printers can't read your carefully formatted documents, so they charge you to reformat them.

But wait! Beyond the borders of WordPerfect, there are also Useful, Friendly Things like spreadsheets, databases, and graphics programs. There's even the whole, new, overeager world of multimedia, where really weird stuff lives — like sound and animation — ready, willing, and able to be part of your electronic documents.

Part III is your travel companion as you explore this outside world. Chapter 14 talks about the types of file formats you may encounter and how to read information into WordPerfect documents, reformatting as needed. Chapter 15 tells you how to turn WordPerfect files into other file formats, so that other programs, even Macintosh programs, can read them. And Chapter 16 talks about how different Windows programs can be linked together, each providing information that appears in your WordPerfect documents.

Chapter 14

Files from Outer Space

• •

In This Chapter

▶ Types of foreign files

▶ Importing a foreign file

▶ Dealing with white space: reformatting ASCII files

• •

*1*f you work with folks who use other word processors, or if you use a
spreadsheet or database program, or if you get information from on-line
services, you may be called upon to use information from these other programs
in your WordPerfect documents. WordPerfect is good at *importing* other types
of files (that is, reading the files into WordPerfect documents), but you may run
into some snags along the way.

Exotic Files Galore

There are lots of different types of files in this world:

- ✔ **Other word processing files:** Each word processor stores its files in its
  own unique format. You'd think that folks could get together on this kind
  of thing — no, you wouldn't. You've been around computers too long to be
  fooled by that kind of pipe dream. The major word processors are
  Microsoft Word (whose files end with the extension .DOC), Ami Pro
  (extension .SAM), and Microsoft Write (extension .WRI).

- ✔ **RTF files:** These so-called Rich Text Format files are actually ASCII text
  files that contain all kinds of formatting. Many word processors can both
  read and write RTF files, including WordPerfect.

  Note: Don't confuse RTF files with RFT files (who picks these names,
  anyway?). RFT (revisable form text) is a format invented years ago by
  IBM — it's also called IBM RFT/DCA (document content architecture,
  believe it or not). WordPerfect can read this format, too, but it's not used
  much any more.

- **Spreadsheets:** Each spreadsheet program stores its information in its own way, of course. WordPerfect can read information from the most popular spreadsheets, including Lotus 1-2-3, Excel, and Quattro Pro.

- **Databases:** Yes, you guessed it — most database programs store information in their own format. Actually, dBASE III was such a successful program in its day that many databases use its format for their files. WordPerfect can read dBASE III, dBASE IV, and Paradox files, among others.

- **Graphics files:** If you want to include a picture in your document, see Chapters 1 and 3. WordPerfect can read most standard graphics file formats and stick them into graphics boxes, and you can fool around with them in WP Draw.

- **Text files:** Text files, also called *ASCII files* or *ASCII text files* or *plain vanilla text files* (an insult to us vanilla-lovers), are files composed entirely of ASCII characters, that is, letters, numbers, punctuation, and not much else. They can't include formatting (no boldface, italics, headers, footers, and the like). WordPerfect can easily read text files — the question is what happens to any formatting (tabs and line-endings) that they contain.

Let's talk about how to import these files — that is, how to copy the information from the original file into a WordPerfect document. If you want to *link* to the original file so that WordPerfect connects to the file without copying it, see Chapter 16.

Paste that data in here

The easiest way to import some data from another program is to display it on the screen using the other program, copy it to the Windows Clipboard using the other program's commands, switch to WordPerfect, and paste the information into your WordPerfect document using the Edit⇨Paste command. Be sure that your cursor is where you want the information to appear before you paste it in. Don't use the Edit⇨Paste Special command to import information — this command creates a link, which is described in Chapter 16.

Importing Foreign Files

Sounds like you should pay duty, doesn't it? Maybe worry about the emission standards? Check to make sure that the steering wheel is on the left side? Oh, never mind ...

Word processing files and RTF files

This is really too easy.

1. **If you want to import the file into a new, blank WordPerfect document, choose File⇨Open from the menu bar or press Ctrl+O.**

   — or —

1. **If you want to insert the file into an existing WordPerfect document, move the cursor to the place where you want the file to appear, and choose Insert⇨File.**

2. **Choose the name of the file you want to open or insert, and choose OK.**

   You see the Convert File Format dialog box, shown in Figure 14-1. WordPerfect guesses the format of the file you are importing, based on the filename extension.

Figure 14-1:
WordPerfect makes its best guess as to the format of the file you are importing.

Convert File Format	
File: C:\MARGY\CAREER.DOC	**OK**
Convert File Format From:	**Cancel**
MS Word for Windows 2.0, 2.0a, 2.0b or 2.0c	**Help**

3. **If WordPerfect asks if you really want to do this, choose <u>Y</u>es.**

   It asks when you are inserting a file into another file, not when you are opening a file.

4. **If WordPerfect didn't guess right about the file format, choose the right format.**

5. **Click on OK.**

   WordPerfect displays a little `Conversion in Progress` box while it does its thing. Then the file appears in all its converted glory.

If the foreign word processing document used styles, WordPerfect creates the same styles and inserts the proper style codes in the converted WordPerfect document — truly awesome.

If you use File⇨Open to import a foreign word processing document, WordPerfect remembers where it came from. The original filename appears in the title bar, with its original filename extension. When you choose File⇨Save or press Ctrl+S to save the file, WordPerfect asks how you want to save it (see the Save Format dialog box in Figure 14-2).

Figure 14-2:
Since this was originally a Microsoft Word document, do you want to save it in that format again, or save it as a WordPerfect file?

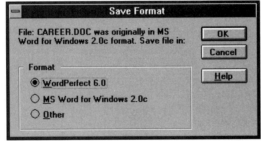

If you want to save the file as a WordPerfect document, or in some other format, it's better to choose Cancel, then use the File⇨Save <u>A</u>s command. Here's the reason: If you choose <u>W</u>ordPerfect 6.0 from the Save Format dialog box, WordPerfect saves the document as a WordPerfect document, all right, but uses the *original name*. For example, if you import a file named `CAREER.DOC`

into WordPerfect, then save it as a WordPerfect document, it will be named CAREER.DOC, not CAREER.WPD. Very confusing. To avoid this situation, use the File⇨Save As command, which lets you specify both the file format and the filename.

Although WordPerfect does a pretty good job at converting files from other word processors, nobody's perfect. Be sure to look through the document carefully, checking for font changes, page breaks, headers and footers — you name it. You may need to clean up a bit.

Spreadsheet files

Spreadsheets can be big and wide and usually contain lots of information that you don't care about. You will probably want to import just part of the spreadsheet. Most spreadsheet programs store information in a grid of *cells,* with lettered columns and numbered rows. A1 is the cell in the first column (A) of the first row (1). You can import just a *range* of cells, rather than the whole spreadsheet. For example, if you want all the information in the cells in the first five columns of the first 30 rows, you can import the range whose upper-left corner is A1 and lower-right corner is E30.

The range of cells you import must be contiguous, in one big rectangle. To import ranges of cells that aren't together, you have to import each contiguous range separately.

When the spreadsheet data arrives in your document, you can put it in one of three places:

- ✔ A table, laid out in rows and columns more or less like the original spreadsheet. A table can have only 64 columns, so don't try to import more than that (hey, they'd never fit across the page anyway).

- ✔ Text, with each row on one line, and tabs between the columns (you will probably have to adjust the tab settings for the columns to line up right).

- ✔ A merge data file, with one record for each row of the spreadsheet and one field for each column. See Chapter 18 of *WordPerfect for Windows for Dummies* if you forgot how to use merge data files.

No matter which way you import spreadsheet data, WordPerfect imports the value in each spreadsheet cell, not the formula that gives the value. For example, if a spreadsheet cell contains the formula +G47*H2*100, and the current value of that formula is 16.7, WordPerfect imports the value 16.7, not the formula.

Here's how to read in your spreadsheet data.

1. **Move your cursor to the place in your document where you want the information from the spreadsheet to appear.**

2. **Choose Insert⇨Spreadsheet/Database⇨Import.**

   You see the Import Data dialog box, shown in Figure 14-3.

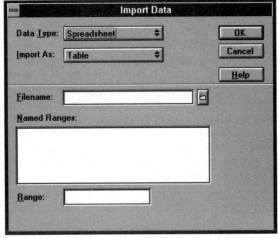

Figure 14-3:
Here's how
to import
some or all
of the data
from a
spreadsheet
or database
file.

3. **Make sure that the Data Type is set to Spreadsheet.**

   The Import Data dialog box is also used for importing data from database files.

4. **Set the Import As option to Table, Text, or Merge Data File.**

   These three options are described earlier in this section.

5. **Enter the filename in the Filename setting or click on the folder icon to choose the filename from a dialog box.**

   When you have entered the filename, WordPerfect reads the spreadsheet file and looks for any *named ranges*, that is, rectangular ranges of cells to which you (or the spreadsheet creator) gave names. It also tells you the size of the entire spreadsheet (for example, A1:D8, which means a rectangle with the upper-left corner at A1 and the lower-right corner at D8).

6. **Choose the range of cells you want to import.**

   You can choose a range from the Named Ranges list or you can enter the range in the Range box. Enter the upper-left and lower-right corners of the range, separated by a colon. To import the entire spreadsheet, don't change anything.

7. Choose OK.

WordPerfect flashes its `Conversion in Progress` box, and then your data appears in your document.

Once WordPerfect imports data from a spreadsheet, you can reformat the data, edit it, delete it, or do anything you like to it — these operations have no effect on the information back in the spreadsheet. WordPerfect copies the information when it imports it. The fact that importing data has no effect on the original spreadsheet also means that if you or someone else updates the spreadsheet, the updated information does *not* automatically appear in the WordPerfect document — you have to import it again.

If you want to create a *link* between the spreadsheet and the WordPerfect document so that updates to the spreadsheet *do* appear in the document automatically, see Chapter 16.

Database files

Databases are organized into *fields* and *records*. A *record* is a set of information about one thing, like about one person, one payment, or one item in inventory. A *field* is a single fact about that thing, like the person's last name or the amount of the payment. Database files usually are rather large, and you probably want only selected fields or records.

If you are not a database guru, or if you are using data from a database that someone else created, you may need to call on their expertise to help you select just the information that you want to bring into your WordPerfect document.

When you import a database into a WordPerfect document, you have three choices of where to put the data:

- ✔ A table, with each record stored in one row and each field stored in one column. A table can have only 64 columns, so you can't import more than 64 fields, but who would want to?

- ✔ Text, with each record on one line and tabs between the fields (adjust the tab settings for the fields to line up in columns).

- ✔ A merge data file (see Chapter 18, "Creating Your Own Junk Mail," in *WordPerfect For Windows For Dummies* if you forgot how to use them).

WordPerfect can import these types of database files:

- ✔ Clipper
- ✔ DataPerfect
- ✔ dBASE
- ✔ FoxPro
- ✔ Paradox
- ✔ SQL (structured query language), from a number of different programs (Oracle, Informix, Sybase, and some others)
- ✔ ODBC (Open DataBase Connectivity), which allows you to import data from any Windows program that supports ODBC, like Microsoft Access

If your data lives in a database file that WordPerfect can't read, don't despair. Most database programs can export data in dBASE format. Create a dBASE file (referring to the documentation for your database program, or to the appropriate ...*For Dummies* book), then import it into WordPerfect.

Here are the general steps for importing a database file into your WordPerfect document:

1. **Move your cursor to the place in your document where you want the information in the imported file to appear.**

2. **Choose Insert⇨Spreadsheet/Database⇨Import.**

   You see the Import Data dialog box, shown back in Figure 14-3.

3. **Set the Data Type to the type of database file you want to import.**

   See the list of database file formats earlier in this section.

4. **Set the Import As option to Table, Text, or Merge Data File.**

   These three options are described earlier in this section.

5. **Enter the filename in the Filename setting or click on the folder icon to choose the filename from a dialog box.**

   As soon as you select the database file (press tab if need be, to tell WordPerfect that you are done selecting it), WordPerfect displays a list of fields in the Fields box, as shown in Figure 14-4.

6. **Select the fields to import.**

   To start out with, there is an X in the box beside every single field in the database. Click on any fields you don't want to clear away the X.

7. **If you want to import only selected records from the database, choose Query. Otherwise, skip to Step 11.**

   You see the Define Selection Conditions dialog box, shown in Figure 14-5.

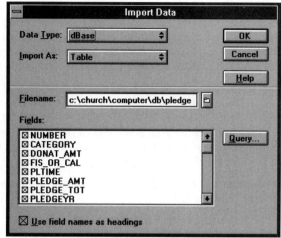

Figure 14-4:
WordPerfect
lists the
fields in the
database so
that you can
choose the
ones you
want to
import.

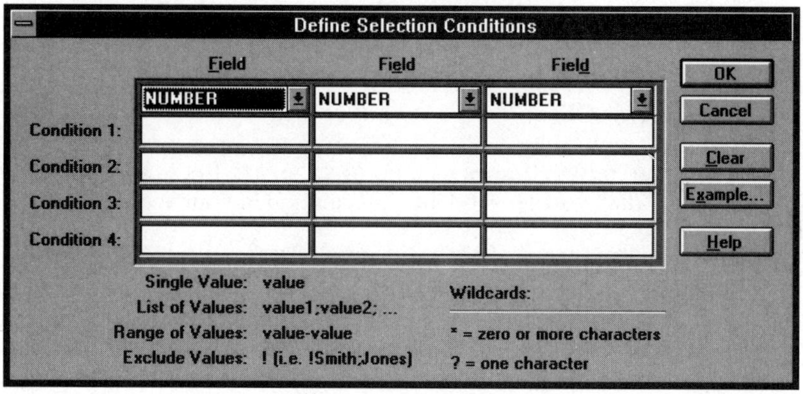

Figure 14-5:
Which
records do
you want to
import?

8. **For each field that contains information on which you want to base your selection, select the field name in the first box at the top of a column.**

   For example, if you want to select people in certain states, set the field name box at the top of a column to the state field. If you want to select payments made during a certain range of time, set a field name box to the date field.

9. **Enter the conditions for the records that you want to import.**

   This is where things get tricky. You need to think about exactly which records you want to import, and how to describe them to WordPerfect.

   Each row of the little grid on the Define Selection Conditions dialog box describes one set of records that you want to import. For example, to import payments made in 1995 or later, enter the condition >=**1/1/95** under the date field name. This tells WordPerfect that dates must be greater than or equal to 1/1/95.

You can also enter more than one condition. For example, if you want to import payments made after 1/1/95 for more than $100, enter the condition **>=1/1/95** under the date field name and the condition **100** under the amount field name. Enter the two conditions on the same row of the grid, so that WordPerfect knows that *both* conditions must be true for you to want the record.

Setting up the conditions just right can be tricky, and you may have to try it several times. Call on a database guru if you can't get the records you want. Choose the E̲xample button to see some examples of how to enter selection conditions. Or just import all the records and delete the ones you don't want in WordPerfect.

10. **When you have entered the conditions that describe the records that you want to import, choose OK.**

    You return to the Import Data dialog box.

11. **If you want the field names to appear at the first row of the table (if you are importing the information as a table), or the first line of text (if you are importing the information as text), or the first record in the merge data file (if you are importing for merging), select the U̲se field names as headings box in the lower-left corner of the dialog box.**

12. **Choose OK.**

    WordPerfect flashes its `Conversion in Progress` box while it converts the data you selected into information in your WordPerfect document.

Now you can reformat the data, edit it, delete it, or do anything you like to it. Changes you make to your WordPerfect document don't affect the information back in the database file — WordPerfect copies the information when it imports it. Keep in mind that if someone updates the database, the updated information does *not* automatically appear in the WordPerfect document — you have to import it again.

If you want to create a *link* between the database and the WordPerfect document so that updates to the database *do* appear in the document automatically, see Chapter 16.

Text files

Hey, text is just ... text, just letters and spaces and stuff that you see all the time in WordPerfect documents. So what's the big deal?

Actually, it's a snap to import a text file into a WordPerfect document. The problem comes when you look at it — text files tend to be full of all kinds of formatting that doesn't work very well in WordPerfect:

- ✔ **Carriage returns at the end of every line.** Once the text arrives in WordPerfect, you should get rid of these. WordPerfect, like all modern word processors, expects carriage returns only at the ends of paragraphs.

- ✔ **Extra spaces.** Many text files don't contain tabs because there's no way to specify the positions of the tab stops. Instead, text files frequently contain lots of spaces, which look crummy in WordPerfect. It's far better to turn all these spaces into tabs, or to turn the text into a table.

- ✔ **Bunches of dashes used for underlining text or for drawing lines.** These dashes don't look nearly as good as the real underlining and line drawing that WordPerfect can do.

- ✔ **All CAPITAL LETTERS used for emphasis.** You may want to turn these capital letters into lowercase letters and use italics — it looks less like shouting. Sometimes people enclose words in asterisks or underscores to emphasize them, like *this*.

- ✔ **No fonts or other formatting.** This lack of formatting goes without saying, since text files can't contain fancy formatting characters. If you import a file that contains headings, the headings may be formatted by leaving a few blank lines above them, capitalizing them, and underlining them with a line of dashes. Your document will look better if you use a larger font, or boldface, or both, for headings.

Here's how to import and clean up a text file. Since there are a lot of steps, we've broken them up into several stages: importing the file, fixing the stray carriage returns, converting spaces to tabs, and other stuff.

Get that text in here!

The first step is to import the text file.

1. **To import the text file, choose File⇨Open from the menu bar or press Ctrl+O.**

   You see the Open Files dialog box.

   It's a good idea to import the text file into a new, blank document so that you can clean it up. Once it looks good, you can insert the text file into another WordPerfect document, if you so choose, by copying and pasting or by using the Insert⇨File command.

2. **Choose the file that contains the text you want to import.**

   If you can't see the filename in the list of files, make sure that the List Files of Type box is set to All files (*.*).

3. **Click on OK.**

   You see the Convert File Format dialog box, shown in Figure 14-1.

4. If WordPerfect doesn't guess that it's an ASCII (DOS) Text file, choose ASCII (DOS) Text from the Convert File Format From list.

Another option, ASCII (DOS) Text File CR/LF to SRt, looks promising, suggesting that it converts hard carriage returns to soft ones, but we haven't had any luck with it. Try it yourself!

5. Click on OK.

WordPerfect imports the file. The text should look peachy, but the paragraph formatting, tabs, and so on, may look crummy. Read on for suggestions on how to clean up.

6. Choose File⇨Save As and save the file as a WordPerfect document, using the file extension .WPD.

If you don't usually use .WPD as your WordPerfect document file extension, use whatever you normally use.

Straighten up those carriage returns!

If you don't care about removing the carriage returns from within paragraphs, skip to the next section. For example, if the text file contains lists of stuff, rather than paragraphs of text, it's not worth the bother of following these steps. Otherwise, read on.

1. Look through the file, and wherever you see adjacent lines of text that *shouldn't* be connected together into a paragraph, insert lines between them (by pressing Enter). Similarly, make sure that there is a blank line between each paragraph.

For example, if there is a list somewhere in the document, insert blank lines between the lines of the list, so that the lines don't end up getting wrapped together into one paragraph.

The next step is to replace all pairs of carriage returns with a bizarre and unique set of characters, like !@#. Pairs of carriage returns represent the ends of paragraphs.

2. With your cursor at the top of the document, choose Edit⇨Replace from the menu bar (or press Ctrl+F2).

You see the Find and Replace Text dialog box, shown in Figure 14-6.

3. With your cursor in the Find box, choose Match⇨Codes.

You see the Codes dialog box, shown in Figure 14-7.

Figure 14-6:
Finding and
replacing all
paragraph
endings,
then line
endings, to
clean them
up in an
imported
text file.

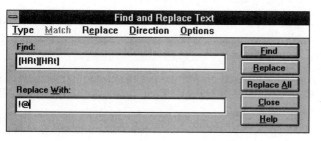

Figure 14-7:
Replacing
secret
codes, like
hard
carriage
returns, in
imported
text.

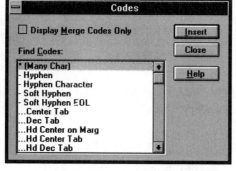

4. **Choose HRt from the Find Codes list (it's in the H's) in the Codes dialog box and choose Insert twice.**

   You should see [HRt][HRt] in the Find box of the Find and Replace Text dialog box. Leave the Codes dialog box on the screen — you'll need it later.

5. **With your cursor in the Replace With box, type !@# or some other bunch of characters that never appears in your document.**

   Be sure to remember what bizarre characters you entered to take the place of pairs of carriage returns.

6. **Choose Replace All.**

   WordPerfect replaces all the paragraph endings with these weird characters. Why? Now you can blow away all the carriage returns in the document, that's why.

7. **Back in the Find and Replace Text dialog box, delete the second HRt in the F̲ind box, so that there is only one.**

8. **In the Replace W̲ith box, delete everything and press the spacebar once.**

   This types a single space, which is what you want to replace all those carriage returns with.

9. **Click on your document and press Ctrl+Home to move back up to the top. Then choose Replace A̲ll in the Find and Replace Text dialog box.**

   WordPerfect deletes all the carriage returns in your document, replacing them with spaces. Yikes! Don't worry — now you can put your paragraph endings back. You should still see the Codes dialog box on your screen — you're going to need it again.

10. **In the F̲ind box, delete what's there, and type !@# or whatever bizarre characters you used in Step 5.**

11. **With your cursor in the Replace W̲ith box, choose HRt and I̲nsert twice from the Codes dialog box, so that** [HRt][HRt] **appears in the box.**

    If you don't want a blank line between each paragraph (we usually don't), insert only one [HRt] in the Replace W̲ith box.

12. **Again, click on your document and press Ctrl+Home to move back up to the top. Then choose Replace A̲ll in the Find and Replace Text dialog box.**

    WordPerfect puts in your paragraph-ending carriage returns.

13. **Choose C̲lose in the Find and Replace Text dialog box.**

Thus endeth fixing the carriage returns. You'd better look through the document and fix the line-endings that didn't work out right — there are always a few.

Fix that table!

If your document contains tables of columnar information, consider converting the tables to real WordPerfect tables, or at least separating the columns with tabs rather than spaces. Either way, the first step is to replace the spaces with tabs. If you don't have tabular-type stuff in your document, skip this section.

1. **Edit the table by hand, deleting the spaces and inserting one tab between each column.**

   Don't worry if the columns don't line up — we'll fix that next.

   If the table is enormous, you might be able to use the E̲dit⇨Replace command to replace spaces with tabs. You'll have to copy the table to its own document, do the replacing, and copy it back.

Once the columns in the table are separated by tabs, you can easily convert it to a table.

2. Select the whole table using the mouse.

3. Choose Table⇨Create from the menu bar.

You see the small Convert Table dialog box.

4. Choose Tabular Column, then OK.

WordPerfect converts the text to a table.

5. Clean up the table, formatting it, deleting extra rows and columns, and doing whatever else it needs to have done.

Refer to Chapter 7 for information on formatting tables.

No more extra spaces!

Your document may still have lots of extra spaces. Here's a (tedious) way to get rid of them:

1. With your cursor at the top of the document (or at the top of the part of the document with the extra spaces), choose Edit⇨Replace from the menu bar.

You see the Find and Replace Text dialog box, shown in Figure 14-6.

2. In the Find box, type ten spaces. In the Replace With box, type one space. Choose Replace All.

WordPerfect replaces all groups of ten spaces with one space. If there are huge groups of spaces, move to the top of the document and choose Replace All again, until WordPerfect says it can't find any more bunches of ten spaces.

3. In the Find box, type five spaces. In the Replace With box, type one space. Choose Replace All.

Keep choosing Replace All until WordPerfect refuses.

4. In the Find box, type two spaces. In the Replace With box, type one space. Choose Replace All.

Again, keep choosing Replace All until WordPerfect refuses.

Now, there are no groups of spaces in your document. All those of you who learned to type two spaces after each period, you can relax. In these modern days of proportionally spaced type, the new rule is to type just one.

Lines that used to be centered using spaces are now sitting at the left margin. Center lines that need to be centered by moving your cursor to the beginning of the lines and pressing Shift+F7. To right-align a line of text, press Alt+F7.

Clean it up!

Here are tips for other types of cleanup your text file may need.

- ✔ If the text uses dashes to draw lines or to underline headings, delete the dashes. To underline text, select it and press Ctrl+U. To draw lines, choose Graphics⇨Horizontal Line from the menu bar (or press Ctrl+F11).

- ✔ If a heading or other text is typed in all capital letters, you can switch it to initial caps (that is, the first letter of each word capitalized and the rest in small letters) by selecting the text and choosing Edit⇨Convert Case from the menu bar.

- ✔ Some paragraphs may be preceded by an asterisk or dash in place of a bullet (since text files can't contain bullets, which aren't standard ASCII characters). To convert these paragraphs to bulleted, indented paragraphs, delete the asterisks or dashes, select the paragraphs, and choose Insert⇨Bullets & Numbers from the menu bar (or click on the Bullets button on the Button Bar, if it is visible).

- ✔ Sometimes the first line of each paragraph in a text file is indented by a bunch of spaces. After blowing away all multiple spaces (in the section "No more extra spaces!" earlier in this chapter), each first line will begin with just one space. If you don't want your paragraphs to be indented, Use the Edit⇨Replace command to replace all occurrences of [HRt] and a space with just [Hrt].

Chapter 15

Sending Documents into the Cold, Cruel World

• •

• •

*L*ife is good in the warm, fuzzy world of WordPerfect. You are in control. Documents print out pretty much the way you want them. Now you want to enrich someone else's life by gracing them with a file containing your beautiful work of text and graphics. You want them to share and appreciate the tasteful formatting, the eye-catching graphics, the visually appealing layout of your document.

Well, forget it, Charley! You'll be lucky if the words alone survive intact. Large documents won't fit on a disk and will have to be chopped up; other word-processor users will gripe that they can't read your file; Macintosh users will sneer at you for using a PC and refuse to even discuss using your grody PC file; professional printers will charge you for retypesetting, redesigning, and re-laying out the document; and Internet users will be mystified by your document files. It's ugly out there. Here are a few ways you can prepare your document to survive in this hostile environment.

Giving Documents to Other WordPerfect Users

Giving documents to other WordPerfect users ought to work pretty well, as long as the version number you use is the same as the other user's. The only thing you should have to do is get the document onto a diskette and give it to them. Even if they're using WordPerfect for Windows 6.0 and you are using 6.0a, only a few minor things may not work quite right.

People who are a little behind

If, however, their version number is lower than yours, other WordPerfect users won't be able to read your files. To prevent problems, find out what version number they're using. Save your document in the format for that version number, using the File⇨Save As command (or F3). Click in the Format window to see if their format is available. The farther away their version number is from yours, the more likely it is that some things won't translate well. For ways to handle a few specific instances of things that don't translate well, see the sections near the end of this chapter.

Divide and conquer

In this age of killer graphics and other memory-hogging features, WordPerfect files can occasionally get too big to fit on a diskette! What do you do then?

One obvious solution is to split the document into several documents and let your recipient piece them back together. Load your document and save a copy under another name, just in case things go wrong. Delete the back half and save the remaining front half (using File⇨Save As), typing in a descriptive name like **front.wpd.** Then close this file, saying No to the question about saving your changes. Reopen the original file. This time, delete the front half and save the remaining back half with a creative name like **back.wpd**. The recipient opens the front-half file, places the cursor at the end, inserts the back-half file (with Insert⇨File), and saves the whole thing with a new name.

If your file is overweight because of graphics, you can use object linking and embedding and send the graphics files separately. See Chapter 16 for a discussion of this topic.

However, the solution we like best is to *compress* the document files. This means using a special program that stores the data more efficiently, creating files that are much smaller than the original. There are various programs out there for doing this. The most famous is PKZip, running under DOS, or under Windows in the guise of WinZip. Both are available on many bulletin boards and on-line services as shareware. Or you can order WinZip from Nico Mak Computing, Inc., P.O. Box 919, Bristol, CT 06011-0919. Nico also makes a free evaluation copy for trial use. This evaluation copy can be legally copied and passed around, so you may be able to get a trial copy from someone else. It's even possible to create self-extracting files that your friend can run to decompress without having PKZip or WinZip.

Giving Documents to People Using Other PC Word Processors

It's sad, but true. There are a few unenlightened souls out there who haven't your perspicacity and sagacity, and don't own WordPerfect for Windows 6.0. Heck, there are some folks who can't even spell perspicacity, and it's not in their spell-checkers. For these folks (the non-WordPerfect-owners, that is), you generally have two alternatives:

- ✔ Save your document as *their* file-type (format).
- ✔ Save your document as a version of WordPerfect that their word processor can read, like 5.1 or 5.2.

Generally, the second approach will work somewhat better. (Our guess is that since the software vendors are inclined to encourage people to use their software, they do a more careful job of importing documents than of exporting.) As long as the other person doesn't mind doing the one or two extra steps necessary for translation, give 'em a WordPerfect file.

Word documents

Most likely, you will encounter WordPerfect's nemesis, Microsoft Word for Windows, which, coincidentally, is also currently in release 6.0. Word 6.0 can read WordPerfect 5.0, 5.1 or 5.2 files fairly well, so you can save your document as one of those file-types. (Your Word-6.0-using colleague may have to install the WordPerfect *import filters,* however.)

If you don't want to burden the Word user, you can save your work in MS Word for Windows 2.0a, b, or c format. For that matter, you can save it as 1.0 or earlier. Higher-numbered versions of Word can read these lower-numbered versions. To save your work in these formats, use the File⇨Save As command (or F3). When you get the dialog box, click in the Format window to see if the format your friend wants is available.

Translation problems

Such translations are rarely perfect. The more you use advanced features in WordPerfect, the more your (former) friend will experience problems like these:

- ✔ One common casualty in file translations is fonts. If your acquaintance doesn't have the same fonts you do, her program will guess; perhaps well, perhaps not. If you use the TrueType fonts that come with Windows, and she uses Windows, she has a fairly good chance at having the fonts come out intact.

- ✔ Another casualty is paragraph and line formatting. Your acquaintance (now a distant acquaintance) may have to adjust spacing, indentation, and justification. If you use styles, there's a chance that the other person can change fonts by just changing the style settings, which is easier.

- ✔ Graphics are a gamble. WP Draw figures may be converted into some other form, like Microsoft Draw, or not appear at all. Same thing for charts. Graphics qualities like shading, colors, and special borders or fills will quite probably be lost. Your acquaintance (now a mere correspondent) may need your graphics in separate files in a new format.

A printout of your document is essential if your (by now) opponent is to sort things out and reconstruct them. Check out some of the later sections in this chapter to help this person (now a sworn enemy) use the work you've done.

Giving Documents to Macintosh Users

Macintosh folks are so snooty you probably shouldn't give them the time of day, let alone your precious document files. Actually, no, they are generally very nice, intelligent people, many of whom just happen to be computer bigots. They will tell you that no, they couldn't possibly use (sniff) *PC* files; and if you say, "but *PCs* can use *Macintosh* files," they will miss the point altogether. We have had Macintosh users refuse to consider using disks and files from a PC, even though they were Mac-formatted disks and files. There's a lot of fear out there.

The 5th Wave
By Rich Tennant

"I'LL BE WITH YOU AS SOON AS I EXECUTE A FEW MORE COMMANDS."

Exchanging diskettes between Macs and PCs

A certain amount of trepidation is justified on both sides when attempting to cross the great Mac-PC divide, but it has nothing to do with the Mac user's claimed superiority of the Macintosh. It has to do with the fact that these systems were originally designed without even the barest consideration of each other.

For instance, PCs and Macs can't even determine the contents of each other's diskettes without help. Fortunately, most modern Macintoshes now come with a little software package that lets them read PC (MS-DOS) diskettes (the little, 3.5-inch ones). If your Mac user doesn't have this, you can, for under 75 bucks, get software that lets you read and write modern Macintosh diskettes just like PC diskettes.

We use MacDisk by Insignia Solutions, which does its work quietly in the background and can read, write, or format Mac diskettes. (Insignia Solutions, 1300 Charleston Rd., Mountain View CA 04043; 415-694-7600. In the U.K., +44-494-459426. And no, we aren't being paid.) Any Windows application (or the File Manager) can read or write a Macintosh diskette using MacDisk. Another product that looks interesting is Conversions Plus, from Dataviz. It's not as slick and easy as MacDisk, but it claims to do all kind of file translations so that all of your formatting stays intact.

Older Macintoshes use low-capacity disk drives for diskettes of about 720K capacity. These drives cannot read PC diskettes under any circumstances that we know of. Nor can you read these diskettes on a PC without a special disk drive adapter. The software we describe here for reading Mac diskettes is only for the contemporary 1.44MB diskettes.

If you can get your PC and your friend's Mac to communicate over a wire, phone line, local network, or communications service, you may not even have to worry about diskettes. You will have to worry about other things. See the following discussion and the sections on communications at the end of this chapter.

Creating Mac-readable files

Once you solve or bypass the problem of creating a *diskette* that the Mac user can read, that user may still have a problem reading your *files*. WordPerfect 6.0a offers no file translation explicitly for Macintosh word processors.

If your Mac-using colleague has Microsoft Word on her Mac, you can save your document as an MS Word for Windows 2.0 file and she can probably read it. As for the other word processors on the Mac that also have a PC version, we don't know; but we suspect that if you can save your document as a PC version of that program, the Mac version may be able to do something with it.

When you give a file to a Mac user, suggest that she not double-click on it to open it, as she probably does with her regular files. Instead, have her launch Word, or whatever her word processor is, first. (She can double-click on another Word file to do this.) Then she should open your file from within her word processor with the File Open command. When done, she should save the translated document as she does her normal documents. This precaution is because the Mac may not recognize your file and not know what program to launch when she double-clicks on it. Once she's using the program, though, it does its best to translate your file, guessing what kind of file it is, and asking her to confirm that guess.

If the Mac user has a word processor that can't read WordPerfect files, and you can't translate to its format, see the next section, "Giving Documents to People Using Heaven-Knows-What."

Fonts often get messed up between the Mac and PC. The word-processing software that's doing the file translation has to guess at whether Arial on the PC should be Helvetica on the Mac, or something else. Between these fonts, special symbols often don't translate at all. To minimize problems, if you know that a file is going to a Mac user, avoid using special symbols (like registered trademark symbols). Or, before you give the file to the Mac user, find and replace those symbols with some unique combination of standard characters, like *** The Mac user can then replace the *** with the Mac trademark symbol.

Giving Documents to People Using Heaven-Knows-What

In the File⇨Save As dialog box in WordPerfect, the Format box lists a variety of general-purpose formats that you can give to both Mac and PC users. To preserve your text formatting and fonts, try RTF (Rich Text Format); many word processors can deal with this. If that doesn't work, try the ASCII Generic Word Processor or ASCII Text versions. These will lose your font specifications and most of your formatting, however. Some white-space formatting will remain, but using characters like tabs. Indentations, for instance, will turn into first-line indents using tabs.

If the other person is running under Windows, try using the ANSI versions of these same formats. These will retain a few more special characters common to Windows applications.

If the other person is using something besides a word processor, like a spreadsheet, that person may just want your tables. See "Giving Tables to Spreadsheet Users," up next in this chapter, if that's the case.

Giving Tables to Spreadsheet Users

If you do your organization's entire budget planning, or something else huge and gigrondous, in WordPerfect tables, first of all ... shame on you. We told you not to do that in *WordPerfect for Windows for Dummies*. Now, someone else is likely to want your table, and he is likely to want it in a for-real spreadsheet program.

One solution is to get your table into a spreadsheet format. Every spreadsheet program known to humankind should be able to read Lotus 1-2-3 format. WordPerfect lets you create a Lotus 1-2-3 file. It also lets you convert your table into Quattro Pro for Windows, or, if all else fails, into a sort of old-fashioned generic spreadsheet form called Spreadsheet DIF.

Here's how to create a spreadsheet file for your PC-using friend:

1. **Select the entire table.**
2. **Copy your table to the Windows Clipboard by pressing Ctrl+C (or by choosing Edit⇨Copy from the menu bar).**
3. **Open a new document and paste the table in it, using Edit⇨Paste.**
4. **Press F3 to save the document in a new format.**
5. **In the Format box, choose whichever form of spreadsheet your friend has, or Spreadsheet DIF. If WordPerfect doesn't exactly match the version your friend has, try an earlier version.**
6. **Choose OK.**

If these approaches don't work, and your friend is working in a Windows spreadsheet, try the following.

1. **Copy your table again with Ctrl+C.**
2. **Rummage around in the Windows Program Manager (the place where you launch programs), probably in the Main group, for *Clipbrd*, the Windows Clipboard Viewer icon. Double-click on it.**

   Your table will appear in it, rather munged-up, but ignore that.
3. **Now choose File⇨Save As in the Clipboard Viewer and type in a file-name like MYTABLE.CLP, with .CLP as the file extension.**
4. **Copy this file to a diskette and send or give it to your friend.**
5. **Your friend can launch *his* clipboard viewer, File⇨Open your file, then paste the darned table into his accursed spreadsheet, for cryin' out loud!**

   Whew! What a lot of work.

If your friend is not using Windows, do pretty much the same procedure but use the Notepad. (It's probably in your Accessories group. If it's not there, you might have to install it by running Windows Setup, under Options, Add/Remove System Component, then click on the Files button next to Accessories.) With the Notepad, you have to paste your table in with Ctrl+V, then save the file with a .TXT extension instead of a .CLP extension.

A final resort is to save the table document in ASCII (DOS) Delimited Text format, one of the other Format selections in the Save As dialog box. This format saves each cell in your table as a separate line; the spreadsheet user must "import" this, telling the spreadsheet program that the file is a delimited text file. As a result, your table becomes one long column of data in the spreadsheet; not optimal, but it beats retyping all the data.

Giving Charts to People

(It occurs to us that you can use these same techniques to give charts to animals, but animals don't seem to appreciate charts as much. Except for kittens, who enjoy the heck out of them, but only if they're on paper. The charts, that is, not the kittens.)

Unfortunately, while WP Chart is happy to import a number of foreign charts (see Chapter 4), it is not so sanguine about exporting them. Must be a weird balance-of-trade problem. Unless you run into somebody who can import WordPerfect charts from WordPerfect documents, you have only two solutions, neither of them particularly good.

First, you can give someone else the chart data. At least they will not have to type the data in again. This is probably not worth the trouble unless you have more than about 50 cells of data or a lot of very precise numbers that are likely to get typed wrong. To give someone your chart data, highlight your entire data area in WP Chart (Edit➪Select All) and press Ctrl+C. Now, you basically have a table in your Windows Clipboard, and you can use the techniques described in the previous section, "Giving Your Tables to Spreadsheet Users." Most chart software either works with spreadsheet data or is part of a spreadsheet program, so this should work out fine.

Second, you can give this putative person a picture of your chart. See the following section, "Giving Illustrations to People."

Giving Illustrations to People

At first glance, this is a no-brainer. Illustrations are graphics files — you give the person your graphics file. End of story. The only sad part of the story is that any fancy stuff you did to the graphics box, like borders, fills, or contrast adjustments, are lost.

But what if your illustration is in WP Draw, and it only exists in your document? You still only need half your brain. (You get to choose, left side or right.) Just double-click on the illustration; then press F3 to Save Copy As in WP Draw and type in a filename. Click on the Save button in this dialog box, and there's your WordPerfect graphics file.

But what if the other person can't read WordPerfect graphics (.WPG) files? Hmmm. OK, here's what you do:

1. **Select the illustration in the document and copy it with Ctrl+C.**

2. **Rummage around in your Program Manager (probably the Accessories group) to find Paintbrush (which comes with Windows) and double-click on it.**

   (If it's not there, you might have to install it by running Windows Setup under <u>O</u>ptions, <u>A</u>dd/Remove System Component, then click on the Files button next to <u>A</u>ccessories.)

3. **In Paintbrush, press Ctrl+V to paste your illustration.**

4. **Then choose <u>F</u>ile⇨Save <u>A</u>s in Paintbrush. Type in a file name and press OK.**

   You've now got an illustration file in Windows Bitmap, or .BMP format. Most modern graphics programs can read these.

If the other person can't deal with .BMP files, tell him to go get a real computer and call you when they're both ready.

Working with Designers and Printers

For the highest-quality documents, you are going to have to deal with these fine people: designers and printers.

You may think your document looks snazzy, and maybe it is indeed snazzy. But compared to what a graphic designer and professional printer can do with it, it ain't nothin'. Sorry, but it's true. Graphic designers (at least, the ones who do document layout) are trained in how to make the document feel just right. Every advertisement, magazine, or begging letter you get has almost certainly been professionally designed, or *laid out,* and professionally printed at high resolution.

Professional printers use a resolution of thousands of lines per inch, compared to the 300 or 600 lines per inch a typical laser printer can deliver. They can do tricks that you can't, like having color or graphics go all the way to the edge of the paper. Obviously, they can also print something bigger than a single 8$^{1}/_{2}$"-by-11" page; do photographic-quality color; print on heavy stock; go "glossy"; lots of stuff.

It is an unfortunate fact of life that most designers and printers, if they can read any files at all, can only read Mac files. While they are not usually Mac snobs, some of these folks are utterly terrified of files from a PC and will have nothing to do with them. A few enlightened printers hire people who can (but don't want to) deal with PC-to-Mac translation.

Graphic designers

If you're working with designers (also called *layout artists*), file translation is not going to be much of a problem. They only want your basic text, anyway. They care nothing for your fonts, layout, margins, typesetting adjustments, and illustration placement. Give them a printed copy, a file from which they can read the text, and your illustration files (if any), and they'll be happy. A simple ASCII text file will often do the job. See the preceding sections, "Giving Documents to Macintosh Users," and "Giving Illustrations to People."

If you are not going to give them an ASCII text file, it helps if you use only the simplest formatting. Otherwise the graphics designer has to remove tabs and extra spaces, bullets, underlining, and other such things. This is time-consuming and error-producing, depending on the page layout program being used. If your text is going to be laid out by a graphics designer, it's best to use unformatted typing and add special notations about format, unless you know that the formatting will translate properly.

The main problem is with illustrations. Unless the designer works with Windows graphics software, the few illustration files of yours that the designer can read do not provide very high quality. If the designer works with Windows, a Clipboard file (.CLP) may a better solution than a bitmap (.BMP) file. The designer may need to redraw your illustrations.

When the designer gives you back a "proof" copy of document, check to see that your text styles, like bold, are duplicated correctly. Especially make sure that special symbols like trademarks are properly interpreted. Let the designer take care of working with the printer. If the designer starts talking about galleys and bleeds and kerning and stuff, ask the dear soul to speak English.

Printers

Folks turn to professional printers for either higher quality or higher quantity, or both.

If you want to get higher-quality printing, you must give your document and graphics files to the printer. If you give printers a printout to reproduce, they can't make it look any better, except maybe to color certain parts. You can try to find a printer that can handle WordPerfect for Windows 6.0 files, but don't count on finding one. Your best alternative is to try the techniques mentioned previously for giving a file to someone who doesn't have WordPerfect.

If you don't need great quality but just quantity, by all means just give your printout to the local copy shop or small print shop. Even for color output, copiers can do a fair, if expensive, job. Small print shops can often do *spot* (unmixed) color inexpensively. Just mark up the color each piece of text or graphics should be on a copy of your black-and-white printout, and give the clean printout to the printer as camera-ready copy.

Do not use the color features of WordPerfect if you are going to give the print shop black-and-white printout as camera-ready copy. The colors come out of your printer as shades of gray, which will make your colored text or graphics too light.

About Photographs: If you plan to have a document professionally printed, don't go to the trouble of scanning in a photograph so that it appears in your document electronically. Have the printer insert the photograph mechanically. Scanning just makes more work and reduces the final quality. You can leave space for the photograph and wrap text around the space by creating a blank WP Draw illustration, with no border. Size the box proportionately to whatever size you want for the photo in your document; the printer can adjust it.

Non-color printing

For higher-quality black-and-white printing, one approach is to find out what kind of typesetting machine the printer uses, such as a Linotronic model something-or-other, and give the printer a *print file* for that machine. Ask your printer about this idea. A print file is what you get when you divert all the data that normally goes out to the printer into a file instead. The printer then takes the file and squirts its data into his actual printing machine. You may have to get the printer a Mac disk, or he may have to read your PC disk, but this is manageable; see the section on Mac users earlier in this chapter.

To create a print file, first find out what kind of printing device (typesetter) your printer uses. If his printing device is a hand-carved potato stamp, move on. Next, find out if you have printer software for that device. (You have to convince your PC that you have one of these printers on your PC.) Here's how to install a Windows printer driver for the typesetter.

1. **Choose File⇨Select Printer from the menu bar and click on Add Printer in the dialog box that appears.**

   You are asked to choose between WordPerfect's printer software and Windows' printer software.

2. **Try Windows first (no, we don't mean jump out the window; save that for later). In Windows 3.1, you get a Printers dialog box, where you should click on Add.**

3. **Browse the List of Printers that appears.**

   There could be anything in there from cheap dot-matrix printers to professional high-resolution machines. (If you don't see the right machine listed, and you're going to be working with this printer a lot, you could try calling the manufacturer and asking for a Microsoft Windows printer driver for that machine.)

4. **Click on the machine's name in the List, and then on the Install button.**

   You are prompted to insert a diskette from your set of Windows program diskettes.

   When you're done with the installation, you can now tell Windows to print to a file.

5. **In the Printers dialog box, select the desired machine in the Installed Printers list and click on Connect.**

6. **In the Connect dialog box that appears, scroll the Ports list and double-click on FILE.**

7. **Click on the Select button when you return to the Select Printer dialog box.**

   You only have to do the above setups once — now you're ready to print to a file using this new printer driver.

8. **Choose File⇨Print to print your document.**

   You are asked for a filename.

9. **Enter a filename.**

When you're done with all these steps, give that file to the printer.

If you can't find Windows printer software for the machine, try this:

1. **Choose WordPerfect instead of Windows when you Add a printer in the Select Printer dialog box.**

   (Still with us? This sounds like gibberish even to us.) You get WordPerfect's Add Printer dialog box.

2. **See if you can find the printer's machine here, and click on Change.**

3. **To tell WordPerfect printer software to print to a file, choose File⇨Select Printer, click on the right machine, then click on Setup in the dialog box that appears.**

4. **Click on the Port button and select File.**

5. **Click on the Select button in the Select Printer dialog box.**

Now when you print, you're prompted for a filename. When you're done, give that file to the printer.

Pat yourself on the back, pour yourself a drink, and take a nice, long bath.

If you create a print file for a professional printer, you need to reselect your own printer when you're done. Choose File⇨Select Printer and double-click on your original printer. You can leave the other printer selection alone and use it again, later.

Color printing

You can get significantly higher color quality and graphics resolution over a color PC printer, if you can manage to give the printer your document in electronic form (as a file).

For color printing, you really need the advice of your print shop as to what kind of document file to create, or what sort of printout to give them. If you only need certain text or graphics to be a particular color, try the approaches we just described for non-color printing. Along with your file, give the printer a printout from your machine with the color areas simply marked in pen.

Printing colors come in bizillions of standard inks, and the printer may ask you to choose one from a humongous sample book. Write down the ink name and numbers you use for future reference. The number of different colors you use will dramatically affect your cost, because the paper has to go through the press once for each ink color.

If you need multicolor images or photographic-quality color, you are asking for a *four-color* process. ("Glossy" finish is often a fifth color but may also be done in the paper stock.) To do four-color printing, a professional printer has to create four separate images in cyan, yellow, magenta, and black, called "color separations." Most word processors are not very good at this, and WordPerfect doesn't even attempt it. (Probably a good idea.) If you have to do something like this, leave it to the experts: a graphic designer or a professional printer.

TIP

Crop marks for printing books

Since few books are printed on standard-size paper, and you print out camera-ready copy on standard-size paper, you need some way to indicate to the printer where to cut. Marks that indicate the paper edge are called *crop marks*.

There's no crop mark feature in WordPerfect, but you can try a page border (Layout⇨Page⇨Border/Fill). Check with your printer to see if that will be OK. Set the line to hairline, and use the lightest gray possible. (Click on Customize Style to set line color.)

Documents à la Modem

Computers were supposed to usher in the paperless era, where people just send data to each other. Well, the paperless world of the future is not quite upon us. Nobody's figured out how to make computerized Kleenex yet. (Maybe that's why we have computer viruses?) But we're getting real close. We didn't see any of the chapters in this book on paper until the final book was printed; we wrote and sent them to our publisher all electronically.

You, too, can transmit your documents electronically. You can have your modem call your friend's modem, use a service like CompuServe, or even use the Internet, if you are connected to it.

Hints for sending files

We have to leave most of the details of running your communications software and hardware to you, since we don't know what you're using. But here are a few hints about how to send files. See "Giving Documents to People Using Other PC Word Processors" for information on how to save your file in different file formats.

✔ Regular WordPerfect document files are *binary* files (not readable by humans) that have to be sent in a special way, using some sort of *protocol* (agreement between computers) like Xmodem, Ymodem, Zmodem, or Kermit. Both you and your friend need to have software that speaks the same protocol for sending and receiving binary files.

✔ You can't send a binary file across the Internet; you can send one across certain commercial dial-up services, like CompuServe, but not all. For Internet mail, you have to convert your binary document file to an ASCII file, transmit it, then convert it back to binary. One set of programs for doing this is called uuencode and uudecode, most commonly found on UNIX workstations but also available for PCs now. Pick up *Internet For Dummies, Modems For Dummies,* or *UNIX For Dummies,* all published by IDG Books Worldwide, for more information on these.

✔ If both you and your friend have WordPerfect, you can convert your binary document files into ASCII by choosing File⇨Save As and using a Format of Kermit (7-bit transfer). (This doesn't mean you have to use the Kermit transmission protocol, by the way.)

✔ A good general-purpose approach is to save your file in RTF format and transmit that (see "Giving Documents to People Using Heaven-Knows-What," earlier in this chapter). RTF is a text file, not a binary file, so you can send it using your software's text file transmission method without any special protocol. Moreover, the RTF format often bridges the gap between different word processors and even between the Mac and the PC, and it doesn't lose all your formatting like other text (ASCII) files.

✔ If all the other person wants is your text, not your graphics or formatting, save and transmit your file as an ASCII file.

✔ If you are transmitting a text file (like a Kermit 7-bit file or RTF file) to a Mac user, you may need to adjust for the difference in the way PCs and Macs end a line of text. PCs send two characters, called CR (carriage return) and LF (line feed); Macs use one character, CR. You or your friend may have to figure out how to *strip LF characters* from files you transmit. Check your communications software manual for this phrase.

Steps for sending CompuServe files

If you and the lucky recipient of your document have CompuServe accounts, you can exchange actual document files. (This is how we sent chapters in this book back and forth to our editor.)

Your communications software has to be able to speak one of two file exchange protocols, either Kermit or Xmodem. To find out if it does, look in your menus for something about setup or binary files; poke around until you can choose one of these protocols. If all else fails, read the manual. The Terminal accessory that comes with Windows offers both protocols, if your software does not.

Figure out what commands to use to transfer, send, or transmit binary files using your communications software before you dial up CompuServe.

Here's the process:

1. **Log into CompuServe**

2. **Type** go mail.

3. **Type** upload.

   CompuServe asks for your protocol, either Xmodem or Kermit.

4. **Choose whichever protocol your software uses. If you have a choice, Xmodem is typically faster than Kermit.**

   CompuServe asks for transfer type: Text (ASCII), Other Text, or Binary.

5. **Choose Binary.**

   CompuServe says Starting Xmodem tranfer (or Starting Kermit Transfer).

   CompuServe says key <CR> when transfer is completed.

6. **Start sending the document file (a binary file).**

   CompuServe says File transfer completed.

7. **Tell CompuServe where to send the file. In response to** Send To, **give the person's name or user ID (CompuServe number).**

8. **Fill in the subject line.**

9. **When asked, confirm that everything is OK by typing Y for Yes and pressing Enter.**

The size limit for such files is 2MB. You can't use these files for faxing or for transmission across the Internet.

Chapter 16
Documents with Connections

● ●

In This Chapter

▶ OLE!

▶ Connecting to other Windows programs in general

▶ Connecting documents to spreadsheets

▶ Connecting documents to databases

▶ Connecting documents to graphics programs

▶ Multimedia documents

● ●

*T*his chapter could be subtitled, "Good Ideas That Sometimes Work." The original good idea here was to let you connect WordPerfect documents to other useful programs. So, for instance, if you wanted to show an Excel or Quattro Pro spreadsheet in your WordPerfect document, you could just do it. When the spreadsheet file changes, so would your document change. If you wanted to change the spreadsheet file while you were working in WordPerfect, you would just double-click on the spreadsheet in your document, and pfzap! you would be in Excel, or whatever. Update or close your spreadsheet file, and your changes would automatically appear in your document.

Even more cool, this connecting feature would allow electronic documents (documents you only read in WordPerfect or through some other piece of software) to do "multimedia." Click on something in the document, like an icon, and you would see a video or listen to a sound clip. (This is what the Media Player and Object Packager are for, if you've ever noticed it in your Accessories program group in the Program Manager.)

This was the dream of the guys who invented Windows. They were so excited, they called it OLE! (Actually they called it OLE for Object Linking and Embedding, but that's boring. "Objects" are the spreadsheets or graphics or whatever that you're trying to put into a document.)

Unfortunately, in many instances this dream has turned into a confusing, compromised mess that only works sometimes or works incompletely. It is often too baffling to bother with. But it's the wave of the future, they say, so grab your surfboard.

When OLE does work, it can be worthwhile. The times when you should consider using it are:

- ✔ If you have a spreadsheet or database that's regularly being updated, and you need to use the spreadsheet or database in regularly produced documents or several documents, like monthly sales reports, reports by product, or mailing list merge files

- ✔ If regular old copy-and-pasting doesn't do a good job (that is, copying something onto the Windows Clipboard from another Windows program and pasting it with Ctrl+V into WordPerfect)

- ✔ If you want to do gee-whiz electronic multimedia documents with bells, whistles, voice, music, movies, or animation

If you simply want to import a spreadsheet, database, or other kind of file, you don't have to use the somewhat complicated methods described in this chapter. Check out Chapter 14, instead.

When you connect your WordPerfect documents to other files, it makes it hard as heck to give your document to somebody else. You have to give the person all the files, and he or she will have to put the files in identically named directories or else change the "links."

What's the Connection?

This connecting business is a Microsoft Windows feature. Everybody else who sells software, like WordPerfect, is supposed to make connecting work in their Windows programs. If everybody did, the world would be a happier place. Unfortunately, everybody does not. So what you read here is the general idea about how things are supposed to work with other programs. If they don't work that way, don't call us.

If you want to connect your document to a spreadsheet or database, you can use the procedure described in this section. In fact, we use a spreadsheet as an example. You may be happier, however, if you use the procedures described in a later section, "Linking Spreadsheets or Databases." WordPerfect has special features for dealing with these kinds of programs, and that's where we talk about them.

There are several different ways (groan) that your WordPerfect document can connect to stuff from some other Windows program. Here are the main ways, the better ways being given first:

Linking

If you can succeed in linking to a file created under another Windows program, Microsoft's dream is truly realized. Your spreadsheet or graphics or whatever remains in its customary file and is displayed in your WordPerfect document. When someone updates that file, your document can display the most recent information. What's more, several documents can share the same, central spreadsheet or graphics or whatever file.

Linking is done by *special pasting* (using the Edit⇨Paste Special command), wherein you copy something from the other program to the Windows Clipboard in the usual way, then "paste the link" into your WordPerfect document. Whenever you reopen your document, the linked objects can be updated to display the most recent information.

Embedding

If you can't link, you can probably embed. This means that the object (spreadsheet or graphics or whatever) is stored in your WordPerfect file, but you get to use the other Windows program (for example, Excel) to create it and work on it. Since it's *embedded* in a WordPerfect document, you can't really work on the object outside of WordPerfect.

Once you create the object in your document, the object behaves sort of like WP Draw drawings do with WP Draw: When you double-click on the embedded object (the spreadsheet or graphics or whatever), the other program (say, Excel) fires up and you can change stuff. Embedding is done either by special pasting or by the Insert⇨Object command.

Other forms of special pasting

If it turns out that either WordPerfect or the other program doesn't let you paste a link or embed an object, there's a sort of consolation prize in the special pasting department. WordPerfect recognizes data from certain types of other programs, and if you use the special pasting command, it can occasionally do a better job than ordinary pasting with Ctrl+V. Sometimes it fails to do anything at all, however.

Packaging

Packaging is used for electronic documents that you read on the computer when you want gee-whiz stuff like animation. You first use the Windows Packager Utility to stuff an animation or something into an icon, then you copy it to the Windows Clipboard and paste the sucker into your document. When you double-click on it, your animation runs, music plays, whatever. You can package darn near anything that runs under Windows this way.

Sound

WordPerfect has a special sound feature that lets you run sound clips (.WAV or MIDI files, if you're hip to computer sound terms) by clicking on a special WordPerfect sound icon in the margin. WordPerfect also lets you record sound clips using the Windows Sound Recorder, if you've got the necessary hardware.

Connecting to Stuff in General

If you're connecting to a spreadsheet or database, the following general procedure works just fine, but WordPerfect also has special procedures for spreadsheet and database files. See the later sections of this chapter for more information.

In principle, the process of connecting your WordPerfect document to something that was created in another program is simple. It's very much like copying and pasting. In this case, however, we call the thing you're pasting an *object*.

Here's how to connect a file from some other program to your document:

1. **Create your object (a spreadsheet, database report, document, graphics image) using whatever Windows program you have.**

2. **Still in that Windows program, save your work as a file.**

   You must save to a file in order to create a linked object. For embedded or otherwise pasted objects, you don't have to save to a file.

3. **Still using that other program, copy your object (usually by selecting it and pressing Ctrl+C).**

4. **Fire up WordPerfect if you haven't already done so, and start a document.**

   Don't put away the other program; leave it running. If you put the other program away, you won't be able to link your object; you'll only be able to embed or paste it.

5. First, try to link the object to your WordPerfect document.

Use the Edit⇨Paste Special command in WordPerfect. This brings up the Paste Special dialog box in Figure 16-1. Try clicking on each type in the Data Type box to see which ones do not gray out the Paste Link button.

If you find a data type for which the Paste Link button is not grayed out, click on the button. Your object is now linked. You're done, go celebrate.

Figure 16-1:
Connecting
a foreign
object to a
WordPerfect
document.

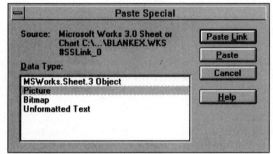

6. If linking doesn't work, look for an "object" in the Data Type box; click on it and then on Paste.

If you can find a something-or-other object in the Data Type list, you can Paste it to get an "embedded" object, as we described earlier in this chapter. If this works, you're all set. Go home.

7. If there's no "object" in the Data Type box, click on something else in the box (as long as it doesn't gray out the Paste button), then click on the Paste button.

This may or may not be an improvement over simply pasting with Ctrl+V, but at least you're done.

Don't worry too much about what data type you choose, at first. Some, like Picture and Bitmap, often give barely distinguishable results. Others will be clearly inferior: For most purposes, unformatted text or RTF formatted text will not work out so well.

If you make a mistake or don't like the results, just press Ctrl+Z to undo the paste and try again.

For a file to be linked, it has to be open in its native program and saved as a file when you do the copy and Paste Special.

There's another way to connect to another program from WordPerfect. Use this way if you want, say, a spreadsheet in Excel, but you haven't made the spreadsheet yet. Choose Insert⇨Object, then choose the program you want to run. Do your spreadsheet or whatever, then exit back to the document. You end up with an embedded object, described in more detail in the next section.

What you've got

Now that you've made some sort of connection from your WordPerfect document, let's see what you've got and what you can do with it.

A linked object

If you ended up with a linked object (Step 5), you've got the best result. You can double-click on the object in WordPerfect, and Windows will kick you over to the original program so that you can edit the object and store it as the file you created in Step 2.

Moreover, any time you run that other program and change that file, those changes will ultimately appear in your WordPerfect document. If you update a linked sales spreadsheet using Quattro Pro, for instance, the results will appear in the WordPerfect document when you next open the document. The spreadsheet file is linked to the document.

An embedded object

If you ended up with an embedded object (Step 6), the object data (spreadsheet, image, whatever) has now been copied into your WordPerfect document, and *that* is what WordPerfect hereafter shows. If you go back to the original program (in Step 1) and change the data, WordPerfect is utterly ignorant of the fact. There's no link between your document and that original file.

If you double-click on this embedded object, the data or image or whatever will be copied back into the original program you used, so you can work on changes. But you're *not* working on the file you started with — only on a copy stored in WordPerfect. If you want to store a copy as a separate file, use File⇨Save As in the non-WordPerfect program.

When you're done working in that other Windows program, do a File⇨Exit or Close. You will zoom back into WordPerfect, and the changes will be displayed. Some programs also let you do a File⇨Update, which squirts the new data back into your document without your having to leave the program.

Something else altogether

If you ended up at Step 7, neither pasting a link nor Pasting an object data type (which embeds it), you've got something else altogether. You may have plain old text, in which case there's nothing special about it at all. Double-clicking on it doesn't kick you into some other application, it just selects something, as usual.

You may have ended up pasting a bitmap, which is a photograph-like image. If you double-click on a bitmap, you end up editing it in WP Draw.

Updating and changing links

The whole idea of linked objects is that the WordPerfect document should always show what's in your spreadsheet or graphics or whatever file. WordPerfect gives you both an automatic and a manual way to make sure that your document always shows what's in your spreadsheet or graphics or whatever file.

Only linked objects show changes to the spreadsheet or graphics or whatever file. This is not true for embedded or otherwise pasted objects. Those objects only change when you edit them in WordPerfect.

So, whenever you open a document in WordPerfect that contains links, WordPerfect prompts you to ask if it should update its links. Respond "Yes," and your document will update the document to display exactly what's in the linked file. (Or, at least, will display the piece that you selected in Step 3 to link to the document.) If you don't want to be prompted, choose Edit➪Links from the menu bar. The Links dialog box of Figure 16-2 appears. Click on Manual, then on OK.

It's generally not a good idea to have the linked file open in its native program when you open the WordPerfect document. If you do, in some cases the program will complain that `the file is already open` and whine about opening another file by the same name. It probably won't hurt anything, but who knows what an annoyed program will do out of spite. So close your linked file and save the changes before opening your document.

You can update the links manually at any time if, say, the document is open and you want to see the results of changes to the file immediately. (No patience, eh?) Here's how:

1. **First, make sure no objects are currently selected in your document.**

   Click somewhere where there's plain text.

2. **Choose Edit➪Links from the menu bar to get the Links dialog box.**

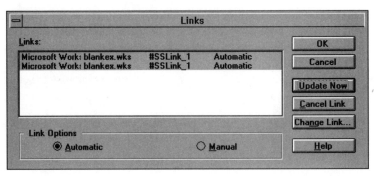

Figure 16-2:
The place to
go to
update,
cancel, or
change your
links.

3. **Select the links you want to update**

To select all the links, hold down the Shift button and drag across all the lines in the Links box. To select certain ones, hold down Ctrl and click on the ones you want.

4. **Click on Update Now and, after a brief delay for updating, click on OK.**

If you only have one link selected, WordPerfect mentions that there are other links and asks if you want to update them.

If you move or change the names of the linked files, WordPerfect's going to have a tough time finding them. So if you move the files or change the names of the files, you have to change the links themselves, using the Links dialog box of Figure 16-2. (The tricky part about using the Links dialog box is telling one link from another, because if you have several links to the same file, as in Figure 16-2, they all look alike.)

Here's how to change a link:

1. **Make sure no objects are currently selected in your document.**

2. **Make sure the file that you're linking to is not already open in some other program.**

3. **Choose Edit⇨Links from the menu bar.**

4. **Select a link, then click on Change Link in the Links dialog box.**

You get one of WordPerfect's customary file selection dialog boxes, where you can choose the file in its new location or under its new name. Double-click on the file.

5. **If there are other links to the same file in the document, WordPerfect asks if you want to update those, too. This is a nice time-saver; tell it "Yes."**

Now it's great that linking always reflects the latest changes to the linked file, but what if you don't want that? For instance, what if you've created a document that uses a current-sales spreadsheet file, and for each quarter, the document shows all the previous quarters, too? You don't want the earlier quarters updated, but you do want the current sales constantly up-to-date.

For this situation, just cancel each of the earlier links at the end of the fiscal quarter. The spreadsheet data will remain in your document, but it won't be linked. To do this, repeat Steps 1 through 3 in the preceding Tootorial; then in Step 4, instead of clicking on Cha_n_ge Link, click on _C_ancel Link. (Step 5 doesn't take place.)

Linking Spreadsheets or Databases

There are two ways to link a spreadsheet or database to your document:

✔ The general way we described in "Connecting to Stuff in General," using the _E_dit➪Paste _S_pecial command

✔ The special way WordPerfect provides, using the _I_nsert➪S_p_readsheet/ Database command

The first way lets you edit your spreadsheet or database file right from WordPerfect, using the spreadsheet or database program: Double-click on the spreadsheet or database object in your WordPerfect document, and you are zapped right into Excel or FoxPro. You can't just type stuff in from WordPerfect. You have to have Excel or FoxPro, or whatever, running on your PC to use this approach.

The second way doesn't let you zap into the spreadsheet or database program from WordPerfect. If you want to change the data in the file, you have to run the program yourself. This approach does, however, give you a little better control over exactly what data gets put in your document. For spreadsheets, it lets you choose named or specified ranges. For databases, you can pull in specific fields such as "lastname," querying the database for specific conditions or records.

Linking spreadsheets the general way

When you link a spreadsheet using the _E_dit➪Paste _S_pecial command, you will end up with something that looks like a table, but isn't really. It's really a graphic image specially drawn to look like a table. For instance, if you copy a piece of a Microsoft Works spreadsheet, when you do your _E_dit➪Paste _S_pecial command, you can choose to link either a Bitmap data type or a Picture data type. The difference between these really doesn't matter worth a hoot unless you do something weird like copy the object into WP Draw, but these data type names suggest that there's something graphical, not table-ish, going on here.

In fact, the image is in a graphics box, in the *OLE object* style. See Chapter 6 if you want to change the style of these boxes in general. If you want to change the appearance of an individual object, you can move, shrink, or expand the image, change its border — all the usual graphics box stuff (see Chapter 1). Be careful, though, because the OLE object style lets you distort the image by changing width and height independently. If you mess up, click somewhere off the box and press Ctrl+Z to undo the change.

Any other changes, such as fonts and column widths, have to be done in the spreadsheet program. Double-click on the image if it's linked or embedded; this will launch the spreadsheet program so that you can make the changes.

Since you are connected only to certain cells in the spreadsheet (the ones you copied), you will only see changes that affect those cells. What happens if you move the cells depends on the spreadsheet program. Some programs let WordPerfect follow those same data values around, no matter where in the spreadsheet the data values are located. Other programs always show WordPerfect the same cell addresses, so if that you move data to other cell addresses, the data may no longer appear in the document.

Linking spreadsheets the special way

WordPerfect's special way of linking a spreadsheet to your document is the Insert⇨Spreadsheet/Database command. See the beginning of this section, "Linking Spreadsheets or Databases," for a discussion of how this approach is better or worse than the general way of linking.

This approach uses exactly the same command described in "Spreadsheet files," in Chapter 14, for importing a spreadsheet or database, but with one difference. Instead of choosing Import after Insert⇨Spreadsheet/Database, you choose Create Link.

Here's a quick summary of how to link a spreadsheet to your document. For more details on each of these steps, see the Tootorial in "Spreadsheet files" in Chapter 14.

1. **Move your cursor to the place in your document where you want the information in the spreadsheet to appear.**

2. **Choose Insert⇨Spreadsheet/Database, then Create Link.**

3. **Make sure that the Data Type is set to Spreadsheet.**

4. **Set the Link As option to Table, Text, or Merge Data File.**

   Table is one of our favorites.

5. **Enter the filename in the Filename setting or click on the folder icon to choose the filename from a dialog box.**

6. **In the Named Ranges or Range boxes, choose the range of cells you want to import.**

   Cells that have been previously linked to something else are also shown among the named ranges.

7. **Choose OK.**

Now see "Using specially linked spreadsheets and databases" for more information.

Linking databases the special way

WordPerfect's special way of linking a database to your document is the Insert⇨Spreadsheet/Database command. See the beginning of this section, "Linking Spreadsheets or Databases," for a discussion of how this approach is better or worse than the general way of linking.

This approach uses exactly the same command described in "Database files," in Chapter 14, for importing a spreadsheet or database, but with one difference. Instead of choosing Import after Insert⇨Spreadsheet/Database, you choose Create Link.

Here's a quick summary of how to link a database to your document. For more details on database files, the terms we use, and on each of these steps, see "Database files," in Chapter 14.

1. **Move your cursor to the place in your document where you want the information in the linked file to appear.**

2. **Choose Insert⇨Spreadsheet/Database⇨Import.**

   You see the Import Data dialog box, shown back in Chapter 14, Figure 14-3.

3. **Set the Data Type to the type of database file you want to import.**

4. **Set the Link As option to Table, Text, or Merge Data File.**

5. **Enter the filename in the Filename setting or click on the folder icon to choose the filename from a dialog box.**

   WordPerfect displays a list of fields in the Fields box.

6. **Select the fields to link.**

7. **If you want to link only selected records from the database, choose Query. Otherwise, skip to Step 11.**

8. **For each field that contains information on which you want to base your selection, select the field name in the first box at the top of a column.**

9. **Enter the conditions for the records that you want to import.**

10. **When you have entered the conditions that describe the records that you want to import, choose OK.**

11. **If you want the field names to appear on the first line, select the "Use field names as headings" box.**

12. **Choose OK.**

Now read on, in "Using specially linked spreadsheets and databases."

Using specially linked spreadsheets and databases

As WordPerfect creates the link to your spreadsheet or database, it flashes its `Conversion in Progress` box, and then your data appears in the document. In page view, WordPerfect also sandwiches the data between cute "link" icons in the left border, then cleverly slides your document over so you can't see them! Grab the scroll box in the slider doohickey at the bottom of the WordPerfect window and slide the doohickey to the left. Click on the top icon to see what file and ranges you're linked to. In draft view, there's a gray line under the linked spreadsheet showing the name of the linked file.

What you see here is real, ordinary WordPerfect text in some form or other, like a table. You can edit the WordPerfect text or format it, but when you update the link, your changes will be blown away and replaced with the data and the formatting from the spreadsheet or database file.

To update the link (that is, retrieve data from the linked file and display it), choose Insert⇨Spreadsheet/Database again, then Update. When you're asked `Update All Data Links?` click on Yes. Wait a long time.

If you want WordPerfect to update the links whenever you open the document, choose Insert⇨Spreadsheet/Database, then Options. In the Link Options dialog box that appears, click on Update on Retrieve, then OK. (The Link Options dialog box is also where you can get rid of the margin icons if you like; click on Show Link Icons.)

To change the link to refer to a different file, or if you have moved the file to a new directory, first click somewhere in the linked area (between the link icons in page view). Choose Insert⇨Spreadsheet/Database, then Edit Link. The Edit Link dialog box duplicates the one you used to create the link, so you can change anything you specified at that time.

Connecting to Graphics

Normally, most people are quite happy to copy and paste a graphics image into WordPerfect or simply do a Graphics⇨Figure command to insert a graphics file. But if you have a graphics image that's constantly changing or is used in a lot of documents, you may prefer to have one central image and link it to your WordPerfect documents. A company logo, for instance, or drawings or screen-captures of your products are typical subjects. If your computers run on a network, the powers-that-be can maintain their dictatorial control over corporate images by having everyone link to a single, central file.

To connect to a graphics image, follow the Tootorial in the earlier section, "Connecting to Stuff in General." You end up with a graphics box in the OLE object style. You can do anything to this image that you can do to images in other graphics boxes, except that the WordPerfect image tools won't work with it. See Chapter 1 for more information on graphics boxes.

Things can sometimes seem a little weird if you connect to an image in another word processor or a spreadsheet program, but it's really OK. If your object is linked or embedded, when you double-click on the object you may end up in a little graphics subprogram of that word processor or spreadsheet, even if the word processor or spreadsheet isn't running. For instance, if you link to a Microsoft Draw figure from a Microsoft Word file, when you double-click on that object in WordPerfect, you'll run Microsoft Draw — but not Word. This may seem weird, since you normally don't see Draw outside of Word, but it's OK. Go with the flow.

Multimedia Documents

If you're a trendy, with-it, 90s kind of person, you absolutely must make multimedia documents: documents that are only read electronically in WordPerfect; that play sound clips, show animations, run slide-shows, whatever. Heaven knows why, but you absolutely must. So put your hand-blown-crystal glass of designer bottled water into your terra-cotta evaporative water-glass cooler, and tighten the Velcro straps on your Tevas. Here we go.

First, see if you can satisfy your trendy taste buds with hypertext (no, it's not caffeinated, don't worry). Turn to Chapter 20. If that doesn't do it for you, read on.

 If you're really going to be dealing with sound and multimedia stuff, pick up IDG's *MORE Windows For Dummies* by Andy Rathbone and check out Chapter 8, "Sound! Movies! Multimedia Stuff!" This explains a lot about how your PC deals with sound and multimedia. WordPerfect has its own sound-playing feature, so you can learn that in this chapter; but WordPerfect relies on Windows for other stuff, so Andy's book is the place to go.

 Multimedia is so young, no one has figured out a generic noun to describe "the animation, sound, or video that happens when you push some button or click on some icon in your document." We're going to call it an "event" here, whenever we need such a noun.

Sound advice

If you feel compelled to make your documents squeak, moo, sing, talk, or play music, you've come to the right place. We will indulge your fantasy here, but be warned: You are treading on the limits of reasonable expectations for word-processor technology. Be prepared for things not to work.

First off, for this to work at all, you need to have some sort of audio electronics in your computer. (There is some software around that turns your PC speaker into a sound-output device, but the result sounds like a telephone does at arm's length — if the software works at all with WordPerfect. Ours didn't.) If you want to record sound, you need recording electronics in your PC, plus a microphone. Shouting or singing at your PC screen is fun, but fruitless.

Second of all, you need to install a sound *driver*. A sound driver is a hunk of software that understands your PC's particular audio electronics and generally comes with the electronics. There should be instructions with the sound driver, probably written in several languages by someone whose principal language is none of them. Hack your way through these.

Adding a sound clip

Still with us? Such persistence! Now you can (maybe) insert a sound clip in your document. A *clip* is a file, by the way — a short recording of sound. Unless you have recording hardware in your PC, you generally get these files from a friend or off the Internet. Which reminds us, be sure to buy *Internet For Dummies* and *MORE Internet For Dummies* by noted world experts Levine and Young. (Hey, if you can't plug your co-authors' books, whose books can you plug?) WordPerfect can use two types of clip: a .WAV file or a MIDI file. What you can use depends on what your audio hardware can deal with. RTFM — Read That Fine Manual.

Here's how to add a sound clip to your WordPerfect document:

1. **Move your cursor to the place in your document where you want the sound clip to appear.**

2. **Choose Insert⇨Sound.**

   The Sound Clips dialog box of Figure 16-3 brightens your day.

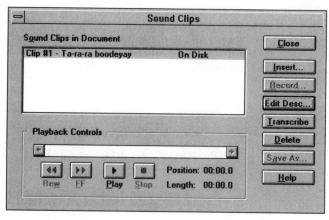

Figure 16-3: The Sound Clips dialog box. When it first appears, there's nothing in the sound clips list.

3. **Click on the Insert button.**

   The verbosely titled Insert Sound Clip Into Document dialog box appears.

4. **Enter the filename in the File text box.**

   You can also give the sound clip a descriptive name in the Name box. If you want the clip to be copied into the document file (a good idea if you'll be giving the document file to someone else), click on Store in Document; otherwise the document file relies on the separate (linked) file.

   Click on OK, and you're back in the Sound Clips dialog box.

5. **Click on the Close button.**

   In page view, a speaker icon appears in the left margin (but you have to slide the document to see it). In draft view, a shaded line appears with the sound clip name in it.

Playing the clip

To simply play the entire clip, double-click on the icon. (In draft view, single-click on the gray bar.) If you want to play parts of the clip, stop the clip midway, or play other clips currently in the document, you need either the Sound Clips dialog box of Figure 16-3 or a Sound Clip Feature Bar.

To get the Sound Clips dialog box, click on Insert⇨Sound. Select the clip from the list and click on Play. The other controls are just like those on a tape player, except for the slider, which lets you set the starting point for playback. There are similar controls on the Sound Clip Feature Bar, which like all Feature Bars remains on screen until you Close it. To get the Sound Clip Feature Bar, either click on Transcribe in the Sound Clips dialog box, or in the document, click with the right mouse button on the sound icon and choose Transcribe off the QuickMenu that appears.

Recording a clip

If you have sound-recording hardware in your PC, you can make your own sound clip. Follow the installation and recording instructions that come with the sound-recording hardware; we can't possibly guess at your particular procedure.

If you can't decipher the recording instructions once your sound-recording stuff is installed, you can try to launch the Windows Sound Recorder from WordPerfect. Choose Insert⇨Sound, then Record. For instructions on using the Sound Recorder, click on Help when the Sound Recorder window appears and choose Contents. In the Sound Recorder Help window that appears, click on Record a Sound File (in green, underlined).

Other multimedia

Yes, OK, WordPerfect can put multimedia-like animation in your documents, but WordPerfect really can't take a whole lot of credit for it. It (and you) really uses Windows' Media Player and Object Packager, available to any Windows program. For the full, gory details on Windows' Media Player, pick up IDG's *MORE Windows For Dummies*, by Andy Rathbone, and check out Chapter 8, "Sound! Movies! Multimedia Stuff!" We stick to the basics here.

The procedure that follows works with other Windows programs, too! Not all of them, mind you, but lots of them.

In order to do anything at all, you gotta have the right stuff. That is, you need the hardware and software that can record and/or play back whatever animation, movie, or sound you want. You especially need a driver — software that knows about your particular hardware and software. This driver typically comes with your hardware, with instructions; to learn more about drivers, see *MORE Windows For Dummies*.

If you're going to do video or animation, you need a new Windows Media Player to replace the one in your Accessories group! The Windows Media Player comes with the special Video for Windows that Microsoft created. Fortunately, you can get a "play only" version of the Media Player for free from Microsoft (from its bulletin board), or it may come with the video/animation stuff you bought.

To play anything, you gotta have the media. No, we don't mean ABC news and the *Times* of London, we mean video, sound, or animation. Some multimedia devices called *compound* devices use computer files for their media; others, like CD players, are called *simple* devices and just play regular CDs or tapes.

If you are using a compound device, there are lots of different types of media files, so check your hardware and software documentation to see what kind of files you can use. Shmooze around the Internet a bit and you'll be able to download a few files, but the files are BIG and often compressed, so you'll need a decompression program like WinZIP. You can download a trial version from nearly any on-line service, or send $29 to Nico Mak Computing, Inc., P.O. Box 919, Bristol, CT 06011-0919.

If you have the new Media Player, here's how to put a clip of video or whatever into your document:

1. **Find the Media Player icon in the Program Manager and double-click on it.**

2. **Choose D̲evice; then, from the pull-down menu that appears, select whatever device you're using.**

   If your device plays computer files (a compound device), you get an Open dialog box to choose the file from. If the device is V̲ideo for Windows, look for files ending in .AVI. Double-click on the file.

3. **Choose E̲dit⇨C̲opy Object.**

   If your Media Player doesn't offer this command, it's not the fancy new one, and it won't do the job.

4. **Click in your WordPerfect document where you want the multimedia event to appear and choose E̲dit⇨P̲aste.**

   Something will appear in this location, depending on the type of multimedia you're doing. Typically, you will either get a picture of the first video/animation frame or a Windows Sound Recorder icon.

5. **Double-click on the picture or icon to play the event.**

If you don't have the new Media Player that Microsoft offers, try the following. It may work if you happen to have the program that created your media file, or if you're just playing a .WAV or MIDI sound file.

1. **Launch the Windows Object Packager.**

   Look in the Accessories group of your Windows Program Manager; the icon looks like a box full of stuff. Double-click on it.

2. **Choose File⇨Import from the packager's menu.**

   One of WordPerfect's file selection dialog boxes appears. Choose your media file. (Or you can skip the File⇨Import command, open up Windows File Manager, click on the media file and drag it into the packager's Content window. Very cute.) This is called *packaging* a copy of the file.

3. **Choose Edit⇨Copy Package.**

   The media file, packaged with the application that created it, is now on the Windows Clipboard.

4. **Click in your WordPerfect document where you want the media event.**

5. **Choose Edit⇨Paste Special in WordPerfect.**

6. **Click on Package Object in the Data Type text box, then click on the Paste or Paste Link button.**

   Paste gives you an embedded object; Paste Link gives you a linked object. See the section "What's the Connection" for the difference.

An icon is inserted into your document. Double-click on it, and it might just play the clip you want! It might not, too. It's probably not your fault, if you followed our instructions. Remember, we warned you: This multimedia stuff still doesn't have all the bugs ironed out.

This Object Packaging thing works for other types of objects besides video and animation. If you package a .BMP file (Windows bitmap) made with Paintbrush, for instance, you get an icon that launches Paintbrush with the file in it. Or if you want an icon that blasts you into your project management software and your current project plan, you can do that, too!

Part IV
More Automation and Customization

In this part ...

*A*utomation, customization: words that suggest being productive, efficient, or perhaps *in charge*. Unfortunately, when one reads about the automation and customization features of software like WordPerfect, one tends rather to feel, um ... cowardly ... tentative ... and sort of like ignoring the whole thing and hoping it goes away.

Well, quite honestly, automation and customization in WordPerfect are not for the faint of heart. But "faint heart ne'er won fair lady," and if you spend a good part of your day lashed to the keyboard, using WordPerfect, here are some ways to take some drudgery out of your day. Here's the "Dummies" way to make your own custom commands, to re-assign keys on your keyboard to do your bidding, and to use buttons that you really need, not just the ones WordPerfect thinks you need. Here also are the secrets of hypertext, a way to automate electronic documents to take the tedium out of both reading and updating documents. Pour yourself a nice cup of tea, take heart, and read on!

Chapter 17
Macros for Non-Programmers

. . . .

In This Chapter

▶ Why and when to use macros

▶ Creating macros

▶ Testing macros

▶ Fixing macros

. . . .

*Y*ou might as well hear the bad news first — writing macros is actually a type of *programming*. OK, OK, stop screaming. We know that you don't have much interest in being a programmer, despite their sexy, charming image in the national press recently. But macros are a special category of programming, namely, pretty *easy* programming. And macros can be very useful. So stick around long enough to give them a try. Also, check out Chapter 22 for a list of our favorite macros.

Whatizzit?

You can think of a macro as a player piano roll — a recording of a series of keystrokes that do something useful. Actually, WordPerfect doesn't record the exact keys that you press when you record a macro, it records the results. It doesn't matter if you use the menu bar, a QuickMenu, or some other way to give a command — WordPerfect just records the command you give.

For example, let's say that you have a document that sorely needs formatting. In many places in the document, there is a line that should be formatted using the *Heading 1* style, followed three lines later by a line that should be formatted using the *Heading 2* style. You get tired of choosing Layout⇨Styles from the menu bar, or even pressing Alt+F8 and choosing these two styles. You want the machine to do the work — a perfect job for a macro that does "apply *Heading 1*, move down three rows, apply *Heading 2*."

Here's what you do:

- ✔ Do the formatting commands once or twice by hand, until you are sure exactly what commands to choose.

- ✔ *Record* the macro, that is, tell WordPerfect to store the series of commands as a macro.

- ✔ Test the macro, to make sure that it does what you want, rather than, say, deleting your whole document.

- ✔ Run (or *play*) the macro as many times as you want.

If you want, you can also assign the macro to a special keystroke, like Ctrl+Alt+Z, to make it very quick and easy to play back, or to a button on the Button Bar. See Chapters 18 and 19.

The rest of the chapter describes these steps in excruciating detail, so you can turn into a real (macro) programmer. It's never too late to become a nerd!

Make Me a Macro

Poof! You're a macro! Oops, sorry — we couldn't resist.

To make a macro, follow these steps:

1. **Make sure that you know exactly what commands you plan to use in the macro.**

2. **Move your cursor to the position in your document at which you want the series of commands to begin.**

   For example, if you are recording a macro that formats a paragraph, move the cursor to a paragraph that you want to format.

3. **Choose Tools⇨Macro⇨Record (or press Ctrl+F10).**

   You see the Record Macro dialog box shown in Figure 17-1.

4. **Give the macro a name, typing a filename into the Name box.**

   The name will be used as the filename in which WordPerfect stores the macro. Either leave out the filename extension, or use the extension .WCM. To see the macros that already exist, click on the little folder button to the right of the text box. WordPerfect lists all the .WCM files in your macros directory. A bunch are already there — these are macros that WordPerfect provides with the program (see Chapter 22 for a list of our favorites).

But what is a macro, really?

If you must know, a macro is actually a special kind of WordPerfect document that contains a list of WordPerfect macro commands. They are stored in your WordPerfect macro directory, which is usually a subdirectory named MACROS in your WordPerfect program directory. Each macro lives in its own file, with the filename extension .WCM.

To change the usual place where WordPerfect stores and looks for macros, choose File⇨ Preferences from the menu bar, double-click on File, choose Macros, edit the Macros Default Directory, and choose OK.

TIP

If you leave the Name box blank, WordPerfect makes a *temporary* macro, one with no name. You can have only one temporary macro at a time, and WordPerfect deletes it when you exit from the program, so don't make a temporary macro for any task that you may want to do later.

5. Choose Record.

You can tell that WordPerfect is now recording your macro because the message Macro Record appears on the status bar (on our status bar, it appears in a barely-readable gray). Also, the mouse pointer turns into a circle with a slash through it (this is the international *Do Not* icon — wonder why WordPerfect uses it for *Recording a Macro*? Maybe you can think of it as a little tape recorder reel.) Everything you type and every command you give will be recorded as part of the macro until you tell WordPerfect to stop recording.

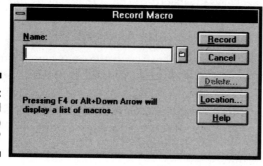

Figure 17-1: What should this macro be named?

6. Give the commands and type the characters that you want in your macro.

For example, if you want a macro that formats the current line using the *Heading 1* style, moves down three lines, and formats that line using the *Heading 2* style, choose Layout⇨Style (or press Alt+F8), choose *Heading 1,* choose Apply, press the down-arrow three times, choose Layout⇨Style (or press Alt+F8) again, choose *Heading 2,* and choose Apply.

7. Choose Tools⇨Macro⇨Record (or press Ctrl+F10) again to stop recording.

WordPerfect stores the macro in the file — it's done.

Now the question is — does it work?

While you are recording a macro, you can't use the mouse to move the cursor. You have to use the keyboard. This is because WordPerfect doesn't have a good way to record mouse movements, but recording keystrokes works fine. It makes sense, actually. (The Windows 3.1 macro recorder *can* record mouse movements — read *Windows For Dummies,* from IDG Books, for more information.)

Lookit That Mackerel Run!

To run a macro:

1. Put the cursor where you want it to be when the macro starts.

For example, if you created a macro that formats a paragraph, move the cursor to a paragraph that needs to be formatted.

2. Choose Tools⇨Macro from the menu bar.

WordPerfect usually lists the macro you just created at the bottom of the Macro menu.

3. If the macro you want appears on the Macro Menu, choose it.

WordPerfect runs the macro, giving exactly the same commands and typing exactly the same characters that you did when you recorded the macro.

4. Otherwise, choose Play and either type the macro name or click on the little folder icon so you can choose it from the alphabetical list of macros. Then click on Play again.

WordPerfect runs the macro.

To run a temporary macro (one with no name), choose Tools⇨Macro⇨Play without entering a macro name.

What's that WordPerfect Macro Facility icon doing on my screen?

When you record or play a macro, WordPerfect secretly runs another program to do some of the work, the WordPerfect Macro Facility. It appears as an icon on your screen. Don't worry — it's just helping out, and you don't need to do a thing with it. When you exit from WordPerfect, this other program goes away, too.

An easier way

You can tell WordPerfect which macros you want to see at the bottom of the Macro menu, up to nine of them.

1. Choose Tools⇨Macro⇨Menu from the menu bar.

You see the Assign Macro to Menu dialog box, shown in Figure 17-2.

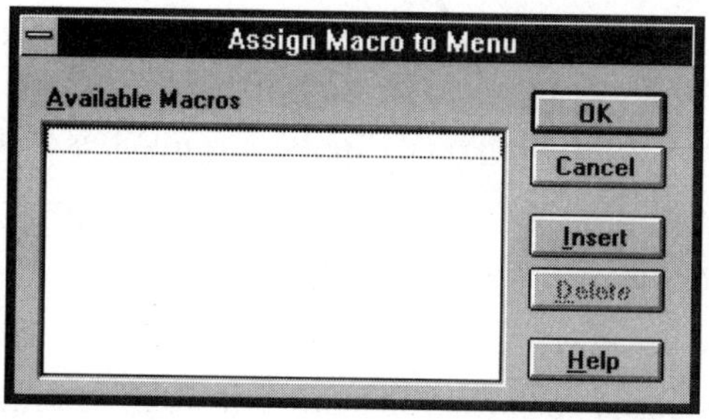

Figure 17-2:
Which macros would you like to see on the Macro menu?

Assign Macro to Menu
Available Macros

OK
Cancel
Insert
Delete
Help

2. Choose Insert.

You see the Select Macro dialog box, which looks exactly like the Record Macro dialog box shown back in Figure 17-1.

3. Type the macro name or click on the little folder icon and select it from the list.

4. Choose Select.

You see the Assign Macro to Menu dialog box again, with your macro listed.

5. **Repeat Steps 2 through 4 for each macro you want to add to the Macro menu, up to nine of them.**

6. **Choose OK.**

You can delete macros from the Macro menu by choosing the macro you want to dispose of and clicking on the <u>D</u>elete button on the Assign Macro to Menu dialog box. This doesn't delete the macro, it just removes its name from the menu.

Running macros lots of times

If you want to run a macro a bunch of times in a row, you can use WordPerfect's Repeat command. This is great if you want to correct the formatting of a bunch of paragraphs or change the punctuation in a whole list of items.

1. **Move the cursor to where you want the macro to run a bunch of times.**

   Using this method, you can't move the cursor, or type anything, between times that the macro runs.

2. **Choose <u>E</u>dit⇨Repe<u>a</u>t from the menu bar.**

   You see the Repeat dialog box, shown in Figure 17-3.

3. **In the <u>N</u>umber of Times to Repeat box, type the number of times you want to run the macro.**

   WordPerfect guesses eight, but you can enter any number (within reason).

4. **Choose OK.**

   The dialog box goes away.

5. **Run the macro the usual way.**

   Instead of running just once, it runs as many times as you requested.

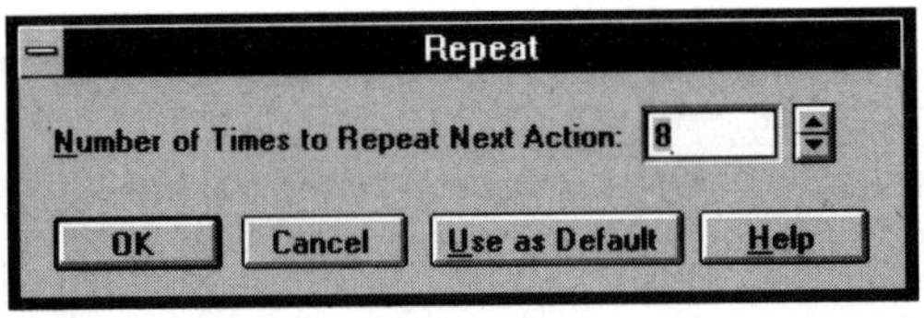

Figure 17-3:
How many
times would
you like to
run your
macro?

Repeat
<u>N</u>umber of Times to Repeat Next Action: **8**
OK Cancel Use as Default Help

You can use the Edit⇨Repeat command to do anything a bunch of times. First you tell WordPerfect how many times to do it (Steps 1 through 4), and then you give any command or type any single keystroke. (Yes, this seems a little backward to us, too.) WordPerfect repeats the command or keystroke the requested number of times. This is great for typing a long row of asterisks or other repetitive jobs.

Running a macro automatically when you start WordPerfect

What if you want to create a macro that always runs when you start up WordPerfect? For example, if you usually work on the same three documents, you could create a macro that opens up all three (one after another).

For example, say you always open STATUS.DOC (with the status of the various projects you are working on), TODO.DOC (with your to do list), and NOTES.DOC. Then you open whatever document(s) you are working on today. You can make a macro that opens the first three documents. To tell WordPerfect to run the macro automagically when you start the program, you can modify the WordPerfect program icon in Windows Program Manager.

Here's how to tell WordPerfect to run a macro automatically as soon as the program is done loading.

1. **Create the macro that you want to run each time you start WordPerfect.**

   For example, make a macro that opens the three files you always open (choosing the File⇨Open command and typing the filename).

2. **Exit from WordPerfect.**

   You can modify the WordPerfect program icon without exiting from WordPerfect, but you'll want to make sure that the modified icon works by running it.

3. **Switch to the Windows Program Manager.**

   Click on the Program Manager window if you can see it or press Alt+Tab until you switch to it.

4. **Click *once* on the WordPerfect program icon.**

   Don't double-click on it, or you'll just run WordPerfect normally.

5. **Choose File⇨Properties from the Program Manager menu bar (or press Alt+Enter).**

   You see the Program Item Properties dialog box, shown in Figure 17-4.

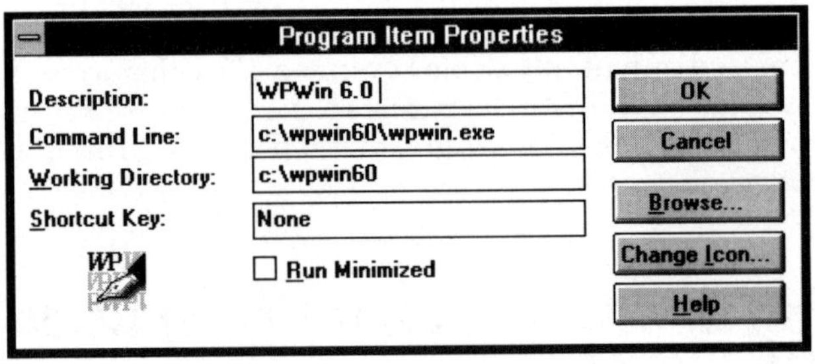

Figure 17-4:
Changing
the
properties of
the
WordPerfect
for Windows
program
icon.

Program Item Properties

<u>D</u>escription:	WPWin 6.0	OK
<u>C</u>ommand Line:	c:\wpwin60\wpwin.exe	Cancel
<u>W</u>orking Directory:	c:\wpwin60	
<u>S</u>hortcut Key:	None	Browse...
	☐ <u>R</u>un Minimized	Change <u>I</u>con...
		Help

6. **At the end of the <u>C</u>ommand Line box, type a space, then /m- and the name of your macro.**

   For example, to run a macro named OPEN3.WCM, you would add a space followed by this:

   ```
   /m-OPEN3.WCM
   ```

   The macro must be in your usual macros directory — otherwise, type its entire pathname.

7. **Choose OK.**

   The dialog box goes away.

8. **Double-click on the WordPerfect program icon to run WordPerfect and then the macro.**

   When WordPerfect is done loading, *Macro Play* appears on the status bar, and it runs your macro.

If you later decide that you don't want to run this macro automatically any more, follow the same steps, but remove the */m-macroname* that you added in Step 5.

Recycling macros

What if you have some macros that you (or someone else) created using an older version of WordPerfect? Well, some are converted automagically, and some will need work.

WPWin 5.2: Macros created using WordPerfect for Windows 5.2 should work just fine with no changes.

WPWin 6.0: If you use version 6.0a, macros created using version 6.0 work fine.

WP for DOS 5.1: For macros created in WP for DOS 5.1, you have to run a separate program, called MCVWIN. In the Windows Program Manager, choose File⇨Run, type **mcvwin**, and press Enter. The program should be in your C:\WPC20 directory — if Windows can't find it, use the File Manager to find it and type the entire pathname into the File Run box. MCVWIN asks you for the names of the macros to convert — type in the names and choose Convert.

Testing Macros

Every programmer knows that you can spend at least as much time testing a program as writing it in the first place, sometimes far more. The more complex the program, the more rigorous the testing. Also, a program with a mistake in it can do lots of damage, deleting information by accident. The same rules hold true for macros.

Here are some tips for making your macros "robust," as they say in the programming biz.

✔ Before you run an untested macro, be sure to save whatever documents you are working on. A untamed macro can type in the wrong places, format the wrong text, or give the wrong commands.

✔ If the cursor has to be in a particular position for the macro to work, include the commands to move it there. For example, if the cursor should be at the beginning of the line for the macro to work properly, press the Home key as the first command in the macro.

✔ If you can't figure out what is going wrong with a macro, record another one that performs just the first few commands, up to the point where the problem occurs. When this test macro stops, you may find that your cursor is in a different place than you expected or that some other condition is different.

The Ultimate Challenge — Fixing Broken Macros

What if your macro doesn't work right, and you need to change it? There are two approaches:

- ✔ Record the macro again, using the same name. WordPerfect asks if you want to replace the old macro with the new one — tell it "Yes."

- ✔ Edit the macro. Choose Tools➪Macro➪Edit from the menu bar, enter the name of the macro you want to edit, choose Edit again, and the macro commands appear on the screen. Next, get a degree in computer science to be able to understand them.

Seriously, editing macros is not for the faint of heart. The commands for a very simple macro (the one we made earlier, that formats one line as *Heading 1* and another line as *Heading 2*) look like this:

```
Application (A1; "WordPerfect"; Default; "US")
StyleSystemOn (Heading1Style!)
PosLineDown ()
PosLineDown ()
PosLineDown ()
StyleSystemOn (Heading2Style!)
PosLineDown ()
```

You can kinda make out what's going on, but it would take a lot of care and study to be able to write this stuff on your own. One parenthesis out of whack, one missing exclamation point, and Blammo! You get an error message from the macro compiler (the part of WordPerfect that reads the commands in a macro and figures out what to do).

To avoid macro problems, we recommend that you stick with recording macros, rather than editing them or typing in the commands from scratch. Life is too short to learn this kind of stuff!

Still curious about macros?

We've only covered the basics of writing and using macros. The WordPerfect reference manual doesn't say much more. If you want more information, including all the gory details of the programming language that macros use, read the special on-line help file about macros that comes with WordPerfect.

To read it, choose Help⇨Macros. You see the WP Macros Manual help file. It works just like all other Windows help files and contains tons of information on macro programming, including the terrifying details about each and every macro command.

Note: If WordPerfect can't find the macros help file, you probably didn't install it. To install it, exit from WordPerfect and double-click on the WPWin Install icon in Program Manager. Choose Custom, then Files, then Unmark All; then choose only WordPerfect Help Files. Then click on OK and Start Installation to install the macros manual.

Tip: Normally, the WP Macros Reference window insists on remaining in the foreground, on top of all other windows. If this annoys you as much as it annoys us, choose Help⇨Always on Top from the menu bar of the WP Macros Manual to remove this always-on-top setting.

Chapter 18
This Key Does What?

- -

In This Chapter

▶ Understanding keyboard definitions

▶ Using WordPerfect predefined keyboards

▶ Making your own keyboard definition

▶ Fooling with key assignments

▶ Making a key give a commands

▶ Making a key run a macro

▶ Making a key type some text

▶ Making a key run another Windows program

▶ Using a keyboard in a template

- -

Hey, I Already Have a Keyboard!

If you are like most of us, your computer has a keyboard. One keyboard. It contains a bunch of keys. You would think that that would be the end of the subject, but with WordPerfect, you would be wrong.

WordPerfect lets you decide what each and every key on the keyboard should do. For example, you can determine what happens when you press the *J* key. Most people prefer for the *J* key to type a *J* — we certainly do. But if you want it to type a *Q*, it's up to you.

Naturally, almost nobody actually changes which keys type which letters. But you might well want to change how key combinations work, like Ctrl+Shift+P or Alt+Shift+E. No problem — this chapter tells you how.

The Keys to the Kingdom

First, some definitions (we hate to throw boring definitions at you, especially this late in the book, but here are two useful ones).

- ✔ A *key assignment* is how you tell WordPerfect what one key does or what one combination of keys does. For example, the Ctrl+O key combination usually is assigned to display the Open File dialog box. You can assign any command, or any macro that you create, to any key.
- ✔ A *keyboard definition* is a full set of key assignments, one for each key on the keyboard, and one for each combination of keys with the Ctrl, Alt, and Shift keys.

Keyboard definitions you've already got

Wow! Sounds like a lot of work, deciding what all these keys should do. Luckily, WordPerfect comes with three (count 'em) keyboard definitions already defined:

- ✔ **Equation Editor Keyboard:** We've never used this, since we don't edit equations much. If you do, follow the instructions later in this chapter to take a look at this keyboard.
- ✔ **WPDOS Compatible:** If you are used to the DOS version of WordPerfect and are constantly confused by the key combinations used in Windows, try this keyboard definition. It defines the keys to work as much as possible like the keys in WordPerfect for DOS.
- ✔ **WPWin 6.0 Keyboard:** This is the keyboard definition that most WordPerfect users prefer. When you install WordPerfect, this definition is the one that is selected.

Throughout this book (and its predecessor, *WordPerfect For Windows For Dummies*), we assume that you are using the WPWin 6.0 Keyboard definition. For example, way back at the beginning of the first book, we told you that you can press Ctrl+S to save the current document, because this is the key assignment for Ctrl+S in the WPWin 6.0 Keyboard.

Where do keyboard definitions live?

WordPerfect stores a keyboard definition as part of a template. (Remember templates from Chapter 10?) In fact, for each template, you can define a different keyboard. If you have a template for creating newsletters, it can use a keyboard definition just for making newsletters, in which the styles the newsletter uses are assigned to convenient key combinations. If you have another template for creating press releases, it can contain a keyboard definition in which useful macros are assigned to keys. If you don't specifically define a keyboard with a template, the template uses the regular old default keyboard that you usually use.

The three keyboard definitions that come with WordPerfect are stored in the standard template, standard.wpt.

Well, enough theory. Let's take a look at these babies.

To do anything with keyboard definitions, choose File⇨Preferences from the menu bar, so that you see the Preferences dialog box. When you double-click on the Keyboard icon, you see the Keyboard Preferences dialog box, shown in Figure 18-1. This is Keyboard Mission Control.

WordPerfect lists all the keyboard definitions that are either stored in the template you are currently using or stored in your default template (which is usually standard.wpt). As you highlight each keyboard on the list, WordPerfect tells you (below the list) which template the keyboard is stored in.

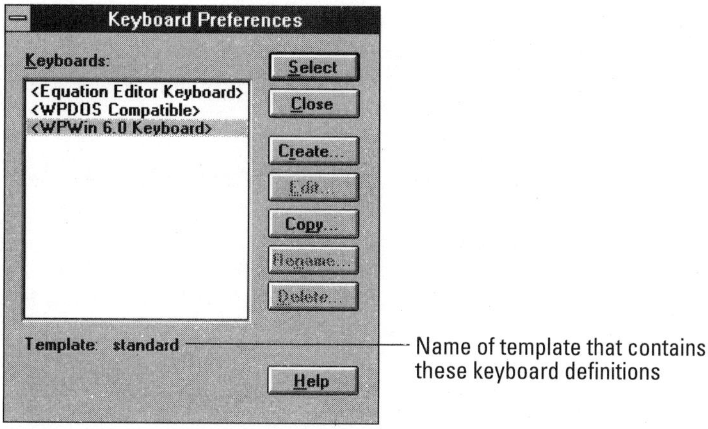

Figure 18-1:
Here are the keyboard definitions that come with WordPerfect, along with any new ones that you make.

Keyboard Preferences

Keyboards:
<Equation Editor Keyboard>
<WPDOS Compatible>
<WPWin 6.0 Keyboard>

Select
Close
Create...
Edit...
Copy...
Rename...
Delete...

Template: standard ——————— Name of template that contains these keyboard definitions

Help

Choosing a different keyboard definition

If you want to use a different keyboard definition, here's what to do:

1. **If you haven't already done so, choose File⇨Preferences from the menu bar and double-click on Keyboard.**

   You see the Keyboard Preferences dialog box shown in Figure 18-1.

2. **Choose a keyboard from the list.**

3. **Click on Select, then Close.**

Now all the dialog boxes are gone, and you are using the keyboard definition you chose. The keys on your keyboard work accordingly. You continue to use this keyboard definition until you either switch to another one or use a different template.

What if you have selected a keyboard definition and you don't like it? You can switch back to the WPWin 6.0 Keyboard by pressing Alt+Ctrl+Shift+Backspace.

Forging Your Own Keys

You can't change the three keyboard definitions that come with WordPerfect. It's probably just as well, since you might mess them up. Instead, you can copy them to create your own keyboard definitions, and then edit the copies.

Usually, it's a good idea to start with a copy of the WPWin 6.0 Keyboard definition, then modify it as you wish. However, you can start with a copy of *any* keyboard definition if you like (we'll tell you how later in this chapter).

Making a new keyboard definition

Here's the easiest way to create a new keyboard definition:

1. **If you haven't already done so, choose File⇨Preferences from the menu bar and double-click on Keyboard.**

   You see the Keyboard Preferences dialog box shown in Figure 18-1.

2. **Choose Create.**

   WordPerfect asks for the name to give to the new keyboard definition.

3. **Type the new keyboard name and choose OK.**

   WordPerfect creates the new keyboard definition, and you see the Keyboard Editor dialog box, as well as a little picture of a keyboard (are these graphics cute, or what?). Before you make any changes, the keyboard definition is an exact copy of the WPWin 6.0 Keyboard.

4. **Skip to the section "Fooling with the keys," later in this chapter, for instructions on how to make changes to the new keyboard you just created.**

Copying a different keyboard

Here's how to copy any keyboard definition so you can create a new one:

1. **If you haven't already done so, choose File⇨Preferences from the menu bar and double-click on Keyboard.**

   You see the Keyboard Preferences dialog box shown in Figure 18-1.

2. **Click on the Copy button.**

   You see the Copy Keyboard dialog box, shown in Figure 18-2.

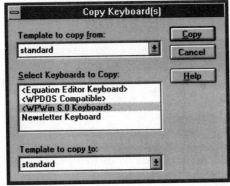

Figure 18-2: Making a new keyboard by copying one that's similar.

3. **If you want the keyboard definition to be in the same template that you are using, make sure that the Template to copy to is the same as the Template to copy from.**

4. **Choose the keyboard from the list that is most like the keyboard you want to make.**

   Make sure that one keyboard is selected from the list.

5. Choose **C**opy.

You see the Overwrite/New Name dialog box shown in Figure 18-3.

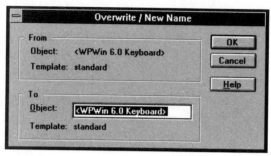

Overwrite / New Name

From
Object: <WPWin 6.0 Keyboard>
Template: standard

To
Object: <WPWin 6.0 Keyboard>
Template: standard

OK
Cancel
Help

6. **In the To O**bject box (actually, it's the only box on the dialog box), enter the name for the new keyboard definition.

7. **Choose OK.**

You return to the Keyboard Preferences dialog box, and your new keyboard definition is listed.

Editing a keyboard definition

Once you make your own keyboard definition, you can edit it like this:

1. **If you haven't already done so, choose F**ile⇨**Pr**eferences **from the menu bar and double-click on K**eyboard.

You see the Keyboard Preferences dialog box shown in Figure 18-1.

2. **Choose the keyboard you want to edit.**

You can't edit the three keyboard definitions that come with WordPerfect. Choose one that you copied.

3. **Click on the E**dit **button.**

You see the Keyboard Editor dialog box. You're ready to fool with some keys.

Fooling with the Keys

Once you see the Keyboard Editor, shown in Figure 18-4, you can make changes to your keyboard definition. Below it is a picture of your keyboard (more or less) as shown in Figure 18-5.

List of keys on keyboard, including key combinations

What the currently selected key does

Figure 18-4:
Who ever heard of editing a keyboard? Well, you can — you can decide what each key on the keyboard will do.

Keyboard Editor - Newsletter Keyboard

Choose a Key to Assign or Unassign

X+Alt+Shift
X+Alt+Ctrl
X+Alt+Ctrl+Shift
Y+Ctrl
Y+Ctrl+Shift
Y+Alt
Y+Alt+Shift
Y+Alt+Ctrl
Y+Alt+Ctrl+Shift
Z+Ctrl   Undo
Z+Ctrl+Shift   Undelete...
Z+Alt
Z+Alt+Shift
Z+Alt+Ctrl

Unassign

☐ Assignment Appears on Menu
☐ Allow Assignment to Characters

Assign Key To

◉ Activate a Feature
○ Play a Keyboard Script
○ Launch a Program
○ Play a Macro

Feature Categories:
File

Features:
Address Book...
Address to Merge
Button Bar Preferences...
Cancel
Close

Assign Feature

OK
Cancel
Help

Figure 18-5:
A darling picture of your keyboard, for use when editing your keyboard definition.

Newsletter Keyboard

To make changes to the keyboard definition, you choose the key or key combination that you want to assign meaning to, then you decide what kind of action it will cause, and then you give WordPerfect the specifics of exactly what the key should do. As it turns out, pressing a key can cause one of four kinds of actions (we'll describe exactly how to use each one later in this chapter):

- **Activate a Feature:** That is, run a WordPerfect command. For example, the Ctrl+S key combination usually activates WordPerfect's Save command (just like choosing File⇨Save from the menu bar).

- **Play a Keyboard Script:** That is, type a bunch of text. You can decide what text to type, of course. For example, if you want the Ctrl+Shift+N key combination to type your name, you can do it with a keyboard script.

- **Launch a Program:** That is, run another Windows program. For example, you could make Ctrl+Shift+C run the Windows Clock program.

- **Play a Macro:** That is, run a macro that you have already created. (Refer to Chapter 17 for how to make macros.)

Let's look at how to choose the key combination you want to change and how to make keys do each of these four types of actions.

Which key do you want?

WordPerfect shows a list of all the keys and key combinations that you can define. It's a long, long list. There are three ways to tell WordPerfect which key combination you want:

- Choose the key combination from the list. WordPerfect lists the function keys first, then letter-key combinations, then number-key combinations (using the number keys above the letters on your keyboard), then numeric-keypad combinations, and then miscellaneous punctuation and cursor-motion keys.

- Use the diagram of a keyboard shown in Figure 18-5. When you click on a key on the keyboard, WordPerfect automagically selects that key from the list. To choose a key combination, click on Ctrl, Alt, or Shift first, then the key you want. For example, if you click on the Ctrl key, then the Shift key, and then the P key, WordPerfect selects the Ctrl+Shift+P key combination from the list.

- Type the key or key combination. For example, if you press Ctrl+B, WordPerfect selects that combination. This doesn't work for all key combinations, though, particularly not for Alt-key combinations.

Some keys can't be reassigned, including Esc, Enter, Space, Tab, and Backspace. Makes sense to us.

Whatever you do, _don't_ choose the Allow Assignment to Characters box in the lower-left corner of the Keyboard Editor dialog box. If you choose this option, WordPerfect lets you assign meanings to plain, unadorned letter and number keys. For example, you could make the _P_ key play a macro. The problem here is that you would no longer have a way to type a _P_. Except under very unusual circumstances (like playing cruel practical jokes on your coworkers), leave this option alone.

Making a key give a command

Once you've told WordPerfect which key (or key combination) you want to use, you tell it what you want the key to do. Here's how to tell it to make the key give a command:

1. **Select the key or key combination you want to define in the Keyboard Editor.**

2. **Choose Activate a Feature.**

   If they weren't there before, WordPerfect displays two list boxes, named Feature Categories and Features.

3. **Choose the category of the feature (command) you want, using the Feature Categories box.**

   WordPerfect divides its commands into File, Edit, View, Insert, Layout, Tools, Graphics, Table, Window, Help, Navigation, Selection, and SubMenus. The first ten correspond to the commands on the menu bar, and the others include other commands.

   When you choose the category, WordPerfect displays that category's commands in the Features box.

4. **Choose the command from the Features box.**

   When you select a command, its description appears at the bottom of the dialog box.

5. **Click on the Assign Feature button.**

   WordPerfect assigns the command to the key combination, and it appears in the key list.

Making a key run a macro

If you want a key combination to run a macro, here's what to do:

1. **Select the key or key combination you want to define in the Keyboard Editor.**

2. **Choose the Play a Macro option.**

3. **Click on the Assign Macro button.**

   A dialog box appears to ask you which macro you want to assign. The macro must already exist and should be in your macro directory. (See Chapter 17 for how to make a macro.)

4. **Type in the macro name, or click on the little folder icon to choose from the macros in your macro directory.**

5. **Choose Select.**

   WordPerfect asks if you want to save the full pathname of the file that contains the macro, or only the filename.

6. **If the macro is in your macro directory, you can choose No. Otherwise, choose Yes.**

   WordPerfect assigns the macro to the key combination, and the macro name appears next to the key combination in the list.

Making a key type some text

If you want a key or key combination to type some text, here's what to do:

1. **Select the key or key combination you want to define in the Keyboard Editor.**

2. **Choose the Play a Keyboard Script option.**

   WordPerfect displays a little box in which you can type the text.

3. **Type the text in the box.**

   For example, if you want the key to type your name, then type your name in the box. Include spaces and punctuation. You can even press Enter to start a new line.

4. **Make sure that the key you want to assign this text to is still selected.**

   If you've pressed any key combination since Step 1, the key selected may have changed.

5. **Choose <u>A</u>ssign Script.**

WordPerfect assigns the text to the key combination. The first word of the text appears in the list of keys and key combinations.

Making a key run another Windows program

For the truly ambitious, you can make a key run a Windows program. You have to know the filename of the program. Here's how to do it:

1. **Select the key or key combination you want to define in the Keyboard Editor.**
2. **Choose the <u>L</u>aunch a Program option.**
3. **Click on the <u>S</u>elect File button.**

WordPerfect lets you choose a program file.

4. **Choose a program file, either by typing its full pathname or by selecting it from the directory and file listings.**
5. **Click on OK.**

WordPerfect displays the name of the program next to the key combination in the list of keys and key combinations.

If you want to run a program but you don't know its filename, choose its icon from the Windows Program Manager and press Alt+Enter. Make a note of the command line, which is the full pathname of the file that contains the program. Then press Esc or choose Cancel so that you don't change the icon's definition.

Making a key meaningless

If you don't want a key or key combination to have a meaning, you can unassign it. Choose the key, and choose the <u>U</u>nassign button. WordPerfect removes the assignment. Pressing the key combination now does nothing.

All done fooling with keys?

When you are done changing the key assignments in your keyboard definition, choose OK. Then click on <u>C</u>lose from the Keyboard Preferences dialog box. You can edit the keyboard definition again whenever you want. Click on <u>C</u>lose in the Preferences dialog box.

Using a Keyboard in a Template

If you have made a template (as explained in Chapter 10), you can tell WordPerfect to use a particular keyboard definition with that template. For example, if you make a newsletter template, you can make a keyboard that has key assignments for stuff you do when creating a newsletter — like a key assignment for each of the newsletter's styles.

Here's how to use a keyboard definition in a template:

1. **Create the template, or edit it if you have already created it.**

   Refer to Chapter 10 for details. Make sure that you can see the Template Feature Bar.

2. **If you haven't already created the keyboard definition that you want to use with the template, make it now.**

   Choose Create Object from the Feature Bar and choose Keyboard. WordPerfect shows you the Keyboard Preferences dialog box. Follow the instructions in the sections "Making a new keyboard definition" and "Fooling with the Keys" to create the definition. Click on Close in the Keyboard Preferences dialog box when you are done.

3. **If you have already made the keyboard definition you want to use, but it's not in the right template, choose Copy/Remove Object from the Feature Bar.**

   You see the Copy/Remove Template Objects dialog box, shown in Figure 18-6.

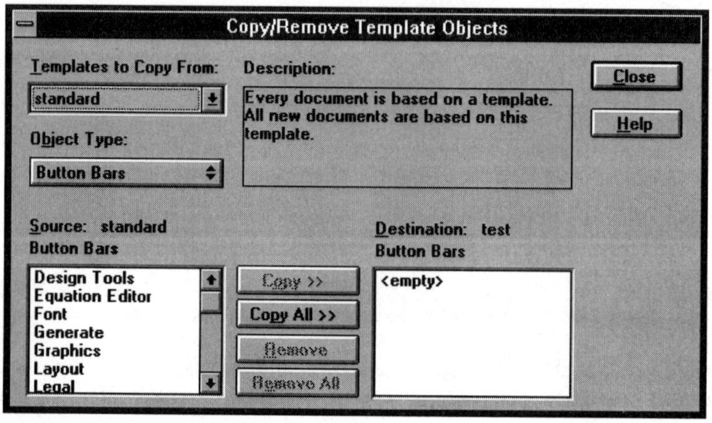

Figure 18-6:
You can
copy
keyboard
definitions,
Button Bars,
and other
things from
one
template to
another.

Copy/Remove Template Objects	
Templates to Copy From:	**Description:**
standard	Every document is based on a template. All new documents are based on this template.
Object Type:	
Button Bars	
Source: standard	**Destination: test**
Button Bars	**Button Bars**
Design Tools / Equation Editor / Font / Generate / Graphics / Layout / Legal	<empty>

Buttons: Close, Help, Copy >>, Copy All >>, Remove, Remove All

For the Templates to Copy From setting, choose the name of the template that contains the keyboard definition. Choose Keyboards for the Object Type setting. Choose the keyboard definition name from the Source list, and click on the Copy button to copy it to the current template. Then click on Close.

4. Choose Associate from the Feature Bar.

WordPerfect shows you the Associate dialog box, shown in Figure 18-7.

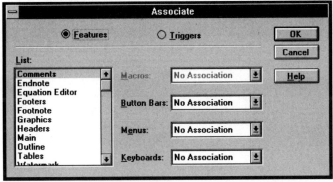

Figure 18-7: Here's how to tell WordPerfect which keyboard definition to use with this template.

5. To tell WordPerfect which keyboard definition to use for general editing when using this template, choose Main from the List.

Actually, you can associate different keyboard definitions to the various editing windows that WordPerfect uses, but this sounds way too confusing for our tastes.

6. From the Keyboards list, choose the keyboard definition you want to use.

The one that you created or copied in Step 2 or 3 should be on the list.

7. Click on OK.

Our favorite key assignments

We use styles a lot, and we like to make assigning styles easy. When we create a template, we also create a macro for each style that we use frequently. Then we assign each of these macros to a key combination in the keyboard definition for that template. For example, if we use the styles *Heading 1, Heading 2,* and *Heading 3* a lot in a particular template, we make macros named HEADING1, HEADING2, and HEADING3 that apply the styles to the current paragraph. Then we assign these macros to the key combinations Ctrl+1, Ctrl+2, and Ctrl+3.

Using key assignments and macros, it takes just one keystroke (assuming that you don't count Ctrl and 1 separately) to apply a style to a paragraph.

Chapter 19

Customizing Your Button Bar

● ●

In This Chapter

▶ Where does the Button Bar appear?

▶ Making your own Button Bar

▶ Making buttons run macros, give commands, type text, or run other Windows programs

● ●

*I*n *WordPerfect For Windows For Dummies*, we told you how to choose which Button Bar WordPerfect displays above your document (check the section "The button bar" in Chapter 20). Now we're ready to go further and talk about how to use different Button Bars in different templates, as well as how to make your own buttons.

By the way, if you've gotten to this advanced topic, we figure that you are out to get some serious work done. So we'll dispense with the obligatory jokes about buttons and bars. By now, you can make up better ones than we can anyway.

The Floating Button Bar

Before we talk about different Button Bars and the buttons that are on them, how about changing where on the screen the Button Bar appears? You're used to seeing it horizontal, just below the menu bar. But you have some other choices:

▸ At the bottom of the WordPerfect window

▸ Vertical, with the buttons running down the left or right side of the WordPerfect window

▸ In a clump, in a floating window that you can position anywhere

To move the Button Bar, use the mouse to point to a blank area on the Button Bar, so that the mouse pointer appears as a hand. Then drag the Button Bar to its new location.

- ✔ If you drag the Button Bar to the left or right side of the WordPerfect window, the Button Bar appears vertically on that side.

- ✔ If you drag the Button Bar to the top or bottom of the WordPerfect window, the Button Bar appears horizontally in that location.

- ✔ If you drag the Button Bar to the middle of the document window, it appears as a floating clump of buttons (referred to artistically in the WordPerfect manual as a *palette*).

Another way to change the location of your Button Bar is by using the Button Bar Options dialog box, described in the next section.

Creating a New Look for Your Button Bars

You can change the appearance of all of your Button Bars by setting your Button Bar preferences.

1. **Choose File⇨Preferences from the menu bar, and double-click on the Button Bar icon.**

   You see the Button Bar Preferences dialog box, shown in Figure 19-1.

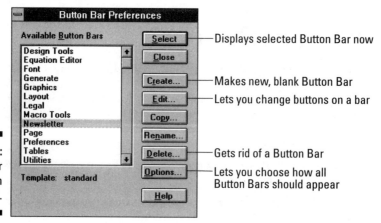

Figure 19-1:
Button Bar
Mission
Control.

Button Bar Preferences

Available **B**utton Bars

Design Tools
Equation Editor
Font
Generate
Graphics
Layout
Legal
Macro Tools
Newsletter
Page
Preferences
Tables
Utilities

Template: standard

Select —— Displays selected Button Bar now
Close
Create... —— Makes new, blank Button Bar
Edit... —— Lets you change buttons on a bar
Cop**y**...
Re**n**ame...
Delete... —— Gets rid of a Button Bar
Options... —— Lets you choose how all
Button Bars should appear
Help

2. Choose Options.

You see the Button Bar Options dialog box, shown in Figure 19-2.

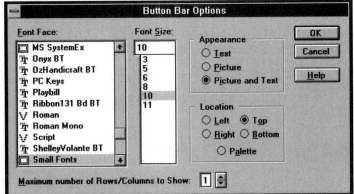

Figure 19-2:
How do you
want all
Button Bars
to look?

3. Choose the font you want to use for the text on the buttons, using the Font Face list.

WordPerfect normally uses the Small Fonts font for buttons. If you find the text too small, try MS FixedSys or MS Sans Serif.

4. Choose the font size from the Font Size list.

This font size isn't measured in points, the way fonts in your document are. We're not sure what the measurement means — maybe the height in screen dots? The Small Fonts font isn't available in larger than size 11, so switch to another font if you want larger letters. WordPerfect adjusts the size of the buttons and truncates the text as you change fonts and font sizes.

Note: When you choose a font from the Font Face list, WordPerfect lists the available sizes in the Font Size list.

5. If you want the buttons to show only the text, not pictures, choose Text in the Appearance area of the dialog box. To show pictures only, choose Picture. To show both, choose Picture and Text.

6. To change the location of the Button Bar (as described in the preceding section), you can choose Left, Right, Top, Bottom, or Palette from the Location area of the dialog box.

7. **If you want the Button Bar to expand to two rows (or two columns, if you display it vertically), set the Maximum number of Rows/Columns to Show to 2.**

   WordPerfect expands the Button Bar only if there are too many buttons to fit in one row (or column).

8. **When you are done, click on OK, then Close to return to the Preferences dialog box. Click on Close again to dismiss it.**

The changes you make to your Button Bar preferences apply to *all* Button Bars, not just the one you are currently using.

Buttoning Your Own Bar

You can make your own Button Bars, with whatever combination of buttons you want. Later in this chapter, we tell you how to create new buttons, too.

Like keyboard definitions, Button Bars are stored as part of a template. Each template can contain one or more Button Bars.

Here's how to make a new Button Bar:

1. **Choose File⇨Preferences from the menu bar and double-click on the Button Bar icon.**

   You see the Button Bar Preferences dialog box (refer to Figure 19-1), listing all the Button Bars that exist in the current template. If you're using a template other than the default template (standard.wpt), the dialog box lists the Button Bars in the default template, too.

2. **Click on the Create button.**

   WordPerfect asks you to name the new Button Bar.

3. **Enter a name for the Button Bar and click on OK.**

   In the WordPerfect window, the Button Bar that was there disappears, to be replaced by a new, totally blank Button Bar. You also see the Button Bar Editor dialog box, shown in Figure 19-3.

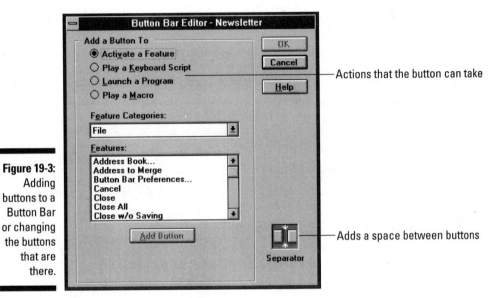

Actions that the button can take

Adds a space between buttons

Figure 19-3:
Adding
buttons to a
Button Bar
or changing
the buttons
that are
there.

Sewing on buttons

If you read Chapter 18, you know that keys can do four kinds of actions. It turns
out that buttons on a Button Bar can do the same four types of things:

- ✔ **Activate a Feature:** This runs a WordPerfect command, like Save or Open
  or Print.

- ✔ **Play a Keyboard Script:** This types a bunch of text. You can decide what
  text to type.

- ✔ **Launch a Program:** That is, run another Windows program.

- ✔ **Play a Macro:** This runs a macro that you have already created. (See
  Chapter 17 for how to make macros.)

The next four sections show you how to make buttons that do these four types
of things. To make these buttons, you must be using the Button Bar Editor
dialog box, shown in Figure 19-3. If it's not on your screen, choose
File⇨Preferences, select the Button Bar you want to create the key in, and click
on Edit.

Making a button that gives a command

It's easy to make a button that gives a command:

1. **Choose Activate a Feature option from the Button Bar Editor dialog box.**

   WordPerfect divides its commands into File, Edit, View, Insert, Layout, Tools, Graphics, Table, Window, Help, Navigation, Selection, and SubMenus. The first ten correspond to the commands on the menu bar, and the others include other commands.

2. **Choose a category from the Feature Categories box.**

   When you choose the category, WordPerfect displays the commands in that category in the Features box.

3. **Choose the command from the Features box.**

   When you select one, its description appears at the bottom of the dialog box, along with the graphics that will appear on the button.

4. **Click on the Add Button.**

   WordPerfect adds the button to the Button Bar, complete with a cute little icon.

Making a button that runs a macro

You can use a button on the Button Bar to run a macro. The macro must already exist (see Chapter 17 for how to create a macro).

1. **Choose Play a Macro option from the Button Bar Editor dialog box.**

2. **Click on the Add Macro button.**

   A dialog box appears, asking which macro you want to assign. Remember, the macro must already exist and should be in your macro directory.

3. **Type in the macro name or click on the little folder icon next to the Name box to choose from the macros in your macro directory.**

4. **Choose Select.**

   WordPerfect asks if you want to save the full pathname of the file that contains the macro, or only the filename.

5. **If the macro is in your macro directory, you can choose No. Otherwise, choose Yes.**

   WordPerfect adds a button to your Button Bar. The name of the macro appears on the button.

Making a button that types some text

If you want to make a button that types some boilerplate text, like the closing to a letter or the name and address of your organization, here's how:

1. **Choose Play a Keyboard Script option from the Button Bar Editor dialog box.**

   WordPerfect displays a little box in which you can type the text.

2. **Type the text in the box.**

   For example, if you want the key to type your name, then type your name in the box. Include spaces and punctuation. You can even press Enter to start a new line.

3. **Click on the Add Script button.**

   WordPerfect adds a new button to the Button Bar and uses the first word of the text you typed as the name of the button. Don't worry — you can change it — see the section "Button, Button, Who Changed the Button?" later in this chapter.

Making a button that runs another Windows program

If you want a really fancy button, you can make one that runs another Windows program. You need to know the filename of the program.

1. **Choose Launch a Program option from the Button Bar Editor dialog box.**

2. **Click on the Select File button.**

   WordPerfect lets you choose a program file.

3. **Choose a program file, either by typing its full pathname or by selecting it from the directory and file listings.**

4. **Click on OK.**

   WordPerfect creates a button for the program. It may even display a version of the same little icon that the program uses in Windows Program Manager.

Swapping buttons, throwing them out, and leaving spaces

Here are ways to spiff up your Button Bar while you are using the Button Bar Editor dialog box:

- ✔ To get rid of an unwanted button, drag it off of the Button Bar. The mouse pointer changes to an adorable little picture of garbage landing in a wastebasket.
- ✔ To switch the order of the buttons, just drag them around on the Button Bar.
- ✔ To leave a little space between buttons, drag the Separator from the lower-right corner of the Button Bar Editor dialog box to where you want it on the Button Bar. These spaces are useful for separating buttons into groups.

Done adding buttons?

When you are, you can make the pile of dialog boxes on your screen go away by clicking on the OK button on the Button Bar Editor dialog box, then Close, then Close again.

Button, Button, Who Changed the Button?

Actually, there are two things you can edit: a whole Button Bar (like changing the order of the buttons) or an individual button on a bar (like changing its label or icon). Either way, you use the Button Bar Editor dialog box, shown back in Figure 19-3.

Messing with a Button Bar

To make changes to an existing Button Bar, either one that came with WordPerfect or one you made yourself, choose File➪Preferences from the menu bar and double-click on the Button Bar icon. Choose the Button Bar you want to modify and click on Edit. Once again, you see the Button Bar Editor dialog box.

There's a faster way to edit the Button Bar that is currently on-screen: Click the right mouse button on the Button Bar and choose Edit from the QuickMenu.

Messing with one button

When you are editing a Button Bar, you can even edit the way individual buttons look. This is a good thing, since buttons that run macros or type text can look a bit funky if you don't improve them.

Here's how to edit a button:

1. **Edit the Button Bar that contains the button (click on the Button Bar with the right mouse button, and choose Edit).**

2. **Double-click on the button you want to change.**

   You see the Customize Button dialog box, shown in Figure 19-4.

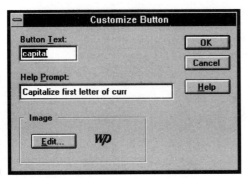

Figure 19-4:
What do you want to do to this button?

3. **To change the text that appears on the button, edit the text in the Button Text box.**

   Keep it short. Those buttons are small. Buttons look better if the text uses initial capital letters.

4. **To change the help prompt that appears in the title bar when the mouse points at the button, edit the text in the Help Prompt box.**

5. **To edit the icon image that appears on the button, click on the Edit button.**

   You see the Button Bar Image Editor, shown in Figure 19-5. Choose the color you want to fill in (by clicking on the color you want), and then click on the image to draw squares of that color. Figure 19-5 shows other ways to edit the icon.

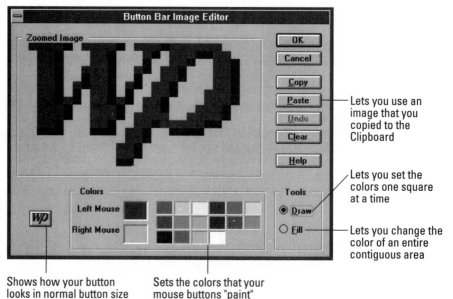

Figure 19-5:
Button Bar
icons look
crude when
you blow
them up.

Lets you use an
image that you
copied to the
Clipboard

Lets you set the
colors one square
at a time

Lets you change the
color of an entire
contiguous area

Shows how your button
looks in normal button size

Sets the colors that your
mouse buttons "paint"

6. **When you are done editing the icon, choose OK.**

   You return to the Customize Button dialog box.

7. **When you are done making changes to the button, choose OK.**

   You return to the Button Bar Editor dialog box.

8. **When you are done making changes to the Button Bar, click on the OK button. If dialog boxes are still open, click on the Close button until they go away.**

Using Button Bars with Templates

If you have made a template (as explained in Chapter 10), you can tell WordPerfect to use a particular Button Bar with that template. For example, if you make a newsletter template, you can make a Button Bar with buttons for stuff you do when creating a newsletter, like creating graphics boxes and applying styles.

Here's how:

1. Create the template or edit it if you have already created it.

To create a template, choose File⇨Template from the menu bar, then choose Options⇨Create Template. To edit a template you already created, choose File⇨Template from the menu bar, then choose Options⇨Edit Template. Refer to Chapter 10 for details. You should see the Template Feature Bar.

2. If you haven't already created the Button Bar that you want to use with the template, choose Create Object from the Feature Bar and choose Button Bar.

WordPerfect shows you the Button Bar Preferences dialog box. Follow the instructions in the section "Buttoning Your Own Bar," earlier in this chapter, to create the Button Bar. Click on Close in the Button Bar Preferences dialog box when you are done.

3. If you have already made the Button Bar you want to use, but it's not in the right template, choose Copy/Remove Object from the Feature Bar.

You see the Copy/Remove Template Objects dialog box, shown in Figure 19-6.

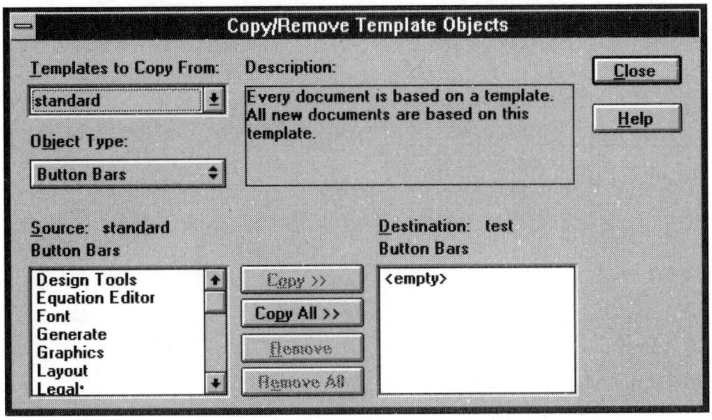

Figure 19-6:
You can copy keyboard definitions, Button Bars, and other things from one template to another.

Copy/Remove Template Objects
Templates to Copy From: standard
Description: Every document is based on a template. All new documents are based on this template.
Object Type: Button Bars
Source: standard Button Bars	Destination: test Button Bars
Design Tools, Equation Editor, Font, Generate, Graphics, Layout, Legal	Copy >>, Copy All >>, Remove, Remove All	<empty>
Close	Help

For the Templates to Copy From setting, choose the name of the template that contains your Button Bar. Choose Button Bars from the Object Type pop-up box. Choose the Button Bar name from the Source list, and choose Copy to copy it to the current template. Then click on Close.

4. Choose Associate from the Feature Bar.

WordPerfect shows you the Associate dialog box, shown in Figure 19-7.

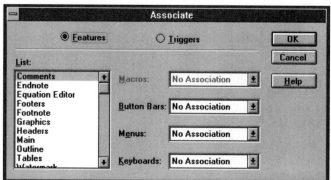

Figure 19-7:
Here's how
to tell
WordPerfect
which
Button Bar
to use with
this
template.

5. **To tell WordPerfect which Button Bar to use for general editing when using this template, choose Main from the List.**

   Actually, you can associate different Button Bars with the various editing windows that WordPerfect uses, but this sounds way too confusing for our tastes.

6. **From the Button Bars list, choose the Button Bar you want to use.**

   The Button Bar that you created or copied in Step 2 or 3 should be on the list.

7. **Click on OK.**

Now this Button Bar appears whenever you use the template.

Chapter 20

Hyped-Up Text

. . . .

In This Chapter

▶ The hype about hypertext

▶ Going places with a "hot" word or button

▶ Getting back from where you went

▶ Making hypertext work better by using macros

. . . .

*W*hen you read something that references a topic you know nothing about, do you ever wish that you could just press a button and read about that topic? Well, us neither. We are just curmudgeonly enough to like nice, printed, bound books that just sit there. Especially since that's the kind of books our publisher prints.

But we grudgingly admit that the idea of pressing a button to read more about something has a certain appeal to it, and we suppose that if we're reading a document on a computer that's already got lotsa buttons and stuff, then a few more buttons wouldn't kill us. And, further, we admit that for serious business-type reading, this push-button reference may even be a good, time-saving idea. Of course, you first have to be happy with the idea of reading stuff on a computer, not on paper. Nobody's figured out how to put electronic buttons on a piece of paper. Yet. Except for Hallmark and their talking greeting cards.

While it's reasonably simple to do hypertext, it's pretty tricky to do it well. Doing it well involves dealing with some technical stuff that is very much like programming. The further you read in this chapter, where we talk about doing things well, the more technical it gets.

What Good Is It, Anyway?

What would you do with a feature, popularly called *hypertext*, where you can click on a word or labeled button and read more about the topic? Consider, if you will, a product guide for a company's sales trainees. The poor shmucks don't know a "turbo agitation prosthesis" from a "vortex reversal armature," and the training manual is full of references to this stuff. They'd love to be able to click on the words they don't recognize and read a description of the whatever, then return right to the main document.

Of course, in the reference document, there could be references to yet more documents and more references within those, *ad confusium*. That's one of the big challenges of using this hypertext thing: keeping people from getting hopelessly lost in "cyberspace" (this vast array of electronic documents) with no hope of ever returning to the original document.

You, too, can enter the exciting, hyperkinetic world of hypertext by creating hypertext *links* between ordinary documents in WordPerfect. (In fact, you've already used this sort of feature if you've ever used Help in WordPerfect or any other Windows software. You just click on a word in green, or a button, and pwfzap! You're reading something different.) If the people you're writing for all have WordPerfect — and especially if you're all using WordPerfect on a network — you can impress the heck out of people by linking corporate reference material together with hypertext. And maybe even help them.

However ... and this is a big however ... *everybody* has to have access to WordPerfect, because that's the only way to read these documents unless you print them out. It is very unlikely that another brand of word processor will be able to translate WordPerfect hypertext documents into its own hypertext document format. It's possible, but then so are lower taxes. Don't count on it.

The idea of hypertext was invented by Theodor H. Nelson way back in the early 1970s, believe it or not. The guy's a visionary — he was also involved in the invention of word processing itself. It's time he got some credit for his invention!

The hottest new hypertext application is on the Internet and is called the World Wide Web, a system of pages of hypertext that are stored on computers all over the world.

A Few Rounds on the Hypertext Links

The only special thing about documents that use hypertext is that there are certain words in the document which, if you click on them, cause WordPerfect to jump to another point in that or some other document. In order to give these words their special ability, you create hypertext *links* between these words and another document or a particular place in the same document.

Sometimes these words that the reader clicks on are called *hot words*. Hot words can be anywhere in the document: the body, the footnotes, the headers — wherever. The words generally have some special formatting so that the reader can tell that they're "hot." Unless you tell it otherwise, WordPerfect formats the hot words green and underlined.

To change the formatting of hot words, use the <u>S</u>tyle button on the Hypertext Feature Bar. See the following section, "Fooling with Links — the Hypertext Feature Bar."

If you want a really high-tech appearance, you can make the hot word look like a labeled button (actually, a form of text box). This button appearance is a little distracting if the hot word is in the body of the text, so it's better to put these buttons somewhere else, like in the margins or just under a section heading (see Figure 20-1).

Figure 20-1: What hypertext looks like. Underlined words are hot words in the text that give more information. The button format is used here for other actions.

> Quit
>
> The Forbisher Co.
> ## Interactive Sales Training Manual
> by Fred Forbisher, III
>
> Welcome to the Forbisher Interactive Sales Training Manual! Modern technology helps keep this manual perpetually up-to-date. When you see a word in green and underlined, you can click on it for more information. Buttons labeled "Back" in the document will return you to this document. "Quit", above, exits the manual. Following are topics covered in this manual:
>
> - The <u>sales cycle</u> of <u>framistats</u>
> - Qualifying a sale
> - The sales cycle of <u>interdigitated</u> framistats

Making a link

Hypertext links are actually pretty simple to make. There are three basic kinds:

1. Links to a particular place in the same or another document

2. Links to another document — no particular place

3. Links that don't necessarily take the reader anywhere, but run a macro instead. (See Chapter 17 for more information on macros.)

To do the particular-place kind of link (1)., you need to first create a bookmark in the place you want the reader to jump *to*. If you don't know how to do that, check out the following sidebar. You don't need a bookmark to jump to the beginning of another document or to run a macro from a hot word or button.

TOOTORIAL

Bookmarks for hypertext

When you want the reader to jump to a particular place in a document, you need to mark that place with a bookmark. Here's how:

1. **Click in the place you want the readers to jump to.**

   If you want the readers to jump to another document, open that document and click someplace there. This place should probably be at the beginning of a heading or other line summarizing the topic, so the readers know what they're reading about when they arrive there.

2. **Choose Insert⇨Bookmark; then click on Create in the Bookmark dialog box that appears.**

   The tiny Create Bookmark dialog box swings into action. It helpfully (sort of) suggests a

Bookmark Name, made up of a few words copied from your document just after the cursor position. Change this name if it doesn't help you remember what this part of the document is about; then click on OK.

Now you're all set to create a link to this bookmark. If you later need to find this bookmark, delete it, or change its name, use the Insert⇨Bookmark command again (even though you're not inserting anything at this point) to open up the Bookmark dialog box. Click on the bookmark name in the Bookmark List and choose Go To, Delete, or Rename. To move the bookmark, click in the new location *first*, before you use the Insert⇨Bookmark command. *Then* select the bookmark name and click on Move.

Here's how to create a hypertext link and its associated hot word or button:

1. **Select the word or phrase that the reader will click on in order to jump.**

2. **Choose Tools⇨Hypertext from the menu bar.**

   The Hypertext Feature Bar appears at the top of the WordPerfect window. See the next section, "Fooling with links — the Hypertext Feature Bar" for more information on it.

3. **Click on the Create button in the Feature Bar.**

   The Create Hypertext Link dialog box appears.

4. **Specify where the link is "to."**

   If you're making a link to a bookmark in the same document, click on the down-arrow next to the box on the line labeled Go To Bookmark to see a full list of bookmarks. Click on the one you want.

   If you're making a link to another document, click on the button labeled Go To Other Document. You must enter the document's full filename and path in the box to the right of that label. You can type this stuff in, but it's safer to use one of WordPerfect's file selection dialog boxes: Click on the button with the file folder icon to get one of these dialog boxes and choose a file.

   If you're making a link to a bookmark in that other document, specify that bookmark's name in the box labeled Bookmark. Click on the down-arrow on the right of the box to see a full list of bookmarks.

5. **If you want the hot word (the one you selected in Step 1) to be a button instead of specially formatted text, click on the Button button (who's got the button?) at the bottom of the dialog box.**

6. **Click on OK.**

   WordPerfect leaves a Hypertext Feature Bar on your screen. Leave it there for now — you may need it.

7. **Save your work with Ctrl+S.**

   Or perhaps save it under a new name using F3. That way, if you've messed up the document, you won't hurt the original.

If you don't save your work now, WordPerfect will ask you if you want to save your work when you test your link. If this happens, answer Yes, or WordPerfect will toss your carefully crafted link into the bit bucket.

Fooling with links — the Hypertext Feature Bar

Yes, as *Mad Magazine* might put it, here's "another furshlugginer Feature Bar," as shown in Figure 20-2. The darned thing pops up every time you use the Tools⇨Hypertext command. Apart from the Create button, what good is it?

Figure 20-2:
Yawn ... another Feature Bar.

Well, if you find it utterly annoying and useless, get rid of it, for heaven's sake. Click on Close. But we suggest you leave it up until you've got your links running well.

When you're fooling with a hypertext link, don't try to select the hot word or button by clicking on it with the mouse. All you will do is execute the hypertext jump! Very frustrating. Instead, carefully click just after the hot word, then hold down the Ctrl and Shift buttons and press the left-arrow navigation key on the keyboard to highlight the word.

Like most Feature Bars, the Hypertext Feature Bar lets you fool with one thing at a time ("things" in this case being hypertext links). If you have more than one link in your document, it's helpful to figure out which link the Feature Bar thinks it's working on. To be sure, click on Next and then (unless WordPerfect is on the last macro and tells you it can't find any more) click on Previous. The cursor appears next to the hot button or word the Feature Bar is currently thinking about. Next takes the Feature Bar to the next hot button or word; Previous, to the preceding one.

Here's what the other buttons do:

- **Perform:** Just the same as clicking on the hot button or word in the document: Perform executes the hypertext jump.
- **Back:** Used after a hypertext jump, Back takes you back where you came from. See "Getting back home," following.
- **Edit:** Edit lets you fool with the stuff you set up when you created the link in the first place. See the preceding "Tootorial."

- ✔ **Delete:** Delete blows away the current link altogether. In some early versions of WordPerfect 6.0, Delete may blow away other things, too — like text! Use Ctrl+Z to undo any goof-ups.

- ✔ **Deactivate:** Deactivate temporarily turns off all hypertext links; jumps no longer work, although buttons and hot words are still visible. To restore the jumping ability, click on this same button, which is then labeled Activate.

- ✔ **Style:** In case you don't like green and underlining, Style lets you change the formatting associated with a hot word. This button brings up the Styles Editor dialog box, with the Hypertext style ready to be edited. See Chapter 10 for more information on the Styles Editor dialog box.

  If you've got a hot button, not a hot word, and you want to change its style, you must edit the Button graphics style. Choose Graphics⇨Graphics Styles from the menu bar, double-click on the Button style, and you get the Edit Box Style dialog box discussed in Chapter 6. You can treat this style like most other graphics, editing the border, fill, or size. You can even change the content to, say, use a picture icon instead of a word.

Testing your link

The moment of truth or consequences has now arrived. It's time to test your little wormhole in cyberspace and see if you end up where you had hoped to.

Click on the hot word (in green, underlined) or hot button you just created. WordPerfect should jump to the document or bookmarked point you chose.

If, instead of jumping, you get an error-message box, check your link by clicking on the Edit button of the Hypertext Feature Bar. (If you closed this bar already — and we've closed many bars, ourselves — reopen it by choosing Tools⇨Hypertext from the menu bar.) The Edit button gives you a dialog box identical to the one you used to create the link. If you're jumping to another document, make sure you have specified the full path of the file (probably starting with **C:** or **D:** and ending in the filename with its .WPD extension).

If you move a linked document (a document that the reader is supposed to jump to in a hypertext link), WordPerfect won't be able to find the document. Make sure that no one moves the linked document from the original directory that you specified in the Create Hypertext Link dialog box.

If the jump works, your cursor appears at the bookmarked point (or the start of the other document, if that's the kind of link you created.) If the jump is to another document, what actually happens is that WordPerfect closes the first document and opens the new one.

Take a moment to admire your cleverness. Now take a moment to ask yourself the question, "If I'm so darned clever, how do I get back to where I was?"

Getting back home

The first time one of us went sailing (and we won't say which one of us), we went happily cruising downwind in a tiny Sunfish, out of a bay, in the wake of a bunch of friends in a larger sailboat. These so-called friends then happily forgot all about this little tagalong and proceeded to the open sea, where Sunfish must not go. Of course, the hapless pilot of this tiny craft had given no consideration to how to find the way back home. Or how to dodge cruise ships in the narrow channels. Or even how to sail upwind. Needless to say, many terrifying and sunburned hours followed. With this moral lesson firmly in mind, let us avoid leaving your hapless hypertext reader in similar (if less sunburned) straits.

With hypertext, there is a way back, but your reader has to use the Hypertext Feature Bar, and this is definitely not a great solution. To go back, your reader must click on the Back button on the Hypertext Feature Bar. Fortunately, if the Hypertext Feature Bar was on the screen before the jump, then it's still there. If the Feature Bar isn't there, your reader has to choose Tools⇨Hypertext from the menu bar to get the Feature Bar. As best we can tell, the Feature Bar approach works no matter how many jumps the reader makes — it eventually takes the reader back to the original document or location.

One trouble with having your readers use the Hypertext Feature Bar is that you have to make sure that the Feature Bar is on their screens and that they know enough to use the Back button. You can try to make sure it's on their screens by saving the initial document with the Feature Bar on. It's quite possible that your readers may accidentally close the Feature Bar and save the changed document, however, leaving subsequent readers up the creek without a Feature Bar.

The other trouble is that the Feature Bar also lets your readers do things like Edit and Delete your hypertext link. Because of these kinds of problems, we've come up with what we think is a better solution: See "Better ways to get back home," following.

Better ways to get back home

Here are two good solutions to the problem of getting your readers back home, other than letting them use the Hypertext Feature Bar. The first one is pretty simple; the second one requires more technical work.

✔ Create a new hypertext button or hot word in the destination location or document that takes the reader back to the original location or document. Call it "Go Home" or something like that. That way, if readers have been jumping around several documents or locations with hypertext, they know this button doesn't just back them up to the last place they've been, but takes them all the way back to the place where they started.

✔ Create a new hypertext button or hot word called something like "Back Up" that secretly runs the Hypertext Feature Bar's <u>B</u>ack function without putting the Feature Bar up on the screen. Creating this new button involves using the third type of hypertext link we mentioned earlier but you've probably forgotten about: running a macro. See the next section, "Hypertext and Macros," for more information.

For the purpose of getting back home, hot buttons are actually better than hot words. See Step 5 in the preceding "Tootorial" on making hypertext links for information about creating a button.

Place these hot buttons so that the reader knows they exist and can find them easily, like at the beginning of the document. (You can put them in a header or footer, but remember that headers and footers aren't visible in draft view.) To make a hot button that isn't in the middle of a line of text, just put the word that you're using for the hot button label on a separate line. Use the <u>L</u>ayout⇨<u>L</u>ine command to center a hot button or make it flush with the right margin.

Hypertext and Macros

Here's the news in a nutshell: You can run a macro from a hypertext hot word or button. (If you're not already familiar with macros, you should probably take a look at Chapter 17.)

Besides being a cute approach to executing macros, the ability to run a macro by clicking on a hypertext button can also help make your hypertext work better. That's what we're going to focus on here.

Running macros from hypertext

The difference between a regular hypertext link and one that runs a macro is pretty simple: When you create the link in the Create Hypertext Link dialog box, you use the Action called <u>R</u>un Macro rather than Go To <u>B</u>ookmark or Go To Other <u>D</u>ocument.

Here's how to create a hypertext link that runs a macro:

1. **Create your macro.**

   You have to do this first. See Chapter 17 if you need a refresher. See stuff after this Tootorial for suggestions about things you can have your macro do.

2. **Select the word or phrase that the reader will click on in order to jump.**

3. **Choose Tools⇨Hypertext from the menu bar.**

   The Hypertext Feature Bar appears at the top of the WordPerfect window.

4. **Click on the Create button in the Feature Bar.**

   The Create Hypertext Link dialog box appears.

5. **Specify the macro you want to run.**

   Click on the button labeled Run Macro. You must enter the macro's full filename and path in the box to the right of that label. You can type this stuff in, but it's safer to use one of WordPerfect's file selection dialog boxes: Click on the button with the file folder icon to get one of these dialog boxes and choose a macro file. Usually macros are stored in the directory `C:\WPWIN60\MACROS`, or `Macro Directory` in the QuickList.

6. **If you want the hot word (the one you selected in Step 1) to be a button instead of specially formatted text, click on the Button button at the bottom of the dialog box.**

7. **Click on OK.**

   WordPerfect leaves a Hypertext Feature Bar on your screen. Leave it there for now — you might need it.

8. **Save your work with Ctrl+S.**

   Or perhaps save it under a new name using F3. That way, if you've messed up the document, you won't hurt the original.

Now, when you click on the hot word or button, the macro runs. That's it.

Why run macros from hypertext buttons?

The question that ought to be in your mind at this point is how on earth (or the planet of your choice) is this at all useful for really doing hypertext? Put one finger in Chapter 17 to refresh your memory on macros as you go. Here are a few ideas for things you may do:

✔ Show multiple documents at once. Instead of creating a real hypertext link to a destination document, open the destination document with the macro; then you can show both the original document and the destination one at the same time by executing <u>W</u>indow⇨<u>T</u>ile with the macro. Have a hypertext button labeled "Close" in the destination document; it would execute a macro that closes the destination document and expands the original one to fill the window (Alt+-, then Alt+X).

✔ Create a "Print" hypertext button that prints out a referenced document rather than displaying it. The macro would execute a <u>F</u>ile⇨<u>P</u>rint⇨<u>D</u>ocument on Disk command, then type the filename of the document, and finally, <u>P</u>rint.

✔ Create a "Go Back" button that invisibly runs the <u>B</u>ack feature of the Hypertext Feature Bar. Referring to Chapter 17, record a macro that executes a <u>T</u>ools⇨<u>H</u>ypertext command. Then edit the macro. Choose <u>T</u>ools⇨<u>M</u>acro⇨<u>E</u>dit from the menu bar, enter the name of the macro you want to edit, choose <u>E</u>dit again, and the macro commands appear on the screen. Delete every line but `HypertextReturnFrom ()`. Click on the Op<u>t</u>ions button in the Macro Feature Bar and choose <u>C</u>lose Macro. You're asked if you want to save your changes to the macro; choose Yes.

Making Hypertext Work

Hypertext is a way-cool 90's sort of high-tech feature, but don't get carried away. If people get lost or confused, they won't have anything to do with your hypertext hobby. Here are a few hints and reminders to keep you squared away:

✔ Create a "main" document to which all the others are subordinate. Don't create a tangle of cross-references with no clear top or beginning.

✔ Always give the reader at least a "Go Back" button that is easy to find and use.

✔ Don't cross-reference enormous documents. They take too long to load.

✔ If you are familiar with "file protection," don't be too hasty to protect your hypertext files; the file protection gets in the way of easy use. Instead, keep a backup copy of your files in case somebody zaps them.

✔ If you're really serious about hypertext, create a macro that turns off the WordPerfect menu bar and buttons when someone starts your hypertext document. This gives people an uncluttered screen and discourages editing of your files. Create a button that executes a macro giving the command Alt+Shift+F5. Call it "Start Hypertext" or something like that to ensure that people use it.

Part V
Shortcuts and Tips Galore

The 5th Wave   **By Rich Tennant**

In this part ...

What a long, strange trip it's been.

Here we are at Part V; we've touched on everything from book bindings to multimedia, and there's still stuff to talk about! Here you'll find hints on various and sundry, including some nifty new things in release 6.0a of WordPerfect, shortcuts like clever macros to automate your work, and tips on where to find yet *more* information on WordPerfect. Gee, maybe it's time for *Yet More WordPerfect For Windows For Dummies*!

Chapter 21
Cute Tricks

*H*ere's a roundup of other nifty things that you can do with WordPerfect, along with some things that are new in version 6.0a.

QuickCorrect

We don't konw about yuo, but we maek a certain numbr of typing mistaeks. A hot new feature in WordPerfect 6.0a, called QuickCorrect, has changed our lives. QuickCorrect silently corrects many of our typos, without complaining to us about it. We have gotten so used to this feature that we now get annoyed at other programs that don't have it.

Here's how to tell WordPerfect about your favorite typos:

1. Choose Tools⇨QuickCorrect from the menu bar.

You see the QuickCorrect dialog box, shown in Figure 21-1. It already contains a long list of the most popular typos in American English, as compiled by that crackerjack WordPerfect Corp. staff.

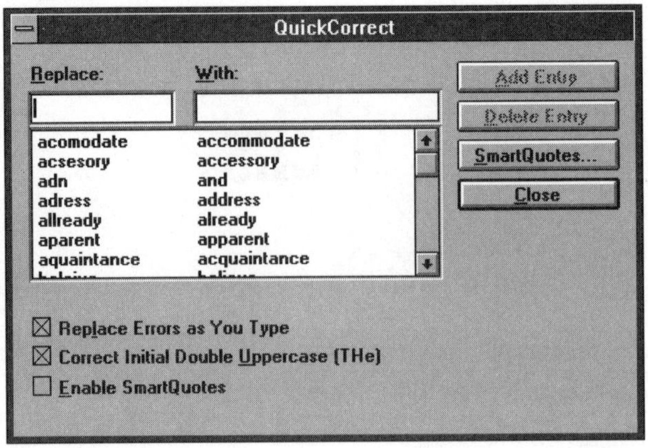

Figure 21-1:
WordPerfect's
favorite
typos.

2. **To add a favorite typo of your own, type the typo in the Replace box, type the correct spelling in the With box, and click on the Add Entry button.**

   The Replace box can contain only a single word. The With box can contain multiple words. For example, you may frequently type *inthe* instead of *in the*.

3. **Make sure that the Replace Errors as You Type box is selected (that is, contains an X).**

4. **If you frequently capitalize the first *two* letters of words, instead of just the first letter (we do — our fingers aren't as fast off the Shift key as they used to be), make sure that the Correct Initial Double Uppercase box is selected, too.**

5. **If you want to use real quotes, instead of straight quotes, select the Enable SmartQuotes box.**

   Straight quotes are the ones that are vertical — many people call them *inch marks*. Real quotes are the ones that slant one way for the opening quote and the other way for the closing quote. They look much classier.

6. **When you are done, click on Close.**

Now, as you type, WordPerfect corrects your words. It waits until you type the space, punctuation, or carriage return after the word, then checks to see if the word is a typo on its list. If the word is on its list, WordPerfect makes the correction without bothering you about it.

You can also use QuickCorrect to expand abbreviations. For example, if you have to type *WordPerfect for Windows* a lot, you can tell WordPerfect to replace *wfw* with *WordPerfect for Windows*.

What Changed in This Document?

If you write by committee (as we do), others may revise your finely crafted prose (like ours). When you get the edited version of your document back, you may want to see what changed.

Comparing two documents

Here's how to compare the edited version to your original version of your document:

1. **Open the newer (edited) version of your document.**

2. **Choose File⇨Compare Document from the menu bar and then choose Add Markings.**

   You see the Add Markings dialog box, shown in Figure 21-2.

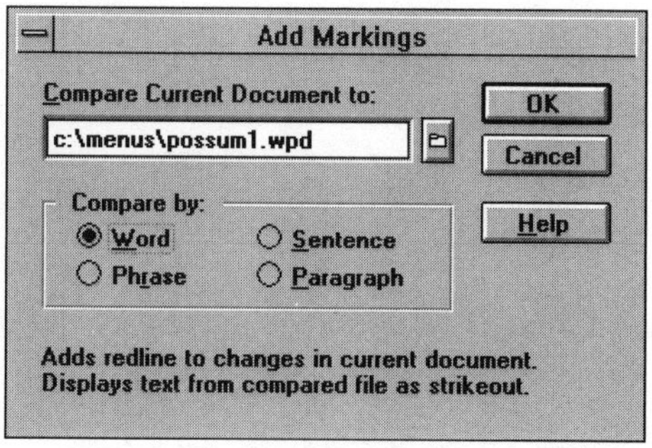

Figure 21-2: WordPerfect can tell you what changes have been made to your perfect prose.

Add Markings
Compare Current Document to:
c:\menus\possum1.wpd
OK   Cancel   Help
Compare by:
⦿ Word   ○ Sentence
○ Phrase   ○ Paragraph
Adds redline to changes in current document. Displays text from compared file as strikeout.

3. **Choose Word, Phrase, Sentence, or Paragraph.**

   This choice tells WordPerfect whether to compare the documents word by word, phrase by phrase (a phrase ends with a comma or other punctuation), sentence by sentence, or paragraph by paragraph. We always choose Word.

4. **In the Compare Current Document to box, type the filename of the original version of the document or choose it by clicking the little folder icon.**

   If you leave the name of the current document in the box, WordPerfect compares the version you are editing to the version stored on disk.

5. **Click on OK.**

WordPerfect displays a message while it compares the documents. Then you see the edited document with redlining and strikeouts to indicate what text has been deleted or added. Text that has been added appears in red, and text that has been deleted appears struck out (that is, with a line through it). Text that has been moved is enclosed in comments that tell you about it.

Looking at the changes

Once you have compared the documents, you can take a look at the changes. If you don't like the text that was added, you can delete it! If you want to keep text that has been struck out, you can remove the strike-out codes, using the Reveal Codes window (you see StkOut codes surrounding the text).

Don't worry about removing the red color from the text you want to keep, or about removing the struck-out text you want to delete — WordPerfect can do that for you.

Removing the markings

When you've decided which changes to accept, do the following to un-red the redlined text and delete the struck-out text:

1. **Choose File⇨Compare Document⇨Remove Markings from the menu bar.**

   You see the Remove Markings dialog box, shown in Figure 21-3.

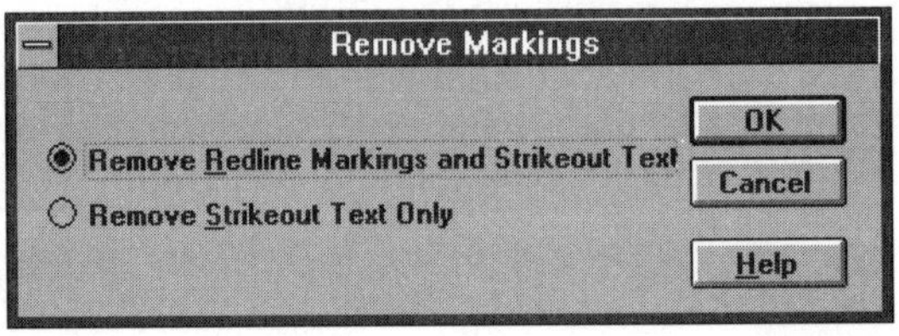

Figure 21-3:
Which
changes do
you want
WordPerfect
to make?

Remove Markings

◉ Remove Redline Markings and Strikeout Text
○ Remove Strikeout Text Only

OK
Cancel
Help

2. Click on OK.

When you compare documents, WordPerfect doesn't compare the contents of graphics boxes, headers, footers, watermarks, or comments. Check 'em yourself.

Getting Your Text Organized with an Outline

Old Mrs. Bottlenose, your sixth grade English teacher, always used to nag you to use an outline when you wrote. She made you hand in outlines so that she could check them for quality and wholesomeness before you wrote the actual essay she had assigned. Of course, since then you probably haven't gotten within 20 yards of an outline.

However, for writing long documents or documents whose structure may change, outlines are actually terrific. And WordPerfect can help you make them. To use WordPerfect's outlining feature, choose Tools⇨Outline from the menu bar. You see the Outline Feature Bar, shown in Figure 21-4.

Figure 21-4:
Yet another Feature Bar, this one for organizing text into an outline.

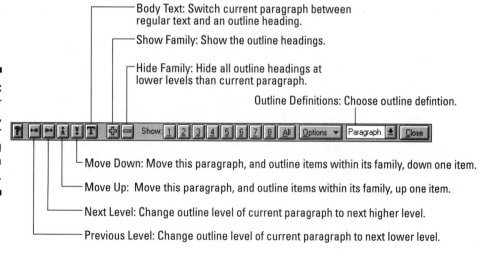

Body Text: Switch current paragraph between regular text and an outline heading.

Show Family: Show the outline headings.

Hide Family: Hide all outline headings at lower levels than current paragraph.

Outline Definitions: Choose outline defintion.

Move Down: Move this paragraph, and outline items within its family, down one item.

Move Up: Move this paragraph, and outline items within its family, up one item.

Next Level: Change outline level of current paragraph to next higher level.

Previous Level: Change outline level of current paragraph to next lower level.

Outlining theory

As you remember from sixth grade, outlines are arranged with major and minor headings. The first-level headings — the most important headings — are usually numbered with capital roman numerals (like *I.*). The second-level headings — the next-most important — use capital letters (like *A.*). The third-level headings use small roman numerals (like *i.*), and the fourth-level headings use small letters (like *a.*). The more important a heading, the *higher level* it is. WordPerfect uses the term *family* to mean an outline heading and all the lower-level headings just under it.

You can also have just plain text under any level heading. In fact, nine out of ten sixth grade teachers (and our editors!) insist that there should be some text after *every* heading, no matter what its level.

WordPerfect tells you what level heading each paragraph is by displaying little symbols in the left margin. Numbers indicate the heading level, a *T* indicates just plain text (see Figure 21-5). A plus-sign after the number means that the outline heading has subheadings beneath it.

Plain old body text

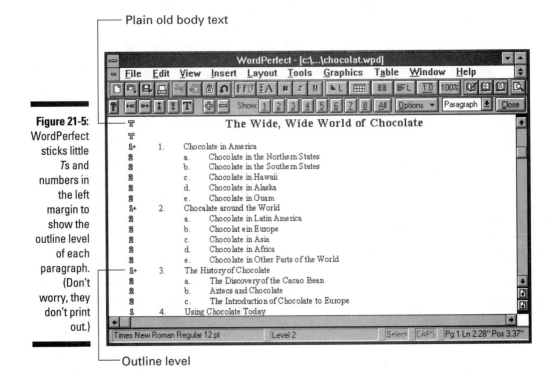

Figure 21-5: WordPerfect sticks little *T*s and numbers in the left margin to show the outline level of each paragraph. (Don't worry, they don't print out.)

Outline level

WordPerfect automatically assigns styles to outline headings — *Level 1* to first-level headings, *Level 2* to second-level headings, and so forth. You can change the styles that it uses and the way headings look — read on.

Outlining practice

Here's how to apply the theory of outlines to your WordPerfect document, using the Outline Feature Bar:

- ✔ To make a heading, just type the line of text and press Enter. If WordPerfect thinks it's text (it has a *T* in the left margin), click on the Body Text button on the Feature Bar to make it a heading. (The Body Text button is a toggle — you click it to switch between body text and headings.) Then use the Previous Level and Next Level buttons on the Feature Bar to set it to the right outline level.

- ✔ To type just plain text (not a heading), just type the text. If WordPerfect thinks that it's a heading (it has a number in the left margin), click on the Body Text button to switch it to body text.

- ✔ To see just the headings of your document, choose the number on the Feature Bar that corresponds to the most minor-level heading you want to see. For example, if you want to see first-level, second-level, and third-level headings, click on the 3 button in the Feature Bar.

- ✔ To see all the headings and the body text of your document, choose the All button on the Feature Bar.

- ✔ To change the way outline headings are formatted, you can change the definitions of their styles (usually *Level 1, Level 2,* and so on). Choose Layout⇨Styles from the menu bar. If you can't see the level styles on the styles line, choose Options⇨Setup and make sure that the System Styles box is checked. See Chapter 10 for information on editing styles.

- ✔ If you want to use other types of numbers for your headings, choose a different outline definition from the Outline Definitions box in the Feature Bar (it usually starts out set to Paragraph). If you don't like any of the options, you can define your own — choose Outline, then Define Outline from the Feature Bar.

- ✔ If you want additional text at the end of the document, which is not included in the outline, move your cursor to where you want the outline to end and choose Options from the Feature Bar, then End Outline, then Close.

Moving WordPerfect to Another Machine

If you need to remove WordPerfect from your computer (presumably because you are getting a different computer), version 6.0a comes with a nice new feature — Uninstall. Double-click on the WPWin Install icon in Program Manager, or stick the Install 1 diskette into your diskette drive, choose File⇨Run from the Program Manager menu and type **a:setup** (or **b:setup** if the diskette is in Drive B). You see the WordPerfect Setup dialog box, shown in Figure 21-6 (it's different from the one you see if you have version 6.0).

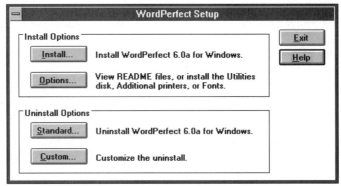

Figure 21-6:
It's easy to remove WordPerfect from your old machine when you move to a new one.

If you want to remove the WordPerfect program, choose Standard from the Uninstall Options area of the dialog box. To remove only certain parts of the program (for example, the thesaurus, if you never use it), choose Custom. WordPerfect removes not only the files in its own program directories, but the files that were installed in your Windows program directory (and maybe other places — who knows?).

More about Version 6.0a

If you are using WordPerfect for Windows 6.0, it is worth getting version 6.0a. It's a little faster, the WordPerfect folks fixed some problems, and — most importantly — they added the QuickCorrect feature described at the beginning of this chapter.

Another reason to get version 6.0a is that it's free to registered WordPerfect for Windows 6.0 users (at least it is within the United States). Just call 800-321-4566 (to talk to a human being) or 800-228-1157 (to talk to a machine) and be prepared to read them your license number. Or write to WordPerfect Corp., 1555

North Technology Way, Orem, UT 84057-2399. If you are calling from outside the U.S., call WordPerfect's international department at 801-226-6800, or contact the local WordPerfect office (addresses are listed in Appendix F of the WordPerfect manual).

There's a bunch of new stuff in Version 6.0a; most of it you probably won't care about. Here are a few of the more useful things, in our opinion. (Some we've already mentioned in earlier chapters.)

- **Fonts:** Click the Font Face button on the Power Bar and WordPerfect shows you the last four fonts you used, displayed at the top of the font list. This way, if you're constantly switching between, say, Arial 12-point italic and Times Roman 10-point bold, you don't have to change all these settings in the Font dialog box. (If you don't see the Font Face button on your Power Bar, you can add it — see Chapter 20, "Improving WordPerfect's Behavior," in *WordPerfect For Windows For Dummies*.)

- **Graphics:** You can now save a WP Draw graphic as a separate graphics file; choose File⇨Save As in WP Draw.

- **Import/Export:** You can now convert Professional Write and Lotus 1-2-3 Version 4.0 spreadsheet files. If your database supports Open Database Connectivity (ODBC), you can import or link your database information through WordPerfect. (Check your database manual to see if it knows about ODBC.)

- **Transition Advisor:** If you've been using your old word processor for years and recently switched to WordPerfect, the Transition Advisor helps you find the equivalent features in WordPerfect. Choose Help⇨Transition Advisor.

- **Network Stuff:** You can now use Novell and Universal Naming Conventions (UNC) in place of path and filenames. This is a method of referring to files and directories that are anywhere on your local area network, not just on your own hard disk. (We don't really know what these fancy names look like, but if you are a network administrator, you will.)

Chapter 22

Our Favorite Macros

● ●

In This Chapter

▶ Macros you'll want to make for yourself

▶ Macros that come with WordPerfect for Windows

● ●

*1*n Chapter 17, we told you how to make and run a macro. Without becoming a member of the dreaded species of programmers, you can really speed up repetitive work in WordPerfect by using macros.

Here are some of our favorite macros. First, there are some macros that almost everyone ends up making — such as a macro that types your name and address. Then we list our favorites among the macros that come packaged with WordPerfect.

Macro-It-Yourself

Here are popular macros that many people create for themselves:

- ✔ A macro that types the closing to a standard business letter, including the *Yours truly* line, the blank lines, your name, your title (if you use one in your letters), and anything else you type at the end of a letter. Alternatively, you can create a letter template that contains this stuff (see Chapter 10).

- ✔ A macro that saves the current document, prints one copy of it on the default printer, and closes the document. This is really handy.

- ✔ A macro that types a long, complicated phrase. Alternatively, you can use the QuickCorrect feature (new in version 6.0a) to allow you to type a few letters and have WordPerfect "correct" it to the long phrase. (See Chapter 21).

- ✔ A macro that types your name and address. You never know when you're going to need it in a document.

One Macro, to Go

In addition, WordPerfect for Windows comes with a bunch of prewritten macros that do all kinds of nifty things. Here are some of our favorites (listed by filename, omitting the .WCM extension). To run any of them, choose Tools⇨Macro⇨Play from the menu bar (or press Alt+F10), enter the name of the macro, and choose Play.

ALLFONTS

This macro makes a document listing every font available to the current printer and some sample text in each font. Open a new, blank document before running it. The result looks like Figure 22-1 (at least it does if you have an elderly HP DeskJet).

CAPITAL

This macro capitalizes the first letter of the current word. If the first letter or the whole word is already capitalized, it doesn't do anything.

CLIPBRD

This macro runs the Windows Clipboard Viewer program, which displays the current contents of the Clipboard. Handy.

Figure 22-1:
The
ALLFONTS
macro
shows you
the fonts
that your
printer can
handle.

CLOSEALL

This macro closes all of your open documents. It displays the dialog box shown in Figure 22-2 to find out which documents to save.

Figure 22-2:
Which
documents
do you want
to save,
asks the
CLOSEALL
macro.

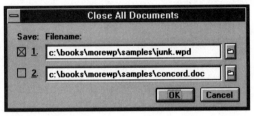

FILESTMP

(File Stamp) This macro puts the filename of the current document in a header or footer. This macro displays its own little dialog boxes, allowing you to choose which header or footer the filename appears in, and gives you instructions to save the document when the macro is done. Before running this macro, move your cursor to the top of the first page on which you want the header or footer to appear.

PAGEXOFY

This macro puts *Page x of y* (or other pagination formats) in a specified position on the page. It displays a cute little dialog box (shown in Figure 22-3) that lets you tell it where to put the page numbers and exactly how to format them. It doesn't matter where your cursor is when you play this macro — it sticks the page numbering codes at the beginning (where they belong).

After you play this macro, if you edit the document so that the number of pages changes, you must play the macro again. Nothing looks dumber than a page numbered *Page 6 of 5.*

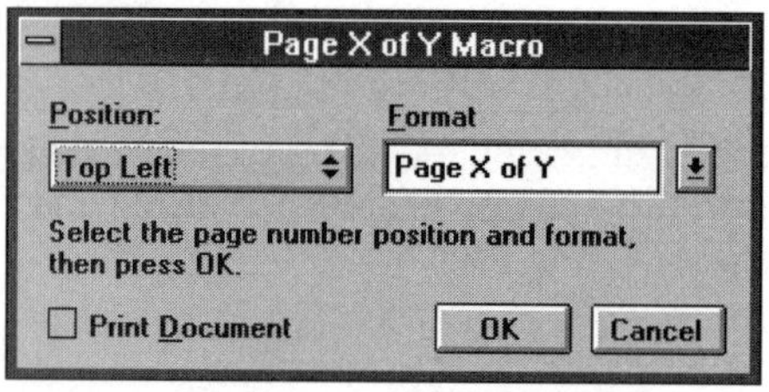

Figure 22-3:
The
PAGEXOFY
macro
displays this
dialog box.

Figure 22-3:
The
PAGEXOFY
macro
displays this
dialog box.

> **Page X of Y Macro**
>
> Position: Format
> [Top Left]   [Page X of Y]
>
> Select the page number position and format,
> then press OK.
>
> ☐ Print Document   [OK] [Cancel]

REVERSE

This macro creates white text on black, gray, or colored background.

- ✓ If your cursor is sitting in some regular old text when you run the macro, it reverses the current word.

- ✓ If you select some text first, it reverses the text you selected.

- ✓ If you want to reverse a whole paragraph, move your cursor anywhere in the paragraph and choose the Apply attributes to the whole Paragraph setting.

- ✓ If your cursor is in the cell of a table, it reverses the cell, as well as offering you some other table-related options.

It displays the dialog box shown in Figure 22-4 (or a similar one if your cursor is in a table). Super-cool!

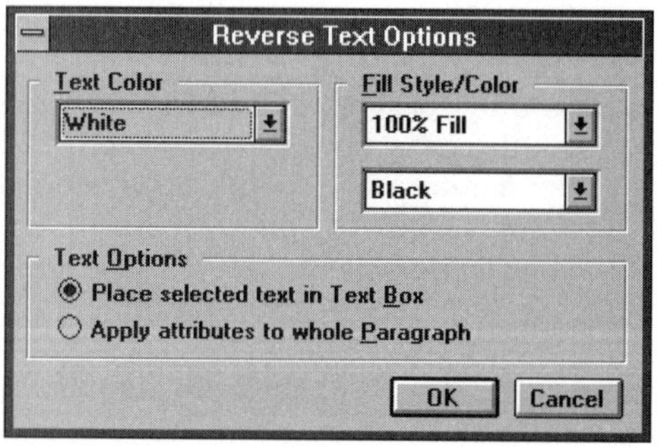

Figure 22-4:
Fancy
macros can
display their
own dialog
boxes, like
this one
from the
REVERSE
macro.

> **Reverse Text Options**
>
> Text Color   Fill Style/Color
> [White]   [100% Fill]
>   [Black]
>
> Text Options
> ● Place selected text in Text Box
> ○ Apply attributes to whole Paragraph
>
>   [OK] [Cancel]

SAVEALL

This macro displays almost the same dialog box shown back in Figure 17-6 to find out which documents to save. It's just like the CLOSEALL macro, except it doesn't close the documents after saving.

TRANSPOS

This macro switches the two characters just before the cursor. Some people transpose letters all the time, and this macro is a godsend.

Chapter 23

More Sources of Inside Information

"*W*hat the heck is going on?" This cry is heard hundred, nay, thousands of times a day throughout the world by the users of WordPerfect (not to mention all the other fine programs that run on personal computers.) The WordPerfect Corp. provides a wealth of information over the phone, including technical support and faxes that contain the answers to frequently asked questions. Check out the beginning of your WordPerfect manual for the phone numbers — there are pages of them. You might also look at the README.WP file in the WordPerfect program directory (usually C:\WPWIN60).

However, you may need to fall back on other sources of information if you need an unbiased view of the product, or help at odd hours, or general inspiration and encouragement. This chapter lists both printed and on-line information that is specifically about WordPerfect for Windows.

The Magazine

WordPerfect Corp. produces a magazine especially about WordPerfect for Windows. Not too surprisingly, it is entitled *WordPerfect for Windows Magazine*. It's a little rah-rah (in fact, sometimes we think we are paying to receive a monthly advertisement), but it does contain useful tips and tricks. As of this writing, the magazine costs $24 per year.

To subscribe:

WordPerfect for Windows Magazine
Circulation Dept., MS 3232
1555 N. Technology Way
Orem, UT 84057-9912
801-228-9626
Fax: 801-221-8449
Internet: *wpwinmag@wordperfect.com*

You can also get most of the information in *WordPerfect for Windows Magazine* on-line — see the next section.

On-Line

To use on-line services, such as CompuServe and WordPerfect's own bulletin board system (BBS), you need a modem, a phone line, and a terminal program. You certainly have the last item since Windows comes with one — Windows Terminal. Other on-line services, like SpaceWorks, provide their own terminal programs.

If you haven't used on-line services before, you might want to refer to *Modems For Dummies* (Tina Rathbone, IDG Books Wordwide).

WordPerfect's BBS

To dial directly into WordPerfect's own BBS, get your computer to dial 801-225-4414 (for modems that can communicate only at 1200 or 2400 baud) or 801-225-4444 (for 9600 baud modems). You can use this BBS to ask questions of the technical support folks and to get their answers.

Once you make the phone call and your modem connects, follow the instructions on the screen to register as a BBS user (this is free). Then the BBS displays the main menu, shown in Figure 23-1. You can ask questions, read press releases, or download text files and programs. When you are done, press *g* (for *Good-bye*) to log off.

Although the bulletin board is free to use, you'll be paying long-distance telephone charges to lovely Orem, Utah.

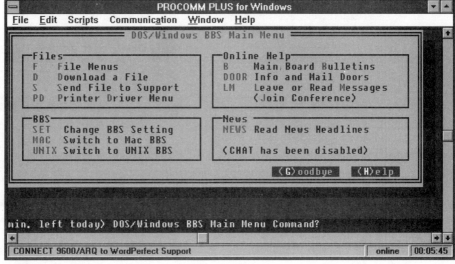

Figure 23-1:
WordPerfect's
own bulletin
board
system
displays this
main menu.

CompuServe

CompuServe is a dial-up service for which you pay by the hour. It has a wide array of services, including e-mail to the Internet, on-line chatting with other users, and games, but for our purposes you are interested in two *forums:*

- ✔ **WPFILES:** WordPerfect Corporation's official forum, in which they provide files you can download. However, don't bother asking questions here, because no one is listening.

- ✔ **WPUSERS:** The WordPerfect technical support forum. Interestingly, it is *not* run by WordPerfect, but by Support Group, Inc., a private company independent of WordPerfect Corp. You can ask questions, and you get quick (usually within a day or so), fairly accurate, and friendly replies. When we wrote this book, section 5 of the forum was specifically for WordPerfect for Windows, but this may change.

You can also send CompuServe mail messages to WordPerfect Corp. The address to use to suggest product enhancements is 73447,754.

To access CompuServe, you can use a regular terminal program, like Windows Terminal, or you can use a program designed specifically for use with CompuServe. CompuServe provides two such programs: WinCim (which is faster but racks up higher connect charges) and CSNav (which lets you gather your messages, hang up, and then read them later when you are not paying by the minute). Other programs, like TapCis (which runs under DOS) and WigWam (which we use — see Figure 23-2), are also available right on CompuServe. To download WigWam directly from CompuServe, type **go ukcomp** (because a British company wrote it) when you are on-line with CompuServe. To download TapCis, type **go tapcis.**

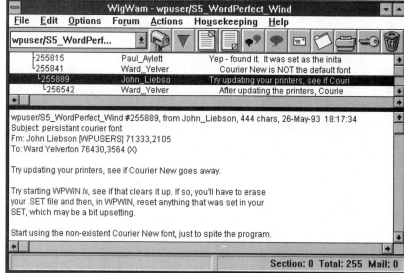

Figure 23-2:
Getting on-
line support
for
WordPerfect
from a
bunch of
technical
hotshots.

You can buy WinCim and CSNav directly from CompuServe (they're cheap). Type **go wincim** or **go csnav** when you are on-line with CompuServe.

You'll also need an account. Within the U.S., call the CompuServe membership sales number and talk to a human being by dialing 800-848-8199 (or 614-457-0802). CompuServe will be happy to send you a free sign-up kit. CompuServe has modem access numbers all over the U.S. and in many other countries, so you can frequently reach CompuServe with a local call from where you are.

If you have problems, you can also call 800-848-8990 (or 614-457-8650), another voice line. Once you know how to connect to CompuServe, you can get help with CompuServe itself by typing **go questions** or **go helpforum** while you are on-line.

SpaceWorks

SpaceWorks is another on-line information service that charges by the hour.
Luckily, any time you spend getting information about WordPerfect is free
(amazing!). Although using the WordPerfect support part of the SpaceWorks
service is free, you still have to give them a credit card when you sign up, in
case you use any of their other services.

To get an account, call 800-5-SPACE-5 (that's 800-577-2235). They send you
special Windows communication software with which you access their system,
along with instructions for installing it and the phone number of their location
nearest you.

Once you follow their instructions for enrolling, you can call up, connect, and
choose the WordPerfect Technical Support forum (Figure 23-3). It contains a list
of open bug reports and enhancement requests, a question-and-answer area,
and a library of files that may be useful.

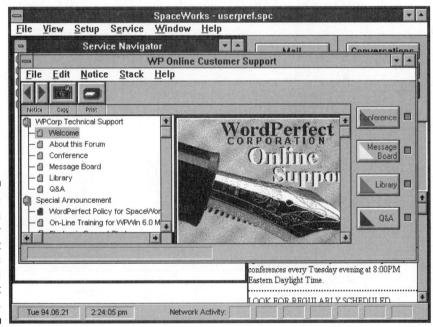

Figure 23-3:
SpaceWorks
is another
service that
provides
information
about
WordPerfect.

The Internet

Well, we don't know of any fancy Internet sources of WordPerfect information, but you can certainly send e-mail to the WordPerfect support folks via CompuServe. To suggest product enhancements, mail your message to _73447.754@compuserve.com_. To let us know how you like this book, use the address _dummies@iecc.com_.

The magazine on-line

For information about how to get _WordPerfect for Windows Magazine_ on-line, send an e-mail message to this Internet address: _emag@wordperfect.com_. (If you use MCI Mail, CompuServe, America Online, Prodigy, or most other on-line services, you can send messages to Internet addresses.)

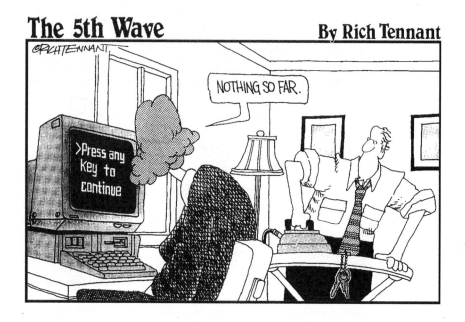

Index

IDG BOOKS WORLDWIDE REGISTRATION CARD

Title of this book: MORE WordPerfect 6 For Windows For Dummies

My overall rating of this book: ❑ Very good [1] ❑ Good [2] ❑ Satisfactory [3] ❑ Fair [4] ❑ Poor [5]

How I first heard about this book:

❑ Found in bookstore; name: [6] ❑ Book review: [7]

❑ Advertisement: [8] ❑ Catalog: [9]

❑ Word of mouth; heard about book from friend, co-worker, etc.: [10] ❑ Other: [11]

What I liked most about this book:

What I would change, add, delete, etc., in future editions of this book:

Other comments:

Number of computer books I purchase in a year: ❑ 1 [12] ❑ 2-5 [13] ❑ 6-10 [14] ❑ More than 10 [15]

I would characterize my computer skills as: ❑ Beginner [16] ❑ Intermediate [17] ❑ Advanced [18] ❑ Professional [19]

I use ❑ DOS [20] ❑ Windows [21] ❑ OS/2 [22] ❑ Unix [23] ❑ Macintosh [24] ❑ Other: [25]_____
(please specify)

I would be interested in new books on the following subjects:

(please check all that apply, and use the spaces provided to identify specific software)

❑ Word processing: [26] ❑ Spreadsheets: [27]

❑ Data bases: [28] ❑ Desktop publishing: [29]

❑ File Utilities: [30] ❑ Money management: [31]

❑ Networking: [32] ❑ Programming languages: [33]

❑ Other: [34]

I use a PC at (please check all that apply): ❑ home [35] ❑ work [36] ❑ school [37] ❑ other: [38] _____

The disks I prefer to use are ❑ 5.25 [39] ❑ 3.5 [40] ❑ other: [41]_____

I have a CD ROM: ❑ yes [42] ❑ no [43]

I plan to buy or upgrade computer hardware this year: ❑ yes [44] ❑ no [45]

I plan to buy or upgrade computer software this year: ❑ yes [46] ❑ no [47]

Name: _____ Business title: [48] _____ Type of Business: [49]

Address (❑ home [50] ❑ work [51]/Company name: _____)

Street/Suite# _____

City [52]/State [53]/Zipcode [54]: _____ Country [55] _____

❑ **I liked this book!** You may quote me by name in future
IDG Books Worldwide promotional materials.

My daytime phone number is _____

IDG BOOKS

THE WORLD OF
COMPUTER
KNOWLEDGE

 # YES!

Please keep me informed about IDG's World of Computer Knowledge.
Send me the latest IDG Books catalog.